DIARY
OF AN OLD
CONTEMPTIBLE

DIARY
OF AN OLD
CONTEMPTIBLE

Private Edward Roe
East Lancashire Regiment
From Mons to Baghdad
1914–1919

Edited by

PETER DOWNHAM

Pen & Sword
MILITARY

First published in Great Britain in 2004 by
Pen & Sword Military
an imprint of
Pen & Sword Books Ltd
47 Church Street
Barnsley
South Yorkshire
S70 2AS

ISBN 1 84415 135 2

A CIP catalogue record for this book is
available from the British Library

Typeset in Bulmer by
Phoenix Typesetting, Auldgirth, Dumfriesshire

Printed and bound in England by
CPI UK

Pen & Sword Books Ltd incorporates the imprints of Pen & Sword Aviation, Pen
& Sword Maritime, Pen & Sword Military, Wharncliffe Local History, Pen &
Sword Select, Pen & Sword Military Classics and Leo Cooper.

For a complete list of Pen & Sword titles please contact
PEN & SWORD BOOKS LIMITED
47 Church Street, Barnsley, South Yorkshire, S70 2AS, England
E-mail: enquiries@pen-and-sword.co.uk
Website: www.pen-and-sword.co.uk

DEDICATION

To the memory of Lieutenant Colonel Le Marchant D.S.O.
1st Battalion Regiment

Mr Parkinson 6th Battalion East Lancashire Regiment

My friend 'Horatius' 6th Battalion East Lancashire Regiment

And my fallen comrades of the 1st, 2nd and 6th Battalions
of the East Lancashire Regiment

I dedicate all my War Diaries to the above.

E. Roe (Private)

Contents

Foreword

There are very few diaries written by private soldiers in the First World War, and certainly not by a Private who was an 'old contemptible', one of Britain's small professional pre-war army.

This diary is a rare example of a private soldier's account of the fighting in France in the early years of the war, of Gallipoli, and finally the campaign in Mesopotamia, which is now modern day Iraq.

To begin with I would like to introduce Edward Roe and let him tell you in his own words as to how he came to enlist for the army.

'As a youngster I read with a thrill, the charge of the Light Brigade at Balaclava, the 16th or 17th Lancers at Omdurman and the exploits of Wellington's cavalry in the Peninsular campaign and Jeb Stuart's cavalry in the American Civil War. So I intended to be a cavalryman at all costs. I made a dash for Longford early in 1905 with full intent to enlist in the 16th Lancers. The recruiting sergeant major informed me that the 16th were closed to recruiting for a time at least.

"Well the 5th Royal Irish Lancers will do then, Sir."

"They are also closed", he replied. "In fact all cavalry regiments are closed against recruiting. How would the Irish Guards suit you?"

I told him 'straight' that it had to be a cavalry unit, or none at all.

He considered for a moment and then replied, "Well I think I can fix you up 'sonny'. How would the East Lancers suit you? If you do not like them you can transfer to the 16th Lancers", he advised.

"They will do 'bloody' fine, so long as it is a cavalry regiment," I replied, although I have never come across them in all the history books I have read. There and then I took the King's shilling and became an East 'Lancer' as I thought.

When I arrived in Preston and again passed a doctor I was conducted to the Quartermaster's stores to draw my kit.

"Do I get no Wellingtons, spurs, jack boots or stable kit?" I asked 'Ginger' Parkinson who was store man.

He looked at me for a moment and then replied, "Oh, you'll get them tomorrow morning." – and I did – I was arrayed in a canvas suit and a pair of size nine army boots completed my riding school outfit. Swords and Lances were conspicuous by their absence. I was doubled around the barrack square at Preston about seventeen times by the Depot Sergeant Major, 'Billy' Horan. If I write that I was doubled until I dropped 'stone dead' it would be nearer an explanation.

So, this is the East 'Lancers', one to you recruiting officer Sergeant Major Smith. Of course, I was rather green at the time but Mr. Smith has two black eyes to come if I ever drop across him in my travels. Yes, he swindled me all right.'

So writes Edward Roe, army number 7041678, Private of the East Lancashire Regiment, on how he came to enlist for the cavalry and was duped into the infantry.

He enlisted on 27 April 1905 at the age of nineteen years and described himself as a labourer on his enlistment forms. These papers described him as 5 feet 9½ inches tall, a fair complexion, dark brown hair and grey eyes.

Born in 1886, his home town was Castlepollard in the County of Westmeath in Ireland.

It took six months hard training at the Regimental Depot before a recruit was considered ready for transfer to his service battalion. During this time the military authorities sought to educate the recruit, in addition to making him into a soldier. The recruits were forced to go to school every day for an hour, except Saturdays, in order to win a third class certificate of education. Hours were spent practising simple addition, multiplication and division, and writing imaginary letters to imaginary friends on titles such as 'Why I joined the army'. Roe writes in his introduction that he gained a third class certificate of education at the Regimental Depot (Fulwood Barracks, Preston) in June 1905. This was his only educational achievement.

During his nine years with the colours, before the war, Roe served in India and South Africa.

The diary starts when he has just been put on the Active Reserve list in March 1914 and he travels home to Ireland, but has hardly arrived before he is recalled with the mobilization in August 1914 at the outbreak of World War One.

The 1st Battalion East Lancashire Regiment moved to France as part of 11 Brigade of the 4th Division of the British Expeditionary Force (BEF).

Roe describes graphically the 'almost triumphant' advance towards Mons and, although the battalion was not involved in the battle, his account of the 'sleep-marching' retreat from Mons is impressively described.

As a private in 'A' Company of the East Lancashires during the retreat he was ordered to guard the transport column. They were involved in several skirmishes that are graphically told, particularly the action at St-Sauveur, where his use of the first person present tense makes the description appear very immediate.

The BEF, and the French, then counter-attacked and Roe was in the midst of the crossing of the Marne and the BEF's first experience of trench warfare after crossing the Aisne in mid-September 1914.

One month later, in October, the 1/East Lancashire was transferred to Armentières and an area of the trench line known as Ploegsteert, or 'Plugstreet' to the men who fought there. Roe gives a fascinating and detailed insight into the daily life of the infantryman in the line and at Xmas 1914 he describes the meetings in 'no-man's-land' and lists the 'Unofficial truce' to be observed by both sides. When hostilities resumed we are then told of life behind the line and a little market that the East Lancashire's established for frostbite fat.

Finally in April 1915 the 1/East Lancashire is moved to Ypres and the bloody battlefield around Shell Trap Farm. Gas attacks, listening posts and German attacks are all detailed in the diary, along with observation on the war and trench life.

In mid-May 1915 Edward is wounded in the arm during a German assault on his trench. He manages to scramble back to the support trenches and then on to the field ambulance. Eventually reaching hospital in England, we are told of the admission procedures for men from the front and the way they were nursed.

Following his convalescence Roe was drafted to the 6th Battalion East Lancashire Regiment in Gallipoli, arriving in early December 1915. He was one of the firing squad who executed a young soldier accused of twice being absent from his unit. Roe's description of the event, and his thoughts about it, leave you in no doubt as to what he felt of the whole sad affair.

Roe was then part of the rearguard as the whole army re-embarked and evacuated Gallipoli in late December 1915, the 6/East Lancashire being taken to Mudros Bay on the Greek Island of Lemnos.

In January 1916 the battalion was posted to Egypt where, for a short period, they were guarding the Suez Canal. During these periods Roe gives us many stories about his comrades and everyday life on campaign.

A month later, in February 1916, the battalion was sent to Mesopotamia to be part of 38 Brigade in the 13th Division of the Tigris Corps in an attempt to relieve General Townshend besieged in Kut.

Again the daily diary and observations are fascinating as the Tigris Corps moves up the Tigris River. The attacks at El Hanna and Sannaiyat are detailed from the meeting of the order groups to the 'dressing' for the attack and the final advance itself.

At Sannaiyat Roe was wounded again and taken, by a hospital steamer, back down the river to Basra where a cholera outbreak caused him to be put in an isolation camp. During his recovery he hears of the fall of Kut and the death of Lord Kitchener. He reflects upon these and many other aspects including the land of Mesopotamia.

Roe writes about the Lewis gun being introduced and many of the 'old sweats' being dubious about its value, and aerial combats he observed, with justifiable criticism of our aircraft.

In November 1916 he was fit enough to be involved in the operations on the Hai. Roe writes of the attack on the Hai and operations around the Dahra Bend, forcing the Turks from their defensive positions around Kut.

In January 1917, much to his reluctance, Roe was made a Lance Corporal and a company stretcher-bearer. The Mesopotamian Expeditionary Force continues its advance to Baghdad with actions at Shumran Bend and crossing the Diyala River. Finally Baghdad is reached in March 1917, but the city itself is a disappointment to Roe and many in the army. However, he does not have too long to explore the city before they are off again after the retreating Turkish forces. The crossing of the Shatt-al-Haim, driving the Turks from the Dahuba, and the action at Adhaim village are again all graphically described, followed by a note on how dangerous it is being a stretcher-bearer and how he is going to try and transfer back to being an ordinary infantryman.

In between the action Roe writes of the countryside, the Arabs, the seasons and individuals in his unit.

In June 1917 he is given leave to go to India and there we are told of some events such as the amusing account of dinner with the Mahratta Rifles and a party with 'the ladies of the Kirk'.

Returning to Mesopotamia in April 1918 Roe is not involved in any more active service, but his diary tells of the influenza pandemic, remarks on Mesopotamia and finally the surrender of the Central Powers, with Germany being last of all, in November 1918. By this time Roe was a Corporal and acting Company Quartermaster Sergeant. In February 1919 the adjutant of 6/East Lancashire was trying to persuade him to stay on in the army and complete twenty-one years with the colours. He was promised a confirmed promotion to sergeant if only he would stay. But Roe refused, feeling that after all his experiences during the war he had had enough of army life and wanted to return home to Ireland.

His diary describes his return to England, the demobilization process and his eventual sailing home to Ireland. Sadly, Roe had no sooner returned home than he was missing his 'chums' in the battalion and, with the rise of

Sinn Fein in Ireland, having fought for England, he felt an outsider in his own country. He decided to re-enlist but first he spent a couple of months' trout fishing in the lakes and rivers of Westmeath.

Roe re-enlisted at Dover on 29 October 1919 as a private in the South Lancashires, who were on garrison duty at Dover Castle at the time. His new tours of duty took him back to India, South Africa and Palestine before he was finally discharged on 12 April 1933 having completed a total of 27 years and 205 days service with the colours.

Staying a bachelor and with no family, it has been difficult to trace details of his life after discharge from the army, but we know that he lived and worked in Warrington for the rest of his life.

Edward Roe died in 1952, aged sixty-six, and was buried at St Benedict's, Orford, Warrington.

It seems surprising that at the end of nearly twenty-eight years' service in the army Roe was discharged still at the rank of private. He was experienced and intelligent but he was still in a period when the idea of promotion was scorned by the ordinary 'professional long service' soldier and to seek promotion was to lose caste and numerous friends. During the war Roe was finally forced to accept promotion as one of the few pre-war professional soldiers left in the battalion, but he complained bitterly that he lacked moral courage and initiative to lead and should not be considered. He writes that he was 'always content to plod along and leave the leading and responsibility to somebody else'. Having accepted a promotion, he proved very successful and was acting Company Quartermaster Sergeant at the end of hostilities, but, on re-enlisting with the South Lancashires, and for the rest of his career, he was a private.

As one reads the diary there is no denying he was a brave man by anybody's definition and yet in his writing he makes no attempts to disguise the fears he felt at various times. He was both shrewd and sympathetic in his analysis of people and events, and gifted with an observant mind and a story-teller's heart. His pleasant and easy sense of humour comes through in his writings and his descriptive gifts give the reader a vivid picture of events. This remarkable narrative gift was well recognized by his peers and he was known as the 'Battalion diarist' as well as being in great demand as a 'letter writer' for the men to their families and sweethearts.

In his introduction, Roe tells us that he was no great scholar. He writes, as he would have spoken, which gives us an immediate liveliness about his writing.

In the transcribing of this diary there is no pruning; everything is as it was written apart from some alterations to punctuation, as he was no great believer in a full stop. In the editorial task I have also provided 'background' notes on people and events. I have not changed his spelling but any correction, or other editorial comment, is put in brackets after the word. The parentheses are used for Roe's own comments within his diary.

As mentioned previously, the diary is written in a very immediate style, sometimes as short notes and at other times more fully but in the present tense. It appears, from what is written in the diary, that Roe made notes on events or impressions at the time of their occurrence and then, when time permitted, usually in the *Estaminets* or cafes behind the lines, he would write out his notes more carefully. The final two handwritten books, which have been transcribed for this book, appear to have been written in 1919–20. These diaries were deposited at the Regimental Depot, Fulwood Barracks, Preston, after his death. Small sections of the diaries have been published in the *Army Quarterly* and regimental magazines but this is the first time they have been fully reproduced.

I hope you will enjoy reading this diary as much as I have in the work of transcribing and editing his original notes.

Author's Preface

By a Private and as a Private went "through it".

When the Russo-Japanese War began I had just passed the school stage. Sir Ian Hamilton was military attaché to the Japanese armies operating in Manchuria. Mr Bennet Burleigh, that brilliant war correspondent, wrote articles which appeared in the *Daily Telegraph* and were eagerly devoured, by me at least. Later I read a book by Sir Ian Hamilton on his experiences. It appeared in diary form and I there and then swore by Saint Patrick, 'Mick' and John that when I became a soldier, and if it were my luck to be engaged in active service, I would keep a diary, at least until I got killed.

Dear reader if you expect anything like what Sir Ian Hamilton wrote, or Hilaire Belloc writes, you will be extremely disappointed as my sole treasure in the educational line is a somewhat antiquated Army 3rd [Class Certificate of Education] obtained in Preston in June 1905. I therefore request all and any who may, through lack of anything else to do, read it, to gloss over bad spelling, rotten English and a host of full stops, split infinitives, commas, colons and semi colons. Some may be in the right place, but the majority are where they should not be 'at all'.

I have tried on several occasions to obtain a 2nd Class Certificate of Education, but inverted and flying fractions let me down on the mathematical side. On the historic side, Oliver Cromwell, Marlborough, Guy Fawkes, young Wolfe, 'Billy' the Conqueror and old 'Bobby' Roberts let me down, so there you are.

So dear reader you will know what to expect.

Unit Organization

France
3rd Corps
4th Division

	10th Brigade	
	11th Brigade	1st Somerset Light Infantry
		1st Hampshire Regiment
		1st Rifle Brigade (Prince Consort's Own)
		1st East Lancashire Regiment
	12th Brigade	

Gallipoli and Mesopotamia
13th Division

	38th Brigade	6th King's Own Royal Regiment
		6th **East Lancashire Regiment**
		6th Prince of Wales (South Lancashire)
		6th Loyal Regiment (North Lancashire)
	39th Brigade	
	40th Brigade	

Glossary

APM	Assistant Provost Marshal
AR	Army Reserve
AT	Army Transport
BEF	British Expeditionary Force
BG Hospital	Base General Hospital
Bn	Battalion
BOC	Battalion Orderly Corporal
CB	Confined to Barracks
C in C	Commander in Chief
CO	Commanding Officer
CQMS	Company Quartermaster Sergeant
CWGC	Commonwealth Graves Commission
DSO	Distinguished Service Order
DCM	Distinguished Conduct Medal
EP (tent)	Despite extensive research and enquiries I
EPIP (tent)	was unable to find the full meaning of
EPSP (tent)	these abbreviations.
FF	Field Force
FGCM	Field General Court Martial
FOO	Forward Observation Officer
GMP	Garrison Military Police
GOC	General Officer Commanding
GS	General Service
HE	High Explosive
i/c	In charge (of)

KD	Khaki Drill (uniform material)
LCpl	Lance Corporal
'M & D'	Medicine and Duty
MO	Medical Officer
MP	Military Police
NCO	Non-Commissioned Officer
OBE	Officer of the Order of the British Empire
Pte	Private
PRI	President of Regimental Institutes
PT	Physical Training
QM	Quartermaster
RAMC	Royal Army Medical Corps
RE	Royal Engineers
RC	Roman Catholic
RFC	Royal Flying Corps
RHA	Royal Horse Artillery
RIF	Royal Irish Fusiliers
RQMS	Regimental Quartermaster Sergeant
RSM	Regimental Sergeant Major
SAA	Small Arms Ammunition
SD	Service Dress
Sgt	Sergeant
SSgt	Staff Sergeant
S & T	Supply and Transport
VC	Victoria Cross
VD	Venereal Disease
WOAS	While on Active Service (on a disciplinary charge sheet)
YMCA	Young Men's Christian Association

Maps

I

Mobilization

(March – August 1914)

'On the Reserve' in Ireland – War Clouds Gathering – The Call up –
Preston – The 1st Battalion – 'The Harrow Flappers'

'On the Reserve' in Ireland

I was transferred to AR[1] (1st Class) in March 1914. My Regiment, the 2nd
Battalion East Lancashires, was then stationed in Wynberg, South Africa.
Wynberg might be called a suburb of Cape Town, as it was roughly seven
miles from the city. I soon regretted leaving the Army. Every weekend my
mind was in Cape Town; Adderley Street, the Grand Parade, Buitengraft
Street, Mick O'Grady's pub of jovial memories, the Ancient Order of
Hibernians, the races at Newlands every Saturday, the first class rugby and
cricket matches and other forms of amusement. I could visualise Mick
Cunningham, 'Spike' West, 'Paddy' Wade, 'Snowy' Parsons and the
'Bullock' Masterton walking down Adderley Street, Yes! They've turned to
the left on passing Van Riebek's statue; they're making for 'Mick' O'Grady's.
I can imagine the night they will have.

And here I am living on the borders of the Great Bog of Allan. I have no
one to talk to that has had any military experience – except the 'Peelers'! –
and I don't like 'Peelers' (Royal Irish Constabulary); they prevent me from
getting a drink on Sundays. They are not popular. Guardians of the peace
never are as a rule – at least not in Ireland. I cannot partake in a debate in the
local pub on the virtues of the latest variety of seed potatoes, or whether
Beauties of Kent grow better in moorland than in uplands, whether the Buff
Orpington is a better layer than the Spanish Minorca, or which is the best
milker, the Jersey or the Hereford. I don't know anything about the subjects
brought forward, so I sit dejectedly in a corner and talk to myself. What the
devil tempted me to leave the Army? The Colonel asked me to 'take on', I
left with an exemplary character, admitted I was slightly neglected (badly
neglected). I have had an official communication from the Record Office,
Preston informing me that I can re-enlist for another two years if I wish, but

1

I cannot carry on for twenty-one. That was no use to me, so I declined the offer.

I have written to the Secretary, Department of the Army, USA [United States of America] for instructions and conditions to joining the American Army. In due course I received a bulky letter from the Secretary of the Army Department, USA. It contained several typewritten sheets explaining the conditions of service, rates of pay and the advantages of joining the American Army, if only for a period of two years. On the expiry of two years I would be granted citizenship papers and would have first claim for employment in any Government department. British ex-service men were preferred. I was instructed as to where to report on arrival at New York. Yes! I'll give the American Army a trial. I know I will have to soldier with black men, Poles, Swedes, Italians, Greeks and Spaniards – well they cannot eat me in two years; besides it will be an experience. But I am not going to cross the Atlantic until the beginning of August. I must have July at home; the perch-fishing season is in, I'm fond of fishing. I have borrowed a boat and intend to have a good month.

I have kept my intentions a profound secret in case the 'Peelers' might get wind of them and have me arrested when embarking at Owenstown. I would naturally be tried as a deserter if caught. Yet I cannot remain here for three years after the life I have been accustomed to over the previous nine years. Just imagine, half a County without a cinema or a place of amusement of any kind. 'Poole and Boscos' and 'Gennets' travelling circuses visit us once yearly, then all the excitement is over until the following year.

War Clouds Gathering

The never to be forgotten month of August came in all its summer glory. The oldest inhabitants declared it was the finest summer they had seen. But what had happened in the Bosnian town of Sarajevo? An Austrian Arch Duke had been assassinated. Austria held Serbia responsible and declared war upon her; the 'Russian Steam Roller' and Germany (Austria's ally) are 'stuck into it'. France has been dragged in. Could England keep out? I demobbed my fishing rods and soaked them in linseed oil, gave away all my hooks, gut, flies, minnows and spoon baits to a local disciple of Isaac Walton's. Maybe I won't have to enlist in the Goddamn Yankee Army after all.

I awaited on the mail car every day and bought the *Irish Times*. I was quite well aware that if a German soldier put his foot on Belgian soil, England would be 'into it'.

I am in great demand in Tom the Blacksmith's Smithy. I am a 'Military Man' and am supposed to know the strength of the belligerent armies and what type of rifle they are armed with, how many men they can put in the field and how many guns they've got.

In the village pub, for a wonder, I'm not allowed to pay for a drink.

'Did I ever see a "Rhoosian"(Russian)?'

'Was it true that the Czar had a bayonet for every star in the sky?'

Ireland was on the verge of Home Rule. Bad luck to Carson, Craig, Galloper Smith (Sir F. E. Smith, later Lord Birkenhead) and the Kaiser, they would not get Home Rule now until the war was over. If England could keep out of it Home Rule was a certainty, as she could not break her promise, but if she got involved she might make it an excuse for delaying the measure. I am compelled to let my imagination run riot in order to answer questions fired at me with Maxim gun velocity from all corners of the tap room, such as,

'Were the Serbians Catholics?'

'Would Catholic Italy take sides with Catholic France and Belgium or would she sit on the fence until she saw which way the "cat jumped"?'

'Surely England and Germany would never go to War. Were not King George and the Kaiser first or second cousins? Cousins might disagree and have a few hot words but they would never go to war and get each other's subjects killed. Blood runs thicker than water.'

'How long would the war last?'

'Would the price of bacon, tobacco and flour go up?'

'Would I have to go if England declared war?'

'Didn't I do 9 years, was not that long enough?'

The Call up

On **4 August** war was declared between England and Germany. The early morning post [**5 August**] brought my mobilization order to rejoin at Preston at once, so I will have to take the earliest train to Dublin. Well, the earliest train is the 2.00 pm. Irish Railways are famed for punctuality, therefore instead of leaving the local station at 2.00 pm it might be 2.30 or 3.00 pm or, if it came to a push, 3.30 pm before she steams out of Float Station. So I had six hours to spare. After breakfast I went around and shook hands with all the neighbours. One or two asked me, did I think I would be killed? The only answer I could give was that I did not know, quite a number will be killed for certain. I wended my way to the village smithy after duly fortifying myself with the necessary amount of espirit-de-corps in Mrs Early's pub en route. I found quite a considerable gathering there considering the early hour and the fine working day it was. No one was getting horses shod or farm implements repaired, but all were talking war. Fifteen pairs of critical eyes were directed on me simultaneously to see how I was 'taking it'. Would I break down and cry? Would I start blubbering because I was going out to be killed? Well I did not start crying, neither did I 'blubber'. I was quite cheerful. I told them it would be over in six months and that I would consider myself lucky if I could get a shot at a Jerry before it was all over. Tom the Blacksmith stated that it would not last three months. How could it last any longer with millions of Prussians on one side and the French, English and Belgians on the other side? We'd go through them like a 'dose of salts', or a wedding through a town, or the Devil through Athlone, maybe. Well, let us hope so.

The country people's conceptions of the German soldier are based on the German bands that used to travel around Ireland up to 1913. The musicians were square-headed, pot-bellied men without either shape or make, and therefore all Germans must be alike. The German Bands were not popular, as they played music, which the country people did not understand. Did any farmer, shopkeeper or labourer know anything, or in fact ever hear of Schubert, Mozart, Beethoven, Wagner, Offenbach or Verdi? No! – certainly not. The Germans could not play the 'Wearin' of the Green', 'The Rocky Road to Dublin', 'The Wind that shed the Barley' or 'Brian Boru's March'; therefore the half-pence they picked up were few, as no one understood classical music or opera. Major Dease, the Earl of Longford, Colonel Pollard-Urquart and Major Boyd-Rochford did, and used to keep the Germans playing for hours outside the hall doors of their country mansions. I am told that if I let such apologies for men beat me then I need never show my face in the Parish again. 'If I ever come across the Brandenburgers, to give them what the women of Limerick gave them when they were engaged in the siege of that city in the turbulent past.' I have not been informed as to what the women of Limerick gave the Brandenburgers from the city walls – but I can give a good guess.[2]

I am called into the house and conducted to the parlour. I was requested to 'eat that breakfast, as God himself only knows when I would get another one, and a war on.' I informed Mrs Fagan that I had already partaken of breakfast. 'Twas no use as the breakfast was prepared for me and I would have to eat it. Four green duck eggs boiled, a plate of home made bread, well buttered, and an enormous teapot (I am sure it contained half a gallon of strong tea) confronted me. A hungry ploughman would consider twice before launching an attack on it.

'Four duck eggs is really too much, Mrs Fagan,' I protested.

'Well,' she considered, 'two would not be enough, three was an unlucky number to start a war on, therefore it had to be four.' I managed one egg and one slice of bread in her presence, when she was called away to attend to some turkeys and geese. During her absence two greyhounds, two Irish terriers, a setter and a pointer made short work of the breakfast. I was complimented on my appetite; although I was going out to be killed I had not lost it. Cheerful, was it not?

At 12 noon I made my adieus to all and set out for the station, which is three miles away, and I have to make some halts before I entrain at 2.00 or 3.00 pm. Everyone is going to pray for my safe return, I am presented with rosary beads and medals that were brought from the miraculous grotto of Lourdes in France. Three briar pipes, enough Gallagher tobacco to last me six months, a quart bottle of John Jameson 'three swallow' whiskey as an antidote against *mal-de-mer* (sea sickness) when crossing the channel, and a parcel of ham sandwiches complete my campaigning outfit.

The train arrives at 2.40 pm <u>punctual</u> instead of 2.00 pm. It is crowded with reservists. Every unit in the army is represented; the majority are uproariously drunk. I was struck by the various stages of prosperity displayed by the reservists. Some were well dressed and looked exceedingly smart, some just managed to maintain an appearance of respectability, whilst others had not a boot on their foot and just the semblance of a coat on their backs. The latter category were almost stupefied with liquor and gave me the impression by their general run down appearance that they could not stick a long march in full marching order. The occupants of every carriage were singing. The crowd of country people who were assembled on the platform were truly amazed, I overheard such observations as, 'They must all be mad; fancy men singing and they going off to be killed, for killed they will surely be as the English always put the Irish in front of the battle'. 'Twas a common belief in the country places in Ireland that the English always put the Irish in front in every engagement in order to get as many Irishmen as possible killed, so that if Ireland ever had to fight England for Home Rule they would have less Irishmen to oppose them. I do not know who originated this quixotic idea, or when it was originated. In any case it is a popular belief and I have been listening to it for as long as I can remember.

With a mighty effort the train moves out of the station at 5.05 pm. I managed a corner seat and in twenty minutes time all familiar landmarks connected with my youth flashed past. The train stopped at Clonhugh. Lord Greville's mansion and estate adjoins the railway. My mind wandered back to the many pleasant Sundays I had spent at Clonhugh when Major Dease's cricket eleven came up to play Lord Greville's. Well, I'm off to play a sterner game than cricket now.

More reservists entrain; I give all my sandwiches away, but hang on to the quart bottle of whiskey. The train pulled up at every station, and every station vomited forth its quota of reservists. By the time we reached Broadstone there was not standing room in the carriages.

Detrained at Broadstone at 5.50 pm, the majority of reservists make for the public houses in the vicinity of the station – just to have a last one in 'Dear

5

old dirty Dublin'. I made for North Wall. En route who should I meet but 'Paddy' Phipps, my company cook orderly in the 2nd Battalion in India. He was accompanied by his better half and an imposing array of young Phippses. Male and female relatives completed the retinue. We shook hands and, of course, advanced on the nearest pub. Dublin is the most convenient city I have ever been in, in the line of pubs. They are conveniently and strategically placed. We discussed old times over a couple of bottles of Guinness. I enquired, 'What time does the boat sail?' He replied, 'Eight o'clock. We'll make a move down there now'.

When we arrived at the docks the scene was one of wild confusion. The boat was already overcrowded, yet crowds were breaking through the military picket and rushing on board. In the end it was given out that no more reservists could get across until tomorrow.

So Phipps invited me to his house for the night. We duly arrived at his house at 8.30 pm. I was introduced to the Dublin Belles as Mr Roe 'from the country', and the piano was set in motion at 10.30 pm, but the music did not suit Phipps's ear, it was not sweet enough. The keys were duly baptized with the contents of four bottles of Guinness stout by the method of effusion (pity the old piano). At 11.30 pm Phipps took me to my room. He turned the gas off and I fell asleep immediately. I awoke at 5.00 am. What an awful smell; I could hardly breath; the room was reeking with gas. I staggered to the window; my head was like a lump of lead. I opened the window. What a relief! Mr Phipps turned the gas, or the light out all right, but in his befuddled state must have turned it on again. I thanked my stars that the bedroom was a spacious one.

[6 August] Breakfast [was] at 9.00 am [followed by] a stroll around the city until noon, dinner, and more 'doing the sights'. It was the first time I had a real good walk around Dublin.

Leave for the docks at 6.00 pm, embark at 7.00 pm; there is still a lot of congestion at the docks. I left a quart bottle of whiskey and my overcoat in Mr Phipps's house. The whiskey is not to be uncorked until we arrive home victorious.

We took our own 'rations' on board. An hour before the steamer slipped from her moorings an immense crowd had gathered on the quayside. They indulged in shouting all kinds of encouragement to us. At 8.00 pm, as she slowly warped away from the quayside, the old women 'chucked up' their old green bonnets in the air and implored us to bring them back some German sausages.

A maelstrom of patriotic fervour seemed to prevail all over Ireland, a sort of 'war fever'. Catholic Belgium and France had been invaded. The Germans, so we were told, were shelling chapels, convents and monasteries; they were reducing them to piles of brick and mortar. It was not love of

6

England that inspired the 'war fever'. No, it was religious sentiment; the war was looked upon in Southern Ireland as a sort of Jihad (Holy War). Well I suppose this 'war fever' will fade out considerably as time passes.

Phipps seems to be considerably 'cut up'; so did Mrs Phipps at the quayside. The young Phippses did not understand the calamity that had befallen their home. I can just imagine his feelings, leaving a wife and family, a decent home and good employment, and it's a 'toss-up' whether he will ever see home or family again. I'm lucky; I have no one to worry about me, not even an old woman, or a young one either.

Violins, mouth organs, concertinas, melodeons and other musical instruments enliven a calm six hours crossing. One would imagine that we were coming home after winning a war instead of going out to fight one.

[**7 August**] Arrive at 3.00 am (Holyhead) disembark and entrain. We have some difficulty in finding seating accommodation. We are turned away from carriage after carriage. At last I come to a carriage, which is not quite full.

I am asked, 'Do I belong to his Majesty's Brigade of Foot Guards?'

'Of course I do,' I replied.

'Well get in here, then.'

Luckily for me they did not cross-question me. Phipps, being only 5 feet 3 inches, could not possibly belong to his Majesty's Brigade of Foot Guards, so he had to take cover elsewhere.

Preston

Arrived in Preston at 7.10 am. Breakfast, a drink or two in the County Arms[3], and after an absence of close on nine years the Barrack gates are closed once more and bolted behind me.

Parade at 9.00 am at Mobilization Stores. Every reservist has a shelf all to himself with a card tacked on to the top portion of the shelf bearing his rank, number and name. Your kit and equipment are stowed away on this shelf; the rifles are in racks, also numbered. There is no delay, you simply file through and get equipped.

I met 'Jock' Wishart from Scotland, Le-Coq from the Channel Islands; 'Cherby' Williams from Kent, 'Cockney' Wadham from Limehouse, Branston from Isle of Wight, O'Toole from Cork and quite a number of others that I said goodbye to years ago and thought I would never see again.

The majority of men who joined up under the Three Years Act (three years with the Colours and nine on the reserve) and have been on the reserve since 1907 do not appear to be very fit. As a matter of fact some men who have only been away for twelve months seem a bit run down. A fortnight's training should pull them together again.

We make bundles of our civilian clothes, address them and hand them into stores for dispatch to our home addresses; or if you wish you can sell them for a song to a civilian who has obtained the contract for buying clothes. One pint per man allowed at 12 noon. Everyone is in uniform once again and all had a stiff medical inspection at 2.00 pm. There is no room in the barracks rooms and quite a number slept on the square. We might as well get used to sleeping out.

[8 August] Four hundred NCOs [Non-Commissioned Officers] and men parade at 11.00 am. We are bound for Colchester to join the 1st Battalion (East Lancashire Regiment).[4] The Corporation kindly placed the tram services at our disposal and the inhabitants of proud Preston gave us a rousing send off. I never saw as many lassies dressed up in clogs and shawls before. Where did they all come from?

Arrive at Colchester at 1.30 pm. We spent an uneventful and busy week at Colchester, route marching and getting rigged out generally. Colchester boasts of a large garrison canteen but we had very little, or no time, to spend in it.

The 1st Battalion

Entrained for Harrow and arrived early on the **16 August [18 August]**[5] and encamped close to the town.[6] The famous school is on a hill some distance from the camp.[7]

Everyone is grousing like hell over not being sent to France. One hears the following remarks with amazing frequency:

'The bloomin' war will be over before we get there, we won't even smell it. What did they call us up for if they don't intend to send us out?'

'The Russians have captured another 200,000 today. God knows how many they have captured and killed in the past week.'

'The French are knocking hell out of them in Alsace and Lorraine. The Belgians are mowing them down from inside the forts of Liege and Namur, and here are we swanking about around Harrow.'

Admitted we get the glad eye from all the 'Flappers'. It is some consolation to know that they think something about a soldier at last, but that's not the thing. We want to get out before it is all over.

We had one route march and a stiff field day at Harrow. We were told that the country around Harrow was similar to the country we would have to fight over in France and Belgium. When we came to hedges [we were] not to make for 'sheep and cattle gaps,' or machine gun fire would mow us down; we would have to force our way through the hedges and not bunch together.

Lieutenant-Colonel Le Marchant[8] (Commanding Officer of 1/Battalion East Lancashire Regt.) gave us a lecture today. He told us we would get out to France soon enough, that there would be enough Germans left to go around. He exhorted us to take more interest in our work [as] we were taking it as a huge joke. He assured us that when we got there we would find it was no joke. That we were up against one of the greatest military powers the world had yet seen. [We were] to play the game and put our hearts and souls into our work.

'The Harrow Flappers'

I went into town at 5.00 pm on the night of **18 August [21 August]**.[9] At 7.30 pm all were warned to return to camp as we move at 9.00 pm. In the street I was surrounded by quite a number of charming 'Flappers' with autograph books. I had to write something in each young lady's book. I felt just like Jack Hobbs would feel after scoring 399 not out and surrounded by a crowd of admirers seeking his signature or autograph. I was in a pretty jovial mood and wrote quite a lot of bombastic nonsense in the dear young maidens' books. I don't know if I was 'ass' enough to put my name and address, at least I hope not. I damn near missed the war all through their 'blink-eyed' requests to write something silly in their books. I grabbed my rifle and equipment. It was lying outside my tent; there was not a soul to be seen. I rejoined just in time to be pulled into a carriage as the train was moving off.

19 August [22 August]: We are moving very slowly, shunted into sidings for hours, off again, halt again, and so on. I had plenty of time to meditate on last night's performance. Did I propose to any of the young ladies in a wave of patriotic fervour, and was [I] accepted? I would like to know what I said, but I cannot rightly remember. Bandsman MacLean was in company with me, but he cannot enlighten me. His memory, if anything, is twenty times worse than mine. I have looked up my notebook, Yes! I've got two young ladies' addresses in it. One of the addresses was meant for MacLean, but which one? MacLean had no notebook, so both addresses were written in mine, hence the confusion. I told MacLean we would have to take 'pot luck'. He could have the one on the left hand page and I would take the one on the right hand page. In any case, the least we can do is to drop them a line.

I found some chocolates and cigarettes in my pockets this morning. I know for a fact that I did not buy either, neither do I smoke cigarettes. I knew Jock was a married man. I jestingly remarked, 'What would the mem-sahib say if she saw you last night?' He replied 'Oh! – Don't make mountains out of mole heaps, Roe, it was only a mild flirtation and a fellow must do something.' The two young dears were inoculated with the germs of 'war-fever' or patriotic fervour. We were two of England's heroes, going out to fight England's battles against England's greatest naval and commercial rival. They fell in love with us on first sight, or at least gave the impression they did. I told Jock not to be alarmed, without a doubt they would soon meet two better looking fellows than we, and would soon forget us. In any case I hope they do, as Jock is about one of the worst letter writers in the British Army. I could visualize what would happen if communications were established. I would have to answer Jock's billet-doux as well as my own.

Notes

1 Army Reserve
2 I believe the ladies of Limerick indulged in what is now termed 'Mooning'!
3 A public house on the way from Preston station to Fulwood Barracks, Depot of the East Lancashire Regiment.
4 The battalion was in garrison at Colchester, part of 11 Infantry Brigade of the 4th Division.
5 Roe is incorrect with a few of his dates, although the timing and events are accurate. I presume a lot of his calculations are from an initial wrong date.
6 The battalion camped in one of the school playing fields. (1st Bn. War Diary, 18 August 1914)
7 The Fourth Division was concentrating at Harrow. It consisted of 10, 11 and 12 Infantry Brigades plus divisional support.
8 Lieutenant Colonel L. St. G. Le Marchant, DSO
9 9.00 pm Battalion . . . proceeded to Southampton (1st Bn. War Diary, 21 August 1914)

II

The Retreat From Mons

(22 – 31 August 1914)

Arrival at Le Havre – Camp at Le Havre – By train to Le Cateau –
Transport Guard – The Retreat – The Poor Refugees –
Old World Town – Re-join the Battalion

Arrival at Le Havre

20 August [22 August]: Embark on *Braemar Castle* for France.[1] Fourteen members of the regiment are still 'Harrowing it,' I mean they are absent.[2] Everyone is satisfied now that we are on our way to France. The fourteen absentees turn up just in time.

Steam up at 9.00 am, arrive at Le Havre at 4.00 pm. The crossing seemed to take years. Got a great reception from French crowds as we 'nosed' in to our berth. I can hear the crowd yelling '*Vive l'Angleterre.*' We seem to be short of French scholars on our boat, as the only reply to the French demonstration is given in two words '*Wee! Wee!*' I am told, on making enquiries, that '*Wee! Wee!*' means, 'Yes! Yes!'

Regimental transport, officers' chargers etc. unloaded by 4.00 am.[3] Had a stiff march up hill to camp (about five miles). We [have now] left miles behind us and have taken over *kilometres*, whatever the devil they are? The camp is well outside the town. Le Havre seems to be a very old fashioned town. The streets are paved and so are the roads for a considerable distance outside the town. It makes marching very difficult particularly for the flank men of each section of fours. Left of the road in England, it's right of the road here. The women kept shouting at us as we marched along but we did not understand what they were saying. The kids kept on shouting '*souvenir*' and '*bully beef.*'

Camp at Le Havre

When we arrived in camp we were detailed to tents and issued out with iron rations[4], which under no circumstances were we allowed to touch unless we

11

got an order from an officer. Any person who loses or eats his iron rations is liable to be tried by court martial. Supposing circumstances arose in which a party of men were cut off, say for two days, and could get nothing to eat, what would happen if they eat their iron rations without an officer's permission? They would get punished, I suppose.

Had a short stroll around camp. I came to an immense ammunition dump of ours. I observed there were no sentries posted. Who is that fellow sitting on an ammunition box at the end of the dump? He is dressed up in a pair of spacious red trousers[5] (they might be described as harem trousers) an ill-fitting blue tunic and a peaked cap. He is rolling and smoking innumerable cigarettes, a firearm of some kind is reclining against the dump on his right. I made enquiries as to whom he was and I was told he was a French sentry guarding our ammunition. 'Good Christ!' I ejaculated, 'You don't mean to tell me he is a soldier! Why he will set the dump on fire!'

Shades of Napoleon, Soult, Massena, Ney, Berthier and Murat, what has come of the French army? I am somewhat appeased on learning that he is only a Territorial. I must admit that my first impressions of the French Tommy fell a hell of a lot short of my expectations.

By train to Le Cateau

[**23 August**] Battalion falls in at 2.00 pm for a lecture by the Brigadier.[6] He gave the battalion a terrible dressing down over the Harrow absentees. He told us we had lost our good name and it was up to us to redeem it in the field. I must admit it was not a very encouraging speech to make to men who were about to entrain for the front. It was something similar to the manner in which the 'Iron Duke' (Duke of Wellington) addressed certain regiments on occasions during the Peninsular campaign. Crauford followed the same method of address in the same campaign. I was not there, but I read all about it.

Full marching order inspection at 4.00 pm, march to the station at 5.00 pm, all entrained by 7.00 pm. Some secured carriages with '*Hommes*' written on them, others were manoeuvred into trucks or boxes labeled '*Chevals*'. We all 'Hurrahed' when the train kicked off: war for a certainty at last. 'Tipperary' was struck up on mouth organs made in Germany. A little advanced knowledge might have done us all the good in the world, but we had none.

[**24 August**] On the way to the frontier, or wherever we were going, I noticed in several instances that women were working in the signal boxes instead of men, owing to the men being called to the colours. They were powerful looking women and sported John L. Sullivan[7] and Bob Fitzsimmons[8] jaws and chins, and wore wooden shoes, which I believe are called *sabots*. Every station presented the appearance of hurry and bustle owing to the enormous amount of war material and troops proceeding to the fighting area. At every station old men in greasy peaked caps and dressed in blue reefer jackets shouted instructions to us in French, which we do not understand. They go through the motions of curling an enormous moustache in line with their eyes, then they draw the index finger of the right hand across their throats and from ear to ear. We understand that part of the business; they are telling us to cut the Kaiser's head off. They have a nautical appearance, although I don't suppose very many of them have seen the sea. They brought back memories of a weekend I once spent down 'Wapping way'.

The progress of the train might be described as a triumphant one, as we were enthusiastically cheered en route by old men, old women and young ones too. We did not see many able-bodied men. The Kaiser, the Crown Prince, von Moltke[9] and Admiral Tirpiz[10] appeared in caricatures everywhere we looked (on walls, doors and wooden hoardings). Count Zeppelin and his airship[11] were not forgotten. Georges Carpentier[12] was caricatured in a position in which I cannot very well describe here; in any case he blew the airship to smithereens.

I found it impossible to keep a daily record of events. I was staggered at the reception the Germans gave us. During the great retreat I did not even know what day it was. It was no use asking Frenchmen, 'What is the name of this village?' as all our enquiries were met with a shrugging of the shoulders and something shouted in French, which I could not comprehend. They might be telling me to go to hell for all I can tell. I may have hit on a date here and there. I have had to be content with a generalization of events. It is almost beyond belief that there are any Germans left, when one considers all that the Russians, French and Belgians have killed and captured, and all that were killed in theory in the public houses and wet canteens in England, Ireland, Scotland and Wales.

On arrival at the little station of . . . [Le Cateau][13] our train ride terminated, and we were not sorry as we were packed like sardines.[14]

The Battalion halted for an hour alongside the station, as there is a big battle taking place on our right front. The gunfire is incessant. Some say they are French guns; others say they are ours. Well, they are making the devil of a row anyway. As twilight approaches six aeroplanes fly in from the direction of the battle and land in a field some distance to the rear of the station.[15] They should have some information.[16]

At last the regiment falls in and we move off accompanied by the distant sound of heavy gunfire. Our first experience of war as we march along the dusty Belgian road in search of billets. Spent the night in a large farm on the outskirts of a large village.[17] Every nook and corner is crammed with troops and transport.

Transport Guard

[**25 August**] Rouse at 3.00 am, a hurried breakfast. We have no sooner finished breakfast than we get a hurried order to charge magazines. It looks like business today.[18] The heavy cannonade has died out during the night. Move off at 7.00 am. My section detailed as transport guard.[19] Jock MacLean is a stretcher-bearer so he had to proceed with the Company. Before parting he requested me to drop a line to Harrow as soon as possible. I told him to talk common sense; didn't we promise not to write until we got to the Linden Strasse in Berlin, or the Ball Platz in Vienna? In any case we had not seen a German yet, let alone kill[ed] the twenty each which we promised the young ladies in Harrow we would do before sending them a postcard.

As the transport moves along the road the inhabitants offer us tobacco, beer, rum and fruit. Good hearted and generous people. I saw some French or Belgian Tommies or *Pilous* [*Poilus*] today and I cannot say that I was impressed by their dress or bearing. They had a 'sloppy' appearance. We trek for thirteen miles and join the Brigade transport, which is parked in a field in the rear of a large village.[20]

The inhabitants of the village from the cradle to the grave turn out to gaze in wonder and admiration at the '*soldats Angleterre.*' '*Souvenir, Souvenir*', they all cry. My titles are deftly removed from my shoulder straps by an old dame of sixty summers, if not more. My cap badge I gave away to a young and pretty filly of seventeen. Who could refuse?[21] The villagers made themselves quite at home with us and, to cement the alliance, partook of our bully beef and biscuits, in wholesome style.

One very old dame asked me was I a Catholic? – '*Wee, Madam*', I replied. She started fumbling at the neck of her bodice, produced a rosary beads from around her neck, took the mother of pearl cross off her beads and gave it to me, and told me in her own language (I could not understand her, but I know what she meant) to keep that cross and the *Bon Dieu* would protect me. Whether there was luck in the old Belgian lady's cross or not I cannot say, but the fact remains that I have been 'through it' on three battle fronts, I'm still alive and 'going strong', and I always carry the old lady's mother of pearl cross on my person.

We will not even have a button left if this souvenir craze does not expire soon.

2.00 pm: Heavy gun and rifle fire has commenced on our right and increases in intensity as the afternoon rolls on.[22] The clerk of the weather lost his temper, opens the floodgates with a vengeance and drenches us to the skin with a real monsoon flood.

4.00 pm: A Regiment of French lancers take up a covering position on our right (at least I presume they are French). It seems strange that before we left

England we were never told or shown by illustrations the multicoloured uniforms worn by our allies. The Germans, we were told, were all dressed alike. French Dragoons[23] are coming in from the direction of the firing, in twos and threes. They are big men on bad mounts. They wear a brass helmet adorned with a long black horsehair plume and breastplate. I noticed that the officer's breastplates were burnished. Was it Gustavus Adolphus that said concealment was the art of war? No, it could not be Gustavus, it's too far back. Anyway, I forget. The English went to the Boer war in review order;[24] the mausers soon made an alteration in the dress. Fifteen or sixteen years later we find a first class military power going to war in uniforms, which no doubt look well on a Presidential review, but in the field they are a direct opposition to 'concealment is the art of war'.

The Retreat

Affairs have taken a serious turn. [At] 7.00 pm, we receive orders to fall-in and move off. We are forced to call a halt a couple of miles outside the village as the roads are choked with kilometre upon kilometre of transport.

[**26 August**] At 3.00 am we move off. Great difficulty in getting along owing to the roads being congested with refugees.[25] Halt at 9.00 pm.[26]

[**27 August**] Next morning we pick up some fifty men of the Lancashire Fusiliers.[27] All bear traces of the previous day's fighting and seem thoroughly 'done up'. Some have rifles and no equipment, others part of their equipment and no rifles. German cavalry are pressing on our rear and every available man has to fall in. We form a line in rear and flanks of the convoy. The convoy is saved as a French or Belgian Cavalry Regiment holds them back.[28]

The enemy has brought his artillery into action and shells are bursting perilously near. However, by assisting the exhausted horses and by much shouting and cracking of whips we manage to get the wagons and limbers over the steep hill that confronted us and get out of one tight corner.

I can hear rifle fire in our rear; one type of rifle seems to have a double report. I cannot tell whether it is the Mauser or the French Lebel. I don't know what type of rifle the Belgians are armed with.

Halt for five hours[29] in order to give the tired horses a feed and a short rest.[30]

[**28 August**] Trek resumed at 3.00 am.[31] Every hour we pick up stragglers of various units, all recounting their own tale of whole Regiments being wiped out in the battle.[32] No one seems to know the name of the place where the battle was fought [Le Cateau]. It is impossible to identify one Regiment from another as all cap badges, numerals or titles have been given away as souvenirs, with the exception of the Scottish Regiments. Of course, they

15

gave nothing away. It cannot be quite as bad as those people state. They gave me the impression that they were all that was left of the British army.

Dead horses, sides of beef, boxes of milk, tea, jam; 'bully' and biscuits mark our line of retreat. Dumps could not be formed owing to the hurried retrograde movement. The difficulty of feeding the retiring troops was solved in the above manner.[33]

The Poor Refugees

We are at present retiring through one of the richest agricultural districts in France. Hundreds of acres of wheat and oats are cut down and bound up in sheaves and hundreds or thousands of acres remain to be cut down. The mowing machines and reapers and binders are lying in the fields unattended. Immense fields of turnips and mangel-wurzel adorn the countryside. Where are the harvesters? The young and able-bodied are in the firing line resisting the invader.[34] The too young, old and infirm are fleeing before the ruthless invader towards the large inland towns with as much of their personal possessions as they can conveniently carry or wheel in box barrows. They have no horses; they tell me Mother Republic requisitioned all their horses.

Here is a young mother wheeling a barrow containing a six-month-old babe, a coffee pot, a bundle of bedding and a few little odds and ends. The grey-haired father and mother follow, struggling bravely on. What's this? A woman has fainted over a box barrow. There are two children in the barrow. She seems in delicate health. We bring her to, place her on a limber and take it in turns to wheel the barrow. An old woman of seventy is struggling along with the aid of a stick, crying and talking to herself. We 'dump' her on the back of the wagon. Scores are carrying bundles. Of course the further they go the heavier the bundles get. The bundles are thrown away in order that they can keep up with the panic-stricken crowd, which comprise war's victims. Incidents like the above are occurring in front of the whole German line of advance. It is a strange sight, in fact some people would be cruel enough to term it loss of dignity, to see British Tommies in full war paint carrying and soothing wailing infants, wheeling box barrows containing a brace of infants, and helping old men and women along the dusty French roads. We have got to clear the refugees off the roads or we would never make any progress. It's cruel; nevertheless it is a military necessity. The unfortunate people stick to their homes to the very last. It is only natural. In fact, some refuse to leave them, with the result that they are caught in the maelstrom and confusion of a retiring army and naturally get wedged in between rear guards of the retiring army and advanced guards of the pursuing army.

I hope I will never witness such heart-rending sights again. The English people should thank God that they made France their battlefield.

Old World Town

At 2.00 pm we enter the old world town of Peronne [Noyon[35]]. A demolition party of French engineers blew up the railway bridge as the last of our wagons entered the town. There is a terrific explosion; the inhabitants rush out of their houses shouting '*Allemandes*! *Allemandes*!' A series of lesser explosions continue. The engineers are demolishing the railway line. Gendarmes explain the cause of the explosions and the inhabitants heave a sigh of relief. There is great military activity in this town. Cycle corps, regiments of cavalry, infantry and batteries of artillery moving out, in a different direction to the one by which we entered the town, to engage the enemy. The gunners slap the muzzles of their field pieces and shout to us '*Bom, Bom Allemandes*!' So I take it they are going to shell the Germans. We halted for about one hour in the town.

A French chasseur and I had our photos taken, had a drink together, and exchanged souvenirs. I gave him a clip containing five rounds of our ammunition and he gave me a clip containing three rounds of ammunition. The clip for the Lebel rifle contains only three rounds of ammunition. The bullets are made of copper and are much heavier than ours. The Frenchman smiled and said, '*Souvenir Angleterre*', and I held up the three rounds and replied, '*Souvenir a-la-Francez*.' My French was rather sickly. The polite cavalryman seemed to understand, as he was quite pleased and smiled broadly. I had to give him my home address, so as he could send me a photo, and he gave me his. Mons Morel, Vailly Suse, Aisne, Department of the Aisne, France. We *au-revoired* and parted. It was evident that Mons Morel intended to hold Peronne [Noyon] against the Germans.

At 2.30 pm an old Frenchman, garbed in an older uniform, parades around the town. He stops about every hundred yards and commences ringing a bell. The inhabitants gather around him and he reads aloud from an official looking paper or document. He is the harbinger of very bad news. I can read it in their faces. I can hear them shouting to one another, '*A-la-bas Prussians*!' or something similar. We of the transport guard think they are calling the Prussians bastards.

What has come over the town? The Café and *Estaminet*[36] proprietors drag us in to their *estaminets* and with a suggestive wave of the arm inform us that all the *vin blanc, vin rouge* and all the other *vins* and gins are ours for the taking. So the old town crier must have told them to clear out. There is much shouting, waving of arms and shrugging of shoulders. It is plain to be seen that everyone wants to clear out but cannot make up their minds what to take or to leave.

Move out of Peronne [Noyon] at 3.00 pm. A couple of miles outside Peronne [Noyon] I observed about 500 French soldiers doubling across the

17

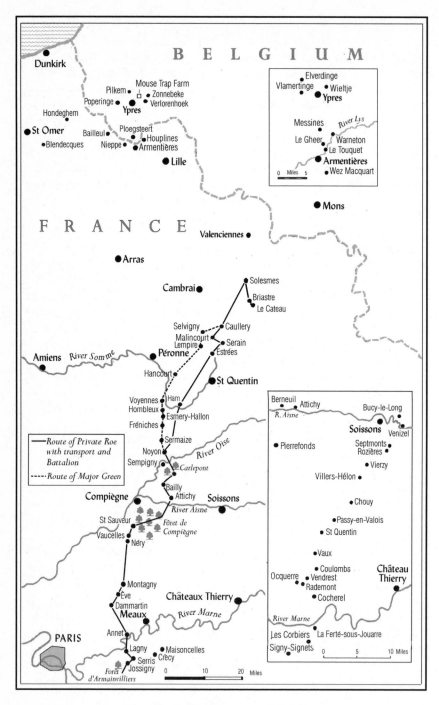

BELGIUM

Dunkirk

Mouse Trap Farm
Pilkem ☐ Zonnebeke
Poperinge ● Verlorenhoek
Ypres

Hondeghem

St Omer
Bailleul ● Houplines
Blendecques ● Ploegsteert
Nieppe ● Armentières

Lille

Inset map (top right):
Elverdinge
Vlamertinge ● Wieltje
Ypres

Messines
Le Gheer ● Warneton
Le Touquet
Armentières
Wez Macquart

0 Miles 5

Mons

FRANCE

Valenciennes ●

Arras

Solesmes
Cambrai ● Briastre
Le Cateau

Selvigny
Malincourt ● Caullery
Lempire ● Serain
Péronne ● Estrées

Amiens River Somme

Hancourt

St Quentin

Voyennes ● Ham
Hombleux
Esmery-Hallon

Fréniches

Sermaize River Oise

Noyon
Sempigny ● Carlepont

Bailly
Compiègne Attichy River Aisne Soissons

St Sauveur
Forêt de
Vaucelles Compiègne
Néry

Montagny
Ève
Dammartin
Meaux River Marne

Châteaux Thierry

Annet
PARIS
Lagny ● Maisoncelles
Serris ● Crécy
Jossigny
Forêt
d'Armainvilliers 0 10 20 Miles

Inset map (bottom right):
Berneuil ● Attichy Bucy-le-Long
R. Aisne
Soissons
Pierrefonds ● Venizel
Septmonts
Rozières
Vierzy
Villers-Hélon ●
● Chouy
● Passy-en-Valois
● St Quentin
● Vaux
Coulombs Château
Ocquerre ● Vendrest Thierry
Rademont
Cocherel
River Marne
Les Corbiers La Ferté-sous-Jouarre
Signy-Signets 0 5 10 Miles

— Route of Private Roe
with transport and
Battalion
----- Route of Major Green

1. North-East France and Belgium

open country on my right and making for the road we were traversing. They appeared to be carrying something on their backs. When they reached the road they unslung a folding bicycle off their backs and in two ticks they were away like hell down the road. 'Very mobile indeed', I commented. [37]

French cavalry are guarding our flanks. There are cavalry regiments in extended order on either flank, so I take it that they are guarding us against an attack by Uhlans.[38]

'*Outspann*'[39] for six hours in a small village [Bailly]. We hand over our charges to their mothers, who will carry on with the retirement. I never dreamt I would perform the duties of nursery maid in France. The Priest or Padre gave us a hearty welcome and did endeavour to make us as comfortable as possible during our brief sojourn. Had a few hours sleep in a school.

I am told on good authority that it is **29 August**. Move off at 7.00 am. The inhabitants of this village are preparing to evacuate and look the picture of despair.

We pick up some of our battalion on the road. Things are not as bad as they were at first painted, as Major Green is 'somewhere in France' with 200 men.[40]

Our transport forms up with the Divisional transport. Our field guns are camouflaged behind stooks of oats and are ranging on some high ground 4000 yards in our rear. The sound of heavy rifle fire in the same direction gently reminds the officer commanding transport to get a move on.

Here there is some confusion as some transport belonging to the 12th Brigade takes the same road as those of the 11th, and we are held up for over half an hour.

The countryside is black with unfortunate refugees. In some cases where there are not a sufficiency of parallel roads, the transport has to find its way across country as to keep to one road would mean a convoy four kilometers long, if not more, and would provide a rather tempting morsel for an enemy cavalry commander.

The burning villages in our rear reflect a ruddy glow on the August sky each night.

Re-join the Battalion

30 August.[41] Join the Brigade at 9.00 am.[42] They are halted for the day outside a small village the name of which I do not know [Sempigny]. We have been on the march for eighteen hours and are done up, so are the animals. Other units have made piles of their packs and burned them.[43] We still retain ours. Full packs, of course, cause what might be called 'lack of mobility'. No man, company or regiment can fight or move with the speed which modern warfare demands and wear a full pack. Even fighting order is rather a strain on a perfectly fit man's stamina.

Major Green arrives with over 200 men and there are some more, wandering about 'somewhere in France'.

I rejoin my Company, 'A', and miss a lot of familiar faces,[44] but the Battalion has not lost so heavily after all.[45]

As we move off at 4.00 pm[46] a French flying machine is chasing a German, which he succeeded in bringing down (so we are told).

Notes

1 'At dawn the battalion embarked on *Braemar Castle* on which were also Brigade HQ, the Somersets Regiment and half a battalion of the Hampshires.' (Hopkinson, p.3)

2 'So hurried [was the order to entrain for Southampton] that some 150 men out on pass in the town had to be left behind and were brought up by the next battalion, joining their own battalion at Havre.' (Ibid, p.3)

3 'Battalion . . . did not disembark until 11.00 pm.' (1st Bn War Diary, 22 August 1914)

4 Iron rations, or emergency tinned rations, could include a 1lb tin of bully beef and a small quantity of tea or cocoa and sugar.

5 The conspicuous colour was supposed to be favoured by the French gunners, whose chief opposed changing it on the grounds that 'the little red backsides gave him a distinguishing line, beyond which to range his guns in battle'!

6 Brigadier-General A.G. Hunter-Weston, commander of 11 Brigade of the 4th Division. The other Battalions of 11 Brigade were 1st Somerset Light Infantry, 1st Hampshire Regiment and 1st Rifle Brigade (Prince Consort's Own).

7 John L. Sullivan (1858 – 1918), nicknamed *The Boston Strongboy*, was the first great American sports idol. He became the world heavyweight boxing champion in 1889 in the last bare knuckle title fight.

8 Bob Fitzsimmons (1863 – 1917), born in Britain, made boxing history by being the first man to be world champion in three divisions – middleweight, light-heavyweight and heavyweight.

9 *Generaloberst* von Moltke, Chief of the German General Staff.

10 Admiral von Tirpitz, Secretary of State for the German Navy.

11 The general population feared the Zeppelin airships. At the opening of hostilities with Germany it was supposed they had fifty Zeppelin airships ready or approaching completion. It was well known the German intention was to employ squadrons of Zeppelins dropping heavy bombs threatening cities and naval fleets. There were some Zeppelin raids, particularly on Antwerp and Ostend in August 1914, but the airships were slow and had poor mobility, therefore were an easy target and were disappointing operationally. Five Zeppelins were lost in the first month of the war.

12 Georges Carpentier (1894 – 1975) was perhaps the greatest European boxer of all time. He competed in virtually every weight class. By 1914 he held the European welterweight, middleweight, light heavyweight and heavyweight titles. During the Great War he served in the French military as an observation pilot and was decorated twice. Already popular, Carpentier was hailed as a true hero in France.

13 Private Roe, as he states in his diary, had no idea of the towns they passed and did not

know the name of their final destination. It was Le Cateau, the General Headquarters for the British Expeditionary Force, 17 – 25 August 1914.

14 'Amiens was reached about noon on the 24th, and Le Cateau at about 7.30 pm, where the battalion detrained.' (Regt. Hist., pp. 2–3)

15 It was not surprising for Roe to see six aeroplanes on 24 August as the Royal Flying Corps [RFC] operated from Le Cateau on 24 – 25 August. There were sixty-three operational aircraft in four squadrons. The squadrons were a mixture of machines, all used for recon-naissance. They performed a very valuable job in enabling the British Expeditionary Force to escape the trap set by the German armies. General Sir John French was to say, in a despatch on 7 September, 'they [i.e. the aircraft of the RFC] have furnished me with the most complete and accurate information which has been of incalculable value in the conduct of operations.'

16 'The only information that reached the battalion that night was that a German Army was marching round the western flank.' (Regt. Hist., p. 3)

17 Briastre, a village five miles to the north of Le Cateau.

18 'During the night of the 24th/25th orders were received for the 4th Division to take up a position just south of Solesmes to cover the retreat of the 3rd Division to Le Cateau. In accordance with these orders the 11th Brigade marched to the high ground on both sides of the Solesmes – Le Cateau road.' (Regt. Hist., p. 3)

19 The first line battalion transport under Lieutenant MacMullen.

20 The village was Solesmes.

21 This was a common occurrence in the villages at this stage of the war. Some of the most competitive village girls managed to secure badges of every unit that passed.

22 'In the afternoon the shells of the German advance guard were . . . bursting over the high ground, north of Solesmes.' (Regt. Hist., p. 3) At Solesmes the South Lancashire and Wiltshire Battalions of 7 Brigade, rearguard to the 3rd Division, stopped the advance of the 8th Division of the German IV Corps.

23 Roe is describing cuirassiers, who at this early part of the war did indeed look to be straight from the Napoleonic period with their horsehair plumed helmets and breastplates. He admits he had no idea of the uniforms of the allies and as the British army had no cuirassiers he most likely assumed they were a type of dragoon.

24 Private Roe is presumably referring here to the red service tunic that was worn in the First Boer War. In the Second Boer War of 1899 – 1902 the British Army wore khaki field service dress.

25 From Solesmes the [Battalion] transport arrived at Caullery about 1.00 pm: about 2.00 pm they were directed by a Staff Officer to go to Malincourt: en route they were directed to Serain. Thence they moved down the Estrées road, which led into the Cambrai-St.Quentin road. On this road they joined a heterogeneous column of troops and transport and moved along the road until dusk, when halted by the roadside near Nauroy for the night. (Regt. Hist., p.10)

26 On 26 August 1/Battalion The East Lancashire Regiment played a prominent part in 11 Brigade's day-long action to hold the left flank of II Corps at the Battle of Le Cateau. The Battalion occupied positions on the Carrière Ridge, one mile north of the village of Ligny. Despite being outflanked, heavily shelled and closely assaulted by infantry, they held their positions until ordered to withdraw on Ligny, from where the Brigade continued its

retirement some time after 6.00 pm. 'C' Company, deployed forward in some gravel pits on the top of the ridge, were the last to break contact and retire at about 5.00 pm, having made an epic defence of a sunken road. The East Lancashires withdrew from Ligny in two parties, but were obliged to leave their wounded in the village. The Battalion's casualties at Le Cateau included Lieutenant Chisolm, the first Australian to be killed in the War.

27 2nd Battalion The Lancashire Fusiliers, part of 12 Brigade of the 4th Division. They were heavily involved in fighting on the left wing in the Battle of Le Cateau against the German 2nd Cavalry Division and Jäger infantry.

28 'A French force of General Sordet's Cavalry Corps and the 61st and 62nd Reserve Divisions were operating on the flank.' (Hopkinson, p. 33)

29 At Ham.

30 'The transport left the bivouac at Nauroy at 7.00 am [27 August] and set out for St.Quentin in the midst of a disorganized crowd of soldiery. About 11.00 am the transport reached St.Quentin, where there was a large notice board directing the 4th Div troops to Ham.' (Regt.Hist., p. 11)

31 'The transport left Ham at 3.00 am passed through Noyon to Bailly (five miles to the south) and bivouacked there.' (Ibid, p. 11)

32 Many units were disorganized following the fighting at Mons and Le Cateau. The dispersal of units naturally bred rumours of regiments being wiped out. In reality, despite heavy losses, only the 2nd Royal Munster Fusiliers, acting as a rearguard, were destroyed as a unit.

33 'The Army Service Corps who had our rations, they couldn't stop. They just threw our rations on the side of the road and left us to pick them up.' (Rifleman E. Gale 1st Battalion The Rifle Brigade, 11 Brigade, 4th Division.)

34 At the age of eighteen every Frenchman did military service and, until middle age released him from his obligation, every Frenchman was on the Army Reserve. There were no exceptions.

35 Almost certainly this is a mistake and the town was most likely Noyon.

36 *Estaminets* were found in every village, near the armies, and were a cross between a café and a pub. It was a focal point for most off-duty soldiers. Wine and beer were cheap and food was available.

37 Each French Cavalry Division had a cyclist battalion, which Roe had just witnessed. This unit would have been from the 1st Cavalry Division of General Sordet's Corps.

38 German Lancer Cavalry.

39 A Boer word which Private Roe no doubt learnt during his service in South Africa. It meant to form a defensive wagon circle during a halt.

40 Following the action at Le Cateau, Major Green ('D'Coy.) was ordered to move south-west for the high ground near Selvigny where, he was informed, the Divisional Commander was forming an infantry rearguard. Major Green took 4 officers and some 280 men . . . 'On reaching Selvigny he found no British troops at all . . . .[He] decided to retire south and eventually reached Malincourt about dusk . . . [where he was joined by] an officer of the battalion and some 50 men . . . .[They] marched on to Lempire and Hancourt . . . reached about noon [27 August] and took up a defensive position to cover the retirement of the II Corps to the Somme . . . .Late in the afternoon . . . [they were] withdrawn without becoming engaged. Voyennes was reached about 5.30 am [28

22

August]. Major Green heard, for the first time, of the survival of the other half of the battalion . . . .[At] 10.00 am, the retreat continued via Hombleux and Esmery-Hallon . . . to Fréniches. [He] continued his march via Compagne to Sermaize, reached at 8.00 am [29 August]. This was the day of the withdrawal and concentration of the II Corps, and 4th Division, south of the River Oise. To cover this 11 Brigade took up a position near Sermaize, which it held throughout the day . . . .[Fortunately the] Brigade was not attacked, and at dusk it succeeded in withdrawing across the river by bridge at Sempigny, where Major Green remained on outposts till the early hours of next morning [30 August]. About 2.00 pm Major Green withdrew from Sempigny and, after a march of five miles, at dawn [6.00 am] the two halves of the battalion met once more. For his work throughout these days Major Green received the DSO'. (Hopkinson, p.p. 32–35)

41 During the retreat Roe writes in his diary that he found it impossible to keep a daily record of events and through this period 'I did not even know what day it was.' As he records later in his diary, he made notes as and when he could and during the retreat these were probably a few days after the events and with tiredness these events must get blurred.
    Particularly towards the end of the retreat he has attributed the wrong dates to some events. However, his sequence of events are in the right order for 25 – 28 August when compared to the Regimental History. The transport rejoined the Battalion on the morning of the 29th and, after resting outside Sempigny for the day, as he states, they marched on the 30th to Pierrefonds and then on the 31st, via the Compiègne forest, to St Sauveur.

42 'The situation for the moment was considered satisfactory, for the advance of the Germans against both flanks of the British force had been held up by the Fifth and Sixth French Armies . . . The situation, however, required a strategic retirement, and during the night August 29/30 orders were issued for the British force to retire to the line of the Aisne from Soissons to Compiègne (as rearguard). The route taken was through Carlepont and Berneuil, across the Aisne at Attichy . . . to Pierrefonds.' (Regt. Hist., p.12)

43 'A GHQ order had ordered all officer's kit and even military material to be burnt on the roadside . . . this order never reached . . . the battalion.' (Hopkinson, p.30)

44 'A' Company had been heavily engaged at Le Cateau.

45 'At the end of the retreat the Battalion was reduced to 22 officers and about 500 men.' (Regt.Hist., p.15)

46 'The Battalion marched three miles further south then bivouacked in a field.' (1st Bn War diary, p.4)

III

Action at St Sauveur

(1 – 5 September 1914)

A Rearguard Action – The Spy – Retire – Barbed Wire – In The Village –
German Guns at Néry – The Retreat Continues

A Rearguard Action

31 August [1 September]:[1] At midnight the Battalion halts in a village,[2] the name of which I am told is St Saviour [St Sauveur]. Outposts are posted on the right flank and in rear of the village. As we are preparing tea, kilometres of transport and Red Cross vans roll by. My Company, 'A', are in supports to 'D' Company. We lie down for a few hours sleep on the roadside and are in a constant state of alarm from 1.00 am onwards owing to repeated bursts of rifle fire on our left front.

At dawn we heard a tremendous burst of machine gun fire and after a few minutes artillery chimed in. It lasted almost half an hour. We were told that 'L' Battery RHA [Royal Horse Artillery] and the 5th Dragoon Guards were taken by surprise and cut up by a force of 2000 Germans with a lot of machine guns and three batteries of artillery. The French cavalry regiment which held the ridge in front and acted as a screen withdrew during the night and did not think it worth their while to inform anybody, with the result that the Germans took possession peaceably and when dawn broke the Dragoons and artillery bivouacs were at their mercy.[3]

Our outposts have opened fire, and so has somebody else to judge by the volume of sound. My platoon is ordered in the firing line to support 'D' Company.[4] We advance at the double under fire and form line on the edge of a mangel-wurzel field in rear of the village. We form a continuation of the line held by 'D' Company. The German rifle fire is very erratic. We cannot locate the enemy as the country is heavily wooded and he has had the advantage of taking up his position unobserved. By keeping up a brisk fire on the edge of a plantation on our right front, 500 yards away, we succeeded in reducing the enemy's fire somewhat.

They have brought some horse or field guns and also a couple of machine guns into action. Quite a number of men have been hit including Captain Seabroke.[5] The inhabitants have evacuated the village in our rear, also the village on our left front. Their shrapnel is bursting 600 yards in our rear around the steeple of the village church. I distinctly heard the clock on the church tower chime the hour of nine. It was the last nine it ever chimed as it went 'bang' with the next salvo of shells. They are now shelling the village, which is about 180 yards in our rear.

My section are on the extreme left of the line so we swing back so as to form a flank facing the village on our left front in case the Germans might work their way into the village and enfilade or surround us. The German shells are bursting well in rear of our line and we suffer no losses from their shrapnel, although their rifle and machine gun fire is getting more accurate.

The Spy

After we had formed a flank facing the village we distinctly saw a civilian standing on the road leading into the village. He was weighing our position up. He took two slow paces forward, halted and put his right hand above his head. He was signaling to the German observing officer that he was 200 yards over range.

We drew our platoon commander's attention to the civilian and explained his actions, but he would not allow us to open fire on him. We told Sergeant Hall that we were positive he was signaling to the German artillery and that there should be no civilians in the village as all had orders to clear out. It was no use; he would not let us fire on him.

The next salvo from the 'Jerries' burst beautifully in front of our line, wounded six and killed two in my part or section of the line. The spy still stood on the middle of the road, gloating over his handiwork. He was 200 yards away so we determined to shoot him, permission or no permission. He turned around and commenced to run towards the village. Three of us opened rapid fire on him; he crumpled up on the middle of the roadway. We gave him another five rounds each to make certain, or in case he was playing 'possum'. Fancy his damned cheek! Standing on a roadway 300 yards away from a platoon of British infantry and deliberately signaling to the 'Jerry' forward observing officer. Well, he will give no more 'tips' to an observing officer. The sergeant wanted to know what we were firing at. We told him we saw three or four 'Jerries' in the village. It was a good job for us that they did not work their way into the village or they would have made our line untenable by enfilade fire.

Retire

They are giving us a pretty rough time. Their shrapnel is doing most of the damage as we have no cover and are lying in the open. Their machine gun and rifle fire is not very accurate; nevertheless an odd bullet here and there finds a billet. We are fighting an uphill fight as we have no artillery support – not even a Maxim gun. I have not seen a German yet. Our volume of fire is decreasing owing to the practice of two men taking their equipment off and 'dumping' it in the firing line in order to carry one man out. Apart from the loss of fire effect, two lives are being risked, (as they offer a better target when walking) in order to bring one man to safety.

Captain Clayhills DSO ['A' Coy] dashes down to the firing line and orders us to get out of it as quickly as possible. He told us we should have retired over half an hour ago.

The village, the houses rather, are built in one continuous line, one house adjoining the other. He warned us not to make for each end of the village; if we did the 'Jerries' would mow us down with machine gun fire. He advised us to force a way through the houses.

Platoons by now were just a little over the strength of sections. It was no use retiring by sections under covering fire, as the last two sections would remain there for 'keeps'.

Word is passed along to retire through the village and form up on the road on the Captain sounding a long blast on a whistle. Meanwhile we redouble our fire on where we think the enemy is concealed.

The blast sounds and the line arose as one man and doubled back across the 'blasted' mangel-wurzel field to the gardens in rear of the village. The Germans redoubled their efforts to put a stop to our gallop. They did not meet much success as running targets are very hard to hit.

Barbed Wire

A serious obstacle confronted us when we came to the orchards (or gardens). They were wired with a fence of barbed wire, five feet high and one foot between strands. Shrapnel and bullets flew all around us. We cannot get over the wire, we cannot get through it, as we have no wire cutters; therefore we must try and get under it.

The Germans have come into the open and are pursuing us. We can hear strange shouts of command and whistles blowing. A glance to the rear and there they are, advancing in line and firing from the hip as they advance.

'Dusty' Millar tries to wriggle through under the bottom strand of barbed wire and gets hopelessly entangled in the wire. He implores me to cut his pack off, which I do with my clasp knife. The Germans are getting closer as there is no covering fire from our side.

In desperation I hurl myself body and soul beneath the bottom strand. I get hopelessly stuck. I undo my shoulder straps and belt and wriggle out of my equipment. I am one side of the barbed wire fence and my equipment is the other side. I shove my hand through, undo the flap of a pouch and transfer the remaining fifteen rounds to my pocket.

The Germans are about 100 yards away. They look pretty formidable in their picklehaubes and bearskin packs. I have got to leave my equipment and Millar his pack as to retrieve either means that we are either going to be shot or taken prisoners. In any case, we should have been shot thirty seconds ago if the 'Jerries' could shoot. We dash through the orchard to the back doors of the houses. A shell bursts overhead and we are smothered in a shower of ripe apples, which fell off the trees owing to the concussion. We did not stoop to pick any up. The back doors are locked. I curse the back doors, the French and the barbed wire.

In The Village

Nothing for it but the butts of the rifles; we soon splinter the back door and dash into the house. We are gasping with thirst; a bottle and three glasses stand on a table – anything in the bottle? Yes! It is half full, I pour out a glass each. It is a white liquid and has a fiery taste. I called it white whisky. We made for the front door; it is locked. Smash a window then and get through to the road. I observed a canary in a cage and boxes of rabbits or hares in rear of the house. A girl of about ten years runs up to the house; she is breathless. She grabs the cage and makes off. Where did she come from? I hope she gets through.

I must get a set of equipment at all costs. There are some dead and wounded lying under cover of the houses, but their equipment has been dumped at the place where they got wounded. Who's this? 'Cockney' Williams.[6] My God! the last time I saw him he was having a 'burst up' in Maxim's Cafe in Cape Town. He got hit in the chin and the bullet ricocheted into his chest. He is well bandaged up and it does not seem likely that he will need equipment for some considerable time, if at all. In any case, it will only fall into the hands of the Germans, so I annex it. We smashed up six of our rifles that we found lying up against the wall of the house.

We double up the road to the right as per instructions from the Captain, and join the Battalion, who are under cover of a hedge on the roadside facing the enemy's line of advance.[7] We had to leave our wounded in the village. The Germans have ceased firing and everything is strangely quiet. We can see Germans on horseback in the distance scanning the country with glasses.

27

The Germans who chased us into the village are very quiet; probably they have no ammunition as they were very lavish in their expenditure upon us. The results did not justify the expenditure.

I am <u>praying</u> hard as I have left eight ounces of Gallagher's Plug (tobacco), three briar pipes, a butler and a Kropp razor, soap, towel and everything I possessed in my valise and haversack. I had no option of course. That scrap left me with quite ¾ of an ounce of tobacco and a wheezy old pipe.

Dear reader, don't be under the impression that because I have used up quite 800 words in describing what happened from the time Captain Clayhills signaled the retire to the time I rejoined the Battalion on the road a mile away from the village that it took me two hours. Nothing of the kind, I did it in well under the half hour. The bullet is the finest incentive in the world for making men 'get a move on'.

I reflected on my boasting in Mr Fagan's smithy on August 4, 'We'll swamp hell with German sausages etc. etc.' Well thank God neither Tom the Blacksmith or my fourteen neighbours who were assembled in the forge that morning could see Roe on the morning of August 31 running like Hell and the despised 'Jerries' running after him. If they could see, – well my cup of disappointment would overflow indeed.

German Guns at Néry

The Battalion waited for half an hour on the roadside in order to give stragglers time to come in as all were instructed in the firing line as to where to rendezvous. We form up on the roadside and act as rearguard in artillery formation.[8] As we moved across the plain we came across eleven German guns out of action and abandoned. They are German and no mistake; the double-headed eagle and the manufacturer's name (Krupp Essen) are engraved or emblazoned on the muzzles close to the breach. The remains of mangled horses and gunners are strewn around the guns, so this must be where the 'scrap' took place this morning at daybreak.[9]

The Retreat Continues

We carried on without incident until 5.00 pm in the evening, although at times during the day (or afternoon, I mean) we could see the enemies cavalry well away on our left rear. Sometimes they seemed to be parallel to our line of retreat. At 5.00 pm a French force wedges itself in between pursuers and pursued and engages the enemy.[10] We reach a small village [Rosières], with a quaint old church built in the Norman style of architecture, and 'bed down' with the cows, calves and poultry until early next morning.

An elderly Frenchman, who could speak English, told us that an Uhlan patrol had been in the village one hour before the arrival of British troops and had abused (I might as well call a spade a spade and say that they raped) two of the village maidens. They must have worked around our flanks.

The Middlesex or Essex, I am not quite sure which, are on outpost duty.

1 September [2 September] The Battalion moves off at 5.00 am,[11] no sooner are we on the road than we are spotted by an enemy flying machine.

A French dragoon was picked up in the village and brought along by our transport. He cannot walk as his spinal column is injured. He told our interpreter that he got injured whilst charging with our cavalry against the Prussian horse. We think he has had a bad fall as his brass helmet is out of shape, badly bent and his sword badly buckled.

For two days we marched through an immense forest and strike open country on the third day.[12] No sooner do we cross a bridge than French demolition parties demolish it.

French engineers, aided by the civilian population, are throwing up defensive works with feverish haste, and mounting guns. We ask ourselves the question, are we going to keep on retiring forever? When are we going to make a stand? We have had hardly any rest for the past seven days and are marched off our feet. We have daily passed groups of men of various units lying on the roadside thoroughly 'done up' and unable to march another yard. Generals and colonels have threatened and cajoled them in turn, but it was no use, they are 'dead beat'.

In my own unit when we get a halt at night men drop where they stand. Others crawl into the wood and fall asleep. When we fall in again it is reported that six or maybe eight men are missing. We cannot stop to look for them, as we must keep moving. The Uhlans picked them up I suppose, immediately we moved off.

When we halt for an hour to make tea, we open the tin of bully (between two or three as usual) and get our biscuits out of our haversacks. Three or four of us may be lucky and be in possession of a loaf of bread each, which we 'scrounged' at some farmhouse. The camp kettles are boiling at last, the tea is about to become a reality, when the order is issued 'empty the camp kettles, pack up at once, the Uhlans are only three miles in the rear'. So we have to fall in and eat a dry breakfast as we march along. This scare occurs daily, the word Uhlan seems to be a form of terrorism. I suppose they are half starved like ourselves, and if they suddenly came upon us they would turn and bolt on sight.

The Brigadier (Hunter-Weston) is a pest. For the past two days he has been riding up and down on the flanks of the Battalion shouting 'Cover off, by the left, hold your heads up, swing your arms, Left, Right, Left, Right!' Everyone is grumbling and remarking, 'It's all right for you Hunter, you're on horseback, your feet are not sore, you have not averaged thirty-five miles per day for the last nine days in full pack and almost nothing to eat, if we had, we had no time to cook or eat it. If you cannot give us encouragement for Christ's sake don't bully us, we're bad enough.'

We marched past three generals today. They were sitting around a camp table, flagging maps. The expressions on their care-worn faces did not give us much encouragement. I enquired who the stout general in the centre was? I was told it was General Snow,[13] the Divisional Commander.

As we march through the villages the inhabitants are the picture of despair. What a contrast; thirteen days previously we were hailed as the deliverers of France, 'Long live England, *Vive-la-Angleterre*.' Instead of delivering France, we are retiring by forced marches in the direction of Paris. There is no enthusiasm now, no '*Vive-la-Angleterre*, no Tipperary.' No! – nothing but black despair. The Prussian jackboot, Prussian soldiers and the Prussian cannon are going, so it seems, to repeat the performance of 1870. The oldest inhabitants of the villages, who remember that black page in France's history, ask us as we march through, 'Are the Prussians going to take Paris?'

Our Adjutant, Lieutenant Belchier, wears a comical appearance. He attempted a much needed shave four days ago, but only succeeded in shaving one side of his face when he had to 'pack up', as the much dreaded Uhlans were only supposed to be half an hour in the rear. He has not had time since to finish the operation, with the result that there is a ten days growth on one side of his face and a four days growth on the other.[14]

I shall never forget the unbounded hospitality of the French people on the retirement. The poorer the people the more generous. Had it not been for their generosity we would have to perform many a long march hungry and thirsty.

At last we march under cover of the fortress of Lagny,[15] one of the chain of fortifications defending Paris.

Someone with a keen sense of humour spread the 'yarn' that we were going to take over the defence of Paris. He could not have perused the evolution of tactics or strategy, whoever he was, although tactics and strategy differ a hell of a lot. Yet a commander, to ensure success, has to combine both. In the field we can manoeuvre, in the first we are stationary objects. Metz and Paris were two glaring examples of French strategy in 1870. We are told that German tactics forced Bayerne [Bazaine][16] into Metz in 1870. Let us hope that 'Jacky French' wont be 'gulled' into slipping into Paris in 1914.

It is amazing the colossal ignorance of 90% of the Battalion regarding military history. They never heard of Hadrian, Hannibal, Gustavus Adolphus, Wallenstein, Nero, Alexander the Great, the De Lacys, Macks and Dauns of Austria. Their knowledge of the Duke of Marlborough, one of the most brilliant soldiers of his age, is very remote. They will admit that the versatile Winston[17] is a descendant of Marlborough. Mention Stonewall Jackson and the Valley Campaign, 'Oh! You mean him who plays full back for 'D' Company at Hockey.' If you told them that the Hanoverians bore Gibraltar as a Battle Honour on their Colours and that they took part in the defence of Gibraltar, they would call you a damn liar.

Of course, the soldier is not to blame. As, for example, on numerous occasions on manoeuvres, I have been on outposts [and] group sentries were posted in a bad position by the sergeant. By simply moving a little forward, or to the right or left, they got better observation or a better field of view. They shifted accordingly, but when the sergeant came around again he, of course, noticed that the sentries had changed position.

'What the hell are you doing there? I did not post you there!'

'No sergeant, but we thought we could get a better observation here.'

'You're not supposed to think. As long as you have the necessary brains to execute your drill movements that is all that is required of you. I do the thinking my lads, I'm paid for thinking, so in future cut thinking out.'

Of course it never entered the sergeant's head that even a private's brain and intellect should be as highly trained as his own and that some day owing to casualties, as in the present case, privates have to take command of sections and platoons. The private is still under the impression that he is not allowed to think and naturally lacks initiative.

From my experience of the army, the literature most favoured by ninety per cent of the Tommies is Buffalo Bill's wild-west yarns, penny novels and famous crimes. Ah yes, Clive! 'Bobby' Clive, that laid the foundations of our great Indian Empire. An odd one here and there heard something about Clive, but gave him no credit for defeating the Nabob of Bengal at the Battle of Plassey. Clive according to their ideas did not win the Battle by fair means, as he 'squared' Meer Cassim, who commanded the Nabob's centre, with five bullock carts full of rupees. As soon as the Battle commenced Meer Cassim naturally withdrew his centre and retired from the field and left the poor old Nabob at 'sixes and sevens'.

On entering the defence area, which is heavily wooded, a vast multitude of civilians of both sexes were engaged in felling trees in order to afford a better field of fire. The roads at frequent intervals were barricaded. The barricades were defended by 'mitraleuse' manned by much be-whiskered and rather ancient French soldiers. I believe the French invented the 'mitraleuse'. It was a type of machine gun, which had seven barrels and was manipulated by turning a wheel or crank. They were also armed with the chassepot rifle and bronze guns. The chassepot had a small bore and a longer range than the Prussian Needle gun. The French guns were inferior to the Germans as regards range, precision and weight of metal discharge.

The Brigade bivouacs in the woods.[18] We are 'thoroughly done up'. We are told that we are to have a rest and reorganization.[19]

We have to keep 'shifting' our position owing to the enemy's aircraft keeping us under observation from dawn until dusk. They cannot see us but they can observe the smoke from our fires. We cannot cook without a fire and a fire causes smoke.

My Platoon Sergeant (Sergeant Hall)[20] is missing from August 31, the date on which we fought the rearguard action, and so are a lot more.

We remained for two days in the woods and could do with a change of underclothing badly as we are beginning to get 'lousy'. Our kit bags, containing the remainder of our kit, have not turned up, so it is a case of remaining 'lousy'.

Notes

1 Private Roe, as he admits, makes mistakes with the dates. To be correct it was 1 September.
2 The Battalion was disposed as a covering force to protect the continued retreat of the BEF.
3 At approx. 5.30 am the 1st Cavalry Brigade and 'L' Battery (Royal Horse Artillery) were preparing to continue their retirement when they were attacked by the German 4th Cavalry Division. Guns, machine guns and rifle fire came from the heights above Néry at approximately 600 yards distance. The cavalry brigade and 'L' battery not only halted the German attack, but when reinforcements arrived with the 4th Cavalry Brigade, 'I' Battery (RHA) and a composite battalion of Warwickshire and Dublins, they were counter-attacked, causing the German division to retreat and lose eight guns (destroyed) with the remaining four lost soon after. Three Victoria Crosses were awarded to the gunners of 'L' Battery who fought to the last round.
4 "D' Company became engaged with the mounted troops forming the left of the advanced guard of the German II Corps.' (Hopkinson, p.38)
5 'Captain Seabroke of 'D' Coy was shot in the leg, taken prisoner and placed by the Germans in hospital in Compiègne . . . unfortunately it was found necessary to amputate his leg. He was released by the French on recapture of that town a fortnight later.' (Ibid, p.39)
6 Private Joseph Williams (enlisted in London).
7 'The battalion then retired by the road to Vaucelles, making use of the wooded country, . . . on to the high ground near Néry.' (Hopkinson, p.39)
8 'After reaching the high ground at Néry the battalion took up a position, and the Rifle Brigade retired through the battalion. The Brigade then retired slowly across the open country in artillery formation for some twelve miles south. During this retirement the battalion formed the infantry of the rear-guard behind a screen of the 4th Cavalry Brigade and Divisional cyclists.' (Ibid, p.40)
9 The action at Néry is described in footnote 3.
10 'French troops were on the left flank.' (Hopkinson, p.42) – [Ed. General Sordet's Cavalry Corps]

11 The retreat continued via Montagny-Ste-Félicité to Ève and Dammartin-en-Goële. (Ibid, p.41)

12 The march continued via St Mard and Annet-sur-Marne to Lagny-sur-Marne. (Ibid, p.42)

13 Major General T. D'O. Snow CB, General Officer Commanding 4th Division.

14 The story of Lieutenant Belchier and his 'half shave' are reported as one of the humorous incidents of the war for the battalion. (Hopkinson, p.30)

15 Crossed the Marne at Lagny on 3 September. (Regt. Hist., p.14)

16 In the Franco-Prussian War the French Marshal Bazaine, faced by the Prussian Army in 1870, had retired into the fortress of Metz. Historians in the 1900's, particularly Sir Edward Hamley, wrote damning judgements of his action.

17 Winston Churchill, 1st Lord of the Admiralty.

18 '[5 September] about 3.00 pm, after a long and trying march of close on twenty miles under a hot sun by Serris, Jossigny and the Forest of Armainvilliers, the battalion bivouacked in the grounds of Marsaudière Château.' (Hopkinson, p.44)

19 'This was the last day of the long retreat from Le Cateau. The Battalion was reduced to 22 officers and 500 men. It had marched 150 miles in 10 days, during the course of which it had fought one pitched battle and several rear-guard actions against superior forces.' (Regt. Hist., p.15)

20 No record of his having been killed in action, therefore presume he became a prisoner of war.

IV

Crossing the Marne

(6 – 9 September 1914)

Advance to the Marne – Devastation in La Ferté-sous-Jouarre – Death of
Lt Col Le Marchant –
Tribute to the Fallen Welshmen – Crossing the Marne

Advance to the Marne

[6 September] On the morning of the third day[1] French[2] orders a 'general advance'. For the first two days nothing of importance happened, although depredations committed by the much-dreaded Uhlans were in evidence in the villages.[3]

[8 September] On the morning of the third day of our advance we were informed that the enemy were strongly posted and occupying the high ground around Chateau Thierry.

On the evening of the same day, as we debouched from a wood into a plain the Middlesex were well in front, accompanied by their transport. The Germans had a battery of horse artillery concealed on some rising ground and opened fire on the Middlesex transport. What is left of the transport retires, carrying the wounded on their carts. The troops in front open out for attack, we lie down on the roadside. Rifle fire has commenced. The German horse artillery limbered up and galloped like blazes over the crest of the rising ground, speeded on by our bursting shrapnel. The advance is resumed.

The French are heavily engaged on our left and their seventy-fives[4] are making a tremendous row.

Our line of advance takes us into another wood. The Battalion wheels to the right and debouch from the wood by platoons and in the rear of three Batteries of our field guns, who are shelling the Germans for all they are worth. The enemy does not reply.

It has begun to rain heavily and the Regiment gets a cheap bath. Wet through, we are marched to a large farmhouse [Les Corbiers] and billeted for the night.[5]

Devastation in La Ferté-sous-Jouarre

[**9 September**] [We] rouse at 4.00 am next morning and deploy into line in a wood overlooking the village of La Ferté.[6] The river Marne runs on the opposite side of the village. The Germans are wide-awake and rake the wood with machine gun fire.[7] The Royal Welch Fusiliers hold the village, as they drove the Germans across the river the previous evening.

The Battalion advances in Indian file down the slopes of the wood and into the village street. We advance under cover of a wall, which ran along a footpath in the village street. There were several wooden doors let into this wall to enable the villagers to gain access to their gardens. The thoughtful 'Jerries' had the doors marked and we had several casualties, as they kept up a continual rifle fire on the wooden doors from the heights beyond the river. One poor fellow, Private Roak, got hit in the left side as he dashed past a door. The bullet exploded his ammunition, blew his left side away, and set his clothing on fire.

We relieved the Royal Welch Fusiliers[8] and commence erecting barricades. Houses, which overlook the German position, are taken possession of, loop holed, and windows barricaded. Bullets are flying in all directions.

The village presents a desperate and desolate appearance. It was the scene of a fierce struggle if appearances are anything to go by, with household property smashed up and strewn in the streets. The Germans could not hold the village, but Attila and his Huns could not teach the 'cultured Jerry' much in the art of devastation and destruction. Tables, chairs, mattresses, bric-a-brac, ornaments, chests of drawers, religious pictures, family photos and crockery were smashed in pieces and hurled through the windows into the streets. They smashed every pane of glass in the windows, relieved the wants of nature on bed sheets and rolled them up. Drank all the wine in the cellars. What they were unable to drink they destroyed or polluted. They commandeered all the coffee, sugar, flour and other commodities on worthless requisitions.

The footpaths are knee-deep in broken bottles and occasional dead 'Jerries', less picklehaubes (German helmets) but with bearskin packs. I never saw such wanton destruction, which served no useful military purpose. I came to the conclusion that they must have a corps of specialists for business like this. Sabotage is mild indeed in comparison to this.

The inhabitants stowed themselves away in their cellars when fighting commenced yesterday evening. We were over an hour in the village before they learned that the 'Jerries' had been chased out. The old men, women and 'kids' emerge from their cellars. "*Soldats Angleterre! Soldats Angleterre!*" they shout from one house to another across the street. They went wild with joy. In twenty minutes time they regale us with coffee.

They tell us they are sorry they have not got bread, as the *Allemands* (Germans) have taken it all.

The Germans are raking the village from every conceivable angle with batteries of machine guns from the heights beyond the river. They cannot get us by direct fire, so they train their guns on the walls of the houses hoping to get some of us by the ricochet of the bullets. Our men are keeping up a heavy and sustained fire on them from the houses, which confront their position. Our artillery are making it hot for them. They do not appear to have any.

Brigadier General Hunter-Weston is running about like a madman in his shirtsleeves, giving advice and encouragement and finding targets for our artillery.

Our Colonel – Yes! If you want to find him, search where the bullets are falling thickest. It is a wonder he has not been 'seen off' hours ago. He has been engaged all morning seeking out positions where rifle fire can be used to the best advantage. He does not say to a section commander, get your section into that isolated house and make loopholes. You should get a good field of observation and fire from it. No! He goes himself first and reconnoitres the enemy's position and if he thinks it is too exposed and they could be enfiladed he will not send them. 'Never send a man where you would not go yourself' is his maxim. He 'choked' off my platoon sergeant this morning over the barricade. We carried stones from a wall and, in a short time, erected a pretty formidable barricade across the street and then manned it. The Colonel came along and 'played up hell' with the sergeant for not utilizing all the mattresses that were strewn in the street, on the barricade. They would be a preventative against splinters from the stones in case the Germans re-crossed the river and opened fire on the barricade. We could have told the sergeant that hours previous, but we are not allowed to think or suggest.

Our casualties are gradually mounting up, as the Germans have spotted all positions occupied by our men in the houses, which face the river. The enemy rearguard is strongly entrenched on the heights beyond the Marne, and only natural to suppose he demolished the bridge in his retreat.

Death of Lieutenant Colonel Le Marchant

We had the misfortune to lose our gallant Colonel. He got shot through the head by a German sniper as he was reconnoitring the German position from the upper storey window of a house on the river's bank.[9] As the stretcher-bearers bore him past our barricade, we asked, 'Who was that?' They replied 'Private Jones!' His body was covered with a blanket but we could see his left field boot and spur. 'Don't tell lies, it's the Colonel.' The stretcher-bearers admitted it was but they were told not to let the men know.

That's done it, what are we going to do now? He was ever where danger was most. We will never get another Colonel like him.

They bore him into the chateau grounds;[10] he passed from our vision forever. That familiar figure, beloved by all, will never lead the old 30th into action again. When I write lead I mean lead in the true sense of the word.

Well I suppose he died, as he would have wished, fighting for his beloved France on the soil of his forefathers. I am told he was a descendant of French Huguenots who were expelled from France by that perfidious Edict of Nantes.

Tribute to the Fallen Welshmen

Our artillery is subjecting the enemy's position to a heavy bombardment. At 4.00 pm we are ordered to evacuate the barricade and man a stone wall which runs along the road some 400 yards in the rear. Are the Germans going to counter-attack? We are told to prepare to receive one anyway.[11]

On the opposite side of the road, to where we are in position, lie five privates and one officer of the Royal Welch Fusiliers. They had been killed the previous evening and their bodies are covered with their ground sheets. On our side of the road lie four Germans.

A procession of women reciting the Rosary and carrying wreaths start from the village and advance up the road. We are dumbfounded, as the bullets from the German machine guns are knocking sparks from the roadway. We crouch close against the wall for cover. Are they mad? They will all be killed. They advance slowly and form a circle around the fallen Welch Fusiliers, cover their bodies with wreaths and recite the rosary, on their knees, on the blood-soaked ground around the fallen Welshmen. During this simple and touching tribute the German machine gunners splattered the roadway and the wall behind which we were taking cover with a continuous stream of bullets. The British soldiers were under cover; the simple and pious women of La Ferté were kneeling in the open and praying for the souls of the departed British Tommies. The sight, I may say, of that touching ceremony, brought tears to our eyes. When they finished the Rosary they stood up and bowed to the dead and slowly filed away, with the German machine gunners still in attendance. 'Twas a miracle how they escaped.

Any of us who survive this war will always retain a warm corner in our hearts for the brave women of La Ferté, who amidst an inferno of German machine gun fire paid their last tribute to the six British soldiers who paid the supreme sacrifice on the battlefields of France.

Crossing the Marne

At 5.30 pm we receive orders to cross the river. We file down past our barricade and reach the end of the village street. The river is on our right. There is no pontoon bridge, but an old Frenchman has 'dug up' a couple of boats. Together with a couple of pontoons they soon get us across.[12] We expected to get 'seen off' by machine gun fire, yet not a shot was fired in opposition. Has he cleared off?[13]

My Company fix bayonets, form line and skirmish up the hill. It was nervy work in the deepening twilight. Half way up the hill we came to a small village,[14] which we thought was deserted. We were mistaken, as soon as we surrounded and entered the village we were surrounded by a crowd of women, old and young, who kissed us several times (I was unlucky again as an old woman about sixty 'grabbed' me) and informed us that the '*Allemands partée*', or something like it. I know they were telling us that the Germans had gone. They gave us all a good 'swig' of Cognac. He must have had to move quickly or he would not leave anything drinkable behind.

We push on to the crest of the hill with renewed energy and post outposts. The night passed quietly.

Notes

1   6 September 1914 was the first day of the advance [Private Roe is incorrect] (Regt.Hist., p.15)
2   Field Marshal Sir John French, Commander of the British Expeditionary Force
3   [6 September] 'March of seventeen miles via Jossigny, a bivouac was reached near Villeneuve-le-Comte about 1.00 pm [7 September] Reached Crècy-la-Chapelle on the Grand Morin about 11.00 am, the march continued to Maisoncelles-en-Brie.' (Hopkinson, p.47)
4   75mm calibre French field guns of the French Sixth Army, which was heavily engaged along the Ourcq.
5   'The battalion passed through Signy-Signets, eventually reaching Les Corbiers farm on the high ground above La Ferté-sous-Jouarre about 6.00 pm.' (Hopkinson, p.48)
6   The task of the 4th Division was to cross the Marne and the 1/East Lancashire was directed to force the passage at La Ferté-sous-Jouarre. Both of the river bridges had previously been blown by the retreating Germans.
7   [The German units] 'were the 4th Jäger battalion and some cavalry.' (Hopkinson, p.55)
8   'A' and 'B' Companies relieved 2/Royal Welch Fusiliers on the river line, with 'C' Company in reserve and 'D' Company and the machine guns detached to occupy high ground at Condetz. 'A' Company was on the left, opposite the destroyed western bridge.
9   'Killed whilst visiting Lieutenant Leeson's post ['A' Company] at 10.30 am.' (1st Bn War Diary, 9 September 1914)
10 Lieutenant Colonel Le Marchant was buried in the chateau grounds, which was used as

the battalion headquarters. Some years later his body was removed to the small Anglo-French cemetery at La Perouse, some five miles south of La Ferté, where it now lies. Major Lambert assumed command of the battalion. (Hopkinson, p.54)

11 All the posts were evacuated to allow two field howitzers to shell the houses north of the river.

12 'About 3.00 pm the Brigade Commander determined to attempt the crossing in small boats, six of which and a barge had been discovered in the Petit Morin at its junction with the Marne, sheltered from the fire of the enemy [The East Lancashires crossed first, with 'A' Company leading]. The crossing was a long and tedious business – the small boats held only six men – but was eventually completed with the loss of only two men from the Hampshire Regiment, drowned by the capsizing of a boat.' (Regt Hist., pp.17–18)

13 The enemy had withdrawn but a few minutes before the crossing was made. (Ibid, p.18)

14 This was probably the northern part of La Ferté, which extends some distance from the river. Hopkinson says they reorganized on the railway embankment, some five hundred yards north of the river, and still in the village of La Ferté.

V

The Passage of the Aisne

(10 September – 9 October 1914)

The Advance Continued – Crossing the Aisne – First experience of
Trench Warfare – Listening Posts – Tobacco – Inniskillings give a
Demonstration – Arrested as a Spy – Hand over to the French – Field
Punishment

The Advance Continued

[**10 September**] At dawn next morning we reform on the railway line and
take the road to the right.[1] Six hundred yards up the road there was a sudden
burst of firing. The cause of this was a couple of debauched Uhlans had over-
slept themselves in a village, at the entrance of which were posted a picket of
the Essex. The Uhlans rode out of a back yard into the street. On the Essex
opening fire the Uhlans turned and charged them with the lance. They fell,
riddled with bullets, and so did their horses. We dragged them to one side
of the road; they were still bleeding.

We advance with extreme caution and fixed bayonets in case there are any
more of those troublesome customers hanging around. In the daylight we
were able to view the destruction wrought by our artillery on the previous
day. What German trenches we could see were full of dead. We are
advancing along the plateau of the Marne. During the day we pass a lot of
abandoned enemy transport and piles of shells, some almost as tall as I am.
The looted vehicles varied from *Monsieur Le Comte's* coach with its armo-
rial bearings to common country carts. All were loaded with 'loot', there were
thousands of wine bottles (all empty of course) and derelict commandeered
motorcars.

We came across a number of graves. Over each grave a wooden slab was
erected. The names on the board, or slab, indicated that there were five or
six buried in each grave. On investigation the 'graves' were found to contain
(artillery) shells.

Battalion halts at 5.00 pm and billeted in a large farm for the night.[2]

11 September: At 5.00 am next morning we resume the advance. Heavy guns fire on our left, it commences to rain in the afternoon and the roads are knee deep in mud, and blocked with transport. Bivouac for the night in a field.[3]

12 September: We resume the advance next morning at dawn.[4] The air of depression has worn away and although we are wet through, cold and hungry, everyone is in the best of spirits. Have we not got them on the run at last? They have had their turn, it's our turn now. The guns are still pounding away on our left. At 2.00 pm the Battalion halts for a few hours in a large farm.[5] A big battle is raging on our left front and we receive the order to prepare for action. Evidently a counter attack is feared, which does not however come off. After lying for one hour in the open the Battalion forms up and marches to the village of Set Mons [Septmonts]. It has been raining all day. General Hunter-Weston informed us in the village that the French had captured 40,000 'Jerries' and close on 100 guns. We found shelter from the teeming rain for two hours in hencoops, pigstys, cowsheds and the village church was crammed.[6] The Battalion moves off at 10.00 pm in the teeming rain.[7] A miserable rain-sodden array of men and animals.

Crossing the Aisne

13 September: Next morning at 3.00 am we reach the village of Venizel on the storied and historic Aisne and rest in a large building until 6.00 am, then rifle inspection. One would imagine that we were hundreds of miles away from the mighty 'Jack Johnsons'[8] and hundreds of guns of smaller calibres that were shortly to pour their death dealing hail on the devoted heads of the British Infantry as they crossed the partially demolished iron and pontoon bridges which spanned the sluggish Aisne.

Presently the enemy commenced to shell the roads and village with heavy howitzers, our first experience of the 'Jack Johnsons', they fairly rattled our nerves.

Regiments in single file are stealing through the village towards the river. Pontoon trains are also sneaking down, and streams of wounded are returning from the river. They are having a hell of a time down there as the Germans are raining a curtain of shrapnel on the village, river and open plain beyond.

The Battalion receives the order to cross. The Germans did not make a complete job of the iron bridge, they must have been too hurried. It is still standing although badly damaged. We cross the tottering bridge, man by man at six paces interval under heavy shrapnel fire. The tottering bridge threatened to collapse at any moment.[9] On the left of the bridge our engineers are manfully swinging a pontoon bridge across in an inferno of high explosive and shrapnel.

41

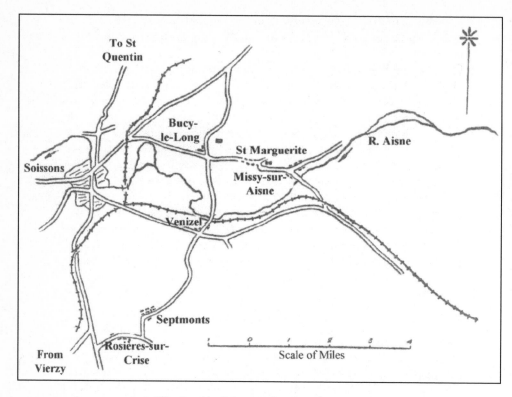

2. The Battle of the Aisne, 13 September 1914

In extended order and under shrapnel fire we skirmished across the plain and up the slopes of the heights. We halted for a couple of hours in the village of Bucy-le-Long.[10] The village was subjected to a bombardment by heavy howitzers. A 'Jack Johnson' killed five men in the blacksmith's shop. The Battalion managed to dig in that night, (scrape in would be a more appropriate term) about 1000 yards from the enemy who held the crest of the ridge or heights. The rain washed us in and out of our shallow trenches. Nature to a certain extent assisted us here as we were on the slopes of the heights. The country was wooded and there were plenty of large caves in which we could shelter. It was wretched weather; it rained continuously for a week.

First experience of Trench Warfare

There was a certain amount of 'wind up' every night, it was our first experi-ence of trench warfare. We wasted a considerable amount of ammunition

42

each night. The French would commence rapid fire at Siossions [Soissons]; it would be carried on without interruption along the whole line. Or our men might start the ball rolling on the right and it would be carried on to the French on our left. Listening Posts and Patrols who imagined that they saw Germans advancing or mistook tree stumps for Germans were responsible for this waste of ammunition, as they dashed back to the trenches and reported that the 'Jerries' were advancing – 'Stand to! Rapid fire!' Our patrols and the 'Jerries' had several little 'affairs' in the woods and on the road leading to the crest. The infantry attack has fizzled out; it is mainly an artillery duel or counter battery work.

Listening Posts

The duties of listening post is one of the most nerve wracking and responsible duties that a soldier is called upon to perform on active service. You crawl out and get as near as possible to the enemies position. As a rule an NCO [Non-commissioned officer] and two men form a listening post – three inspires confidence. You are the eyes and ears of the Company or Battalion in the rear. On your vigilance and judgement depend the lives of hundreds of your comrades. You must not be over confident; on the other hand you must not be 'windy', or in other words suffer from nerves. Don't stare too long at tree stumps or you will find that they assume grotesque shapes. You must not let the enemy get right upon you before giving the alarm; on the other hand you must not dash back with an imaginary attacking force behind you and cause a whole brigade to stand to and blaze away into the blue for twenty minutes before they find out it's a false alarm. Remember, the supports and reserves have to stand to also. You will get soundly 'straffed' by all and earn the reputation of being as 'windy as hell'. You must be prepared to lie out for four hours in all weathers, or all night if circumstances will not allow for you being relieved. I have known of instances where listening posts dashed in, either through fear or their position of isolation, and disturbed the rest of the first line, reserves and supports by giving a false alarm. We get very little rest here at night as it runs about three doses of 'wind up' each night.

If you are not on duty at night, you are down on the plain burying dead horses and gunners or else on RE fatigue [a work party for the Royal Engineers] in the village of Venizel. Our field artillery is unable to compete with the German 'heavies'. I'm sure they have siege guns in the field. Von Kluck[11] has been nicknamed old 'One o'clock' as he shells us every day when we are having dinner. We were under the impression that he was more gentlemanly than to do a trick like that; maybe it's his artillery commander that is responsible.

What it Really Feels Like
To be on patrol duty at night-time

The village baker has stuck to his guns amidst the ruins of Bucy. If you happen along at the right time you can purchase a loaf of French bread. Are we ever going to be issued with bread again, I wonder?

By night our gunners, and the French, change their gun positions leaving dummy guns and men in the abandoned gun pits. Next morning over comes a couple of 'Jerry' aeroplanes; they spot the dummies, hover over the positions and drop what appears to be cotton wool over the dummy gun positions. The 'Jerry' artillery range on the substance they drop and shell the dummy guns delightfully for half an hour or more and so the game goes on daily.

The second week brought bright sunny days, and aeroplanes are active as observation is better. As one glances heavenwards the almost motionless puffs of white smoke, caused by the bursting of anti-aircraft shells, meet the gaze. Water is plentiful and the demolished houses provide a plentiful supply of wood. In a three cornered field about 600 yards in the rear, there are quite a number of empty sardine tins. When the sun is up they reflect its rays like a helio.[12] It is quite laughable to witness the efforts of the German gunners for a couple of hours each day trying to put the empty sardine tins 'out of mess'.[13]

Tobacco

I forget when I last had a smoke of tobacco. I'm smoking, yes! – dried coffee and tealeaves. The smoke I emit is green, yellow and sometimes red. I was smoking in the trench the other day when two Zouaves[14] or Algerians came along, picturesque looking fellows in embroidered waistcoats, flowing trousers and wearing their fezs at a rakish angle. They were scouting for '*Tabaac*' [tobacco]. They thought they were 'quids in' when they saw me smoking. They '*Bon joured*' and '*Bon soured*' me, they were all smiles, they went through the motion of rolling cigarettes with nimble fingers and held out their hands in anticipation. I produced my tobacco pouch and displayed its contents, tea leaves and dried coffee, before their astonished gaze. They lifted both their arms up to heaven in holy horror and bolted down the trench. The cigarette smoker's position is hopeless.

Inniskillings give a Demonstration

During our first or second day [It was the first day, **13 September**] on the Aisne, we witnessed an actual demonstration of infantry advancing under shrapnel. The Inniskilling Fusiliers crossed the river about 7.00 am and adopted artillery formation [diamond]. The 'Jerrys' opened up with shrapnel. The Germans had too many guns and knew the ground too well even for diamond formation, so they broke into line and advanced by a series of rushes, the 'Jerrys' meanwhile decreasing their range. It was an exciting spectacle; at least we were excited, and I expect the 'Skins'[15] were a jolly sight more excited. However, they gained the base of the hill with few casualties. What foolishness to attempt a daylight crossing. Why, if a rat only crossed the bridges by day the 'Jerry' gunners would send a salvo of shells at him.

I omitted to mention that Colonel Lawrence arrived from England shortly after we crossed the Aisne and took over the Battalion from Major Lambert.[16] This oscillation caused an orgy of inspections.

The German 'heavies' give the village baker fewer opportunities of kneading his dough, therefore the price of the French loaf has risen fifty per cent. Tobacco issue: a 2oz tin of 'Navy Cut' per man. We eat it.

We are close on three weeks here now and are likely to remain here forever, as the Germans appear to have chosen to halt their retirement on their previously prepared position, the heights of the Aisne.[17]

Arrested as a Spy

I form one of a party who are sent down to Venizel on RE [Royal Engineers] fatigue tonight. When we arrive at the RE dump Corporal S asked me would I have a scout around the village for some tobacco. It did not matter about the price, or what kind of tobacco it was, only get some and also a couple of loaves of French bread. The French bake their bread in rings; it can be slipped over the head and worn as a necklace for convenience. I set off on my mission, although I had doubts about its success. I wandered up and down main streets and side streets for fully fifteen minutes without achieving anything, when I was suddenly pounced upon by a patrol of the Royal Irish Fusiliers who apprehended me and charged me with being a German Spy. There were at least two companies of RIF [Royal Irish Fusiliers] in the village. They were guarding the bridges and roads. They took me into a house, took my rifle and equipment away from me, and searched me for dynamite, gelignite, guncotton and other explosives, time fuses, detonators, etc, that spies are supposed to demolish bridges with. I was subjected to a cross examination that equalled Sir Edward Carson at his best. I produced my pay book and identity discs; no use, the Germans had thousands of them. The Germans could also equip a Division with our rifles and equipment.

'What was I doing in the village if my unit were in the firing line?'

'If I were on RE fatigue, what was I doing strolling around the village?'

I asked the Corporal, 'Did he ever hear a German talk with an Irish accent?'

'Oh! – That's easy, there were plenty of Germans living in Belfast and Dublin before the war and when one lives in a country for years you pick up the accent and characteristics of the people you are in contact with. Example Gratia: An Irishman enlists in a Scottish Regiment he acquires a Scotch accent in time, or he joins a Lancashire Regiment he will speak 'Lancy' in a couple of years and so on.'

My tale did not work. I was a German spy, and I remained hidden in the village when the Germans crossed the river. I had slabs of guncotton and dynamite hidden somewhere in the village, I was only awaiting a favourable opportunity to blow the bridges up. Who could tell whether I was signalling to the 'Jerrys' every night or not? I was their prisoner and that was all that was about it. I asked the Corporal to send a man up to the RE dump to verify my statement. He did. Unfortunately, by the time he reached the dump the party were gone and the RE corporal heard no remarks being made about anyone being absent from the party. That settled it. One genial soul suggested taking me down the road and shooting me. They could easily explain it away – that they were coming down the road, I dashed out of a house, they challenged me and I ran away and they opened fire. Fortunately there were a couple of men who opposed such a drastic method of dealing with spies, and I am reprieved. I am allotted a straw pallet in a corner and am warned that if I 'stir a peg' they will blow 'my crust off', and I quite believed it too. Spy and all, as they thought I was, they were kind hearted enough to throw me two biscuits and a chunk of 'Bully', with the consoling remark 'Cheer up "Jerry", you'll soon be dead.'

I had an interview with an officer the following morning. He had some sense, as he told the patrol to hand me over to my regimental transport as they passed through the village that night. At 6.30 pm I was duly handed over. The RQMS (Regimental Quartermaster Sergeant) disowned me; he had never seen me before, although I saw him. 'For heavens sake take me up, Sir,' I entreated, 'or I will get shot as sure as fate if I remain another night with those mad men.' He in turn handed me over to the CQMS (Company Quartermaster Sergeant), who handed me over to my Platoon Sergeant. Without a doubt I will be handed over to the Company Commander tomorrow morning, who, without a doubt will pass me on to the Commanding Officer for disposal.

I found my haversack intact, but some rascal 'pinched' my emergency ration of tea and sugar out of my valise. I had to report it, as they were inspected every day. There were no casualties, or I could have made it up, and it is a serious charge being deficient of a portion of your emergency ration. I saw Corporal S, he thought I had obtained the tobacco and bread and made my way ahead of the party. When he got back and I had not turned up he gave me an hour's grace. He then had to report me. He was a decent chap so I told him I will take all that is coming, 'You need not worry, Tom.'

Hand over to the French

For some unexplained reason I was not tried next day, as we were busy preparing to hand over to the French,[18] who were relieving us that night. Old 'one o'clock's' artillery made it hot for us from 1.00 until 2.00 pm, and from 5.00 until 6.00 pm. Had he any 'inkling' that we were going to change over?

47

If he had it would make it awkward for us crossing the bridges tonight and the French are such a noisy crowd they might give the 'whole show' away.

[**5 October**] At 7.00 pm the French arrive. I never witnessed, in all my life, such a conglomeration of tall men and short men, stout men and thin men. Length and rotundity seemed to be very unequally divided. The handing over ceremony commenced with a 'scrap' between a very tall French officer and a very small French drummer. The drummer was very agile and thrice in succession planted his foot in the pit of the officer's stomach. The Officer groaned; nevertheless, he pummelled the drummer's head delightfully. The soldiers took no notice; a senior officer came along and made peace. Some of the soldiers dropped their equipment and rifles and made for the village in search of chickens, wood and bread.

'Jerry' is strangely quiet, the sooner we get listening posts in and away from here the better. Eventually they are settled down and we make for the bridges. Let us hope the French will not start firing until we get across, for if they do the 'Jerrys' can tell by the reports of the rifles that there are French troops in front, and might surmise what has taken place. We cross the river without any '*au-revoirs*' from the German artillery and rest in the village for the night.[19] The relieving party were a Division of Reservists.

[**6 October**] Move early morning with a halt at noon. We are still within sound of the guns. Move off again at 2.00 pm and billet at 6.00 pm in a village.[20]

[**7 October**] Move off at 7.00 am next morning and halt at noon. Move again at 2.00 pm to billets at 7.00 pm. We are gradually getting away from the war area, as the country seems more prosperous and no signs of devastation.

[**8 October**] Move off at 7.00 am and halt in a pretty Cathedral town at 11.00 am I am patting myself on the back as I imagined they have forgotten all about my twenty-five hours absence on the Aisne.

Field Punishment

'Private Roe!'

'Sergeant'

'Company office at once, cap off, quick march!'

I was charged with 'absenting myself from the firing line for twenty-five hours', or from such and such an hour on such and such a date, until reporting in the firing line at such and such an hour on such and such a date. 'Quitting my fatigue without permission. Loitering or loafing (it's all the same) in the streets of Venizel until apprehended by a military patrol' and 'losing by neglect a portion of my emergency ration, (i.e.) tea and sugar ration.' I had visions of the firing party.

'What had I to say?' Well I could not say much unless I gave the Corporal away, and he is a full Sergeant now.

Commanding officer: 'When you went before the Company officer you told him you went to see if you could purchase tobacco? – Without permission?'

'Yes sir'. But the officer was more concerned as to which Battalion I belonged to than he was with the charges. He was convinced that I was a 1st Battalion man, that he knew me well on the Curragh, Woking and Colchester. Fool that I was, I proved to him that I was a 2nd Battalion man. It was my undoing as he awarded me fifteen days Field Punishment No.1 instead of the seven or ten which he would have only awarded me had I left him under the impression that I was a 1st Battalion man. I would not mind twenty days Field Punishment No.1, no matter what Battalion I belonged to. I deserved punishment, but why the animosity between Battalions?

I have the pleasure of being lashed to cart wheels and trees for two hours every day in every village in which we halt. I do not mind being tied up – of course it depends on who ties you up. It's the degradation I feel the most. It does not look very well to see a line of British soldiers tied up to a line of trees in a French village and surrounded by crowds of old men, women and kids.

'Where are we going?'

'Oh! – We are going back fifty miles for a rest and to re-organize.'

My friend Mr Phipps I have not seen since the morning of the Battle of the Marne. I have been told this morning by one of the Orderly Room staff, that he stopped a couple of machine gun bullets in the arm (at La Ferté on the Marne) and has gone to Blighty. I expect he will make an attack on that quart bottle of whisky, as winning the war is a tedious affair after all. We have not heard a gun for over a week.

Notes

1   Northwards to the Cocherel area. (Regt.Hist., p.18)
2   'The Battalion billeted in a particularly dirty farm near Rademont, which had been completely looted by the enemy.' (Ibid, p.18)
3   'From Rademont the Battalion marched via Ocquerre to Vendrest, where it was joined by the rest of the brigade. From Vendrest the brigade marched, in pouring rain, via Coulombs-en-Valois and Vaux-Parfond . . . to Passy-en-Valois, which was reached at 5.00 pm.' (Ibid, p.18)
4   'Brigade moved off at 8.00 am and marched over bad roads and in showery weather via Chouy, Villers-Hélon, Vierzy and Rozières-sur-Crise to Septmonts, which was reached in pouring rain about 7.00 pm.' (Ibid, p.18)
5   'The halt at St Quentin allowed the 12 and 19 Brigades to pass through.' (Ibid, p.18)
6   'The battalion had some difficulty in finding billets, but eventually settled down in a church and an adjoining farm.' (Ibid, p.19)
7   'At 10.00 pm orders were received for the brigade to advance at once, to cross the Aisne

by a partially destroyed bridge at Venizel and make good the high ground above Bucy-le-Long. The brigade moved off, in a howling gale of wind and heavy rain, headed by the 1/Hampshires and the East Lancs in the rear.' (Ibid, p.19)

8 A 'Jack Johnson' was the name given to the shell of a 5.9" Howitzer, from the plume of black smoke which brought to mind a certain tall black American boxer with a big punch.

9 As the British approached the Venizel bridge, the Germans endeavoured to blow it, but only one of the four charges exploded. The remaining charges were removed by an officer of the Inniskilling Fusiliers.

10 'The battalion halted in Bucy-le-Long whilst acting as the Brigade reserve.' (Ibid, p.21)

11 *Generaloberst* von Kluck, Commander in Chief of the German First Army.

12 Heliograph – a signalling device reflecting the sun's rays in flashes.

13 Army slang for 'killing' them.

14 [These men were part of] 'a platoon of Turcos [Zouaves], of the neighbouring French division, who were billeted with the transport in Bucy-le-Long . . . This Turco platoon, when they first arrived . . . caused considerable excitement amongst the men of the transport, as their sergeant gave a sort of juggling display with a string of most gruesome human trophies . . . [This was] too much for the transport officer, who promptly sent them off to Brigade HQ with a note saying, "Herewith fifty Turcos." But . . . they shortly after came back proudly showing a message from the Brigade Major, . . . "Herewith fifty Turcos returned for your retention." So they stayed.' (Hopkinson, pp.61–62)

15 Nickname for the Royal Inniskilling Fusiliers.

16 Lieutenant Colonel Lawrence came from Depot and assumed command of the battalion on 1 October 1914. Major Lambert reverted to second in command of the battalion.

17 'The enemy position in front of the 4th Division was too strong for a frontal attack . . . . The general organisation of 11 Brigade was to have three Battalions in the line and one in reserve. The Battalion when in the line held the centre sector, and when in reserve was accommodated in small caves and shelters in the reverse slope of the ridge three-quarters of a mile north-west of Bucy-le-Long.' (Regt. Hist., p.21)

18 Towards the end of September, active operations against the British front on the Aisne ceased; the situation had become a deadlock. At the same time the enemy was strengthening his troops in the north, presumably with the intention of turning the northern flank of the Allied line and so cutting off the British Expeditionary Force from the Channel ports. Sir John French proposed to General Joffre that the British Army should move to the north of France. This was agreed too by General Joffre, and the transfer of the British Army began.

19 The battalion was relieved by the French shortly before dusk and marched to Septmonts. [Then] commenced its march to an entraining area near Compiègne. (Hopkinson, p.65)

20 La Carrière L'Eveque.

VI

Ploegsteert Wood

(10 October – 24 December 1914)

Move to Armentières – Counter-Attack at Le Gheer – Burial Party –
Trench Life in the Mud – 'Jerry' makes a Big Attack – Piggery Farm –
Counter-attack at Plugstreet – 'Little Willie' – Ration Parties – Relieved by
the Hampshires – The 'Londons' arrive – Making Corduroys – The
Manchester Guardian – Rain and Mud – Rations – Attack on the Salient –
Is there a God?

Move to Armentières

[**10 October**] Entrained today at 7.00 am and detrained at 3.00 am on the
following day [**11 October**].[1]

We are quite a long time getting to whatever place we are going to have
this rest. March out to a large village as soon as we detrain. A fleet of thirty
French motorbuses are drawn up on the village square, and we get 'told off'
to the buses. We set off. The interior of each bus is a seething mass of
Tommies. After a ten hours bumpy and uncomfortable journey we find we
are dumped in the neighbourhood of Armentières.[2] The guns are going like
hell. So this is the 'much looked for' rest we are going to have.

We spent a week here, marching from billet to billet, and on three occasions set out to storm villages which were already in possession of our men.
We are acting as a kind of floating reserve. At Houplines we were called upon
to support the Leinsters. We advanced under heavy shell and machine gun
fire, almost to their position. We were then ordered to retire as our services
were not needed.[3]

We march into Armentières at 8.00 pm. I give a boy my last 'two bob' bit
and borrow the last ounce of Jud Thompson's tobacco to give to the boy so
as he will know what kind of tobacco to bring. The boy, tobacco and 'two
bob' piece never turned up. I don't say that the boy was dishonest; he was
under the impression that I gave him my last 'two bob' and all Thompson's
tobacco for a souvenir.

51

Cannot obtain billets. It is raining heavily and we have to make the best of it on the Market Square. Rivulets ran under and over us but we slept just the same, as we were exhausted. At 4.00 am **[21 October]** a dispatch rider arrives with a message for the CO[4] [Commanding Officer]: 'Come along, fall in, we are off again.'

Counter-attack at Le Gheer

After a four-mile march we arrive in the village of Ploegsteert, or the Bois de Ploegsteert. We call it 'Plugstreet' for short. It is a sombre looking place. It boasts of an extensive and dense forest. Heavy rifle and machine gun fire is on our right flank and an occasional shell bursts in the village. A German high explosive has blown the end out of the village church and the roadway is strewn with broken Saints. I am glad to meet St Patrick once again, although he is in decimal fractions. St Peter's crozier reposes on Mary Magdalene's breast. John the Baptist and St Joseph are hopelessly mixed up. The Soldier Saint's sword is unbroken and Patrick Oates accepts it as a good omen. I carefully pick my steps over Saints' legs, heads and arms.

We meet a crowd of 'Inniskillings' coming down the road which leads alongside the wood. They have lost their trenches and are retiring. They inform us that the Germans have broken through in thousands. Not very encouraging as we are thoroughly done up and wet to the skin.

The East Lancs and Somersets[5] open out for attack. Part of my Regiment are attacking through the wood in which the Germans had obtained a foothold. We can barely force our way through the dense undergrowth and have no field of view. Pheasants are numerous. My Company ['A'] are in support; it is regular hell with bullets and shells. The 'Jerries' have three machine guns in the houses at the crossroads, and are raking the wood. Mr Lewis took my platoon into the firing line. They have two machine guns trained on the edge of the wood and we lose heavily. The enemy held a well-concealed trench in a turnip field eighty yards from the edge of the wood. When located they are charged by a platoon under Mr Hughes, who was shot through the head as he led the charge. The charge failed,[6] and what was left of the platoon had to lie in the open under shrapnel and heavy rifle fire until two sections of the Somersets worked around their flank. The Germans then surrendered as they had run out of ammunition. One man refused to surrender; it took two of our men to put him out of mess. He was a brave man and we recognized him as such. He was a recipient of the Iron Cross. At this stage we were slightly disorganized and fighting in isolated groups and were mixed up with the Somersets.[7] We made a dash across a turnip field and rushed Le Gheer Convent with the bayonet. We bagged twenty Germans who were guarding a ration party, which they captured that

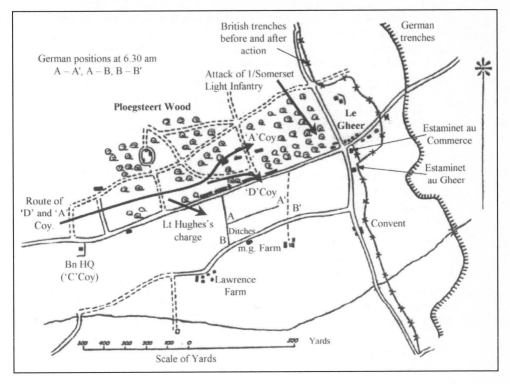

Map labels:

British trenches
before and after
action

German
trenches

German positions at 6.30 am
A – A', A – B, B – B'

Attack of 1/Somerset
Light Infantry

Ploegsteert Wood

Le
Gheer

'A'Coy

Estaminet au
Commerce

Estaminet
au Gheer

'D'Coy
A'
B'

Route of
'D' and 'A'
Coy.

Lt Hughes's
charge

A
Ditches
B
m.g. Farm

Convent

Bn HQ
('C'Coy)

Lawrence
Farm

500 400 300 200 100 0   500   Yards

Scale of Yards

3. Action at Le Gheer, 21 October 1914

morning when they were drawing rations. The Germans drank their rum; otherwise they treated them well and were in the act of making coffee for them when the tables were turned. The Convent was converted into a temporary hospital. It was full of German wounded when we captured it and the German Red Cross flag flew from the roof.[8] It could plainly be seen from the German position, but the humane Germans turned their guns on the Convent. What a spectacle; British soldiers carrying German wounded out of the Convent at the risk of their lives in order to save them from their own artillery fire. The Convent is on fire. German wounded first, British last.

I witnessed another instance of misplaced chivalry at Houplines, when our stretcher-bearers had to carry in the German wounded on their stretchers. The 'Jerries' had the comfort of a stretcher; our men were carried in on doors and planks. Would the Germans treat us in the same manner?

We drove the enemy out of the line of trenches he captured that morning. We dash forward and line a hedge.[9] A heavy fire is opened on us. We cannot locate the enemy as his uniform blends or harmonizes with the turnip and

53

mangel-wurzel tops. Suddenly over forty of the enemy arise from the ground 100 yards in front, throw down their rifles, turn about, raise both arms above their heads and sprint for their own lines. They made a splendid target and the dear boys were also running in the wrong direction. We let them have it. A few got away with it, and the remainder did not. The Boer Commander-in-Chief in the South African war at the Battle of the Tugela River would not, it has been said, allow his men to fire on a retiring foe for biblical reasons. There were no Jouberts amongst us; neither were we biblically minded. The enemy suffered heavily.

The troops against whom we were engaged were recognized as the 104th and 118th Regiments of Saxon Infantry. Why did we go to war with only two Maxims to each Battalion? Why, the Germans seem to have dozens of them. I'm sure they have five to our one at the very least.[10]

Burial Party

I formed one of a party who were detailed for burial fatigue that evening. We buried twenty-one Saxons in two graves in a corner of 'Plugstreet' wood. We had to search them and hand all their possessions over to Major Lambert before 'dumping' them in the pits we had dug. One could open a first class jeweller's shop with the contents of their pockets; gold watches, rings, bracelets, pendants and what not. Major Lambert retained all their papers, but made us bury all the jewellery with them.

Trench Life in the Mud

[22 October] Next morning the enemy counter-attacked.[11] It was a half-hearted affair and was repulsed. Of course 'Jerry' always telegraphs his attacks by a hurricane bombardment.

Our trenches are more or less irregular ditches following twists and angles without any apparent meaning, through turnip fields, across roads, through badly pulverized villages and farm houses; in some places they ran through cemeteries. One would imagine that the trench line was the result of accident; they were not like the elaborate affairs we used to dig on the Curragh or Maryborough Heath, but there was no war on then. 'Dugouts' were muddy alcoves scraped out anywhere on either wall of the trench and contained one or two and sometimes three if we folded ourselves up properly. The roofs were covered with our ground sheets and straw, sometimes with a door from a nearby farmhouse, and tobacco leaves. Muddy rifles rested in slots up against the trench wall.

The wants of nature (latrines and urinals did not exist) for the first week were relieved in empty 'bully beef' and jam tins and thrown over the top, fore and aft. Later, when the 'Jerries' released their pressure we found time to dig slots running back from the trench, which served for 'lousing' ourselves and other purposes.

In rear of our trenches were a number of unshapely irregular mounds, increasing daily. They were adorned with wooden crosses made from biscuit boxes; the black lead wording or epitaphs were almost washed away by

The Fatalist
"I'm sure they'll 'ear this damn thing squeakin'."

55

continuous rain. They could not be buried further away owning to the exigencies of the moment.

Sandbags were arriving each night in bundles of ten. Barbed wire began to arrive ten yards at a time. Corrugated iron had not made its appearance so far.

It rained continuously. We were covered with mud and lice from head to foot. An air of humour and sulkiness pervaded the muddy waterlogged trenches. We had to maintain a ceaseless vigil under awful conditions. The language was awful – but it was not meant. A sentence of five words was embellished with hoary adjectives that in peacetime would get a man seven days CB [Confined to Barracks]; now it seems to give us some sort of relief.

Ration parties parade every night. They have to go back almost a mile over shell and machine gun swept roads. One third of the party invariably get 'seen off' each night. You come across a biscuit box on the road; Tom or Bill or Dick is 'panned out' beside it, the traversing machine gun caught him. A little further on a box of 'bully' tells the same tale. Tom and Bill went 'west' at 7.00 pm; it might be my turn before 7.30 pm. We get back to the trench with our portion of the rations, out again to retrieve Tom and Bill's. Two more mounds and two more wooden crosses adorn the turnip field in rear of our trenches next morning and so the lottery of death goes on.

Water and wood is obtained at the risk of our lives. Empty rum jars serve as receptacles for holding water. The Germans are fighting on interior lines (that is to say we have driven them back over the country we now occupy) and they know the position of every pump. From dusk until dawn they keep up a plunging fire on the sources of our water supply and of course men get killed and wounded each night. That does not act as a deterrent; we must have water. Three men invariably 'muck in' or form a mess, as two men might be on duty at the same time. So the odd man draws the water. We take equal risks. Procuring a rum jar of water means death; in other words, you might get 'seen off' and you might not. If a man tries to shirk his turn he is 'chucked out' of the trinity and blacklisted. The language used in the 'chucking out' ceremony is as follows: 'You go to 'ell and "muck in" on your own. What the bloody 'ell do you think we are? We risk our bloomin' lives every night for water, wood and "*pommes-de-terres*" (potatoes) whilst you hug the trench for safety. Are not our lives as valuable to us as yours is to you? Consider yourself finished with us'.

The wounded have to lie in the muddy trenches all day. We bandage them up as best we can and place them somewhere where they will not be walked upon. There are no communication trenches so you cannot carry a man out during the day in the open or you would get shot. When the shades of night fall the stretcher-bearers come up from Battalion headquarters and take what wounded are still alive away.

'Jerry' Makes a Big Attack

We held the trenches we recaptured for fifteen days in spite of repeated attacks by the Germans. They made one great attack one foggy October morning [Ed: Actually **2 November**]. The bombardment was heavier than usual. The German shells blew the tobacco leaves, ground sheets and doors off the tops of our dugouts; they left us roofless, so to speak. The morning mist lifted and revealed to our gaze lines and lines of solid grey advancing. Our gunners have spotted them; I think it is 66 Battery commanded by the 'Mad' Major, who are in the rear of our position. In any case, they are tearing gaps in the densely packed German lines. Bandoliers of ammunition are feverishly passed down the trench line. Our two Maxims are on them. Captain Clayhills DSO restrains us from firing until they get to within 500 yards of our line. They are advancing with the utmost confidence. 'Now let them have it!' and we did. We are re-loading and firing like mad; still the advance continues. Our rifles get jammed with clay. With the utmost persuasion and much swearing we can only average about eight rounds per rifle per minute. We take our bolts out of our rifles and urinate on them, as we have no rifle oil. Our batteries in rear are sending over a continuous stream of shells and amidst the din we can hear the swish of the Germans shells on their way to our batteries.

On comes the grey wall. The Maxim on our right has stopped and a man dashes down the trench for any water bottles or rum jars that contain water, as the water contained in the jacket of the Maxim has boiled away.

At the same time Captain Clayhills DSO dashes along the trench shouting out 'There must be no retirement from this trench! Fight to the last man! If the Germans get through all is lost!' The German line is roughly 200 yards away now. We can plainly hear words of command being shouted. The Maxim on our right and the one on our left get going; they bring converging fire to bear on the advancing German lines. The lines wither and melt under the storm of well-directed fire. It was too much for the Germans; they break and fall back in irregular lines and groups on their own trenches, leaving the mangel-wurzel field strewn with dead, wounded and dying in bear skin packs. Their artillery open on our trenches again to keep down our fire and a couple of platoons of Germans form line 400 yards away and open a pretty accurate fire on our trenches. A bullet smashes my bayonet, puts my foresight out of action and blinds me with clay.

Our trench line was not half-manned, as two men had to man six yards of trench and in some parts of the trench one man had to man six yards. All dead and wounded men's rifles were shoved through loopholes with bayonets fixed and magazines charged. Several times each day we stole along the trench and fired two or three rounds from each rifle in order to give the

Germans the impression that the trenches were strongly held. We were told that our supports were three miles away, but we knew very well that there were no supports and no reserves. Captain Clayhills DSO, my Company Commander, got killed,[12] as did Captain Coventry[13] and God knows how many more. By degrees we are losing all our old and experienced officers.[14]

We keep a close eye on the Germans in front. I saw one fellow moving; he slowly worked his water bottle up to his mouth. Another fellow's hand steals to his haversack; he has commenced munching a sandwich or something. Everything has gone strangely quiet by now.

Night falls. We get no rations, as every man has to stand to arms. Regimental Police and officers' servants and the sick, lame and lazy are sent in the firing line as we expect another attack.

We look to our rifles during the day; rifle oil is essential and non-existent. The chambers of our rifles are coated with a layer of mud, carried in by successive muddy rounds of ammunition. We have no 'sticks cleaning chamber'.

We lost seven rounds per man per minute this morning owing to dirty chambers. One had to use brute force to load. When you fired you could not extract the empty case, you had to lift the bolt lever then hammer it with your clenched fist or your entrenching tool handle to get the bolt back and the empty case ejected. The attack lasted forty-five minutes; that is to say from the time we opened fire on them until the remnants of the attacking force got back to their trench line 900 yards away. Had conditions allowed, every man could have got 315 rounds more off in that time. We were 500 strong, every man, owing to mud, lost 315 rounds. Just think of the number of Germans that got away with it.

At 7.00 pm we hear a tremendous lot of shouting in front. It seems there is a lot of swearing going on, but we don't understand the language. Our listening posts dash in and report that the Germans are advancing. We 'stand to' and open fire. The Maxims and artillery chime in. Very lights[15] are sent up but we can see nothing. The Germans reply with rifle fire; we can see the flashes and hear the ugly crack made by their bullets as they strike the parapet. We redouble our fire. Our nerves are on edge, but nothing happens. This goes on for half an hour. We are ordered to cease-fire and recon-noitering patrols are sent out. They can see nothing unusual (of course they did not go out far enough). We 'stand to' until dawn when a new trench line is revealed about 450 yards away across the mangel-wurzel field. So that's their game is it? Sapping forward so as they will not have as much exposed ground to cover in their next attack. And where are all the Germans and bear skin packs that were lying out there yesterday evening? Why, there are only about twenty dead Germans where there were hundreds yesterday. I'm afraid they pulled our legs yesterday as quite a number must have dropped down and pretended to be dead, and then took advantage of the darkness to get back to their own trenches, and besides, the German stretcher-bearers must have been at it all night bringing their wounded in.

A section of our trenches around Le Gheer Convent are subjected to a bombardment by German trench mortars (Minenwerfers) that fire a torpedo-shaped shell, which fills in whole bays of our trench system. It kills and buries the defenders and is nicknamed 'the German undertaker'.[16]

The farmhouses in the vicinity of the firing line stench abominably owing to the carcasses of dead cows, calves and pigs, which were killed over twelve days ago when the Germans shelled all the farmhouses on the morning we counter-attacked the Saxons. I released a dozen cows that were chained up in their byres; their udders were bursting with milk. An old sow with a litter of nine pigs patrols the road in rear of our trenches. At least she had nine a week ago. She passed down the road today with only two in attendance.

An amusing incident occurred last night. Lance Corporal Langthorne, Private Mullen and I were sent out on listening post. We advanced seventy-five yards or more from the firing line [and then] we lay down in line. On scanning the ground in front we saw a figure kneeling. He was as steady as a statue. We kept him under observation for ten minutes and then, after a whispered consultation, decided to surround and rush him with the bayonet. We crawled away, one to his right front, one to his rear, whilst Langthorne carried out a 'belly' movement from the centre, keeping our 'lamps' (eyes) on the 'Jerry' all the time. Strange he has never moved, yet he must have heard the rustling. When we got to a pre-arranged distance we jumped up and charged him – 'Good God!' He was stone dead, shot through the heart, the butt of his rifle rested on the ground and he had gripped the rifle with both hands, a death grip. We were greatly dis-appointed as we thought it would be a feather in our caps to capture, and bring in, a real live German. The Commanding Officer would ask 'Who were those men who were on listening post? They are damn vigilant fellows', and it would make a story for the 'estaminet', with additions of course, when we got relieved. As it so happened we cannot very well relate how three of us rushed a dead German with fixed bayonets and captured him. That would only be exposing ourselves to ridicule, so we agreed not to mention the incident.

The rumour is current that we are getting relieved tonight. The listening posts go out at dusk. At 6.30 pm there is a hell of a scatter, the listening posts dash in, in a state of great excitement. The Germans are advancing. We man the parapet. They are, sure enough. One could imagine by the rustling made by the mangel-wurzel leaves that a Brigade of Cavalry are advancing at the gallop. We open rapid fire. It drew forth grunts and squeals from two sows and about twenty young pigs that had taken it into their piggy heads to charge the British line. We laughed heartily at the humour of it, and were immensely relieved. The listening posts got a telling off.

Piggery Farm

[**4 November**] At 7.30 pm on the night of our fifteenth day in the trenches we were relieved by the Hampshires. We are not sorry; it was almost a continual 'stand to' all the time we were in. It rained every other day, shelled every day, [we were] on short rations, attacked twice, and to add to our discomfort, every seam in our shirts were strongly held by platoons of vermin who resisted all efforts to dislodge them and could only be got rid of by the process of cremation, which process, alas, involved the loss of the shirt.

It was raining as usual; it would be something unusual if it were not. 'A' Company marched to a farm called the Piggery farm. After a lot of swearing and messing about, we climb up a ladder to a hayloft. We dare not strike a match as there were holes in the roof and we might draw shellfire or set the barn on fire. Just imagine a Company of men [120] trying to settle down on a loft twelve yards long and five yards wide in stygian darkness. If you lie down too soon someone walks on your 'clock' (face), and if you hang on for position you walk on someone else's. The swearing is incessant and awful. It is well after midnight before we get to sleep.

At 2.00 am we are ordered to 'stand to'. Down the rickety old ladder we shuffle and form up on the dung heap. We are half asleep. It is reported that the enemy has broken through. We are dismissed at 3.00 am and we crawl up the ladder to our kennel, more shuffling and swearing and off to sleep again. At 4.30 am we are up again and 'stood to' until 5.30 am in compliance with general routine orders which state that the firing line and supports will 'stand to' one hour before dawn. What a 'bloomin' nights rest.

Between inspections and digging reserve trenches by day[17] and digging for four hours each night in the firing line and 'standing to' if there was a sudden burst of firing at 1.00 or 2.00 am in the morning and from 4.30 to 5.30 am every morning, the four days rest was a farce.

Counter-attack at Plugstreet

[**7 November**] On the morning of the third day of our so-called rest, we are ordered to 'stand to' again. [We] march to Battalion Headquarters, wait there for an hour, got sent back to get our dinner, fall in again after dinner, back to Battalion Headquarters where we halted for two hours. The situation is then explained to us. It runs as follows: The Ws[18] lost some trenches in front of Ploegsteert wood[19] and they have got to be retaken at all costs tonight. The Battalion marched to the wood, got as close as possible to their objective, made their dispositions for attack, and lay down until darkness set in and then attacked.[20] We drove the Germans out with the bayonet, losing heavily in so doing. There was no end of confusion. Platoons lost direction, and some their heads. The Germans worked their machine guns with deadly effect. Captain Cane [was] killed, Major Lambert wounded.[21] Several sergeants got killed including 'Chicko' Brennan[22] who is married and has eight 'kids' in Preston. These night attacks always entail heavy losses. The objectives are not clearly defined, some get too far ahead others do not get far enough forward. There is a grave danger of shooting and bayoneting your own men.

At dawn no-man's-land is strewn with dead. Germans and British lie in heaps with their bayonets plunged into each other. The Regiment that let the Germans take their trenches should be made to re-take them. This is the second time that we have had to re-take trenches that other units lost, and we have lost heavily each time.

'Little Willie'

Those trenches are hell; we are enfiladed from our right by a small calibre field gun, which we have nicknamed 'Little Willie'. This shell gives you no warning; it is a high velocity shell something akin to what our mountain batteries fire. It bursts right in the trench and 'knocks out' all who are in that particular bay or part of the trench where it bursts. It is close to us as we can hear the report of the gun every time it fires. Anything worse than the trenches we now hold could not be imagined. It is a canal not a trench and it runs in a curve right to the edge of 'Plugstreet' wood. Whole sections of trench parapet fall down by day and by night, owing to continuous rain, and we are enfiladed by rifle fire.

[**17 November**] The casualties average from ten to fifteen daily, Captain Preston got a 'Little Willie' all to himself today. We sleep standing up as we cannot find a dry spot on which to sit down, save on a floating biscuit box. The German snipers are in deadly form. Our Bavarian neighbours are in a devilish mood owing to the inclement weather and give their Mausers little rest.

Ration Parties

It is an agony of endurance trying to get rations up to the firing line. The nights are dark and wet; the turnip field is pitted with shell craters, which are full of water. The dykes on each side of the road to Headquarters are full of water. The Regimental transport dumps the rations on the road opposite headquarters in an indiscriminate pile, and get out of it as quick as they can

"---------- these ---------- rations."

in case they might get shelled or machine gunned. Yes! – There is something
dreadful about the sound of a Maxim. It's our place to find out where those
guns are and avoid, if we can, going over the ground they cover. Yes! – We
shun the ground they cover as if it were plague infested, but on ration fatigue
we cannot. As an alternative to the bullet swept road we can go through the
wood, but we would never get through the wood and carry a box of biscuits
or 'bully'. The mud is knee deep and the shell craters almost adjoin one
another they are that numerous, so it must be the road then. The party gets
loaded up and struggle towards the firing line. Will he open up with his
machine guns before we get there? Or will we be lucky enough to get back
to the trenches without coming under machine gun fire. Those are our
thoughts as we struggle along with our loads. Ping, Ping, Ping, Swish – down
go the boxes, sand bags and rolls of cheese. We dive into the dykes on either
side of the road. We are up to our necks in water, but we're alive. He fires
down the road, traverses left and right then stops. 'Come on lads let us get a
move on before he starts again.' Hello! – What is this? What a smell of rum.

62

Someone is lying on the middle of the road. It's Sutcliffe, they got him through the breast, and he is dead. When hit he dropped the rum jar and smashed it. Never mind, get along with the rations. We get to the corner where there stands a large image of Christ nailed to a cross. 'Now for it', mind the shell holes and for Christ's sake stand still when the Germans throw up their 'Very' lights. There is no moon, one or more flop into a shell hole and flop out again, we curse the moon for not being out, and when putting up barbed wire in front of our trenches, we curse the moon for being out. Eventually we arrive at the Company Quartermaster Sergeant's dugout. 'Any casualties?'

'Yes! – One "K.O'd", two wounded and no rum issue in the morning, it went "west" with Harry Sutcliffe.'

That is only one little job that has to be performed every night; there are a dozen others just as dangerous.

We have not seen the Commanding Officer for the past ten days. Someone enquired from Captain Belchier, the Adjutant, 'How is the CO[23] getting on?'

The adjutant replied, 'He is all right, what do you mean?'

'Oh – we thought he was wounded, Sir, we have not seen him for ages.'

'Well I'll try and get him up tonight,' the Adjutant replied.

He paid a hurried visit to the trenches that night. As he went along the trench line everyone kept on shouting, 'Keep down there, Sir!' and, 'Watch yourself there Sir!' I'm certain he suffered a pain in the back by the time he finished his run through the trenches.

The Brigadier, Hunter-Weston, is a constant visitor and is a source of worry to his staff as he always hangs about the most dangerous points. He remarks to us as he strolls along the trench, 'Well lads you're going through it here, but I'll let you get your own back, I'll let you in with the bayonet on the first opportunity.'

Dear old Hunter, we've been 'in with the bayonet'. We know what it means, Cavalry and Infantry charges are a thing of the past, unless you have an overwhelming preponderance of artillery. Mud, barbed wire, magazine rifles and machine guns have shorn cavalry and bayonet charges of all their glamour and glory. Hunter dear, we may take a couple of hundred yards of waterlogged ditch but our losses are out of all proportion to our gains.

Private Deakin, champion billiard player of 2/Battalion, was on snipers, and got sniped in the ruins of a house in the rear of our trench line.

Relieved by the Hampshires

[17/18 November] The Hampshires[24] relieved us on the twelfth night of our tour of duty in the trenches. The Battalion rendezvous at battalion headquarters and march to Armentières or Nieppe [Ed. It was in fact Nieppe].

We were almost 'done up' before reaching our billet owing to the awful condition of our feet. We have not had our boots off for months. If we risk taking them off, our feet swell and we cannot get them into our boots again.

[We were] billeted in a brewery. When everyone went to sleep a few thirsty souls discovered a small cask of beer that had strayed away from its base. Next morning a torpedo bearded Frenchman, with much shrugging of shoulders, bewailed the loss of the said cask and the contents therein contained. He instituted enquires but he always got the same answer, '*No comprée, Monsieur.*'

The Battalion had a bath in another brewery today (a hot one) and a change of clothing. I heaved a sigh of relief as I parted with an overpopulated shirt and drawers, and so did all of us.[25]

We remained in Armentières for four days. We were allowed out on pass and consumed litres and litres of French beer. It did not inspire either a lively or jovial feeling. No one sang a song, no one gave a recitation, no one staggered, no one had a flushed face, and no one got shoved in the 'mush' (slang for guard room). At least French beer has some good points after all.

At the Brewery Baths
'You chuck another sardine at me, my lad, you'll hear from my solicitors.'

64

The 'Londons' arrive

[**21 November**] On the night of the fourth day we proceeded to the firing line and take over a new line of trenches[26] from the Essex on the right of the barricade on the road and the bicycle shop, or it would be more correct to say, what was once a bicycle shop. They are palaces in comparison to the last lot of trenches we held. We call them trenches out of courtesy, but they are only converted dykes. It is fairly easy here as our neighbours, the Saxons, are not quite so bad tempered as the Bavarians. I'm certain that the Bavarians are a drunken lot, as they never cease volley firing and jeering at us every night they are in the trenches.

We are enjoying fairly decent weather at present. The London Rifle Brigade (Territorials) has arrived from home and is attached to our Brigade. My Battalion has the 'Queen's Westminsters' attached to us. We have got to initiate them into the art of trench warfare. They soon resigned themselves to the hardships of trench, or canal, warfare. They are a fine lot of fellows, well educated. Some can speak three or four languages, all can speak French, and they have a superior bearing. Why send these fellows in to die with people who only possess Army thirds, and most none at all? I do not mean that they should not die or take equal risks, but they could be better employed and would be of more benefit to the State were they trained and employed as officers.

The first day in they lost their rum issue. Hubert S (the young gentleman of the Londons I was told off to look after), the chap I was detailed to coach, commentating on the theft, remarked, 'It was beastly awful.' I told Hubert that 'All new Regiments, or Regiments new to the firing line, are bound to lose rum and other items until they play themselves in; or in other words get used to trench routine. You lose sand bags, beams for making dugouts and straw you collect for your dugout if you don't watch it. Cavalry and artillery have been known to lose horses, transport have lost limbers and your Regiment leave two jars of rum, above all! – on the fire-step with no one looking after it? Why, Hubert it's inviting capture.'

Our casualties were few for the first fortnight owing to the fact that we could use our communication trenches.

Captain Fletcher arrived from second Battalion [**2 December**] and took over my Company ('A'). He got badly wounded in the head on his first tour of inspection,[27] he was too fond of gazing over the top of the trenches, and he underrated the accuracy of the German snipers. He got one poor fellow of the Londons killed, before he got hit himself, as he made him stand up on the fire-step and expose his head and shoulders to the Germans who were only 100 yards away. He got shot through the head right away. The next sentry he came to was one of ours. He made him do the same, Sergeant B

65

told the sentry to stand down when the Captain went past and to take no notice of the 'bloody fool'. We were not allowed to look over the top in the daytime. We were provided with periscopes for observing the German trenches during the day. To expose your head over the trench parapet meant getting it blown off. He must have had no trench experience at all. We all thanked heaven for a damn good riddance. He would have had us all killed in a week and there would not be a German killed in return. A mad man would not order his line of sentries to stand up by day and expose their head and shoulders over the trench parapet for the German to pick them off from behind cover.

We are having it much easier now as some reinforcements have arrived from England, and we are holding a shorter line. Two companies are in the firing line, one in supports and one in reserve, usually at Nieppe (the reserve Company).[28]

I have shown Hubert how to make a 'bully beef stew', or *stew à-la-Plugstreet*. I crawled out last night, got some potatoes from a pit in front of our firing line, [and] some leeks from a cultivated patch, and commenced the stew at 11.30 am, using both our mess tins. He pronounced it, 'Top hole,' gave me his address, and when the war is over we are going to have a 'blow-out' in Frascatis in Oxford Street.

Hubert rose to heights of generous confidence tonight. He was on listening post and gave me his watch to take care of until he returned.

We have a bath and change of washing every fourteen days in Nieppe.[29] The change of washing does not do much good as the straw on which we sleep on in the billets has not been changed for months and is alive with vermin. You come out of the trenches verminous, go for a bath, come back clean, sit down on the straw in your billet and get lousier than ever in half an hour's time.

Making Corduroys

When in supports we have not half an hour to ourselves. If we are not digging communication trenches or reserve trenches to get filled with water as fast as we dig them, we are in 'Plugstreet' wood, cutting down saplings to make what are called corduroys. They are something similar to a ladder, if you nail the rungs as close together as possible. They are made in sections and are laid on top of the sea of mud to form pathways. There are miles and miles of those corduroy roads laid in 'Plugstreet' wood. If there are no corduroys to be made, we are stretching fathoms and fathoms of barbed wire around trestles. These have to be carried up to the firing line at night and placed a certain distance in front of our first line trench.

When in reserves at Nieppe, we start PT [Physical Training] at 6.00 am in the morning, then breakfast, [and continue] from 9.00 am until 12.30 pm. Turning by numbers, sloping arms by numbers and saluting by numbers is from 2.00 until 3.45 pm as platoon and company drill. The Regimental Sergeant Major is permanently billeted in Nieppe and plays his part in the Great War by putting the 'lousy', weary men 'through it' from 6.00 am until 3.45 pm.

The Manchester Guardian

We are thankful to the *Manchester Guardian*[30] for keeping us well supplied with tobacco and cigarettes and also gifts of mufflers, cap comforters etc., which are thrown away as soon as they get lousy. Inside every gift packet there is a postcard and you can write a few lines of thanks to the donor. His, or her address is already written on the postcard. I am in a literary humour and in consequence I wrote a rather long note of thanks to Miss N. C. just to pass the time away. I almost forgot all about Harrow, so I write a rather brief letter. I am plagued by about half a dozen fellows in my Company; I have got to write their letters for them. It is rather a pull on the imagination when you do not know anything about the people you are writing to, and one also has to take the censor into consideration. 'Shall I tell, or rather write, about how nice the French and Belgian girls are and how good they are to us?' I ask those married men of forty years of age or more. 'Oh no Paddy, for goodness sake don't mention anything about the women out here. Don't you know what women are?'

Rain and Mud

We trudge back to our muddy trenches along muddier roads, worse in mind and body than when we came out for our so-called rest or persecution. I can hear men praying for 'Plugstreet' ones (the Battalion graveyard was just outside our Battalion Headquarters) if they cannot get a 'Blighty' one.[31]

On **20 November** the weather broke in earnest; it did not stop raining for a month. The first week's rain turned our trenches into canals.[32] Bale out all day and all night was the order. We are provided with scoops. They are large ladles and are fitted onto a wooden handle about six feet in length. Holes are dug at irregular intervals in the trench. The water drains into those. You set to work with your scoop and empty the water over the parapet. It percolates through the earth in time and finds its way back into the holes in the trench floor; those holes are called sump holes. The object of a six-foot handle is to enable you to throw the water over the parapet without running the risk of getting shot through the hand or arm. I have seen men deliberately hold their hands over the trench parapet, when baling out, with the object of getting wounded. Of course their heads were kept well down. Quite a number get wounded in this manner.

Our dugouts have caved in. You lie down in the water for a couple of hours at night. You must fold yourself up as neatly as possible; if you stretch your legs out they get trodden upon by all who pass up and down the trench. Drip, drip, drip on your ground sheet, that damned rain, will it ever cease? Every ten minutes you have to scratch various parts of your body with dirty clay stained hands. The infernal lice are marching all over your body by platoons.

I felt an infinitive longing to be out of it, out of this useless slaughter, misery and tragedy. I feel that way that I would sign peace on almost any terms.

Parties of men are engaged day and night, filling sand bags in order to repair the parapets and trench walls which are constantly falling in owing to continuous rain and undermined by too many dug outs. The 'Jerries' over the way are just as bad, if not worse, as they are nearer to the River Lys than we are. A good many men are losing their lives through sheer carelessness. Before they will use the communication trenches, which are half full of water, they dash over the top in the open. They invariably get killed or wounded. If you use a communication trench you are liable to get drowned; if you don't use it you may get shot, so you have to choose between the two.

Rations

We read various articles in the papers dealing with the shortage of foodstuffs in Germany. We in the trenches ask ourselves the following questions. Have we lost command of the sea? Have the Germans cut our lines of communication? We did not mind in the early stages of the war when everything was at sixes and sevens, but now when we have settled down in a permanent trench line, why should it run three men to one pound loaf of bread. We 'toss up' to ascertain on whom the unthankful task of trying to cut a sodden loaf into three equal parts will devolve upon. The man who cuts the loaf up takes the portion that is left. Between ten men we have a tin of jam with 1oz of bacon and 1oz of cheese per man. We could eat our day's ration for breakfast, and often have done so.

We are well aware that our ration scale is ample if we got it.[33] I am writing without fear or prejudice. The Regimental Quartermaster Sergeant draws a loaf for each man, or full rations as per indents rendered. The rations are then divided into six portions, transport, Regimental Headquarters and the four Companies according to strength. All rations are dumped at Battalion Headquarters. They are drawn from there by company ration parties and taken to the Company Quartermaster Sergeant's dug out or cellar. They are again divided into platoons after company headquarters have had their pick. Platoon ration parties draw their platoon's rations and put them in the platoon sergeant's dug out. They are subjected to another process here, then section commanders are sent for to draw what is left and issue it to their sections. It is quite common for two sections to toss up to see who takes the bacon and cheese, or we come to a mutual agreement for one section to have all the bacon and cheese one morning and the other to have it the next, as it

The Eternal Question.
"When the 'ell is it goin' to be strawberry?"

is an impossibility to divide one section's bacon and cheese into eight or ten equal parts, it was that small. Rum goes through a similar process; there is no shortage of water in Flanders. Battalion and company headquarters get all the strawberry and blackcurrant jam, platoon sergeants and their hangers on all the raspberry, and the privates all the plum and apple. If you want to lead a life of absolute misery or to die really quick, make a complaint.

The Hampshires, on our left and beyond the barricade, seem to have come to some kind of an agreement with the Germans to fire as little as possible at each other. We have got a battery of mountain guns posted in Le Gheer wood and they give the Germans hell every night.

Attack on the Salient

21 December,[34] Christmas is approaching on a sea of mud, rain, frost, fogs, vermin and sudden death. At 2.00 pm my Company 'A' are detailed as supports to the Somersets and a battalion of the Rifle Brigade who are going to take a line of German trenches in front of Le Gheer wood.[35] This trench is a sniper's paradise and from it they can also bring enfilade fire to bear on a portion or sector of our fire trenches. We take up position in a line of breast-works on the edge of the wood.

Our artillery commence the bombardment at 5.00 pm. At 5.30 pm over they go. They were greeted by an inferno of shrapnel, rifle and machine gun fire from the enemy. They struggled across the shell pitted muddy field and the survivors jumped into the trench. There were no Germans in it. They had retired to their main line, and had turned water into the trench by some means or other. The water concealed layers of barbed wire in the bottom of the trench. The Germans kept on yelling from behind their formidable array of barbed wire and machine guns, 'Come on the 'Sets! Come on the 'Sets!'[36]

Our artillery made a 'bloomer' as instead of increasing their range they decreased it, and what was left of the attacking party struggled back to their original first line.

The shades of night fell on 'Plugstreet' wood and on no-man's-land, on the heroic dead, and on the moaning wounded who had rolled into shell craters full of water for cover. Parties of volunteers and stretcher-bearers carried the wounded in all through the night. The stretcher-bearers of the Londons deserve special mention.

Is there a God?

One brave German carried a badly wounded Somerset in on his back. He was thanked and granted a safe passage back to his own lines. Without a doubt, on the British and German sides of the barbed wire there are educated men; men who fear God; men who try to live up to the doctrines of their religion, faith, hope and charity. On the other hand there are brutes who own neither God or the Devil, who scoff at religion, trample the name of God in the mud and filth beneath their feet, and who live their lives solely to satisfy their carnal passions. I will quote the following as an example. A man's leg or arm is blown off by a shell in either the German trenches or our own. There is no salvation for him unless he gets into the hands of the MO [Medical Officer] straight away. Two men throw off their equipment and volunteer to carry him to the dressing station. No sooner are they clear of the trench than they are shot down like rabid dogs. Is this humanity? We are civilized, at least we are supposed to be. Is it following the teachings of Christ? What did the Redeemer of all Mankind die nailed to a cross between two thieves on Calvary's hill for? It makes one doubt if ever there was a Christ or a Calvary hill.

Notes

1   'The battalion entrained at Compiègne and arrived at Blendecques, 2½ miles south of St. Omer.' (Regt. Hist., p.23)
2   'Bn HQ, 'A' and 'B' Companies (were the first to leave) . . . owing to mechanical breakdowns and loss of direction in the darkness it was not until 2.30 am, 13 October, that the battalion was assembled at Hondeghem.' (Ibid, p.23)
3   'The battalion was called to support 17 Brigade at Wez Macquart as the Leinsters had been attacked and the Germans had broken through . . . they had been surprised.' The battalion put Wez Macquart in a state of defence. A few hours later they were recalled to Armentières to support 12 Brigade. (Lawrence, p.9)
4   'Information was received that the enemy had attacked the 12 Brigade about Le Gheer. . . 2/Royal Inniskilling Fusiliers had been driven out of Le Gheer by the enemy . . . .'D' Coy (Major Green) and 'A' Coy (Captain Clayhills) of the East Lancs were ordered to retake the village and restore the line.' (Regt. Hist., p.25)
5   1/Somerset Light Infantry (Ibid, p.26)
6   Roe did not get this right as the charge of the East Lancs on this occasion restored the line. I suspect that Roe did not see precisely what happened in the heat of the action. The following account was written by Major Green and it was his Company ['D'] that made the charge. 'Almost as soon as the charge commenced, all the Huns in the trench jumped up and held up their hands, except two who opened fire. One of them shot [Lieutenant] Hughes dead, at a few yards, and was then bayoneted, as was the other. The man who shot Hughes was a NCO wearing the 'Iron Cross'. Major Lambert sent the Cross to England, to be sent to Germany for his exceptional gallantry.' (Ibid, p.26)
7   I suspect that this happened when both battalions converged on the Le Gheer/Convent crossroads, the Somerset Light Infantry from the north and the East Lancs from the west.
8   Over 130 prisoners were taken and some 40 or 50 of all ranks of the 2/Inniskilling Fusiliers, who had been captured in the morning, were released. The total loss to the Germans was estimated to be about a thousand.
9   "A' and 'B' companies cleared the trenches south of Le Gheer.' (Regt. Hist., pp.26–27)

10 In fact the Germans in 1914 had only twenty-four machine guns per division, the same as the British.

11 'About 4.45 am . . . the enemy, supported by artillery and machine-gun fire, attacked . . . defeated by rapid and accurate rifle fire.' (Regt. Hist., p.27)

12 'Shot through the head whilst directing the fire of his company ('A').' (Regt. Hist., p.30)

13 'Killed by a sniper' (Lawrence, p.20). Battalion history says he was killed on the 1st November.

14 This was also the day when Drummer Bent earned the Victoria Cross for conspicuous gallantry on several occasions. It was the first Victoria Cross to be awarded to the battalion since the Crimean War.

15 A flare projected into the sky for signalling or temporarily illuminating part of a battlefield.

16 'The trench mortar shell comes without any noise and explodes with a huge detonation and makes a nine foot deep hole, large enough to bury a horse and cart.' (Lawrence, p.20)

17 'Two days were spent digging trenches on Hill 63.' (Regt Hist., p.30)

18 3rd Battalion Worcestershire Regiment

19 'At dawn on 7 November the enemy developed a strong attack on the front from Le Gheer to St Yves . . . The brunt of the attack fell on the 3/Worcestershire, which had suffered severely from artillery fire on the previous day. The result was that the two companies in the front line gave way, and the enemy at this point penetrated some 600 yards in Ploegsteert Wood.' (Regt Hist., p.30)

20 The counter-attack was made by 'A' and 'D' Companies with two companies of the Royal Inniskilling Fusiliers and 'C' Company in support. The advance through the wood commenced at 5.00 pm and by 8.00 pm the enemy was driven out of Le Gheer and the trenches running north from the village about 300 yards east of the wood. The village was captured by 'D' Coy . . . led by Captain Cane, who with his company Sergeant Major, Nolan, was killed. 'A' Company, commanded by Lieutenant Leeson, re-captured the trench running north from the village and released a wounded officer and some sixty other ranks of the 3/Worcestershire who had been surrounded all day.

21 Major Lambert was severely wounded whilst standing next to Lieutenant-Colonel Lawrence. He was evacuated to England and, on his return to France early in June 1915, he was posted to the second Battalion. He subsequently was a successful commander of an Infantry Brigade during the Battle of the Somme, 1916, and advanced to command the 32nd Division. After the war he was killed in Ireland during the Sinn Fein troubles.

22 Sergeant Martin Brennan, aged 35, was a Boer War veteran. Born in Burnley, he lived in Brierfield. He was reported dead on 8 November and is commemorated on a panel of the Ploegsteert Memorial.

23 The Commanding Officer, Lieutenant-Colonel G.H. Lawrence.

24 1/Hampshire Regiment.

25 '19 November was our washing day! The men soaked for thirty minutes in hot water while their clothes were taken away to be disinfected and washed, and clean underclothes were given out in their place; while their khaki was ironed by women. They went into good billets in Armentières.' (Lawrence, p.30)

26 'The battalion went back to the Le Gheer trenches, the centre section of the brigade line.' (Regt Hist., p.31)

27 'Afternoon of 3 December he was sniped in the head . . . now in hospital.' (Lawrence, p.34)

28 'The battalion had two companies in the front line, with their Company Headquarters in the cellars of the ruined Convent and the Estaminet du Commerce respectively. One company was held in support at Lawrence Farm and the remaining company was billeted at Nieppe in reserve. The normal routine for each company was three days in the front line, three days in support, three days in the front line again and then three days in Nieppe as reserve.' (Regt. Hist., p.32)

29 'Huge tubs of hot water to hold about twelve men . . . we got a complete set of under-clothing, which did not necessarily fit. . . . While we were in the baths our uniforms were 'baked' in a kind of oven to disinfect them.' (*Four Years on the Western Front*, by a rifleman, London Rifle Brigade, Odhams Press, 1922, p. 19)

30 'Throughout the first winter of the war the authorities of the *Manchester Guardian* wrote weekly to every Lancashire Regiment in France asking what articles were most required.' (Regt. Hist., p.34)

31 In other words, to be shot and killed if they could not be shot and wounded severely enough to send them home to Britain ('Blighty').

32 'Trenches were waterlogged and even constant draining and bailing had little result. The water in one short forward trench, in front of Le Gheer was so deep that it came up to the breast pockets of the men in the trench. Access to this trench by daylight was impossible and the men had to remain in it from dawn to dusk.' (Regt. Hist., p.34)

33 The daily ration scale per man was: 1¼lb bread or 1lb biscuit; fresh meat 1¼lb., or tinned meat (bully beef) 1lb; 4oz jam; 4oz bacon; 3oz cheese; 3oz sugar; 8oz tea; ½oz salt; ½gill of rum (about a tablespoonful and a half); and, when possible, ½lb of fresh vegetables. Now and then tobacco was supplied at 2oz per man.

34 Incorrect – it was 19 December.

35 'An attack on the (German) salient (north of Le Gheer) was carried out on 19 December by the 1/Somerset Light Infantry, covered by the machine-gun and rifle fire of the battalion from the trenches north of Le Gheer. The attack was a partial success only, owing to the impassability of the ground and lack of adequate artillery support . . . . For some time the available allowance for field-guns was limited to from four to six rounds per gun per day.' (Regt. Hist., p.34)

36 Nickname for 1/Somerset Light Infantry.

VII

Christmas 1914 and Life in 'Plugstreet'

(24 December 1914 – 26 April 1915)

Christmas 1914 – An Unofficial Truce – The war starts again – Frostbite
–Lonely Soldiers – Selection as a Bomber – Nicknames – A visit to the
Estaminet – The 'Learned Divine' – Bombing Raid – The Barber's Shop –
A Brave Man

Christmas 1914

24 December 1914, Christmas Eve: Both sides sang Christmas carols in their respective trenches. The carols were accompanied by uncalled for bursts of machine gun and rifle fire. It looks bad for the morrow as we were hoping to have a peaceful Christmas Day. Old Jim gets 'seen off' just after 11.00 pm by a stray bullet. What a Christmas for his wife and kiddies. Has mankind forgotten the Shepherds, the Magi and the Child that was born in the manger because there was no room for him in the inns of Bethlehem?

25 December Christmas Day: At midnight firing ceased as if by mutual consent. As I stood on the fire step, gazing out into no-man's-land with the point of a spare bayonet underneath my chin in case I might doze, I prayed to God (if there was a God?) in his infinite goodness and mercy to end this slaughter and misery and bring peace and goodwill to all mankind. Someone has started playing 'Home Sweet Home' on a mouth organ, away down the trench on my right. Another fellow starts 'Keep the Home Fires Burning' on my left. They join in chorus – the mockery of it all.

At 5.00 am word has passed down the trench that the Hampshires and the Germans were out fraternizing in no-man's-land. 'Impossible, who's leg are you pulling?' 'If you don't believe me, go down and see for yourself'. And there they were, sure enough, British and German warriors in no-man's-land, unarmed, talking to each other and exchanging souvenirs. There is a Christ after all.

Presently the Germans on our front get up on their trench parapets and

74

commence to wave their arms to us. We do the same [and] in twenty seconds we are out in no-man's-land talking to the Germans, or trying to. They gave us bottles of wine and cigars; we gave them tins of jam, bully, mufflers, tobacco etc. I annexed a tin of raspberry from the sergeant's dugout and gave it to a stodgy and bespectacled Saxon. In return he gave me a leather case containing five cigars. They were a Christmas present he received from Baden Baden. The line was all confusion [with] no sentries and no one in possession of arms.[1]

A party of Saxons has already commenced to bury some of their dead who have been lying in the mangel-wurzel field since we made our first counter-attack in October. We were thankful for that at least, for when the wind blew in the direction of our trenches it made us sick with the foetid atmosphere of decaying bodies.

The awful slaughter had been unable to check the spirit of Christmas. On Christmas Eve something 'went west'. Good Will appeared on the battle-field, which had never previously appeared in any other campaign. Would the Spirit of Christmas be maintained? Would friendliness between mankind again be established on the anniversary of the birth of the Redeemer? Would ambitious Statesmen and Warlords, who only think of the Regimental officer and common soldier in terms of mathematics, cast aside their ambitions, stupidity, pride and hatred and allow the angel of peace, instead of the angel of death, to spread his wings over stricken and bleeding humanity. I, or any of my comrades, as far as I can ascertain, bear no malice or hatred against the German soldier. He has got to do as he is told, and so have we. His methods of fighting, his treatment of the in-habitants of occupied territory and the wanton destruction in which he indulges in when forced to evacuate portions of those occupied territories, leave a lot to be desired, but he is only obeying orders. His acts are condoned by the Highest Military Authority, probably by that Apostle of Culture, the all-highest himself (the Kaiser).

I'm afraid I'm a damn bad soldier. I'm preaching peace in the spirit of Christmas.

An Unofficial Truce

We made an unofficial truce with the Germans.[2]
Conditions: -
1.   Any action taken by the Artillery of either Army did not break our truce as we had no control over Artillery.
2.   If either side received an order to fire, they would fire the first three rounds high in the air so as to give the other side time to get under cover.

3.   The German machine gunners had to expend a limited amount of ammunition daily. They would fire high and would blow a shrill warning blast on a whistle before firing. This waste of ammunition would take place every evening, if possible, between the hours of 5.00 and 6.00 pm.

4   Neither side were allowed to erect barbed wire entanglements in front of their trenches.

5.   If either side fired a shot with intent to kill, the truce was declared off.

Members of the Regimental staff, who in times of turmoil and strife gave the trenches a wide berth, now that the truce was on, got quite bold and came up to inspect our trenches, just to see how we lived – and died.

The civilians who owned the pulverized houses at the cross roads came along to see if they could retrieve any article of furniture from the wreck of their once prosperous and comfortable homes.

We could stand upright and smoke; draw water and rations in security. Would it not be splendid if it was always like this? But then no one would be getting killed and the war would last for ever. Sentries were posted on Christmas night but no one fired a round. We had to keep vigilant, as the agreement was only mutual.

26 December Boxing Day: The dawn of boxing morning broke on a scene of general laxity. The Germans remove their old sand bags from their loopholes and replace them by new ones. They look very conspicuous and we duly make a mental note of their positions. If this is going on through the entire length of the line, and for any length of time, they will never get us to start again. We barter more goods with the Germans today and arrange for a Football match on New Year's Day[3]. Boxing Night passed in a similar manner to Christmas Night.

The war starts again

27 December saw the war start again. On looking towards the German trenches we discovered to our dismay that they have painted, or dyed, the new sandbagged loopholes they made yesterday. Their trench seems all alike to us now and we can spot no loopholes. The Germans don't seem very eager to show themselves this morning, however by 9.00 am everyone is on top.

About 9.30 am a shot is fired from the direction of our Company Headquarters and a German falls. That started the war again. Three of our men, who were out looking for doors to roof some dugouts, were caught in the open coming back, and two were wounded.

We found out who fired the shot. It was a young fellow, about sixteen or seventeen years of age and a Lance Corporal. He was acting as a kind of ration corporal to the Company Quartermaster Sergeant. The only qualifications he possessed for either his lance stripe or his employed job were his good looks. He got a couple of tots of '*bukshee*' rum and he got brave. It was a wonderful achievement to shoot down a man standing behind his trench unarmed and smoking, a man that placed his trust in us. The young LCpl Jack thought he had performed a wonderful deed. We did not like the idea of being the first to break the mutual agreement. The honour of the British Army was at stake, and we lost it. He got told off in proper French style.

The Bavarians have relieved the Saxons and the old game is resumed once more. We are well supplied with tobacco, and have all received a Princess Mary's Christmas Gift box. It is a well got up affair and contains a pipe, tobacco and cigarettes. We have also been issued with sheep or rabbit skin coats or jerkins.[4] Christ, are we not carrying enough already? We christen them 'Louse traps'. Some of them are floating about the trenches now. They are all right for people at the base and on the lines of communication, but it is a waste of public money issuing them out to men in the trenches.

Corporal 'Bag-'em-all'[5] got bagged tonight, he was found at the head of a communication trench leading towards our Company Headquarters. Somebody or something hit him very hard on the head. He was badly stunned and was in a comatose condition when he was taken away on the stretcher. As I walk down the muddy trench, I can hear expressions of sympathy from the denizens of muddy and leaky dugouts, such as, 'Poor old Bag-'em-all,' 'Dear old Bag-'em-all,' 'A good chap was Bag-'em-all.' 'Yes! We'll miss Bag-'em-all' (I don't think), and if Bag-'em-all has any brains left when he recovers he will transfer to the 'Linseed Lancers'[6] for his own good.

Quite a number of men who were wounded early on have rejoined. They tell us that when you are hit you never feel it owing to excitement. Jock McLean has been returned off stretcher-bearers and is posted to my section. He will not tell me definitely what he has been returned for, but I hear remarks being passed about him having a 'rum nose'. At Battalion Headquarters there is always a supply of rum stowed away. Jock must have scented it and helped himself. My section are at present holding a house in the rear of our line as a strong point. Jock, who is very superstitious, related to me about a dream he had. The dream revealed to him his wife, dressed all in black, on Glasgow Railway station awaiting his return home. He took it as a bad omen. I told him not to be 'silly' as only Irishmen were superstitious. He got shot clean through the heart next day by a German sniper. Poor old Jock – never again will the 'Alpine Echoes' resound from your cornet.[6]

Frostbite

We have had quite a number of casualties of late during the winter owing to men suffering from frost-bitten feet. On reaching billets a man who could hardly walk would be induced to take his boots off and 'uncase the colours'. By uncasing the colours I mean taking his socks off. 'Holy Moses! What a sight! For heavens sake go sick, why your feet will fall off.' No! he will let them develop. In another three or four days he will report sick. He makes certain that he will get to Blighty. What does the loss of three or four or more toes matter so long as he gets 'out of it'?

Some benign 'Brass Hat' [slang for a senior officer], in the medical profession I presume, and who sits on the seats of the mighty in Whitehall, has invented a preventative against frostbite. It is a tinned transparent substance and resembles lard. It is called anti-frostbite grease or fat. When in the trenches it is supposed to be applied to the feet daily. We are standing in water up to our knees. We are supposed to take our puttees, boots and socks off, smear our feet with this substance (it is solid and as cold as an iceberg), put our wet socks, boots and puttees on again and stand in water up to our knees. Well we don't do it. Who would?

A couple of enterprising spirits have found a market for our frostbite fat. In a back street in the village of Ploegsteert a stout and genial old woman runs a kind of restaurant. Fried *pommes de terre* and *oeufs* (fried egg and chips) are very popular with the troops. In fact it is the one and only dish available. One night Madame explained the difficulty of obtaining fat to fry the 'spuds'. An inspiration hit 'Diamond' and Daly – the anti-frostbite fat. They told Madame they would get her some fat. Next night they brought her down four tins (less labels). Madame tried the fat; it melted. Madame was intrigued. Madame was delighted. It seemed as if manna had dropped from heaven. Madame there and then offered three *francs* a tin. She wanted '*buckoo*' tins (I think 'buckoo' means plenty) and she got plenty from the syndicate.

It was a favourite resort of the Londons, who were epicures in the 'grub line'. We called in several nights. The place was full of Londons, who were relating their experiences over plates of fried chips and eggs. 'Good night Londons!' 'Good night Lancs'. 'What are the chips like, Londons?' 'Oh! – they are top hole, Lancs. Do try some!' We declined with thanks. Of course, the Londons were not aware that they were consuming eggs and chips fried in East Lancs anti-frostbite fat.

Madame was duly instructed, by signs, and illustrations, not to let any person see, or to reveal to anyone, where she got her supply of 'dripping' from. Madame winked knowingly, closed both her optics, compressed her lips and sealed them with the rather chubby index finger of her right hand.

Madame was duly impressed. Madame would not let anyone see. Madame was not to tell anyone as to where she obtained the 'dripping'. In three weeks Madame had enough anti-frostbite fat, at three *francs* per tin, to carry on for the next five years.

The reliefs take place every fourth or fifth night. The German snipers claim four or five victims daily. We have been issued with iron plates to use in our loopholes. The rifle is pushed through a slot in the plate; even then men are shot through the slot. If you want your cap badge perforated by a German bullet as a kind of souvenir, just put your service dress cap over the edge of the parapet and 'Jerry' will oblige you.[8]

The battered convent of Le Gheer is subjected to its usual evening hate.[9] We have not been shelled for six weeks; our trenches are too close to the Germans for them to shell us. 'Plugstreet' Church is badly knocked about as the Germans suspect our artillery officers use the tower for observation purposes.

The Germans have installed a searchlight in rear of their lines and everyone is remarking, 'Why the 'bloomin 'ell can't we have one?' You cannot move when in supports without being shelled. The Germans have a line of observation balloons, or sausages, strung up over their positions for observation purposes.

The owners of some of the *estaminets* and quite a number of villagers are hanging on to their homes, although the village is barely out of rifle range and is shelled every day. It is quite common to see children playing in the village streets whilst the village is being shelled. Four or five of us were often in an *estaminet* having a drink of beer (of course we were not supposed to be there, but we do a lot of things we're not supposed to do and so do our superiors) and a shell would arrive in the house next door. The proprietor would grab two kids and make a dive for the cellar followed by his better half exclaiming '*Souvenir Allemands, Souvenir Allemands!*' We would all look at each other and remark 'Oh 'Jerry's got his "rag out" again.' Everyone was uneasy and yet none would betray the fact that the five minds had but one thought, where was the next one going to burst?

The Germans kept us well informed about Von Hindleburg's [von Hindenburg's] victories over the Russians.[10] They know when we go out to Nieppe in reserve, for when we return to the trenches, they shout across, 'Have you been to Nieppe to change your lousy shirts?' 'How do you like the beer out here?' and so forth. This badinage leads to unprintable remarks from our side of the wire. Officers check the flow of obscene language, so we take it out of each other by blind and indiscriminate firing. It is now evident that the Christmas spirit has departed.

Lonely Soldiers

'Pincher' Martin and Dick Amos are playing the role of lonely soldiers (No soldier should be lonely; if he is it is his own fault). They write to philanthropically minded old ladies and gentlemen in 'Blighty' stating that they have not a soul belonging to them in the world and have no one to write to them. Of course they are telling damn lies, as men who know 'Pincher' Martin tell me that he has two wives and three families. Dick Amos is known to have at least one wife and a family. They receive parcels every mail. 'Pincher' Martin shares the contents of his parcels amongst us. Dick Amos would not give you good morning and in consequence gets most of the contents of his parcels 'pinched.' I received a photo today from Miss Norah _____, Manchester. Is there going to be a romance attached to that postcard? I wrote thanking her for the tobacco, which she sent through the Manchester Guardian. I showed her photo to Hubert of the Londons. We are deep in each other's confidence and he should be a better judge than I. He remarked, 'Well old chappie, you're in luck; she is a stunner.'

I have not much faith in photos as during my term of service in India I have known men who were ten or twelve years in the country and began to feel sort of lonely like and started a correspondence through exchanging such post cards, or some other agency. They wanted a photo, of course, of their wife to be. The wily ladies in 'Blighty' would send out a photo that was taken twenty years previously. 'Oh! What a peach.' The lonely soldiers would submit an application for permission to get married on the strength [of the photo]. They would 'flash' their future wives' photos around the barrack room.

'Here Roe, have a look at the future Mrs. Mullen.'

'By Jove! Tom she's a "stormer".'

'Here you are, "Buck," this is my future Mem-Sahib, Mrs. Wade'

'By Heck, Pudgy, she's a "Topper".'

The boat with the Mem-Sahibs to be duly arrived in Bombay. Wade and Mullen, agog with excitement, would be waiting at the quayside. The ladies, of course, would be leaning over the rails. Photos and faces would be scanned alternately, 'She is not there Tom,' 'Nor is mine "Pudgy".' In the end the Embarkation Officer would have to untie two knots before the clergyman tied them up again.

'Privates Wade and Mullen.'

'Sir.'

'You belong to the East Lancs and have come down to meet your future wives?'

'Yes sir.'

'Well I must say you are a very lukewarm pair. There are only two ladies left. Don't you know your future wives?'

'Oh – they are not the same as the photos, sir.'

'Well I can't help that; maybe it's the photographer's fault. You will have to have them for better or for worse.'

We did a dry smile when we saw the Mem-Sahibs. Poor old 'Pudgy' and Tom had been had.

The Londons are fully fledged now and have taken over a sector of trench line on our right.[11] Hubert and I say *'au-revoir'*. We will meet again – perhaps. I give him a final lecture on the wiles of German snipers.

February arrived, more rain, fog and dreariness; I cannot imagine a more depressing country than Flanders. Remarks are flung about by cheerful optimists, such as, 'Bear up Joe. The first five years is the worst,' and 'England always loses a war before she starts to win it.'

Von Hindleburg is doing well it seems against the Russians, as the Germans over the way inform us every night, in excellent English, about his progress.

Corporal Lindsay and Private Barker of my Company have been recommended for the DCM [Distinguished Conduct Medal]. The Germans' shells fired a farmhouse in our rear. In the cellar was stored our reserve supply of bombs and ammunition, which would have 'went west' had the fire not been extinguished.[12] Captain Moloney (2/East Lancashires), my new Company commander got mortally wounded as he was superintending erection of barbed wire entanglements. Quite a number of officers and men get shot through sheer carelessness.

A very wet month, everybody and everything suffers through rain. Certain people are in a continual state of joviality, which the regulation allowance of rum issue does not warrant, and some have lost their lives by unduly exposing themselves owing to an 'excess of tots.'

March, and still in the same old network of canals, the same old routine, the same old snipers and the same old scenery. On certain days we get issued out with a Mc.Onnachie Ration [Maconochie].[13] It has got to be heated in hot water to enjoy it but we cannot get hot water. As a rule it is eaten cold. It is a great improvement on the 'bully' as it contains a certain amount of vegetables.

Selection as a Bomber

I have been selected to go on a bombing course.[14] I leave the trenches every day at 9.00 am for Battalion Headquarters. It requires a certain amount of strategy to get out and get back without being shot. I was weak minded. I took an interest in the Hales or stick bomb [and] I was second to the officer, Mr

Penny I believe, in the final throwing test. I was not as well in the know as some of the class, who only threw the bombs as far as was compatible for their bodily safety, and were rejected. I was made a Regimental bomber and I unconsciously increased my chances of 'going West' by about forty per cent.

Showers of hail and cold biting winds chill us to the bone. In our sheep or rabbit skin jerkins we resemble Cossacks from the Urals. Our feet are never warm.

The last time I was in Nieppe I was purchasing a loaf of bread from a baker's shop when about twenty men of the Baluchi[15] Regiment marched past. They were mud from head to foot, they were war weary, and they were fighting in a country the climatic conditions of which they were not accustomed. They did not look to their right or left. It was a matter of doubt if they would ever look cheerful again. Poor devils, I pitied them. Madam (in the bakery) took an altogether different view of the situation. Madam expected them to be singing and playing mouth organs. With a gesture of her left hand Madam exclaimed, '*Soldats Hindustan nappu Tipperary, Soldat Hindustan no bon.*'

Nicknames

Out to Nieppe for a bath and a four days rest. At 3.00 pm on the first day of our 'holiday' in Nieppe I made preparations for going out at 3.10 pm when parades were finished for the day. Out of the corner of my eye, in the school-room in which we were billeted, I saw 'Red' Ned and 'Black' Tom withdrawing packs of stationary from their packs. I was not immediately requested to write a couple of letters each for them, but I knew it was coming. How the devil was I going to dodge them? Well, I smuggled my SD [service dress] cap out to Corporal 'Shady' Fleet, who was Guard Commander. I was not in possession of a 'Pass.' It was all right with 'Shady', as he could trust me if I got caught by the military police – 'Well, I got over the wall'. There was nothing 'Shady' about Corporal Fleet. Perhaps people who did not know him kept their 'lamps' [eyes] on him owing to his nickname. Corporal Fleet was the victim of Tradition. We have our 'Jumper' Wildes, that is to say that if you are unfortunate to bear the name of Wilde in the Army you are adorned with the nickname 'Jumper', even if you cannot jump over a Blanco sponge. All Smiths are nicknamed 'Marrowbone', whether they mash up stewed or boiled bones for the marrow contained therein or not. All persons bearing the name of Andrews are called 'Charzies', although they may never have seen a 4 anna piece. All Browns are called 'Tapper', even if he is a colonel or general he is called 'Ow'd Tapper' when he is a subject for discussion in the barrack room or 'wet' canteen, all Shaws are affectionately dubbed 'Jerrys'.

When I got back to the billet after squaring 'Shady', 'Red' Ned and 'Black' Tom were enjoying a smoke of Rat Tail tobacco from clay pipes and talking about mild and bitter ale, sad cakes and winberry pies. Ah yes, they wished they were back in Chorley again. They would have a 'Minister's Face', spuds and cabbage for dinner, washed down with a couple of quarts of bitter ale. (Without disrespect to a minister of any denomination, a 'Minister's Face' was commonly known as a pig's head. It was boiled with cabbage and served up thus.)

I was asked if I was going out? I was non-committal and replied that I might do so later on. I was in no humour for letter writing anyway. If my memory serves me aright, I heard 'Red' Ned soundly cursing the Army authorities in a public house in Harrow in August 1914 for their tardiness in not sending us out to France. He swore by twenty-seven Gods that we would not be in time to get a blasted 'gong' [slang for medal]. Well, we've got a 'gong' now;[16] whether we live to wear it or not is a matter of luck.

A visit to the Estaminet

I slipped out of the billet in my bare head, retrieved my cap from 'Shady' at the Guard room, and passed into the main street. Nieppe was not shelled by the 'Jerries' in my time, as our gunners and the Germans came to some kind of an agreement it seemed. If you do not shell Warneton (a big town on our front and beyond the river Lys and in 'Jerry' lines), we will not shell Nieppe.

I was in search of a quiet *estaminet*, as I wanted to write up some notes. I gave the sign of the Three Pigeons *estaminet* a wide berth as I knew from experience what was going on in there. The proprietress was an aristocratic looking old dame, but had the business acumen to employ four notoriously good-looking refugees to act as barmaids. They were dressed in the shortest of short skirts. Even then some people were not satisfied. Well, it's the devil to please everybody. In fact I was almost convinced that only French and Belgian ladies could dress. Lizet, Juliet and company were in the habit of going around the tables and asking everyone, in a tone of confidence, had we a fiancée in *Angleterre*? 'No certainly not', no one had. Lizet would then 'pop' the question, '*Après la guerre you will come back and marry me?*' Of course we will all come back and marry Lizet and Juliet. I don't bloomin' well think! Every time we came out of the trenches for a bath at Nieppe, Lizet and Juliet would miss quite a few prospective 'hubbies' that would never see '*après la guerre*'. Certain ancients who would be adorned with mutton chop whiskers had not a benevolent government issued out two pence halfpenny razors, with orders that they had to be utilized 'at all costs', denied the soft impeachment that they had wives and families or even a fiancée in *Angleterre*.

I could not derive any inspirations in the sign of the Three Pigeons, as apart from the attentions of the quartet of Mam'selles, Tommy Carrol would be singing 'Roses in Picardy' at one end of the room, whilst Pat Mayo would be singing 'My dear old Galway Bay' at the other. So I took my notebook and notes down to the sign of the 'Belgian Hare' *estaminet*. Thank Christ no one could get drunk on French or Belgian beer. This *estaminet* sported on its signboard a large and well-fed Belgian hare, sitting on its hind legs contentedly munching a cabbage leaf. There was no other person in.

Madam was tall, Madam was angular, and Madam's hands indicated that she was a daughter of the soil. Madam was dressed in the early or mid-Victorian era. A flowing skirt concealed her ankles, her jacket or bodice sleeves were buttoned very close to the hands. I would not like to stop a right hook from Madam on the point or on the solar plexus. Madam furnished me with a litre of beer and babbled over '*cat sue*' francs. I imagined that I had found the ideal place at last and that I could write in peace and quietness. I was to be sadly disillusioned. Madam talked me to death; will she ever close her 'trap' [mouth]? I asked myself. Ah yes, her 'hubby' was away fighting in all this '*dilu*' (rain), Yes – and I bet he is laughing his socks off to be away from you, I inwardly remarked. 'Was she *bon*?' I told her she was '*tray' bon*. Well she was not, and I'm not hard to please. 'Why do all the soldiers *Angleterre* favour the Three Pigeons? No one comes in to her *estaminet*.' I told her that the Three Pigeons was nearer to our billet in case we had to 'stand to'. Suddenly, Madam raised her right arm, pointed the index finger of her right hand at me, and confidently informed me that the French soldiers were '*no bon*' (no good). In moments of inspired confidence French ladies have informed me that *Belgique* soldiers were '*no bon*'. Who the devil has one got to believe? Of course I have my own opinion and that is – it's hang the devil between them.

Someone came in. 'Good Christ!' it is one of Pontius Pilate's Bodyguards.[17] I greeted him thus, 'Hello Pontius, what are you on?' 'I'm on the staff', he replied. Yes, and I wish to Christ I was on the staff too; at least I would not be as lousy as what I am. Charlie seemed offended over me calling his 'mob' Pilate's Bodyguard, until I explained that the Munsters were nicknamed 'The Dirty Shirts', the Irish Guards were called the 'Moikes' and the Scotch Guards the 'Burgoo Wallopers'. Madam sang. Madam had a terrific voice; the plaster fell off the ceiling.

I saw 'Big Feet' of the MPs [military police] approaching. 'Big Feet' was a GM Provost of the worst type. The devil must have had a 'hell of a liver on' the day or night that 'big feet' was brought into the world. He had a special grudge against the Lancs and made it his business to persecute them in every way. I implored Madam to hide me, as I had no pass. I took cover under Madam's ample skirt behind the counter. 'Big feet' came in and asked was there any of the B . . . . Lancs in? I was damn near emerging from under

Madam's skirt and saying 'Yes! – There is one of the B .... Lancs here. Can you take anything 'out of him'? Had I consumed the same quantity of English beer I would be fired with esprit-de-corps and have done something rash. Would *mon* Colonel, at the compulsory interview the following morning, view it in the light of esprit-de-corps? Would the members of the court martial view it in the light of esprit-de-corps? Without doubt I would be charged with 'WOA [when on active service] Service – Drunk', 'striking a GMP whilst in the execution of his duty' and 'Quitting my billet without permission'. Quite enough to get me 'seen off' at 6.30 am some foggy morning up against the chateau wall and I would go the way that quite a few of my comrades had gone.

One night 'Big Feet' was waiting on the stone bridge, which spans the sluggish River Lys and marks the boundary line between France and Belgium. He was awaiting the return of some adventurous spirits that had gone to visit 'Green Lamps' in Armentières. Only a very poor tactician would cross a stone bridge with a policeman waiting to take his name on the bridge. Such people deserve to be caught as there were other ways of getting across the Lys than by the stone bridge. 'Big Feet' never saw a louse, nor had the guts of one when 'tackled'.

'What about if he cannot swim?'

'That's his own "bloody" look out. Every soldier should know how to swim.'

Next morning, on identification parade, 'Big Feet' picked out three men who were on guard when the incident happened. In any case alibis were prepared. 'Big Feet' got shifted to another part of the line and Nieppe knew him no more. Thank the Lord he had learnt to swim.

Towards the end of March we took over the Hampshires' trenches and had a Regiment of Terriers attached to us (the Lincolns).[18] As it was their first experience in the firing line, they were very anxious to have a 'pop' at the Germans and would blaze away at the German trenches all day, wasting ammunition, if we let them. They were distributed amongst the old hands for tuition. I was unlucky as my Lincoln was a love-lorn swain. The first day in he wrote a letter to his dear, darling loved one, Mabel. It ran thus: 'I am only 100 yards away from the Bosche', full stop: he picked his rifle up and fired twenty rounds at the German trench parapet, then resumed his letter. 'Could she picture her Algy 100 yards away from the Germans and knocking spots off them?' He would then loose off another twenty rounds. I was snatching half an hour's rest in the dugout. I heard the bursts of firing; I got up and went out to see what he was firing at. He showed me the letter as far as he had progressed and was going to blaze away another twenty rounds at nothing. I consigned Mabel and him to the South Pole, or some place hotter. I gave him a good telling off for wasting ammunition, told him he had deprived me of a good hour's hard earned rest, and besides, he was inviting retaliation from the German gunners, and for Christ's sake to cut romance out, Algy. Fritz, our pet sniper, got him after tea, or about 4.30 pm as there was no such thing as teatime in the trenches. I told him never to fire more than a couple of rounds from the same position over the parapet by day, unless the Germans were attacking, or he would get 'seen off'. He would not take advice.

I almost forgot to mention the advent of the Canadians.[19] They were attached to us late in February. A New Brunswick Regiment, [they were] a sturdy lot of fellows, rather careless at first, but learnt to respect the bullet in the course of time. They were armed with the Ross rifle, a cumbersome weapon, excellent for slow firing but useless for the 'mad minute' or rapid firing.

The first night they arrived in the trenches the Germans were aware of it, as they kept shouting over, 'The dollar a day men have arrived. Are you regulars going to fight for a shilling a day whilst they get a dollar?' Next morning they shoved up a screen on which a white horse was roughly chalked.

We are overcrowded, it was very inconvenient, and of course there were more casualties.

The majority of the Canadians 'dumped' their Ross rifle in preference for ours, which could be picked up in scores in the cellars of farmhouses adjacent to the firing line.

April and still alive. Each company take over Nissen huts[20] when in support. They are all over canvas affairs [and] scenic artists have painted them to harmonize with the surroundings. The enemy's airmen cannot spot them. They are erected in 'Plugstreet' wood, or what is left of it. A stove is fitted in each hut. They are very comfortable but we are hardly ever in them.

The 'Learned Divine'

At this stage a learned divine favoured us with a visit, a divine who had his foot on the topmost rung of the ecclesiastical ladder.

He exhorted us not to swear when we fall into shell holes full of water on dark nights, in full marching order and carrying a box of biscuits or perhaps a coil of barbed wire on your 'hump' [slang for 'back']. Swearing offended God – Hell was full of men who swore. He exhorted us, when up to our necks in water in a shell hole with a coil of barbed wire lapped around our necks, to utter that pious ejaculation, 'Oh Lord, not my will be done but thine'.

He paid a visit to the trenches one night. It was very dark and wet [and] he did not keep in close touch with his guide. The communication trenches were half filled with water and could not be used. When in [the] rear of our trenches he slipped, 'up to his neck in it', in a shell hole full of water. We heard some awful language; we knew no one in our company used language like that. Good God! – who should it be? The air was turning blue; all the artillery in Germany will be turned on us. 'Cherby' Williams went out and, with the assistance of the guide, rescued a mud be-splattered and soaking figure from the shell crater. It was our clerical friend. There was no 'Oh Lord, not my will but thine' about it. Oh yes! – he would visit the brave lads who were going through it, just to see how they endured misery, wounds and death. What a fine sermon he would be able to preach to his congregation on his arrival in L . . . , taking as his text – 'In the midst of life we are in death'. We are wondering will he tell them what he said when he fell into the shell hole on his visit to the brave lads.

This time we have been pretty busy in supports. We have had to work for six hours nightly carrying planks from Hyde Park Corner [in Ploegsteert wood] to St Yvson or St Ives, up by Messines. We all have to carry planks except the RE Sapper; he is too fastidious to carry one, I suppose. One feels a supreme lack of mobility when in full marching order and carrying two 8 foot planks for three miles along bullet swept roads and paths.

Sergeant Helm DCM got killed about the middle of the month,[21] as did a lot more. We're always getting killed anyway.

Will it ever stop raining in this sea of mud, filth and misery? It is [so] dark at times, when 'sloshing' our way across the muddy fields to relieve the two companies who are holding the line, that we cannot see the section of fours who are swearing in front.

Everyone, apart from the regulation mess-tin, carries a receptacle of some kind, secured on his supporting straps, for the purpose of 'drumming up'. These tins or 'Billy cans', as they are called, have been annexed from deserted houses contiguous to the line. You never hear the remark, 'Who is going to cook the breakfast, or dinner?' It's 'Who is going to "drum up"?' or 'Have you "drummed up"?' The verb 'to cook' has been stowed away, at least until the war ends. Biscuit tins punctured by bayonet blades serve as braziers. Bayonets are also very handy for opening jam, butter, bully and Mc.Onnachie tins. Charcoal is an issue – we get some.

One has not much need to worry about his shooting abilities, but it is advisable to be an accomplished digger, as for the past 8 months it's dig, dig, dig.

Our new platoon officer has just arrived from England, his name is Mr D[22] . . . but we all call him Joey Chamberlain, as he sports a monocle (of course he does not hear us). I think he is a bit religious minded as he has started an anti-swearing league. We've got to say 'jam and butter it', instead of what we would say, and 'Blink eyed NELL' instead of something else. 'Feel and mind it' is another substitute. Of course his crusade against swearing was not a success and his substitutes are only used when he is within earshot. It has been reported that he has been heard using the word 'damn' with great fervour on two occasions of late. I suppose he will be just as bad as the remainder of us – if he lives long enough.

The owner of the Piggery Farm, where we billet at times, always shows his love for the British troops by removing the sucker from his pump to prevent us from obtaining water. I'm sure he hates the very sight of us, and his better half is the same.

I met a party of the Londons in 'Plugstreet' today. I made anxious enquiries about Hubert; I was informed that he had 'Gone West'. I asked how? 'Sniped in the trenches. He was firing at a dummy "Jerries" head, which was just showing over the parapet. The real "Jerry" was five or six yards to the right or left behind a concealed loophole.' Hubert was drawn and paid the penalty. Ah! Hubert you forgot all that I told you about the wiles of the German sniper. So it's good-bye Oxford Street and no 'burst up' in 'Frascatis' after we had won the war. They took me to their billet and treated me to *vin rouge*. Like our everlasting plum and apple, it inspired no poems in its praise.

This evening a 'Jerry' aeroplane bombed a party of us who were digging trenches away back of Messines. The sickly sound of bombs dropping from the air put the wind up us, but no one was hit.

On April 20 the Fourth Division was relieved by the 4th [46th] Midland Territorial Division.

A Regiment of the Rifle Brigade, the Londons (Terriers), the Somersets and Hampshires, have gone back to Bailleul for the long-talked-of rest, so we are told, and we take over a new line of trenches at Le Touquet, and curse our luck for having to remain behind.

During our first twenty-four hours in our new position the 'Jerries' greeted the Lancs with showers of rifle grenades, which they fired with amazing precision and our casualties were mounting up. Our first experience of those grenades was in Ploegsteert about November 14. We did not know what they were or where they came from. We were looking skywards but there were no aeroplanes and it took us a week to find out what they were. The opposing lines ran so close together in places that when a sentry of ours got shot and his comrades stooped to pick him up, the empty mauser case filled with clay was thrown into the trench and hit one of the men who was assisting him. At 5.00 pm we had two killed and three wounded by another grenade.

Bombing Raid

The Bombing Officer asked four other bombers and I would we go out tonight at 8.00 pm and bomb them by way of retaliation. We all agreed – it would not look well to say no. We made our way to the cellar which was head-quarters at 7.30 pm and prepared our Hales bombs. When the red lines on the base and nose of the bomb were brought into line the bomb was at 'danger'. They were not time bombs; a percussion cap and pin fitting into the nose of the bomb and a slight impact on the nose and off she went. The bomb was fitted on to a wooden handle about 18 inches long. The end of this handle was fitted with tapes or streamers, which caused the bomb to drop on its nose.

The rations have arrived and we are asked will we have our rum issue now or wait until morning? 'We'll have it now in case we might not come back.'

At 8.00 pm we filed down the trench and selected a position from where to throw the bombs. The sentries were ordered to put their rifles against the parados or back portion of the trench. The Germans were keeping up a slow, continuous fire on the trench. We crawled out on our knees and elbows. We could not use our hands as we had a bomb in each hand and had to keep the noses up, as the slightest impact on the nose would set the bomb off and some of us along with it. As we crawled out we cursed the empty jam and 'bully' tins as we made an awful row; empty jam and 'bully' tins were thrown out in front and sometimes hung on the barbed wire in order to give us the alarm if 'Jerry' came over. I had a sort of 'sure to be hit' feeling. When we passed the barbed wire we managed to get three paces distance from each other and carried on crawling until we reached the road. The bullets meanwhile were flying too close to be comfortable.

Mr Wilkinson gave the signal. We all stand up and away goes the right hand bomb. Change from left to right and ensure that the tapes do not get entangled around your wrist – for if they do, it will mean a little black cross and there will be precious little to put underneath it. The second bomb is thrown: crash, crump, crash, bang. We bolt like hell for our trenches. There is a hell of a commotion in the 'Jerry' trenches. We dived over our own parapet just as he opened rapid fire and one of our number lost a boot heel through the action of a Mauser bullet. They were in a continual state of 'wind up' all night. Whether Saint Peter or Satan profited anything by our exertions we will never be able to tell.

The Barber's Shop

When out of the firing line we are billeted in houses and *estaminets* in Le Bizet. We never have any sense of security as our billets are shelled daily. Nieppe was a much safer place. When billeted in Nieppe, 'Pasha' Lindsay, Riley and I used to get permission to attend 7.00 am Mass every morning. There was a barber's shop 100 yards down the street [and] whether we wanted a shave or not we used to visit it every morning. The barber, a man about sixty years of age, stood 6 feet 4 inches in his stockinged feet, wore a round skull cap and wielded a razor the blade of which held some relation to a cook house chopper. A chair was placed in such a position that you could obtain a full view of Madam in the kitchen. Madam was old, Madam was toothless, yet Madam managed to retain a large clay pipe in her mouth and smoked incessantly. Her varied brands of tobacco were supplied by patriotic readers of the Manchester Guardian. As her Lord and Master lathered apace, madam would politely murmur '*coffee*?' We would reply '*Wee wee madam.*' Madam would pour out a cup and hold up two fingers. This signal meant did we want two tots of cognac in the coffee? As a rule we would hold up three fingers. 'twas divine. It is the only method cognac should be drunk, and madam could make coffee. The barber would then remove the lather with a towel and we would proceed to church, renewed in spirit.

We kept it (the barber's shop) a profound secret, as if the men got to know fifty per cent of Mr Canton's company would try and change over to the RC [Roman Catholic] persuasion, as no one was allowed out until 2.00 pm, and only then a certain percentage on pass, and the barber's shop closed down at 11.00 am.

A Brave Man

Nobody tries to 'scrounge' a Divine service parade now. Has the 'Jack Johnsons', the shrapnel, the trench mortars, the bullet and sudden death brought us nearer to God?

One Sunday the padre preaches a sermon, in somber surroundings, first in French and then in English for our benefit. He told us that if ever anyone of us were badly wounded in the trenches by day and could not be got out, to send for him (first line was in telephonic communication with battalion headquarters) and he would come right to the first line. He was as good as his word. A week later we were in supports in a farm alongside the bullet swept road. A gig or pony and trap drove past in the direction of the trenches. Who was that? Had someone gone mad? We watched events from over the parapet of the support trench, expecting to see the driver come to a sudden end, as the German machine guns played incessantly on the road. He drove right up to Le Gheer Convent, alighted from the trap and made for the trenches. He administered the last rights of the church to one of 'C' company who was mortally wounded, and returned unscathed. He was a brave man, anyway, whatever nationality he was. Of course, Paddy Oates and 'Diamond' swore that he was an Irishman.

The Monmouthshires are driving a mine towards the German second line.[23] They have already got past their first line. The clay they excavate has to be carried in sandbags and distributed on the parados. If it were heaped up around the mineshaft the Germans would naturally be suspicious as to why all the fresh earth was heaped in one place.

On **23 April** the battalion handed over the trench line.

24 April: The CO holds a battalion parade in a field in the rear of the village. He had us fixing bayonets and presenting arms. We were expecting the German gunners to cancel the parade any second, as we must have been plainly visible to the 'Jerry' observer in the sausage or observation balloon. We had not long to wait. Crash, bang, wallop – we took cover behind a steep embankment and had no casualties, but the poor villagers suffered, some more houses and lives 'went west'. When one party of twenty got back they had no billet. The house was wrecked; an old man, a woman and one child were killed.

On **26 April 1915** we marched to Bailleul and left old Le Touquet and 'Plugstreet' behind. 'Plugstreet', with its wood of tree stumps, Nissen huts and cemeteries. We almost claim 'Plugstreet'. It is ours – at least in spirit.

Notes

1   'At 10.00 am [Lieutenant-Colonel Lawrence] went round all the trenches and wished the men a Happy Xmas . . . there was a sudden hurrah and rush and our men and the Germans started running to one another and meeting halfway shook hands. I did not like it at first and ordered my men back, then was told the Germans wanted a truce to bury their dead, so I agreed . . . ordering half the men to keep a smart look out in the trenches with their rifles ready, I went forward and joined the crowd . . . for an hour I stood there and took the opportunity of observing their trenches and wire and sent my Subs. to other parts of the line to observe while I kept their men away from our trenches, and we got useful information . . . .I said if they would have an armistice on New Year's Day we would play them at football between our lines – so that remains to be seen . . . should it come off it will be a funny sight as I will keep half my men armed and ready in the trenches, while the others would be encouraging their side. I wonder if it will come off.' (Lawrence, pp.38–39)

2   'Early in January the Second Army issued an order forbidding all informal understandings with the enemy, under penalty of trial by court-martial on any officer or non-commissioned officer who allowed such understandings.' (Regt.Hist., p.35)

3   'We never got our football match [on 1 January], the Germans were not for it and sniped all day. General Wilson and his staff turned up at 11.00 am to see it but were disappointed, as were various other fellows who turned up. As they would not play we shelled their trenches.' (Lawrence, p.41)

4   'Gum boots and goat-skin coats with the hair outside were issued. There were not sufficient gum boots for every man, and the goat-skin coats were not popular and were eventually withdrawn.' (Regt. Hist., p.34)

5   'Bag-'em-all' was an extremely unpopular non-commissioned officer.

6   Royal Army Medical Corps.

7   I believe this man to have been Private Frank McLeod, born in Glasgow, who was reported killed in action 8 January 1915.

8   'The German snipers . . . showed deadly skill and patience. Lying out in no-man's-land

91

for hours, they watched the British trenches, and if they got even a 2 inch bull's-eye for the moment, they got it every time.' (Regt. Hist., p.36)

9   'Whenever you are near the firing-line you can see them shelling the Convent (at Le Gheer) just behind the Lancs' trenches and half of it still stands. Yet the Lancs continue to garrison it [it was company headquarters]. They just turn out, stand behind the wall and smoke a pipe, waiting while they shell the other side of the building, and when it is all over they go inside again. Those Lancs are a cool lot of chaps. (*Four Years on the Western Front*, by a rifleman, London Rifle Brigade, Odhams Press, 1922, p. 23)

10 This was the campaign of Field Marshal von Hindenburg against the Russian 10th Army in East Prussia and Poland, which was very successful for the Germans.

11 'Two companies of the London Rifle Brigade were attached to the Battalion and took over the line between the Warnave brook and Le Touquet.' (Regt.Hist., p.35)

12 'Corporal Lindsay and Private Barker were recommended for the DCM for extinguishing a fire at 'A' company headquarters under heavy fire of all sorts.' (Ibid, p.35)

13 A tin of Maconochie's consisted of meat, potatoes, beans and other vegetables. The best firms that supplied them were Maconochie's and Moir Wilson's.

14 31 January 1915 – 'Discussion on the formation of a Company of Grenadiers in the Battalion. Some ninety-six men are to be trained in the art of throwing bombs.' (Lawrence, p.45)

15 A Regiment of the Indian Army raised in Baluchistan. These men were most likely from the 129th (Duke of Connaught's Own) Regiment, part of the Lahore Division in the area.

16 The Mons Star.

17 Nickname for the Royal Scots.

18 '1/5 Lincolnshire of the 46th (South Midland) Division.' (Regt. Hist., p.36)

19 'The 1st Canadian Division arrived in the 4th Division area and two companies were attached to the battalion for instruction in trench warfare.' (Ibid, p.36)

20 A tunnel – shaped hut named after the British engineer who invented it.

21 8 April 1915 – killed by a sniper.

22 I believe him to be Second Lieutenant W.J. Foster who joined the Battalion on 16 February 1915.

23 It was a counter mine as it was suspected the Germans were mining Le Gheer at Forward House. On 27 April, Lieutenant-Colonel Lawrence went to see how the mining operation was progressing, as both sides were mining, and it was a question of which side would win. 'We had two mines ready. The one at the sniper's house we had to blow up in a hurry as they [the Germans] were about to discover it . . . They retaliated with theirs but it was hopelessly short and only blew up in a field between the opposing lines and did no damage; but at our other mine near the railway barricade it was much more exciting. We had a gallery and cross-gallery – the cross one was really a listening one. The morning after we were relieved [the East Lancs] a miner who was going to the listening gallery heard German voices and saw a light. So he hurried back to give the alarm and Captain Woodgate of the King's Own, who was commanding there, went down the mine with his revolver and with two of his men. He met the Germans at the cross-gallery and they fired at one another. Finally the Germans were driven back to the spot where they broke in. Here they exploded their mine which did no damage to us and left our mine quite intact and ready for any future time.' (Lawrence, pp. 66–74)

VIII

2nd Battle of Ypres

(26 April – 17 May 1915)

Move to Flanders – Ypres – 'Straightening the Line' – Shell Trap Farm –
The Listening Post – The Patronage System –
The 'Jerries' Attack – Wounded

Move to Flanders

Well we're off for our long earned rest anyway; we march cheerfully to the
strain of tunes played on mouth organs that were made in Germany. Mr
'Joey' Chamberlain has left us as he blew three or four of his fingers off with
a 'Very light' pistol accidentally on the night we got relieved in 'Plugstreet'
to take over the Le Touquet position.[1]

Billet in a large farmhouse somewhere near Bailleul on the night of the
26th. Inspections of all kinds on the **27th**, on the **28th** we are hustled into
London County Council motor buses and away to Ypres.[2] So this is our long
promised rest, is it?[3]

The unconscious humour of the Cockney drivers cheered us up somewhat. As we passed through Poperinge headlights were dimmed and the
buses bumped in and out of shell craters. 'Cheer up Bill, we'll soon be dead!'
one bus driver would shout to another. They 'dumped' us close to Ypres, I
do not know what is the proper pronunciation for Ypres (I have heard it
pronounced as 'Yapps', 'Wipers' and 'Snipers'); in any case it's a devil of a
place, if the detonations of Bertha Krupp's heavy pills on the already
demolished and burning town are anything to judge by.

Ypres

On de-bussing [at Vlamertinge] we marched towards the sound of the guns
and rested for one hour in a small field on the fringe or outskirt of the town,
and close to what was at one time a road. The field that once grew cabbages,
broccoli and *pom-de-terres* is now pitted with shell craters. I recline on the
lip of a newly made shell crater. It is not full of water; the earth is fresh and

93

the air reeks with the fumes of gas or acids from the high explosive shells. Shells and still more shells continue to fall on the town. It is nearer my God to thee with a vengeance here. I have a kind of feeling that I cannot last much longer. I mentally examined my soul; it resembled a target that twenty men had fired fifteen rounds rapid at – good shots and bad shots – 'twas stained all over. They tell us there is a recording angel – well he must be a pretty busy spirit. Let's hope he makes a mistake or two, the same as they do in the record and pay offices in Preston.

We have not seen the Brigadier lately. I can hear him discussed thus:

'Oi Paddy, I have not seen the "Brig" lately!'

'Gor Blime, he don't arf chance his bleedin mit, e don't.'

'Faith that he does for sure, Bill, he's not afraid to be killed anyway, like some of them, as you were.'

All the unkind things we said about you on the retirement, Hunter, when we were dead beat and you kept shouting 'Cover off' and 'Left, right, left' – You're a soldier and not afraid to 'chance your arm'.[4]

Fall in at midnight and march through the town.[5] I will not forget the early morning of **April 29** in a hurry. The shell swept streets were blocked with wrecked transport, dead horses, dispatch riders, motor bikes and dead men here and there and what an awful smell. It defies description. The tower on the ruined church of St Martin's still rears its spire heavenwards. We cast a sorrowing glance at the ruins of the famous cloth hall, but the German gunners give us no time for contemplation as they are shelling the town with guns of all calibres. We were lucky to get through the scene of desolation without any casualties.

After marching for two hours we take over some reserve trenches at a place called Zonnebeke.[6] He shells the roads with deadly accuracy every night.

Straightening the Line

On **May 2** [**3 May**] at 7.00 pm we are ordered to advance with fixed bayonets. We thought we were going to attack. It was otherwise, as we had to cover the retirement of a sector of the British Army from an untenable position. In other words, the line was being straightened.[7] We relieved the Londons and had to throw their dead out of the shallow trenches before we could get in. What a lot of dead; in fact the trench was held by dead men, the survivors were like lunatics.[8]

I feel an impact on my pack and hear a rattle. A bullet went through my pack and lodged inside my mess-tin, thus putting it out of mess. It was fired from my right rear. From what I can make out of this position we are too far forward, as the Germans, to judge by the firing are on our flanks and almost directly in rear of us.

At 10.00 pm we retire,[9] each regiment left a sacrifice platoon behind to hold the position until dawn and then retire. The Germans, we are told, have been massing for attack all the evening. We fell back for about 150 yards and lay down in the open and in line with fixed bayonets, then arise and retire through another regiment, who are also in line in the open. Two hundred yards in rear of the regiment through which we retired we get down again, and they retire through us, and so on until we reached a previously prepared position.

The Germans shelled us, not with shrapnel, but with shells that contained some chemical substance as everyone is coughing and crying. We were issued out, some days ago, with a pad attached to an elastic band. We were told to wet the pad if ever the Germans attempt to gas us. If we have no water in our bottles we must urinate on the cotton wool pad as the pad must be wet. We are to place the wet pad over our mouths. The pad is held in position by the elastic band, which fits around the head and over the ears. Of course we have to breath through the nostrils and inhale the gas as the nostrils are not protected. It inflames the eyes. We took it more or less as a joke and christened it laughing gas; it was no laughing matter, as we witnessed the effects of the gas of another type later on in the morning.[10]

Mr Salt's platoon remained behind in the original position.[11] The line retired about 1½miles in this particular sector. The battalion retired into Pilkem Woods. Mr Salt's platoon arrived at 12 noon [**4 May**]. They propped dead men in position in the trench before they retired. So far the Germans are not aware that the position has been vacated.

At 2.00 am this morning we marched past a lot of men who were lying on the roadside in a wrecked village. They were gasping for breath and were tearing at their throats.[12] We were told they were the victims of a new engine of destruction – gas. They seemed to be in great agony.

I had a really inspiring letter from Harrow today. Joyce tells me in her letter that they are raising and training an immense army in England and if only we can hang on until they get out it will be over in no time. She informs me that there are quite a number encamped around Harrow and that times are quite lively. Yes! I can imagine the times you are having in Harrow Joyce dear. I can see through your little game, Joyce. You are like the lonely soldier; you want half the British Army to be in correspondence with you. You will receive a field service post card in reply to this, and then I will fade away.

[**8 May**] We have been in this wood for the last four days[13] and are moving up this evening to attack. At 2.00 pm the RC padre came around and gave all the RCs absolution. He was a genial old soul and asked one and all where they came from. Nobody really cared or bothered about where they came from, but we would be greatly obliged to him if he could tell us where we were going to go to, tonight or early tomorrow morning maybe.

Move at 3.00 pm, reach Divisional headquarters at 4.00 pm, and received orders which were to the effect that the Germans had broken through somewhere east of St Julien. No one seemed to know exactly where. We had to find out, drive them back and restore the line.[14]

We set out to perform our precarious task with the advent of darkness, avoiding roads, as machine guns are always so placed that they can sweep roads. We skirmished over muddy fields with fixed bayonets, into shell holes and dikes full of water and out again. Stygian darkness and the thoughts of coming under machine gun and rifle fire at any moment gave us a very unpleasant feeling. We did not encounter any truant Germans.

Shell Trap Farm

[**9 May**] Dawn is breaking. We can just make out the dim outline of a large group of farm buildings on our left front [Shell Trap Farm][15] and a smudge on our front, which we know represents a trench or breastwork. The straggling line halts, gaps are filled up and we charge at a walking pace as up to the present no shots have been fired. The lines of breastworks are empty. They are ours, or were at one time, as the breast and head cover are facing in the direction of the enemies line. The farm is surrounded by a moat. Around the edge of and in the moat, dead Jerries and British soldiers lie about. Truly a cheerful looking place. We push on and occupy a line of trenches beyond the moated farm and breastwork without opposition.[16]

Dawn has broken and a few Germans have been observed dodging about 200 yards in front. No firing has taken place up to the present. Our new line trenches stench abominably. One encounters or feels a springy feeling underneath the feet when walking along the trench floor. Of course, we are walking on the bodies of men who have been buried there at an earlier date. Patches of field grey (German), khaki (British) and horizon blue (French) cloth show, or appear behind a thin film of clay, on the trench parapet and parados. The ground in front and rear of our trenches is seared with shell craters of huge dimensions. The trench is filled in in places by the action of high explosive shells. The moated, or 'Shell Trap' Farm is a farm no more, or at least not until it has been rebuilt. Broken rifles, bayonets and equipment strew the ground everywhere. The owners of the same are just buried, or a layer of clay scraped over them, on the lips of shell craters or the trench parapet and parados. In some cases they were dumped into dug-outs, the dug-outs were then undermined and allowed to fall in on the dead. It simplified grave digging; in fact I don't suppose there was any time to dig graves.

I counted fifteen dead and bloated figures in service dress lying on the embankment of the moat on our left rear. Barbed wire entanglements there

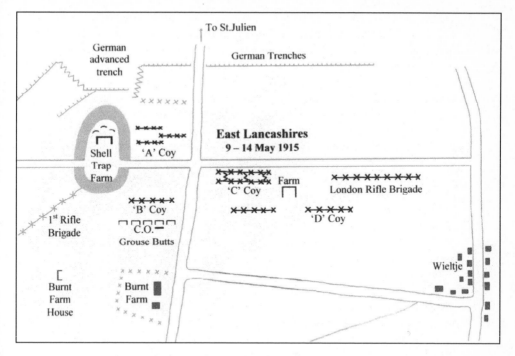

4. A Sketch map of Shell Trap Farm, 9 - 21 May 1915
from the diary of Lt Col Lawrence, 1/East Lancashire Regiment

are none; it is impossible to believe that any entanglements could survive in this paradise for high explosives.

Our left is in the air, so to speak, as we cannot find contact with anybody. Some say that the Hampshires are on our left, others say that the Rifle Brigade are on our left. In any case, as far as I can see there is about 100 yards of a gap on our left occupied by nobody.[17] The trench system is not continuous, yards and yards at a stretch have been blown in by high explosive shells.

We have been trying to improve our trench since dawn without interruption. 9.00 am – Christ, what's this? We can hear a nerve-wrecking sound coming through the air. It seems as if a lot of invisible steam trains are approaching us. We've heard it before, or some of us have. They are 'Jack Johnsons' [5.9 inch howitzer shells]. We crouch down. The concussions take our breath away. Columns of dirty grey-black smoke ascend for a matter of 50 or 60 feet and then the awful explosion. Two of those shells alight almost on the parapet and in comes the trench, burying five men. Two burst in rear, and three men who were in a kind of dugout where reserve ammunition was stored are seen no more and the ammunition commences to go off like a lot of crackers. We start to dig out the men who have been buried and the German field gunners spray our trenches with shrapnel. It is not much use continuing to dig when one pulls out a bloody leg or arm and nothing more. The Germans are near enough to hear the shouting when a party of our men get buried. They can see the entrenching tools at work as we try to rescue the entombed men (that is if they are not already dead). They rain shrapnel, trench mortars, rifle and machine gun fire on our trenches. Of course we suffer casualties, as we have to expose ourselves in order to try and save our comrades. Mr Knight, my new platoon officer, is sticking it well considering it is his baptism of fire, and so is Mr Metcalfe, another young officer who has just joined my company.

We are outgunned here. In fact we always were. Of what use are a battery of field guns here and a battery there against the array of fortress and field guns, which the Germans bring to bear upon us. Our gunners tell us that they are short of shells and always have been.[18] Some days they have been limited to twelve shells per gun. They must keep a certain amount of shells always in reserve in case of an attack. Can 16 pounders compete with 5.9 and 6-inch guns? There is a battery dug in, in what was at one time a small wood, in our rear. They are not allowed to fire unless the German attack.

We suffer a lot from shellfire owing to cramming as many men as possible into the first line. I do not know if the Germans act on similar lines.

Darkness! Will it bring any relief?

Rations have to be drawn and water bottles filled. I volunteer to take the officers' and what is left of the sections' water bottles to the rear and get them filled. I had to go back about 2 miles, then line up for an hour as there appeared to be only one farmhouse with a pump left in this part of the world. On my way back to the trenches the German 'clog dancers' (machine-gunners) have started operations for the night. The Germans hold the high ground and therefore command all the ground in rear of our trenches. So it means a continuation of hops from one providential shell crater to another. I cursed the same shell craters for being there last night and early this morning. I come across a 56lb box of biscuits on the rim of a shell crater. I peer into the cavity and shout 'Anybody there?' I get no response. Hello, what's this? A piece of white bandage, it feels sticky, so someone's got a 'Blighty one'. I have got to leave the biscuits as the ten water bottles and the German shrapnel and machine guns are giving me quite enough to do. I got back to my platoon in safety; nevertheless I feel proper 'browned off'.

The German gunners are sending 'express trains'[19] over to Ypres and the villages in our rear. We can plainly hear our ammunition columns and transport on the roads in our rear. I suppose they are getting their share also. The Germans are aggravating us with trench mortars.

The Listening Post

I am warned for listening post. I have got to go out on my own as two more men cannot be spared owing to sentry duty and repairing our trench, which the 'Jerry' artillery leveled today.

I wriggled out for a matter of 30 yards or more. I cannot crawl on my hands as the town of Ypres is burning like a furnace in rear and all movements above ground are silhouetted. I took up position behind a mound, some soldier's hastily made grave, I suppose. I had an uneasy feeling; something seemed to tell me that I was not quite alone. I can hear our men talking quite plainly in the trench behind me. I hear a slight noise in front. I shove my safety catch forward and stare in the direction of the sound. Presently two heads pop up from behind a mound similar to the one behind which I am taking cover. They are listening to our men talking. I can plainly hear requests for sand-bags and shovels and someone enquires where the Maxim gun is placed 'Oh, 100 yards down the trench on your right.' The heads pop down again. What am I to do? If I open fire on the two 'Jerries' I will alarm the whole trench and give my own position away. On the other hand, they should be warned against talking so loud in case those two 'Jerries' understand English. I know quite well what will be said if I do go in – that I'm 'windy' – so I will stay where I am, that is providing the two 'Jerries' do not come any nearer. I keep a close eye on the heads that kept frequently popping up in front.

An hour or more elapsed when my attention was drawn to someone digging along a hedge in 'no man's land' on my left front. This hedge I noticed during the day. It ran from the untenanted trenches on our left right to the German 1st line. Where there is a hedge you usually find a ditch. I concentrated on the hedge, and although the Germans were working with great caution I could hear the sound of picks and spades and suppressed coughing. Quite a large party of Germans was engaged in converting the ditch into a sap or trench. In a couple of hours time at the most, if they were not stopped, they would be connected up with that part of our trench line which was unoccupied. They must be stopped at all costs.

I began to edge back very slowly. I almost got to the trench parapet when I run foul of a couple of empty 'bully' or jam tins. They made an awful row, or at least I thought they did. I inwardly cursed all tins. A 'Very light' came over, but if you stand or lie still you are quite safe as far as 'Very lights' are concerned. I completed my crawl and found my platoon officer, Mr Knight. I reported what I heard to him. I brought him down the trench; the machine gun sergeant also accompanied us. We listened and could hear the Germans sure enough.

The Company Commander decided to form a post of six men in the trench where the hedge adjoined it and the machine gun sergeant is going to expend a couple of belts of ammunition immediately on the hedge and keep his eye on it all night. All available men chimed in with the machine gun when she opened up and there was quite a commotion along that particular hedge. He 'trench mortared' and shelled us until dawn by way of retaliation.

It is impossible to make a mess-tin of tea in our present position, owing to lack of wood and the enemies' high explosives. Cheese and 'bully' foster a thirst that soon exhausts the contents of our water bottles, and the acrid fumes from high explosives, trench mortars and tear shells cause us to repent for our ever having wasted any water in our lives. No one appreciates the value of water until one cannot obtain it. The men crawl out and drink the stagnant and polluted water in the moat. It is against orders but men must drink something, and pure water is unobtainable.

Today is a repetition of yesterday; we lost about thirty men in the regimental first line and supports. I do not know how the two companies in reserve fared. We have no hand grenades with which to resist a 'Jerry' attack,[20] and the tin which contains a liquid chemical preparation, into which we have got to dip our gas pads if the Germans loose gas upon us, gets buried daily. If not buried it is knocked over by chunks of clay, which the German high explosives fling about.

'Conk' W stopped a piece of shrapnel this morning through the fleshy part of his [– – – –]. He created an awful row. We could hear someone on our right shouting,

'Oh! Doctor! Doctor! Stretcher-bearers! Stretcher-bearers! I'm killed, I'm blown to bits', the din grew nearer. It was Mr 'Conk' crawling along the trench floor, still shouting for the College of Surgeons. We were under the impression that he had a leg or an arm blown off. When we found where he was wounded and the simple nature of the wound we laughed heartily, it was so ludicrous. We told him to 'shut up', that he was like a 'bloomin' big kid'. He was offered £5 for it as a first bid, eventually the offer closed at £10.

The enemy is directing his artillery with devilish system and amazing accuracy. All we can do is huddle down in the trench and await on the pleasure of a high explosive to transfer us to the Flying Corps.

We have not got an abundance of guns of heavy calibre to adequately reply, so 'Jerry' has it all his own way. Why, the Marne, the Aisne and Ploegsteert were paradises in comparison to Ypres.

One cannot fill a sand bag in any part of our trench line[21] without disturbing the last sleep of a German, a Frenchman or a British soldier.

Oats and McCann found a framed picture of the Madonna and child on the road outside a house in Ploegsteert in 1914. They have carried it about ever since. It is always hung up in their dugout when in the trenches. It adorned an apology for a dug out in our trench line. It fell off the dugout wall about 11.00 am this morning. Oats and McCann take it as a bad omen and bolt from the dugout. Luckily they did, and just in time. The dugout got a high explosive to itself and Oates and McCann are convinced that the picture warned them and saved their lives.

The Patronage System

There is some discontent over making NCOs [Non-Commissioned Officers]. The patronage system is responsible for this. Say a reinforcement draft joins the Battalion. One young man of the draft is the Orderly Room Sergeant's wife's sister's brother's son; he gets a tape. Another youth may be a thirty-first cousin of the Company Sergeant Major's; he gets a tape. Another youth may be a forty-fifth cousin by matrimony to the CQMS [Company Quartermaster Sergeant]; he is given a tape. Then there are what we call 'Townies'. The word 'Townies' means men who come from the same town or village. A man comes from the same village as his new platoon sergeant; he is recommended for a tape the second day he is in the trenches. Blackburn owned the Orderly room, Burnley the Quartermaster branch and Preston the Regimental transport.

Those youngsters have had no previous army experience worth mentioning, and have had no war experience at all, don't know how to fill a sandbag properly, don't know what the word revett means and have not the slightest knowledge of barbed wiring, yet they are placed over men with nine and ten years peace time service and over nine months service in the field. I have not got an axe to grind; I do not want stripes and never did. 'To hell' with stripes. But there are people whose record of service and a fine example set in the trenches and who should come before those gentlemen in the line of promotion, but they don't stand a dog's chance. When stationed in Mhow in pre-war days, a *Naik* [an Indian Army corporal] in the S and T [Supply and Transport] pointed out to me with pride some army mules who had partaken in 'umpteen' Frontier Wars. They are still army mules, and so will those privates still be privates when the war finishes, owing to the patronage system. We have no faith or confidence in this type of NCO as they lack experience and just as soon as they begin to pick up routine they are invariably seen off.

This position is a regular death trap, a war of attrition with a vengeance. A whole battalion can be decimated in three days with artillery fire and the enemy suffer no losses. Ypres has been burning merrily for the past four days and nights. We are told that our Engineers have set it on fire in the interests of health, as the dead bodies cannot be recovered from the ruins. The reflections from the burning town in our rear show our working and ration parties up each night. By day the 'Jerries' while away their time by having a little target practice on our dead who are lying on the edge of the moat.

101

The Colonel came up tonight. He wants us to bury an Army Corps of empty tins that have been lying around our position since the war first started. I'm afraid he will be unlucky. The French meat emergency ration is contained in a round tin and weighs about 10 ounces. The French soldiers call it '*monkey*'.

The latest trench story goes around, something the Colonel said to our sanitary man when he first saw him. I don't believe for one moment that the Colonel did say it, but it livens us up to pretend he did.

The French seventy-fives have been barking away all day on our left rear. We have been working from dusk until dawn for the past five days. From dawn until dusk we crouch down and await for what is sure to come, if not today well tomorrow then. We have had well over 150 casualties up to date.

The 'Jerries' Attack

13 May: At 4.00 am we lay down to snatch a few hours rest as on the past five days the Germans did not commence to shell us until 7.00 am, but this morning he started pulverising us at 4.20 am. We thought the world had come to an end. He flattened two dugouts right away and killed six men. I was 'scared stiff'. We all were for a matter of that, but we gave no outward sign. We endured three hours of awful fury. All shelters were blown in or up. Moans and groans – Who is killed now? How many men buried here? Men are going mad; they are running up and down the trench trying to dodge the trench mortar bombs. I implore Mr Knight to take his Burberry off. I told him he would be the first man to be shot when the 'Jerries' came over if he kept it on. He would not take it off.

One man stripped himself naked, scrambled over the parapet and made for the German trench. We do not know what happened to him. Three men in succession have been shot through the head as they peeped over the parapet. The German trenches are fully manned and they are keeping up a continuous rifle fire on our parapet.

'Watch the left! Watch the left! Ah, that infernal left.' Mr Metcalfe's brain has given way; he has gone mad and has to be tied on a stretcher at the breast-work in [the] rear, not a very inspiring sight when an officer goes 'potty' before his men.[22]

There are dead and moaning wounded all around us, and what are left are huddled in groups in parts of the trench that have not been blown in. It seems as if numbers inspire confidence. Our rifles resemble sticks of mud thanks to the rain and flying clay.

It must have been after 7.00 am when his barrage lifted. 'Get ready, he is coming!' Yes, he is! His bombers are advancing, quite leisurely. We cry with relief; at last we call retaliate. We open fire – sights at 250 yards. It could not be described as rapid fire as our rifles are clogged with clay. The Maxim splutters on our right and about twenty 'Jerries' get bowled over. Whistles are blown and they retire on their own trench line.

We were congratulating ourselves on repulsing the attack when his artillery commenced again.[23] They gave us another hour of screaming, shrieking hell. Again his guns lift and someone shouts that they are advancing down the trench on our left and throwing bombs as they advance. The left of the line get out of the trench and form a flank in the open to meet the threatened attack. Shots are being fired in the trench on our right; all is confusion. We shoot down some German bombers who are sneaking down the trench from the left. They are clearing their way by lobbing bombs into the bays ahead. They are pretty small men and are accompanied by riflemen. The machine gun has ceased cackling on my right and the 'Jerries' are on the trench parapet. Mr Knight gets shot on my left.[24] I can hear a German officer shouting out 'Surrender and we will treat you kindly'.[25] Still the firing, bombing and shouting goes on. I am watching the bombers coming up the trench from the left.

Mr Canton dashes from the breastwork with about twenty men. He was wearing a raincoat and got shot right away.

I fired and hit a 'Jerry' bomber as he appeared around a bay. The 'Jerries' are all over us. Our attention is directed to the 'Jerries' in front, some of whom are in our trench and some on the parapet. I reload with one charger. Someone falls on my right; I can hear the impact of the bullet. I fired two rounds at the 'Jerries' on the parapet. In the excitement when reloading, I did not pull the bolt back to the full extent and got a jam. I curse and wrestle fiercely with the bolt. I get it righted and swiftly glance towards the parapet – to find a 'Jerry' has me covered. A young bowlegged 'Terrier' named Bleasdale, who is on my right, drops him – I will never call the Terriers 'Saturday Night Soldiers' again.

Wounded

Stars! Christ, what has happened? I drop my rifle. My right arm seems paralysed. Spasms of pain shoot up my arm. I made a mental note of persons who told me that you don't feel it when you get hit. You are too excited to feel anything. Well, the next man who spins me that yarn I'll tell him he is a damned liar. I am dazed and my vision is dimmed.

Someone shouted 'Retire'. I crawled into a shell crater half filled with water. I have visions or recollections of the remnants of the trench defenders struggling past my shell hole to the breastwork about 50 yards in rear. I can see the Germans in their field grey and round peak-less caps. They are in our vacated trench, searching dead men's pockets for letters and small books.

103

They are heaving the dead out of the trench and are shifting the parapet to the parados. This is termed consolidating.

When a trench is dug, or you are digging a trench, you always throw the earth which you excavate towards that side of the trench from which you expect to be attacked, this gives you head cover, and a depth of 2 feet 6 inches, or 3 feet, of solid clay will stop a bullet. That side of the trench is called the parapet. You do not bother much about the trench wall in the rear, which is called the parados. Well, the Germans were feverishly raising the parados at the expense of the parapet. In other words, they were preparing for a counter-attack.

I was much too close to them to feel comfortable, so I decided to make a dash for liberty and 'chance the ducks'. So I crawled out on the British side of the shell hole and ran like blazes for the breastwork.[26] I did not break any records as I was plastered with mud from head to foot and still wore my equipment and carried my rifle. I was speeded on to liberty by several 'pot shots', fortunately none of which hit me. I gained the breastwork exhausted and had to lie down. There were quite a number of dead here, some wounded, and a few gallant souls who were still resisting.

The breastworks could not be called breastworks any longer, unless one suffered from extreme flights of imagination. The Germans are shelling our reserve trenches and the country in the rear with a view to prevent a counter-attack from developing. The Germans have taken possession of the moated farm on our left.

I have a good view of the country in rear and I can see pairs of wounded hobbling along in the open assisting each other. They are forced to take cover in shell craters owing to the attentions of the German machine gunners. I saw some shot down.

I make for the road on my left and manage to crawl down a ditch to our reserve trenches. On my way down I pass the Essex going up to counter-attack supported by our reserve companies.[27] What a sight – the reserve trench. It was heavily shelled all morning and filled with dead, dying and wounded. The latter can be saved if they can be carried out. The dying and wounded are crying out for water. I have none, but pits or holes are dug on the side of the trench floor to drain away the surface water. The blood from the dead, dying and wounded also drains into those holes. I get a couple of mess-tins and fill them from the muddy, discoloured water. They are glad of it and don't mind the red tinge in the water. Their own or their comrades' blood was responsible for the water being almost the colour of blood; but they don't mind – it is wet. I did not give any to men who were wounded in the abdomen.

When the shelling eased down a little I made my way down the road. Behind a rather delicate hedge about 500 yards from the reserve trenches I was hailed by an authoritative voice. I looked in the direction of the voice and saw it was our Colonel [Lieutenant-Colonel G. H. Lawrence]. He was in a sod-covered hut somewhat resembling an Esquimaux snow hut; it was a wonderful piece of camouflage.[28] I explained to him the position as it stood when I left and scrounged a drink of water from his servant. On my right and in the open a staff officer, he may be a General, is bravely walking through a tornado of shrapnel and high explosives followed by an orderly – to ascertain how the position stands in front, I presume.

I continue on my way and come across the war worn remnants of a regiment in General Reserves. I recognize them as my old friends the Londons (Territorials). Another drink and one kind gentleman makes an improvised sling from a cotton bandolier. Thanks gentlemen, and off I go again. The Germans are shelling a field on the left side of the road unmercifully. There was not a man or gun in the field. I prayed that the 'Jerry' gunners would not 'tap over' to the right. I reach a large farm on the right of the road. All the outbuildings are crowded with stretcher cases and some, for whom no room [inside] can be found, are lying in the open. Our regimental NCO i/c stretcher cases dresses my wound. I asked him to get three field post cards [and] I gave him the addresses of the people to whom I wished them to be sent. He did send the field postcards to the addresses I gave him, but did not erase anything of the cards. Therefore 'I was sick', 'I was well', 'I was wounded', 'I was in hospital', 'I was at the base' and 'I was coming on leave'.[29]

The MO [Medical Officer][30] advises all walking cases to make for the canal as the Germans may shell the farm at any moment, and 'Good God' if he does, I shudder to think of scores of helpless men being blown to bits or cremated inside the burning buildings. Let us pray that he does not.

In company with two wounded Hampshires I make my way as directed to the pontoon.[31] The stretcher cases will have to remain at the farm until night. Just as we arrive at the pontoon, we hear the shriek of a salvo of shells, and dive into an old trench. The shrapnel burst right over the pontoon. We rush across the pontoon and get clear before the next one came over. We make our way to desolate and shell swept Poperinge. The Germans are 'Krupping it' with their heavies. 'Will we get seen off here?' the Hampshires ask. 'We will,' I replied, 'if we do not leave the road and take to the fields,' which we promptly did. We connected with the road again some two miles beyond Poperinge and pass regiments going up. Eventually we get picked up by an ambulance [and] at nightfall we are set down at a large farm on the roadside. It is a kind of advance hospital; at least there are blankets and apologies for bed-cots. Here we get a drink of tea and I broke my fast for the first time that day, and also broke one of my best teeth on an army biscuit. You cannot sit down but you sit on jam. You cannot touch anything but you get smeared with jam; Ticklers' plum and apple everywhere.

After remaining for an hour in this farm an ambulance convoy arrived and we set off for Bailleul, that refuge for torn and bleeding humanity.

On arrival all men who have been wounded file into a room wherein presides a gentleman in a white smock. He is armed with a syringe as big as a football pump. He is very businesslike and wields it as an expert club-swinger wields a club. 'Open your jackets and shirts – First man.' 'Oh! Oh!' He recharges the syringe. 'Next!' I felt myself going white under an eight-day growth of beard. I managed not to faint like some. The contents of the syringe raised a lump on my left breast as big as a toy balloon. We are told this is anti-lockjaw, or anti-tetanus vaccine. In any case, it cannot be anti-frostbite.

The hospital is crowded out with wounded. The dead are laid out on the lawn in a row awaiting burial. I meet some of my own unit wounded here. I hear tales of how Major Rutter smashed our Maxim up with a pick and, a German officer calling on him to surrender, he carried on smashing up the Maxim and got shot. He was a great cricketer in pre-war days in India and used to play for Presidency teams.

Of how our Colonel sent four weak platoons of 'B' company under Captain Smith to re-take the moated farm, held by a German regiment with six machine guns. The Captain and two platoons were captured.[32] McCann [of the framed Madonna story], Captain Leake, Sergeant Cuttle and 'Cherby' Williams from Kent, all old 2nd battalion men, 'went west'.

Of course I could not describe what happened in detail on the 13th. My description is only flashes of memory. No man can fight and describe with accuracy what happened.

On **May 14** I entrained for No4 British General Hospital, Versailles, which is close to Paris. If this old Palace could only speak! What tales it could tell, of Kings, Queens, favourites and court intrigues. This hospital is under-staffed and the nurses are overworked, one nurse having as many as thirty cases to look after. They are not the regulation brand of Army nursing sister, as they are too kind and sympathetic and do not address one in a sergeant major's tone. No praise is too high for those angels of mercy. Just imagine the nature of their work. There are men here less arms and legs and can do nothing to help themselves. The sisters have got to do everything for them and they are only young girls.

On **May 17** the doctor came into my ward and pinned a white label on my tunic. It means a trip to England. I am overjoyed – I'm sure I could leap over a five-barred gate.

At 4.00 pm in the afternoon I leave (per) hospital train for Le Havre. The line ran parallel to the beautiful River Seine for a short distance. It was crowded with barges and pleasure craft. I have heard glowing accounts about private hospitals, I pray God it will be my luck to get sent to one.

Embark on hospital ship and had a calm crossing.

106

Notes

1 'Second-Lieutenant Foster accidentally blew off the thumb and two fingers of his right hand in attempting to uncharge the detonator of a hand grenade.' (1st Bn War Diary, 30 March 1915)

2 Night of 28/29 April the battalion moved in buses to Vlamertinge arriving about 11.00 pm (Regt. Hist., p.36)

3 The battalion was destined for an even grimmer battlefield, for they were immediately committed to the Second Battle of Ypres where the Germans had, for the first time, released poison gas.

4 In February 1915 command of the Brigade passed from Major-General A. Hunter-Weston to Brigadier-General J.Hasler (late Buffs) who was killed by a shell on 27 February 1915. He was succeeded by Brigadier-General C.B. Prowse.

5 'The battalion moved off at midnight and reached Verlorenhoek at 2.00 am, without casualties . . . road and Ypres were continuously shelled by heavy howitzers.' (Regt. Hist., p.40)

6 It was Zevenkote on the Zonnebeke road from Ypres. The Battalion was now in Brigade Reserve.

7 'The pressure on the eastern portion of the salient, in which lay Ypres was so heavy that it was decided to retire to a shorter line.' (Regt. Hist., p.39)

8 'Late in the afternoon I suddenly got orders to take up my remaining two companies, 'A' and 'B', to reinforce the 1/Rifle Brigade . . . we filled a big gap in them [the trenches] as they had many casualties, about 300.' (Lawrence, p.77)

9 'About 10.00 pm . . . the two companies, less one platoon rearguard under Major Rutter, retired to Hill 37, whence they retired to Wieltje and thence to Elverdinge, which was reached at 4.30 am May 4th . . . 1/Somerset Light Infantry and London Rifle Brigade retired about the same time.' (Regt.Hist., p.39)

10 The first 'poison'-gas-filled shells the Germans used contained a chemical agent, known to the Germans as T-Staff [xylyl bromide] and was lachrymatory [tear producing], not lethal. Roe mentions it inflamed the eyes and they did not regard it seriously, but later in the day they saw the effects of chlorine gas shells. Chlorine is a vesicant, which causes death by stimulating over-production of fluid in the lungs leading to drowning in your own secretions. As chlorine is soluble, clothes soaked in water [or urine] were tied around the mouth as a protection. Roe writes about the temporary respirators the men were issued with. These were cotton wool pads impregnated with a neutralizing chemical, which was activated when wet.

11 'Major Rutter, with two platoons, evacuated the trenches at midnight . . . the withdrawal was carefully thought out and was carried out so skilfully that the enemy did not discover that he was facing empty trenches until well into the following day.' (Regt. Hist., pp. 39–40)

12 Victims of chlorine gas.

13 'From 4 – 8 May the Brigade remained in Divisional reserve,' [In a wood west of Elverdinge at 'Dirty bucket' camp] (Regt. Hist., p.41)

14 'During the afternoon [of 8 May] 11 Brigade moved up to Vlamertinge . . . Lieutenant Colonel Lawrence went to Brigade headquarters, where he was informed that Wieltje was still in enemy's hands, and was directed, together with the Argyll and Sutherland

Highlanders, to take up a line running north and south about 700 yards east of Wieltje and to clear the enemy out of Wieltje if still there.' (Ibid, p.41)

15 Later to be known as Mouse Trap Farm.

16 'A trench near the farm was held by a platoon of the Northumberland Fusiliers . . . the enemy's trenches were 300 yards north-west of the farm. Major Rutter occupied a trench, running slightly south of east from the farm with 'A' and 'B' Companies without opposition.' (Regt. Hist., p.41)

17 'On the left of the battalion were the Monmouths holding 'Shell Trap' farm and on the right were the Dublin Fusiliers.' (1st Bn War Diary, 8–9 May 1915). Later the Rifle Brigade took over the farm, but it was never strongly held.

18 The apparent shortage of artillery shells on the front produced a 'Shell Scandal' in the British newspapers against Asquith's Liberal Government. It resulted in the formation of a coalition government on 25 May 1915 and led to the formation in late 1915 of a Ministry of Munitions under David Lloyd George.

19 So called from the noise produced by large artillery shells speeding overhead to their targets.

20 The Commanding Officer writes in his diary that he had repeatedly asked Brigade for hand grenades – 'but none were to be had'. (Lawrence, p. 85)

21 'A' Company was next to the farm in three breastworks immediately to the right of 'Shell Trap' farm, which was held by the 1/Rifle Brigade.' (Ibid, p.84)

22 'Lieutenant Metcalfe went off his head from concussion [shell shock] produced by the bursting shells and was carried down to my headquarters on a stretcher and then on to the doctor.' (Lawrence, p.83)

23 'The men stood the bombardment very well and Captain Dyer relates how in the middle of it he came on a group of five men "arguing the point" fiercely, and on enquiring what it was, was told a loaf was missing from their rations!' (Ibid, p.86)

24 'About 9.00 am a German bombing party got into the first breastwork and with their bombs killed Lieutenant Knight and many men.' (Ibid, p.85)

'The attack . . . was carried out by bombers covered by rifle fire from 'Mouse Trap' farm [where the two platoons of the 1/Rifle Brigade had been practically annihilated by shell fire and the farm occupied]. In the breastwork nearest the farm, manned by two platoons, Lieutenant Knight and many men were killed and Lieutenant Barr and the survivors were driven out. The remaining [two] breastworks, held by 'A' Company, with which were Major Rutter, Lieutenants Canton, Browne and Salt, were enfiladed from both flanks and shelled by . . . artillery.' (Regt. Hist., p.43)

[These two breastworks] 'held fast and it was keeping back the bombers that Major Rutter and Lieutenant Canton, exposing their heads and firing over the . . . breastwork, were shot through the head.' (Lawrence, p.86)

25 'Lieutenant Salt . . . kept back the bombing party by firing over the traverses at them, he was shot through the head but in spite of his wound, when the German officer exposed his head and shouted to him to 'surrender' in English, his reply was to shoot him dead.' [He was awarded the Military Cross for his action that day] (Ibid, pp.85–86)

26 By his account I assume Roe was in the advanced breastwork of 'A' Company with Lieutenant Knight and on being wounded he crawled for one of the other two breastworks

108

held by 'A' Company (some 10 – 15 yards behind) which held fast and kept the bombers back.

27 'Two platoons of 'B' Company reinforced the remnants of 'A' Company and established themselves in the shell holes and ruins of breastworks around 'Shell Trap' Farm. The Essex Regiment sent a Company ['C' Company] who joined 'B' Company in the shell holes round the farm.' (Lawrence, p.86)

28 The 'grouse butts' were built, by the French gunners, of logs, with just room for two people to lie down and sit up in; the sides and top were covered with sods of earth.

29 The Field Post Card was a multi-choice card. The idea was to cross out the phrases which did not apply.

30 Dr Whigham.

31 Yser pontoon bridge.

32 The sequence of events at Shell Trap Farm on the night 13/14 May appears to have been as follows: At 6.25 pm Brigadier Prowse, Commander of 11 Brigade, ordered Lieutenant-Colonel Lawrence to occupy and hold the farm, which had been abandoned by the Rifle Brigade on the evening of 12 May. The order was very explicit: 'It is essential to prevent the Germans occupying Shell Trap Farm. You will take every man you can and hold [it] ... You are personally responsible that this is carried out.' Lawrence tasked Captain Leake to reoccupy the farm with two of his 'B' Company platoons, but Leake was killed, both his platoon commanders were wounded and the attack failed. Lieutenant Palmer, the Adjutant, then took charge and cleared the farm buildings with two platoons of 'D' Company, leaving them in garrison there overnight under command of Captain Smith. The situation appeared to have stabilized, so Lawrence sent back the Essex Company, though he retained two companies of the 5th Battalion South Lancashires as a reserve. However, at dawn the following morning the 'D' Company platoons found themselves in the open and dominated at close range by German machine guns. They were obliged to surrender. The farm was then attacked and occupied by the 5/South Lancashire companies.

IX

Blighty
(18 May – 25 October 1915)

Hospital – The Aussies Arrive – Visitors – Out to Tea –
The Belle of Tavistock – Convalescence – Ireland –
Rejoin the Regiment

Anchor in Plymouth harbour on the evening of **18th**. All walking cases are lined on deck and all are asked, 'What part of the United Kingdom they came from?' The object of this was to send men to hospitals that were as near as possible to their homes. I told the orderly I came from Ireland. He gave me a white ticket marked number nine.

Numbers one, two and three get packed into one train and away they go. Fours, fives and sixes follow half an hour later, followed by numbers seven and eight. I am very uneasy, as the number nines are Hampshire and Devonshire men. The 'bloomin' orderly must have been under a misapprehension over my pronounciation of 'Oireland' and must have understood me to say Isle of Wight.

At last we entrain. We are not twenty minutes in the train when she stops and disgorges her freight on the platform [and] we are hustled into Red Cross vans.

Hospital

After a short drive we are dumped outside a gate let into a high wall. I enquired of one of the drivers what was the name of this hospital? He informed me that it was Devonport Military Hospital. My heart sank; I had visions of old soldier sisters and bees waxing. Presently we are formed up, told off and conducted to wards.

Sister 'Three Badges', Sister 'Two Badges' and an affable lady who is addressed as 'Nurse' run my ward. The lady addressed as 'nurse' is only a probationary, I presume. I do not know if the sisters wear the red rings on the cuffs of their sleeves for qualifications or for every five years service and I'm too crestfallen to enquire.

110

Sister 'Three Badges' examines and dresses our wounds in the passage of the ward. I take my jacket off. I am wearing what I thought was some kind of white shirt. Sister 'Three Badges' declares it to be a chemise and is horrified at the thought of a British soldier wearing a chemise. I was asked where I got it? 'I found it in a shell-wrecked house in Pilkem Woods, Sister. It was clean, it was light and did not take up much space when folded up, so I carried it about with me for a change, Sister.' I did not tell Sister that we could not get a chance to wash our shirts, or when they got too verminous we threw them away. All our clothes and boots are raked away by a sanitary man. All have a hot bath; change into hospital kit and in to supper. Chicken! Well we've made a good start. Then to bed and I cannot get accustomed to a soft bed and therefore cannot sleep.

Next morning the MO comes around and examines our wounds. Mine has turned septic. I have a temperature, and I am marked 'bed'. Around comes the Colonel accompanied by the Matron at 10.00 am. He is a big man and a regular fire-eater. His booming voice brought back memories to me of exploding 'Jack Johnsons'. He told us that the 'Jack Johnsons' put the 'wind up us'. If he does ask 'How are you going on?' tell him you are going on fine and will be better soon. For Heaven's sake don't tell him that you feel poorly, or only middling, or he will eat you up. He does more harm than good when he comes around. If a man is not already suffering from shell shock, well he jolly well soon will be.

Chicken has disappeared from the menu. I am informed by old residents that every patient gets a meal of chicken on being admitted, to give them a good impression. The old system is then reverted to, 4oz of this, 10oz of that and 6½oz of the other; frankly I could eat some more. After the fifth day I am allowed up for two hours. I feel rather shaky on the 'pins' [legs]. This is increased to four hours daily and eventually I cease to become a bed patient.

There are certain hours laid down for smoking. Sister 'Two Badges', a typical Welsh lady, caught me smoking during prohibited hours today. Sister 'Two Badges' did not reprimand me, or pretend she saw me, but reported me to Sister 'Three Badges', a Norfolk lady to judge by her accent. Sister 'Three Badges' came into the ward and asked me had I been smoking? I confessed I had, as I knew she had 'got the wire'. I came in for a severe verbal castigation as to the punishment inflicted on patients who did not comply with hospital regulations. Sister 'Three Badges' informed me that no patient could 'pull her trestle' [leg] as she could tell cigarette smoke from tobacco smoke by sense of smell, in fact she could tell one brand of tobacco from another by the aroma hanging about the ward and that she was too old a soldier to have her 'trestle pulled'. If it occurred again, I would 'hop it' before the Colonel. I therefore resolved not to 'chance my arm' again during prohibited hours, as I have not the slightest ambition to 'hop it' before that

111

gentleman. Sister 'Two Badges', you did not play a straight bat. Why, Nurse puts the 'blind eye to the telescope' (Nelson at Copenhagen), so to speak when she is on duty, and we 'sneak' a smoke.

The Aussies Arrive

A batch of wounded Australians has arrived here from Gallipoli via Malta. They are a wild, devil-may-care lot and have upset the discipline of the whole hospital. They address the Colonel as 'Old Boy', Sisters 'Two' and 'Three Badges' as 'Old Dears' and 'Nurse' as a 'Sweet Young Thing'. Some are minus an arm and some a leg. They broke out into town the second night they were in hospital. Legs or no legs, arms or no arms, they scaled a 12 foot wall, set Devonport on fire and got uproariously drunk. It took the whole crew of a super-dreadnought in combination with the Military Police to shepherd them back to hospital. I am told by Nurse that they are going to another hospital where there are nobody but Australian soldiers.

They turn on the gramophone at midnight. When Sister 'Two Badges' dashes into the ward and orders them to turn it off, they ask her 'What's wrong, Old Dear? Don't you like that tune? Well what one do you like?' They do not understand discipline as it is applied to us. Instead of wearing the red hospital handkerchief in the form of a tie they wear it cowboy style. They are breaking Matron's heart. One of them told the Colonel today that they could do with an Antiphon issue daily as they were 'falling into flesh'. They were transferred to another hospital next day.

Visitors

Visitors are allowed in every Sunday from 2.00 until 4.00 pm. The first Sunday I was in hospital a venerable old lady toddled in at 2.00 pm. My bed was right opposite the door. It was in a bad position as one was always open to a surprise attack. I heard a rattling of beds; on glancing down the ward to my right, everyone was asleep. Imagine my astonishment. Why, before the old lady came in everyone was reading and wore an air of expectation as if expecting young and pleasant visitors. The old lady came towards my bed as everyone else in the ward was in the land of dreams or appeared to be. She wore a pair of spectacles slung around her neck by a black tape. The spectacles were attached to an ivory handle. (Nurse afterwards told me they were called a lorgnette.)

The old lady asked me was I wounded and where? So I told her.

Had I ever been to India?

'Yes Madam'.

'Then you can knit'.

112

I told her it was not one of my accomplishments, but quite a number of soldiers who have been stationed in India can knit. She almost persuaded me that I could knit and she wanted some mufflers, in fact a shipload if she could get them, for her dear sailor boys in the North Sea. She would supply the wool and needles and I could knit to my heart's content. She was most persevering. In the end to convince her that I could not knit, even if I knew how, I had to show her my right arm in splints. Before she took her departure she dived into her reticule. I had visions of some tobacco. No! It was not to be. She gave me a text, or as she called it 'a word from God'. It quoted something that St Paul said to the Corinthians 1900 years ago. When she went out of the ward every one else woke up. I made enquiries as to who the old lady was and was told it was Miss Aggie Weston.[1] Didn't I know her? No I did not, but 'twas apparent that everyone else in the ward did.

Visitors are not allowed to bring in pork pies, mince puffs and jam tarts, or a penny's worth of chips and fish. The hospital regulations forbid the bringing of food into hospital. We are so well fed that without a doubt our digestive organs would be upset if we did partake of a mince puff or a jam tart on a Sunday. Owing to the influx of visitors the top of my locker presents an inspiring sight. A *Strand* magazine dated May 1908 takes pride of place. An orange, kept company by a banana and a packet of Woodbines [cigarettes], complete the day's spoils.

I am quite an expert at bed making now; in fact I am that proficient in the art that Sister 'Three Badges' highly commended me, and Sister 'Three Badges' does not throw any praise away. The blankets are folded and squared with a style and precision that almost demands trigonometry and a spirit level. I always give Nurse a hand and when I cannot help it, Sister 'Two Badges'. I cannot quite forgive Sister 'Two Badges' for 'peaching' (informing) on me when she caught me smoking.

Had my arm X-rayed today. My medical card tells me that I am suffering from a gunshot wound in the right arm and shellshock.

I have been asked to go to the pictures several times. I refused; what do I want to go to the pictures for? Have I not seen enough of human pictures? 'Three Badges' is angry.

I have seen a photo [X-ray result] of my arm today. The bullet went right through the bone, or ulna. It is shattered.

Out to Tea

Two ladies called this afternoon and took a sergeant, a private and I out to tea to some country mansion. We passed grim Dartmoor and drove through and well outside Tavistock. Tea was laid on the lawn, on a number of small tables. I endeavoured to get seated at a table at which a be-whiskered old gentleman sat, but I was foiled by a Sergeant of the Hampshires who was on crutches. I therefore had to sit opposite a lady. I did not feel comfortable.

A dainty maid came around and left a teapot covered with a cosy on the table, and two racks of delicious cakes. I could have drunk four of those tiny cups of tea and eaten five of those glorious 'buns' to the lady's one-cup and one cake, but I felt ashamed to get 'crackin'. I can see the Hampshire Sergeant shouldering his crutch and showing the old gentleman how the Marne and the Aisne was fought and won. Madam nibbles at her cake and keeps up a sustained conversation about France. I nibble also and reply. Her husband is a doctor at Balliol. I can nibble like this for hours and feel as if I have eaten nothing; the drive over the Devonshire Moors gave me a roaring appetite, but I never ate less. I was wishing I had a dirty old black mess-tin full of tea and twenty of those cakes in an old sandbag behind the stables. I would make short work of them.

What did I hear on the next table? Sir John running Billy Gladstone down. Sir John is a Conservative and running Billy Gladstone down, Billy Gladstone that always stood up for Ireland. Billy Gladstone that I heard prayed for, and helped to pray for, every night on bended knees from the time that I understood what prayer was. My Irish blood began to boil. It would be bad manners to interrupt conversation on another table, or I would have championed poor old Billy.

A diversion now occurs. For the past twenty minutes I have been watching the antics of two pretty maids in dainty bibs and frilled caps. They squeezed their heads out of one small window and have been blowing kisses in our direction without cessation. They may be intended for the Hampshire Sergeant, the other Private or I, or for all three of us; they cannot be intended for the Mistress or Sir John. Madam noticed me glance several times in the direction of the maids. Madam is sitting sideways; I am facing the window. Madam turns her head sharply to the right. Alas, poor maids, they could not withdraw in time. Madam asks me to pray excuse her for a couple of minutes and made for the house. I presume that the maids got a scolding whilst I was sampling the varied brands of confectionery during Madam's absence.

After tea we were presented with three bouquets. They were composed of roses, gardenias, etc. We all had to shake hands with Sir John before we entered the limousine. We got back at 6.00 pm, Sister 'Three Badges' met us on arrival and enquired as to the time we had. I emulated poor Hubert of the Londons by replying 'Top hole, Sister', and asked her would she care to accept my bouquet of roses? She condescended and her gracious act brought a pleasant afternoon to a close.

The Belle of Tavistock

Sunday arrives, two o'clock draws nigh. I will try and pretend to the pretence of sleeping during visiting hours, as it is Miss Weston's day for visiting. Visitors begin to arrive.

I can hear dainty footsteps around my bed. I inhale sweet smelling perfumes; it is a trying ordeal, scarcely less than being awake. A tentative eyelid flickers and a charming voice asks, 'Are you winking at me?'

The accusation got me 'stone cold'. I open both eyes, and – lo and behold! There was a charming girl standing at my bedside.

'Why do you pretend to be asleep?' she queried, 'Don't you like visitors?'

'I'd adore them, Miss,' I replied, 'if they were all like you, or anything near approaching you' (I had to pay her a compliment). Fancy I pretending to be asleep, and the Belle of Tavistock standing beside my bed. I really thought an angel had dropped from Heaven when I opened my eyes. She is going to visit the hospital next Sunday and bring in some tobacco and friends.

Convalescence

On **June 20** I was transferred to Orchard Convalescent Hospital in Kent. It is close to the town of Dartford. I was amazed to find that we have lady cooks here, and a lady sergeant cook, I thank you. We are quartered in wooden huts and each hut contains thirty men. There are lady masseurs; they are equipped with electrical appliances. Those appliances soon find out lead swingers who declare that this muscle and that muscle are paralysed. This hospital contains about 1000 convalescents; almost every unit is represented. We have a wet and dry canteen and get paid every week. Every Sunday we get quite a number of male and female visitors who drink beer deliciously in the big marquee that serves as a wet canteen. A lot of our lady visitors come up from London (or down, I do not know which).

The lady cooks are not popular with the London Scottish, who wear kilts. When they are on cookhouse fatigue the lady cooks make them get down on their knees and scrub the cookhouse floor. I've got to admit it is rather embarrassing, having to scrub a floor in a kilt, particularly if you've got nothing on underneath and eight ladies moving around you.

I bade a friendly farewell to Sisters 'Two and Three Badges' before leaving Devonport, and not forgetting Nurse. The Belle of Tavistock I left with regrets – Well, such is life.

I met Daunt, of my company in the second Battalion, here. He was badly wounded at Neuve Chapelle. No Sisters, bees waxing or bed making to worry us here.

On **July 7** I was passed fit and granted seven days leave to Ireland.

115

Ireland

I arrived home on **July 9** at 5.00 pm. This left me only three clear days at home. I developed a rheumatic knee. As I was living fourteen miles from the nearest Military Hospital two local ladies of high social standing took me into Castlepollard in their motorcar to see Dr K. He granted me three weeks extension, although he was rather sceptical about the rheumatics.

The French chasseur never forwarded a copy of the photo we had taken at Peronne [Noyon], so I assume he got killed.

On my seventh day's leave the local sergeant of the Royal Irish Constabulary paid me a visit and informed me that I was an absentee. He had an official letter from Headquarters. 'You will have to go back, Mr Roe. Lord Kitchener says you are only allowed seven days leave.'

'To hell with Lord Kitchener,' I replied, 'Does he think that I've just run home for a breakfast of eggs and bacon and catch the next train back to France to be killed? Take this medical certificate and send it back to Headquarters. In any case, I received £15 from Preston yesterday morning. Does Lord Kitchener expect me to spend that in three days?' 'Oh' – Dr K's certificate was good enough for him. Dr K was a justice of the peace. He went away satisfied.

I was chaffed unmercifully in the village Smithy. What did I boast about in August 1914? – that we'd swamp hell with German sausages; that the British army would go through the Germans like the Devil driving through Athlone – Well, it must have taken the Devil a long time to drive through Athlone as we were not through the Germans yet, and so on. What a change of sentiment since 1914. Home Rule had not materialized; there was a dread of conscription; even my friend Mr Fagan (Tom the Blacksmith) has turned pro-German and cheers for the 'Kaizar' [Kaiser] when leaving the village pub at 'knock out'. The 'Peelers' [police] have threatened to jail him several times, but he still defies them. The only people really anxious for England to win the war are the old age pensioners. They believe that if England loses the war they will lose their pension.

Going down to my uncle's one day I saw another friend, Mr Owen Ward. He was outside his house and exploring the recesses in his back teeth with a whittled down Bryant and May's match stalk. He pounced upon me; he was aged fifty-seven.

'Would there be conscription?' I was asked.

'There might be,' I replied, 'but not for some time yet.'

'What would I advise him to do to "dodge" conscription.'

'Get married,' I replied, 'they will not take you if you are over fifty and married.'

He replied, 'The cure you propose is worse than the disease. Rather than get married or fight for England, I would drown myself in the River Luny.' So I left him to meditate and carry on with the exploration of his molars and grinders.

In the village inn I am put through an inquisition on the fighting qualities of the English, Irish, Scotch and Welsh. I am on my own amongst twenty stalwarts, all of whom carry 'blackthorn sticks'. I have not a Maxim [machine gun], nor yet a dozen of Hales grenades by me and it is more than my life is worth to say it is 'level pegging', that is to say that one man is as good as another. So it works out that one Irishman is equal to two of any of the other three, and all are quite satisfied. (It had to work out at the ratio of one Irishman equals two Englishmen, Scotsmen or Welshmen. If it did not, well, Christ help me then.) Ah yes, they knew, didn't Ireland win all England's battles? Wasn't all her best generals Irishmen, and so I listen on (good generals and bad landlords).

I am in a rather embarrassing position here. In fact, I'm not quite sure that it would be better had I got 'seen off' at Ypres, as I owe my existence to everyone whom I meet. Every individual, particularly the women, all claim that it was 'their' prayers 'alone' saved me. I am led to believe that I was the most prayed-for man in the British army. I am already in possession of a kit bag full of rosary beads, prayer books and medals, all of which have some special miraculous power. When I get back I will have to distribute them amongst my less fortunate co-religionists as I could never carry them all about with me.

The police sergeant and the village schoolmaster keep me in the village inn until midnight. I have got to tell them all about Ypres, which I do with embellishments. We are all 'Government men'. They pronounce Ypres as 'Yapps'.

Rejoin the Regiment

Well it is time I was 'picking them up.' I leave for Dartford in Kent on **August 16**. I entrained amidst a shower of prayers and blessings. I had no time to look up Phipps in Dublin, and then it would mean another week. The Doctor in Devonport military hospital was right, I must be suffering from shell shock indeed, not to have come here sooner. Goodbye Longsight, and regrets. I entrain for Euston. Arrive at Euston at 7.00 am. I have two hours to wait for the Chatham and Dover or South Eastern Express, I don't know which. So I took a trip out to see what London was like. I got hopelessly lost before I got 400 yards from the station. London's mighty whirl of traffic mesmerized and dazed me. I'd have been lost yet had not a woman policeman rescued me and brought me back to Euston – Bless her.

When I reported at Orchard Hospital I was made an accused and charged

117

with being an absentee from 13 July 1915 until reporting at Orchard on 20 August 1915. I requested a postponement of trial until the arrival of Dr K's medical certificate from Preston. Owing to some flaw, I was convicted and fined nineteen days pay.

I rejoin my reserve battalion[2] at Plymouth on **August 22**. I am marked fit before I get inside the gate at Fort Efford.[3]

I immediately get employed as QM [Quartermaster] store-man and had a decent time, although half a dollar a week did not go very far unless one was gifted with being able to tell the tale to 'benevolent civvies' in local pubs. Quite a number were gifted in that direction, although they had never seen a German and did not intend to if they could possibly avoid it. Tales were related that had been told in the wet canteen by people who 'were there'. The re-counters, 'who had never been there,' elaborated them. The 'patriotic civvies' swallowed them and poured quarts and quarts of bitter ale down the gullets of men who pirated the experiences of men who had been 'through it', with the result that those long-range fighters returned to Fort Efford each night as drunk as judges. Oh – I am sorry for the imputation I've cast on judges. Judges could not possibly get drunk. If they did, how could they conscientiously try an offender for being drunk? I should have written as drunk as Lords. Of course no one passes any comment on a Lord getting drunk, as they are always supposed to be drunk, or nearly so.

The RQMS [Regimental Quartermaster Sergeant] sleeps in a bunk let into the stores. It is on the same style as a sergeant's bunk in a barracks.

'Long Bond' of the 2nd battalion is my sleeping partner. I mean to say that he occupies a bed in the stores. He is a full sergeant and is Master 'Moochie' (Indian for shoemaker) or shoemaker. His better half lives in Dublin; nevertheless he is carrying on a mild flirtation with a certain lady who is the property of the middleweight champion of the Mediterranean fleet. Games of bowls are played nightly on the historic Hoe, as in the days of Drake and Raleigh. 'Twas ever thus and I suppose it will so continue.

RQMS 'Charlie' Overton is a damned nuisance in one respect. He 'didders' and shakes. He dislikes rats and hates them as the devil does Holy water. The fort has more than its quota of rats, but the huts outside the fort in which we are quartered literally swarms with them. I am almost positive that every rat in England has taken up his or her abode in the camp or hutments. The floors are of rough wooden planks, which intensify the pest. The rats kick up an awful din each night. About 1.00 am each morning I am awakened by a noise something akin to a bombardment by German 5.9ers; it is only o'wd Charlie battering on the floor with his boots in order to frighten away the rats. The bombardment is kept up until dawn each morning. One would want to be notoriously drunk or drugged in order to obtain a night's rest. I cannot give the RQMS an order to 'shift to hell out of

118

it', but I have the keys of the ration store and will have to bring cheese to my aid so that he will remove his 'carcass out of it'. For two nights I wedged cheese in between the planks, which formed the bunk floor, and in such a position that it could not be seen. The effect exceeded my widest expectations. He 'stuck it' for two nights and then sought shelter elsewhere. Admitted I did not play Kreigspiel [wargames] or Ludo with the RQMS. The tactics I adopted for his removal were rather low-down, but one must have some sleep.

The sword of Damocles is suspended over my head by a single thread that may snap at any moment. I have been marked fit now for some time and am expecting to be warned any moment to proceed with a draft to the front. Every NCO that approaches me with a belt and bayonet on is going to warn me, I imagine, for a draft. On **October 19** I should have gone to France with a draft, but o'wd Charlie used the long arm of influence and 'lifted' me out of it.

I could do with about three months in beautiful Devonshire. I go for long walks on Sundays and visit country pubs, and listen with amusement to country yokels talking in their quaint accent about cows, sheep, oats, cabbages and boars. I could not understand them, as they seem to speak a language all on their own. One Sunday, about 5 miles from Devonport, I got into conversation in a pub with a bewhiskered old farm labourer. The subject we 'were on' was sheep. I could only reply in yes's and no's. I might have said 'yes' a dozen times, when I should have said 'no'. I could not understand a word of what he said. When the pub 'knocked out' at 2.00 pm I was just as wise as when I entered it at noon. I know that he talked a lot about South Down rams and Shropshire ewes, and that is all I do know. I will not enlarge on the delights of Plymouth or Devonport, although I am strongly under the impression that the ninth Commandment is somewhat 'badly bent' in both places.

On **October 24** I am warned to proceed with a draft for Gallipoli at 9.00 am on 25th. [4] The RQMS's arm was not long enough, it seems, to 'wangle' me out of this one. The medical inspection was only a farce. One or two 'climbed it' – teeth of course. In any case I do not mind. It will be a change from the everlasting mud, misery and dreariness of Flanders. I draw 5 shillings pay for once and imagine that I am the Duke of Devonshire. I'll set Plymouth alight tonight, Yes! I will.

At 6.00 pm on 24 October it was raining like hell. However, rain will not deter me from having what may be the last night in old England. Horace B.[5], who I will refer to as 'Horatius' asked me where I was going.

I replied, 'I am going out to get as drunk as Croesus or John the Baptist.' I did not care which.

'Half a mo, old chappie, and I will accompany you,' he said.

119

'Well,' I replied, 'I've only got "5 bob", it will hardly get the pair of us merry, but you can "muck in" as far as it goes.'

When we arrived in the main street he asked me, 'Roe, don't you think it is a "silly" idea on your part to get drunk tonight? Worse might follow and you will wake up in the morning with a head like Howth Head. If there is any breakfast you won't be able to look at it. There will be no dinner for a certainty. Will you feel any better for it when you face the Turks? It is a pound to a pinch of snuff that we will die; well, let us die clean anyway. Surely you have the moral courage to embark on a voyage which may mean the end of all things earthly without getting drunk the night previous. If you have not that courage – well you are not worth one of "Bow and Arrow" Burke's spittles. Come along with me.'

So we went to Chapel and to confession (of course I got a good telling off, but I quite expected it) and had a big fish and chip supper afterwards. My soul was as red as scarlet going out (and might be redder still coming in had I not met 'Horatius'). Now I am returning to the barracks with a soul as white as driven snow, or as white as Father O'Slattery could make it. At 8.20 pm, I suggested to 'Horatius' that we should return to camp and look up number sixteen hut, as a Quaker or Methodist or Shinto society, through patriotic motives, were giving a farewell 'do' in the form of a concert to the 'dear lads' before they went out to be killed. He fell in with my suggestion and we arrived in time to see an adorable 'piece of fluff' dressed in a Stuart tartan with Tam-o-Shanter to match. She was singing – 'Yes! We all love you, but we think you ought to go' – a straight tip, a gentle tip, falling from the lips of one so adorable. So 'Horatius' and I went straight to our barrack room.

No man who has been through the horrors of war likes to face it again, if only he tells the truth. The misery, mud, lice, starvation, out in all the elements: the brains, guts, legs and arms, the disemboweled bodies of your comrades – it's ghastly. Yet we pretend we want to go, we might as well pretend, as we know we've 'bloody' well got to go.

When we arrived in the barrack room, 'Bow and Arrow' Burke was uproariously drunk. He told all and sundry that the Turks were a 'piece of cake', although he never had read anything about the military history of Turkey. Plevna and Osman Pasha, or at least the stand that Osman Pasha made in the mud town of Plevna in the Russo-Turkish war, won the admiration of the world. He did not know that Plevna was on the map of the world, or that such a General as Osman Pasha ever existed. He wished they would let him go. Yes, – it is very well expressing the desire to go when you know damn well that you will never go. It is a kind of 'shouting the odds' from a position of comparative security.

'Horatius' packed the Rubbaiyat of Omar Kyyam [Khayyam], Virgil,

Marcus Aurelius and a lot of classics for the voyage. He seems to have a different literary taste from other people in the barrack room, as the literature which they stowed away might be described as 'fast'.

I have got a tremendous Prayer book that a well wisher presented to me whilst I was on leave. With difficulty I can squeeze it into my haversack. It fits in the pack, but I cannot force a great coat to keep it company, no matter what amount of persuasion I use. I am on the horns of a dilemma; I do not want to leave the prayer book, yet if I take it I will have to leave the great coat. I know from experience that the nights are bitterly cold at certain times of the year out East. I cannot very well put a prayer book on; it will not keep me warm; so I give it away. I hope it is in safekeeping and will be utilized.

25 October: Reveille at 5.30 am, I can see the number on my kitbag, 8557. My name stands out prominently also. I have some breakfast, thanks to 'Horatius' and his benign influence of last night. I must bid goodbye to 'o'wd' Charlie before I go. I know damn well that I am only a 'rookie' in his eye, but still I say goodbye to him. He was a bit 'ratty' at times, but on the whole he treated one as a human being. He was not like some NCOs that I have soldiered under during the war in France and Belgium; NCOs who bullied and trampled on all beneath them and fawned and 'kow towed' to their superiors; NCOs that were confounded bullies when out of the line and arrant cowards when in the line and looking death in the face – if they could look death in the face; NCOs who could not go wrong, who thought they were infallible. When their mistakes were pointed out to them, by their inferiors in rank, [they] fell back on their rank and told the men who were in the right to 'Shut up, who the blazes do you think you are talking to?' They believe in the doctrine of 'might is right'. Thank God such specimens are few and far between, but I suppose a certain percentage of this type is to be met with in all branches of the Services, bluffers who bluff their way through (people in the Army who know 'nothing' but try to make other people believe that they do). I am convinced that one ounce of cheek is worth a mound of brains – well somebody has got to be an NCO.

I knocked at 'o'wd' Charlie's bunk door. He jumped three feet in the air. It was an indiscretion on my part, taking him by surprise, and I, knowing the condition of his nerves. I should have coughed.

'I have come to say goodbye sir and I wish yourself, Mrs Overton and family all the luck that is going.'

'Goodbye Roe,' he exclaimed, 'and I wish you have a jolly good time.' At the same time he presented me with a spanking new wooden pipe to ensure that I would not forget him.

'A jolly good time,' I repeated to myself, and going out to war. As we shook hands I was wandering how many 'liveners' he had that morning or was he a 'three bottle a day man'. Of course I did not mention the cheese incident.

121

I would have been quite satisfied with a safe return – but a jolly good time? – Yes! I can visualize that 'jolly good time!'

Notes

1   Dame Aggie Weston (1840–1918), philanthropist, temperance crusader and founder of "Sailors' Rests" at Portsmouth and Devonport.
2   3rd (Reserve) Battalion The East Lancashire Regiment, a training and drafting 'depot' unit was based at Plymouth throughout the war with its HQ at Laira Battery.
3   Fort Efford, one of the many forts and hutted camps used to accommodate the 3rd Battalion, whose strength often rose to 2–3,000 officers and men. 'The hutted camp outside the fort, known as Efford Camp, was capable of housing about 2,000 men in reasonable comfort.' (Regt. Hist., p.209)
4   At this time the 3rd Battalion was sending drafts of officers and men to the 6th (Service) Battalion, which had suffered severe losses in the August 1915 fighting at Sari Bair.
5   Most likely Private H. Bundy (born in Hornsey, Middlesex) who enlisted in London.

X

Gallipoli

(25 October – 18 December 1915)

Embarkation – At Sea – Mudros Bay – Gallipoli –
The Firing Squad – Evacuation – Impressions

Embarkation

25 October 1915: The draft[1] composed of 120 other ranks and 3 officers of the original BEF [British Expeditionary Force]. We marched from Laira Battery, Plymouth and embark on the troopship *Ausonia* for Gallipoli. The inhabitants en route were not in a very enthusiastic mood. I observed an old lady, in an upper storey window, vigorously waving a small Union Jack.

'Bow and Arrow' Burke accompanied us to the docks. As an Irishman, a Catholic and a very old soldier, he prayed to the Virgin Mary and Saint Patrick to take care of us and bring us all back 'safe and sound'. In the same breath he appealed to our generosity as comrades to give a lame dog 'a lift over the stile', as he had not the entrance fee for beer issue at noon. It meant a small donation from all hands. I doubted very much if Burke's prayers ever reached celestial regions, as one night about a week previous I had occasion to visit a certain building in Plymouth where liquid refreshment was retailed. I heard the said Burke relating with great gusto to two be-whiskered and benevolent 'civvies' how, on the retirement from Mons, he took cover behind a 'kilometre' (a French milestone) and held up an entire German Cavalry Regiment on his own owing to rapidity of fire, ('Drink up, soldier'). As I was leaving the establishment, I heard him darkly hinting that a VC [Victoria Cross] would be a small reward, but as usual in such cases there was no officer present to recommend him. He never saw France; however, it was a strong rumour that he lost Harold the Battle of Hastings owing to his bowstring being slack and his arrowheads rusty.

Prior to embarking, the draft halted at the dock gates in order to allow about thirty ladies, who had lovers amongst the draft, to say their adieu. Bucketfuls of dry tears were shed. Every lady seemed to be crying. Whether they shed any tears or not was a matter of doubt. In any case all had handkerchiefs out and seemed to be making good use of them. I was deeply touched at seeing so much beauty in distress, and remarked to 'Horatius', 'Is it not a pitiful sight?'

'Horatius' replied, 'Don't waste your sympathy, Roe, it is only temporary with a few of them at least. They will soon be consoled. Soldiers come and soldiers go.'

'Well,' I replied, 'probably you know more about the business than what I do; you are more experienced.'

Embark at 10.00 am. Transport steams out of harbour and anchors for the night.

At Sea

26 October: Set sail at 4.00 pm.

27 and 28 October: Weather fair, we partake of our meals in 'catch as catch can' style, as we were the last to embark and have no proper accommodation.

29 October: Anchor in Gibraltar harbour at 11.00 pm.

30 October: Rumoured sinking of *Empress of Britain* by a German submarine. TBDs [Torpedo Boat Destroyers] are patrolling the harbour, also seaplanes scouting around. Set sail at 11.00 am.

31 October: Mountains and barren coastline of North Africa visible from the deck of the troopship.

1 November: Calm. Flying fish and the coast of the Barbary States are the only objects of attraction.

2 November: Getting warmer.

3 November: Arrive at Malta and anchor in inner harbour at noon. A French hospital ship, from Gallipoli, steams in and anchors alongside. The docks are enclosed by solid and impressive piles of masonry. Our ship has been surrounded all day by about forty Maltese 'bum boats' the occupants of whom offer tobacco, cigars and cigarettes at ridiculously cheap prices.

4 November: Two British and another French hospital ship arrive from the Dardanelles. It is evident somebody's getting hurt on the Peninsula. Set sail at 5.00 pm. How many of us will see this island again, I wonder?

5 November: Steam past a convoy homeward bound at noon.

6 November: Sea [was] like glass. Two TBDs appeared at dawn from 'nowhere' and are escorting the troopship. Aegean Islands on our starboard bow. This is a beautiful sea, dotted with small islands, which, from the nature of the climate, are rocky, barren and mostly devoid of vegetation. From what I can observe they should make admirable 'nests' for German submarines.[2] Everyone on board has got the boat fever.

Mudros Bay

7 November: Anchored in Mudros Bay[3] at 6.00 am. Our vision is obscured by a thick fog that, however, lifts at 9.00 am and we get a view of the island and bay. The slate coloured units of our fleet are anchored alongside smutty looking colliers and supply ships. The French 'man-o-war' are stockier in build and not so graceful looking as ours. They have too much super-structure. I can just imagine the damage a 12 inch shell would cause above deck. To me it seems our fleet are thoroughbred racehorses, the French, Clydesdales or Suffolk punches. A person unaccustomed to such sights would imagine that one half of the world's shipping was assembled in the bay and that a mighty host were encamped on the island.

8 November: Rumoured assassination of 'Foxy' Ferdinand of Bulgaria;[4] it is also rumoured that Greece has come into line with the Allies. This important item of news acted like a dose of invigorating medicine on my friend 'Horatius', who has been rather pessimistic of late. He now predicts a series of victories for the Allied armies operating in the Occident.

9 November: I cannot make out the change that has come over my friend 'Horatius' since we anchored in Mudros Bay. I made his acquaintance in England a few days previous to our departure and formed a good opinion about him. His nice manners, obliging ways and polite conversations – devoid of swear words – virtues so rare in His Majesty's Army, commanded my admiration and respect. He may be a gentleman in England and English waters, but now we see him in his true colours in Greek waters, as he swears horribly on the slightest provocation, damns everybody and everything. A mislaid toothbrush brings forth a flow of adjectives that would exhaust a navvies' vocabulary.

The 'Flanders pilgrims' [lice] have put in an appearance again, for on two occasions during the past three days I have observed 'Togo' diligently examining what is supposed to be an army shirt by the dim and uncertain light of a porthole.

The ship is a miniature Monte-Carlo today as all on board have been paid out. Even 'Horatius', who always condemned gambling, has just backed the 'mud-hook' for half a dollar – and lost.

10 November: Dorsets disembark at 10.30 am.

11 November: 'Horatius' lost one of his wristwatches today. He immediately reported the loss to his confidential friends. We held a council of war on the starboard side of the ship, which resulted in the employment of Detective Kelly of Durban fame. Kelly took copious notes and proceeded to investigate in a manner a Scotland Yard man might well envy. At the end of two hours he restored the watch to its owner. 'Horatius' was so overjoyed that he forgave the thief and in a spirit of generosity presented Kelly with the watch. The latter refused the gift but darkly hinted that he would accept a bottle of whisky when we took Constantinople.

12 November: At 8.00 pm a few intellectual members of our draft held a debate on the port side of the ship. The subject was 'Women's rights and is education beneficial to the working classes?' As usual 'Horatius' took up the cudgels on behalf of the opposite sex and proved a worthy champion as in ten minutes time his opponents were scuttling down the hatchways. When this war is brought to a successful conclusion, and if he survives, I can imagine him arm in arm with Mrs Pankhurst preaching equality for the petticoats.

13 November: Lancs draft disembark at 3.00 pm. The *Waterwitch*, a one-time Isle of Man pleasure boat, I believe, took us ashore. We marched to Mudros West camp, which is about two miles from the landing stage.

14 November: Divine service parade at 8.15 am. In the afternoon I took a stroll to the Greek village. Not much to look at from the architectural point of view. The ramshackle cabins are erected in any style or place that suits the owner's taste. Every third house contains a stall, after the Indian bazaar style, where the owners sell their goods at famine prices. The inhabitants of this island are a blend of Jew, Armenian, Egyptian, Greek and other precious products of the Levant. Money is their God, '*Baksheeshs, Baksheeshs*' their everlasting wail. '*Baksheeshs*', like 'Souvenir', means of course that you give something and get nothing in return.

I visited the Greek Church and was shown around by a much bearded and extremely greasy ecclesiastic who spoke French. As my knowledge of French was limited to six words the conversation was a one sided affair and his explanations conveyed no meaning to me. The interior contains some over-done paintings of bygone saints and an altar with more than its quota of icons. Barbarous and showy was my verdict. On showing me out, he produced a wooden platter from God knows where and held it out for the reception of alms. I dumped a handful of shrapnel (coppers) on same and received a profound and courtly bow in return.

The 'flappers' are fairly good looking, but only up to a certain age. They have a fine erect carriage and are not strangled in corsets. 'Tis evident a 16 inch waist is not their ambition. In this respect they differ from their western sisters. Productivity is strongly in evidence on this island if the multitude of grubby brats who disport themselves in the sand is anything to go by. Well, they've never heard of Dr Marie Stopes or birth control.

15 November: Draft inspected by the Commandant at 9.00 am. Sandstorms, flies and fleas are the chief products of this Island.

16 November: As in India, the Greek agriculturist 'sticks' to the wooden plough drawn by two bullocks. It ploughs a furrow about 3 inches deep. If any greater depth is required it is attained by the simple process of the ploughman sitting on the plough, the added weight giving depth and at the same time easing the ploughman's weary limbs.

The male Greek is attired in loose baggy trousers, the seat of which hangs to their calves. I have been told that in case of emergency it fulfils the role of haversack. Their vest is a 'posh' affair indeed. Their headdress is a type of fez and they strut about with infinite swagger.

'Horatius' is a Greek scholar of some repute and is never done singing their praises, Homer, Demosthenes, Leonidas and his 300 Spartans at the pass of Thermopylae, what Lord Byrom did for Greece, and so on. I'm fairly 'fed up' listening to him. I'm afraid if Horace wants to find a Greek he will have to look elsewhere than on this island as there is not a true Grecian profile amongst this rabble.

17 November: Can't see 20 yards ahead all day owing to a sandstorm.

18 November: 'Lightning' Medical Inspection at 2.00 pm. I will explain this 'lightning' process. All drafts before proceeding to the firing line are medically inspected. On this inspection all kinds of diseases suddenly develop just as the man's name is called out. I have known men who have developed heart disease, indigestion, neuritis, Bright's disease [a kidney problem], 'swinging' liver and a host of other ailments in the three seconds which elapsed from their names being called out until they stood before the MO. Our Mudros MO was an 'old bird' and did not give anyone time to manufacture an ailment. As a man's name was called out he dashed into the tent at the same time throwing his helmet on the ground outside the tent. The MO, sitting on a chair behind a table, asks a question and answers it: 'Are you all right? – Yes' – at the same time pointing with his pen at the exit door. If every wise Hakim adopted the same methods as our Mudros Hakim there would be fewer people wallowing at the bases on all battlefronts.

19 November: Draft inspection by the Commandant at 2.00 pm.

20 November: There are nine hospital ships at present in the Bay. It is bitterly cold and a blinding sandstorm is raging all day. Field Marshal Kitchener inspected the Gallipoli position early in November. What does it mean?[5]

21 November: Another day of sandstorms; some people like sandstorms because they cancel parades. For my part I would much rather do four hours parade than lie in a tent all day with a blanket rolled around my head to keep the sand out of my eyes, ears and mouth.

22 November: Company drill from 10.00 am until 12 noon. The only attraction on this island is between 6.00 and 9.00 pm nightly when you can walk to a spare piece of ground outside the camp area 'dubbed' the Casino and watch the 'Auzzies' play Roulette and Crown and Anchor for high stakes. There is the air of a mining camp about it instead of a base for operations. It is quite a common sight on any of the Crown and Anchor boards to see handfuls of sovereigns thrown on the emblem of their (the backers') choice.

To us humble 'bob a day' men the 'Auzzies' appear in the light of bloated capitalists. They can afford to spend a shilling where we could not spend a penny. They have bought the island up, so to speak, on numerous occasions. In the village when we of the 'shilling' had a Greek shopkeeper beaten down to 4 shillings for a tin of salmon, or 2 and 6 [2 shillings and 6 pence] for a tin of sardines, a couple of 'Auzzies' would walk up, 'plank' down twice the amount and walk away with their purchase, leaving us to say all sorts of unkind things regarding '4 bob a day men'.

Bully, biscuits, plums and apples and cheese appear daily on the menu. We can buy black rye bread at 1 shilling per pound, baked in polo ball pattern; hard as a stone, as weighty, and contains about as much nutriment. If aimed with accuracy, it would do as much damage as a Mills bomb. It would tax the digestive organs of an ostrich, yet despite all its disadvantages we have to line up outside the village bakery and consider ourselves extraordinary lucky if we secured 1 pound [weight] of indigestion.

23 November: Rum issue.

24 November: Nothing doing.

25 November: 'Wangled' a Dechie of beer between four of us at 12 noon. Took a lot of strategy to manoeuvre it out of the range of vision but we succeeded thanks to a sandstorm. Sandstorms have their uses after all. Hospital ships look well when illuminated at night. I would not mind being tucked up in a nice berth on one of them with a 'Blighty' one in the leg.

26 November: Football match that was due to take place this afternoon cancelled due to sandstorm.

27 November: Route march in the morning. Heavy rain in the afternoon for a change. Rumours of a move to Egypt.

28 November: Church parade declared off owing to inclement weather. The cold was intense.

29 November: A hard frost last night and snowing all day. The mountains are covered with a mantle of white. It was washing day in camp. Fresh water is unobtainable, and since salt water and soap don't agree very well our shirts retain their usual hue.

30 November: Weather has changed for the better. It is rumoured that scores of men have died from exposure on Gallipoli during the cold snap[6] on the 28th and 29th. 'Flanders Pilgrims' [lice] are attacking in full strength so our leisure hours are fully occupied.

1 December: Route march and kit inspection.

2 December: A draft of 100 officers and men embark for Gallipoli.

3 and 4 December: Nothing doing.

5 December: A lecture today on the care of pay-books, but they are merely an ornament east of Gibraltar.

Gallipoli

6 December: I form one of a draft of two officers and eighty-three NCOs and men[7] who embark for Gallipoli at 8.00 am. The transport anchored in Suvla Bay at 9.00 pm. Everything is in darkness as not a light could be shown. Only hospital ships were illuminated. We were transferred to River Thames barges, which took us ashore. The bargees, to judge by their accent, saw the

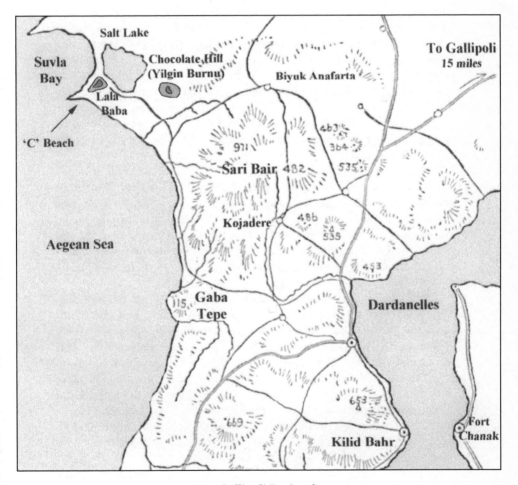

5.   Gallipoli Peninsula

light of day within sound of Bow Bells. They were in the devil of a temper and used language that would sink the *Queen Elizabeth*. I have heard highly placed officers, NCOs and men swear hard when occasion demanded it, to relieve their feelings perhaps, but they could not hold a candle to those 'Angels from Limehouse'. However, they managed to ground their barges under the red light that marked the place of disembarkation, as there were no landing stages.

The hills of Gallipoli were shrouded in mist. An unnatural silence reigned, not a gun or a shot being fired although we were only some three odd miles from the firing line. We would be more at home had we heard some 'fireworks'. Going off the beam of a searchlight, from one of our battleships, that plays at fitful intervals on the hills, by midnight all are disembarked and formed up on Lala Baba [a hill to the south of Suvla Bay]. A guide arrives from the Battalion, who are in supports at Yilgin Burnu (Chocolate Hill), who exhorts us to fall in '*Jaldi*'[8] and get a move on as the Turks have a nasty habit of dropping 6 inch shells at all hours by day and by night on the very spot on which we are standing. As we are not anxious for an introduction to the Sultan's heavy artillery at midnight, he had no need to repeat the 'request'. Sergeant Salisbury, the guide, lost his direction and we were straggling around in circles until dawn found us some 300 yards from the Battalion Headquarters.

7 December: The Battalion are in supports on Chocolate Hill, so called on account of the soil being the colour of ground chocolate. I thought we were quartered in a convalescent camp by mistake as the men were physical wrecks staggering like drunken men as they walked about. I did not recognize some of my old comrades who were wounded at Ploegsteert in '14'. So this is a sample of the army of invasion, a dysenteric, hollow-eyed, sunken-cheeked army more resembling skeletons than men in the flesh. Well, thank God our Navy is within rifle range.

The Turkish positions were pointed out to me at 8.00 am this morning. They hold every commanding spur, ridge and mountain. Their field guns command the beaches; our forces have no commanding positions worth mentioning. Kalyan Dagh on our left, Gaba Tepe on our centre and Sari Bair on our right, all held by the enemy. Truly the Turk is master of this graveyard. Members of the Alpine club in mountaineering rig-out could, with no little difficulty, scale the mountains confronting us, but the half starved dysenteric army that opposes the Turks today, in full war kit and in face of determined opposition, would never achieve the impossible. The 6th South Lancs and Gurkhas who breasted the crest of Sari Bair in August must have been 'super-men' indeed.[9]

At 10.00 am the Turks welcomed us new arrivals with a hurricane bombardment by their field artillery. It lasted twenty minutes and 'KOd' four of my draft. Our navy retaliated by bombarding the enemy's earthworks on Anafarta, the Turkish guns replied forcing one battleship and two colliers to change anchorage.

8 December: Pick and shovel medicine for six hours.[10]

9 December: Turks give us a lively half hour's shelling in the morning; ten casualties – our field guns are pretty active.

10 December: Considerable artillery activity all day. Our fleet shelled enemy works in the Anzac region.

Dr Akerman (or Captain Akerman of the Royal Army Medical Corps), our medical officer, was presumed to be of German extraction and was known to us of the 'other ranks' on Gallipoli as the 'Hun' medico. As there are men dying from dysentery, when they report sick, they are awarded two hours extra trench digging. He uses such expressions as, 'Go and dig your own "bally" grave', followed by a boot up the backside. I am personally aware that at least a dozen of the men in my company sleep every night in the latrine; when they reach the last stages they are sent to hospital by night. The hospital is 3 miles from our position. Some may reach hospital and some may fall into a trench full of water – where they remain. We are well aware that if every man were sent to hospital that is sick, it would be impossible to carry on. Yet some effort should be made to alleviate the sufferings of those unfortunates. I asked 'Horatius' what he thought about it. He pointed towards the sea where our fleet rode at anchor and exclaimed, 'Our salvation'.

The Firing Squad

11 December: Execution of Private Salter[11] at 7.15 am. This youth barely 19 years of age was shot by twelve of his comrades for taking 'French Leave' from his Regiment on two occasions and attaching himself to the Anzacs. Not by any stretch of imagination could my comrades or I catalogue it as desertion, as 'twas impossible to desert from the Peninsula even had he so desired. Our position in comparison to the position that the Anzacs held was as heaven compared to hell. He therefore did not seek safety; he absconded because his life was made a hell by the CSM [Company Sergeant Major] of my Company ['D']. In barrack room parlance he was 'sat upon'.

I was one of the firing party; he was marched from a dugout about 80 yards away, to a kind of disused quarry where the final scene was enacted. A clergyman preceded the doomed youth and his escort, reading prayers for the dying (the mockery of it all). The doomed youth was tied up to a stake, his grave already dug. His last request was, 'Don't blindfold me'. What followed I'll leave to the reader's imagination, in other words, I'll pull the pall of oblivion o'er the ghastly scene – 'If I can ever forget it'. I only wish that the distinguished person who signed the death warrant, without taking into consideration extenuating circumstances, would leave his comfortable island residence and visit the men under his command who were 'going through it'. Well, we'd have a bit more faith in our leaders and confidence in ourselves. I don't suppose for a moment that the executed Salter ever heard the sentence ending read out to him – 'Death or such less punishment' – as in this act mentioned.

A Turkish aeroplane bombed our reserve position, at Lala Baba at 10.00 am; ammunition dumps evidently his objective. Naval 'quick firers' soon shifted him.

In the evening our position was subjected to a heavy bombardment by fortress guns. Fort Chanak on the Asiatic coast and Kalid Behin [Kilid Bahr] on the European side of the entrance to the narrows are held responsible. I do not know the position of the Turkish forts, as I have no maps. I am depending on older residents for the information. Ten of our men were blown to fragments by one shell. What could be collected of their remains were buried in two sandbags.[12]

Evacuation

12 December: Sunday, but the spiritual consolers of any denomination were conspicuous by their absence, with the exception of the clergyman who was at the execution. The Battalion retires to Lala Baba on 'C' beach under the cover of darkness.

13 December: Trench digging has been the order of the day and night since we landed, as we had to prepare a third line of resistance, also dig out lines of communication trenches from Yilgin Burnu to the 'C', or beach, position at Lala Baba.

The daily ration scale would about keep life in a not too energetic white ant, yet we are within a stone's throw of a ration dump that would keep the entire force comfortably for six months. Men fell over their picks and spades, when digging, from sheer hunger. I have known instances were 'half a Bradbury' [10 shillings] was offered for four biscuits. Who is to blame?

We are under enfilade fire here, as the Turks have posted a French 75mm gun (which they captured from the Serbians in the last Balkan War) on a hill on our left. It causes no end of annoyance and casualties.

14 December: Enemy's positions heavily shelled by our field guns all day. The Turkish reply was feeble.

15 December: The Turks made it hot for us all day with small calibre guns. Corporal Spaxman, of my draft, and four privates went 'west'.

16 December: The regiment worked until dawn this morning loading up barges with ammunition and stores. This work commenced at 11.00 pm last night. I observed Royal Engineers, hard at work yesterday, dumping shells into the sea under cover of a cliff. During the past two nights three regiments have embarked, so we light the usual quota of fires along the cliffs every night to give the Turks the impression that the usual number of troops are in reserve. We also have had orders to expose ourselves as much as possible during the day for similar reasons.

17 December: My platoon is detailed for 'sacrifice duty', which means parading along the beach road in parties of eight and in full view of the Turks for four hours. Luckily they did not shoot at us.

18 December: Orders have been issued for the evacuation of Suvla Bay positions. There are about one million pounds worth of stores that cannot be taken away, so the dumps are thrown open to the troops and the Navy. One hundred cases of rum were smashed by the APM [Assistant Provost Marshal], a necessary and much regretted measure. We loaded our valises and sandbags to their full capacity with all kinds of preserved eatables and 'smokables'. 'Horatius' passed in front of my 'funk hole' with a sand bag, which, amongst other items, contained some exceedingly rank and odiferous cheese. It is disgrace the amount of stores that will have to be destroyed by fire owing to the evacuation. Those stores could have been very well issued out the famished, half-starved troops months before, as some of the 'Brass hats' must have known that the evacuation must have been in contemplation.

There are roughly 800 mules in terraces of underground stables. When the Turkish shells burst on Lala Baba, the mules start whinnying although it is not feeding time. Although only animals, they know the devastating and destructive power of high explosives and respect them as much as we do.

At 8.00 pm we get dressed and man the last line of defences, for here we do make our last stand in case the Turks discover our move. Army transport carts wended their way towards the firing line as usual, empty of course; they were nearly always so (as Kelly naively remarked, he would take more rations up in a box-barrow). They creaked and squeaked as of old, owing to a lamentable shortage of lubricating grease [and] they succeeded in drawing the fire of two Turkish field guns posted somewhere on the crest of Kalyan Dagh. The *Packet of Woodbines*, a Russian Cruiser with an unpronounceable name, tried on several occasions to silence those guns, but without success. The troops got over the difficulty of pronouncing, or trying to pronounce, her name as she was conveniently adorned with five funnels and was affectionately 'dubbed' the 'Packet of Woodbines'.

All of our field guns save four, which are worn out and useless, have been removed during the past three nights, their places being taken by wooden dummies or substitutes. Today we have gashed all sandbags in several places with our bayonets in order to render them useless. At 6.30 pm we made bonfires of our picks and spades; useful, but implements of torture at times.

At 9.00 pm our transport returns. The two field ambulances which were left standing 'for a blind' have been saturated in petrol. All is ready, but an unnatural quietness reigns as we await the order to embark on the barges which are ranged alongside the landing stages (impromptu affairs recently erected). Excitement is now at its highest, for if the Turks discover our move, two thirds of us will remain as compulsory landowners on Gallipoli until the Angel Gabriel sounds the trumpet.

At 10.00 pm we receive the order to embark, the North Lancashires, who were holding the firing line, having retired to the third line of resistance without having been observed by the enemy.

By midnight the Regiment was embarked on the transport *Osmalia* without a casualty and at 12.30 am we steamed away from the scene of one of England's greatest blunders and glorious defeats. We left an army behind – Yes, an army of ghosts to bear silent testimony to impulsive statesmen and politicians.

At 2 am 'Horatius' asked me to have a drink. I gave him a withering stare and replied, 'A drink, don't be sarcastic.' Without more ado, he hooked his water bottle out of its carrier and withdrew the cork – the smell was enough – I had a good 'swig' and felt as if I could go back and beat all the Turks on Gallipoli on my own. It was the first time that I had tasted rum, real rum[13], that had not been 'got at' by the quartermaster's staff, or the company quartermaster sergeant. 'Horatius' was the last man, within view of the Plains of Troy, that I would accuse of 'sneaking' rum. So 'twas evident that the APM did not destroy all the rum, but how he came by the 'swag' he would not divulge.

Impressions

The most illiterate private in the army knew that the Turkish positions were impregnable once the element of surprise was lost. The Turks were well entrenched on every spur, hill and mountain. Machine guns by the dozen were emplaced on every coign of vantage. Such positions, strengthened by the mastermind of the German engineers under von Sanders and held by the finest, most ragged and ill-equipped, defensive soldiers in the world, might well be deemed impregnable. Our fleet could not level the mountains and their defenders that intervened between the Golden Horn and us. Military and Naval chiefs and those under their command did more than their damndest, but the impossible could not be achieved. I asked 'Horatius' at 2.30 am, in an atmosphere of submarines, what he thought about it? He simply muttered, 'Another Walcheren expedition.'[14]

The Turks 'played the game'. They respected the Red Cross flag, refrained, as far as necessity allowed, from dropping bombs from their aerial armament near our field hospitals or shelling our hospital ships, even although they were used for purposes other than for what they were intended. Chivalrous Turks in an age when chivalry has departed.[15]

The Germans had expended more shells in twenty-four hours on that 'health resort' Ypres than the Turks have expended during my sojourn on Gallipoli. I noticed a marked increase in the Turkish expenditure of shells from guns of heavy calibre from the date that Bulgaria threw in her lot with the Central Powers.

Notes

1   The draft was to the 6/East Lancashire who were with 38 Brigade of the 13th Division at Gallipoli.

2   Towards the end of 1915 Germany decided to transfer the centre of her submarine activity to the Mediterranean. The dangers to the U-boats were much less as the Mediterranean was comparatively free of anti-submarine devices and, with its long coastlines and many islands, it presented great opportunities for the planting of submarine bases (as Roe observed). It also had the advantage of her ally Austria in the Mediterranean. In October 1915 it was known that German submarines had passed through the Straits of Gibraltar and begun to exercise an 'unrestricted attack' policy (contrary to maritime law) against all shipping including passenger liners.

3   On the Greek Island of Lemnos, the advanced base of the Mediterranean Force.

4   This rumour was not true. King Ferdinand of Bulgaria was the youngest son of Augustus, Prince of Saxe-Coburg-Gotha. On the outbreak of the Great War Ferdinand pursued a policy of caution, but eventually Bulgaria joined the Central Powers, declaring war on 13 October 1915. In September 1918 Bulgaria surrendered and 'Foxy' Ferdinand abdicated and fled to Vienna.

5   Roe was correct in realizing the significance of Kitchener's visit. He arrived at Mudros on 9 November, and on 22 November, following a tour of the Gallipoli position, he signalled London recommending evacuation of Gallipoli.

6   The Regimental History (p.326) records that a blizzard raged on 27/28 November at Suvla, where the 6th Battalion trenches were 'deep in half-frozen slush and such shelters as remained were in little better state, so that a number of men died from exposure'.

7   Private Roe was put in 'D' Company, 6/East Lancs.

8   Another term from the Indian Army meaning 'quick!' or 'Hurry up!'

9   This is a reference to the famous incident on 9 August 1915 when a mixed force of South Lancashires, Warwicks and Gurkhas captured the summit of 'Hill Q' on the Sari Bair Ridge, only to be shelled off it. This episode was the last real hope of victory on Gallipoli.

10 'Digging parties were out daily constructing the defences of Chocolate Hill.' (6th Bn War Diary, 6–11 December 1915)

11 Private H. Salter executed at 7.15 am on 11 December 1915.

12 'We were subjected to a very heavy bombardment of 8 inch high explosive shells. Our casualties on this day were nine men killed in one dugout.' (6th Bn War Diary, 11 December 1915)

13 The rum ration arrived at the front in large earthenware jars marked 'SRD'. It was Navy rum, not diluted, although Roe's remarks suggest that it rarely reached the private soldier before being diluted.

14 The Walcheren Expedition of the Napoleonic Wars was the British landing in the Low Countries in 1809. The reason for the Expedition was to assist Austria and to destroy the French fleet in Flushing. Unfortunately, by the time the British force of over 39,000 men had landed, Austria had been defeated and the French fleet moved to Antwerp. After four and a half months on Walcheren, the British troops were withdrawn, having suffered 4,066 deaths, of which only 106 officers and men were killed in combat. The rest died from Walcheren Fever which was so debilitating that just less than two years later Wellington requested that no unit which served at Walcheren should be sent to him.

15 This statement of the 'clean-fighting Turk' was widely held within the Regiment and was based on the knowledge that the Turks had refused German offers of poison gas and flame-throwers.

XI

Lemnos, Egypt and the Gulf

(19 December 1915 – 4 April 1916)

Return to Lemnos – Christmas 1915 – Embarkation for Egypt – Port Said
– Sailing for the Persian Gulf – The Shatt al-Arab – By Steamer up the
Tigris – Shaikh Saad – Forward to Orah

Return to Lemnos

19 December: *Osmalia* anchors at 5.00 am in Mudros Bay. We are transferred by lighters to HQ Ship *Aragon*, then again on to lighters and barges, which took us ashore. So we are back again in sandy, 'fleay', 'lousy' Mudros, midst cheating Greeks and nondescript Egyptians. Here we can at least eat and sleep in a certain degree of comfort as there are no Turkish gunners to send us our iron rations when we least expect them. Draw tentage. Pitch and arrange camp.[1]

20 December: Usual camp routine. My Platoon Sergeant, Charlie Kay, is a mixed blessing. He is here, there and everywhere in the interests of his men, but has one great failing to which we all strongly object. When issuing out rum he suffers from assumed ague. Our issue is three tablespoonfuls; he 'didders' so much that one tablespoonful in every three finds its way back to the mess-tin from which he doles out the issue. He is extraordinary lively and very hilarious half an hour after each issue. Ague has its good points after all.

21 and 22 December: Nothing doing.

23 December: Lecture by Charlie Kay on interior economy. The lecture was quite uncalled for, as our wardrobe consists of what we are standing up in. There is even an insufficiency of Hardman's cement biscuits and our old favourite 'plum and apple'.

24 December: Mail up. Scraggy chickens that must have been on hunger strike from the minute they popped their heads up out of their shells, cost 10 shillings each.

CHRISTMAS 1915

25 December, Xmas day: Divine Service parade at 8.00 am. One pint per

137

man beer issue at 2.00 pm, but the brothers Walsh 'wangled' a camp kettle full for our tent. It did not go far, but still!

The islanders attended divine service in their own churches. The women-folk were arrayed in all their finery. Gaudy skirts and still gaudier blouses seem to be the fashion here; it gave a kaleidoscopic touch to our usual drab surroundings.

Twelve months ago I was knee deep in Flanders mud. What changes time brings!

26 December: Battalion marches to the sulphur springs, which are situated in the village of Therma [Thermos]. All had a welcome steam or vapour bath.

27 December: Heavy rainfall in the early hours of the morning. All my tent washed in the stream, which flowed through it, an unusual pleasure as spring and washing water is at a premium on this island. I have known twenty men to wash in one galvanized pail of water; the last fifteen had no occasion to use soap.

It is rumoured that we are going up to Cape Helles to cover the withdrawal of the 39th Brigade of our Division.

28 and 29 December: Usual camp routine.

30 December: Route march.

31 December: New Year's Eve. At midnight rockets were sent up in camp and all ships in the bay set their sirens and foghorns a-going. The islanders were unprepared for this demonstration, to judge by the manner in which they tumbled out of their shanties. The 'Flanders Pilgrims', by way of celebration, vigorously attacked throughout the morning.

1 January 1916: Parades declared off due to inclement weather.

2 January: Divine service parade at 9.00 am.

3 January: Usual routine. Everything on the island is bought up save oranges and nuts.

4 January: Extended order drill. After one hour's juggling with the knotty and intricate problem of extended order from column of route, my platoon sergeant, Charlie Kay, solved the problem, much to the chagrin of his brother NCOs.

5 January: Campfire concert.

6, 7 and 8 January: Usual parades and Iron Ration inspections.

9 January: (Sunday) It is rumoured that the Roman Catholic Chaplain has been kidnapped by the Anzacs as he never turned up to celebrate mass. I came across the Carney brothers. They were full-blown sergeants in an Australian infantry regiment. They deserted from the East Lancs in Cape Town [pre-war].

10 and 11 January: Extended order drill.

12 January: Attack practice and bathing parade.

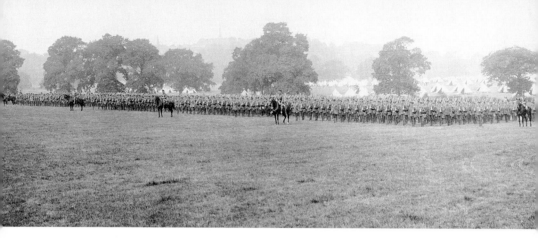

1. 1st Battalion, East Lancashire Regiment, on parade at their camp in Harrow prior to their departure for France on 21 August 1914.

2. The Officers of the 1st Battalion, the East Lancashire Regiment, on embarkation for France, August 1914. From left to right, back row: 2nd Lt W.A. Salt, 2nd Lt R.Y. Parker, Lt F.D. Hughes, Lt H.T. McMullen, Capt. A.St.L. Goldie, Lt E.M.B. Delmege, Lt J.F. Dyer, Lt W.E. Dowling, Lt N.A. Leeson, Lt H.W. Canton, 2nd Lt W.R. Tosswill. Middle row: Capt Walker, Capt E.E. Coventry, Capt G. Clayhills DSO, Lt and Adjt F.E. Belchier, Maj T.S. Lambert, Lt-Col. L.St.G. Le Marchant DSO, Maj. E.R. Collins DSO, Maj J.E. Green, Capt G.T. Seabrooke, Lt and QM R. Longstaff. Front row: 2nd Lt G.H.T. Wade, Lt C.E.M. Richards, 2nd Lt K. Hooper, 2nd Lt T.H. Mathews, Lt E.C. Hopkinson, Lt W.M. Chisolm, Lt R.A. Flood (RAMC). Of the twenty-six East Lancashires in this photograph, nine were killed and twelve wounded.

3. The 1st Battalion, East Lancashire Regiment, 'somewhere in France', 24 August 1914. They are seen at a halt on their train journey to join the British Expeditionary Force. On detraining at Le Cateau they heard the news that 'There's the hell of a German army marching round our flank,' and were in action there on 26 August.

4. *(above)* Private Edward Roe, author of the diary.

5. *(right)* Lieutenant E.C. Hopkinson, MC, 1st Battalion, the East Lancashire Regiment, after the epic Retreat from Mons. His letters are quoted in some footnotes in this book. He earned his Military Cross, a few days before this photo was taken, at the Battalion's gallant rearguard action of Le Cateau. To his left rear, with stick, is Captain Clayhills, Roe's Company Commander.

6. Brigadier General Sir Aylmer Hunter-Weston KCB, DSO. Nicknamed 'Hunter-Bunter', he commanded 11 Brigade in the 4th Division in 1914. As a result of his skilful handling of 11 Brigade he was promoted to major general in the field and took 29 Division to Gallipoli. He finished the war in command of VIII Corps on the western front.

7. Lieutenant-Colonel Louis Le Marchant, DSO. He assumed command of the 1st Battalion, the East Lancashire Regiment, on promotion from the 2nd Battalion on 23 September 1913. During the South African War he was adjutant of the 1st Battalion and was mentioned in despatches and awarded the DSO. He was widely respected by all ranks of the battalion. Roe writes, 'He was ever where danger was most. We will never get another Colonel like him.' He was shot dead by a sniper on 9 September 1914 at La Ferté-sous-Jouarre during the Battle of the Marne. He is now buried at a small cemetery at La Perouse, some 5 miles south of La Ferté.

8. Lieutenant-Colonel George Henniker Lawrence, CMG. Commanded the 1st Battalion, East Lancashire Regiment, from September 1914 to May 1915. His diary is quoted in some of the footnotes in this book.

9. Captain George Clayhills, DSO, commanded 'A' Company of the 1st Battalion, East Lancashire Regiment. He was Private Roe's Company Commander and is often mentioned in the early part of the diary. He was killed in action on 2 November 1914 at Ploegsteert Wood. He is buried in Lancashire Cottage Cemetery, Ploegsteert.

10. A painting by de Walton of British troops crossing the Aisne on 13 September 1914. Some of the demolition charges failed to explode and the iron bridge was not totally demolished. Roe writes, 'We crossed the tottering bridge, man by man at 6 paces interval under heavy shrapnel fire.' *(Waverley, History of the War)*

11. Le Gheer Convent just behind the front line and within 300 yards of the German trenches. The 1/East Lancs had two companies in the front line and one of these companies used the cellars of the convent as headquarters. Every evening the Germans shelled it and when this happened the occupants would turn out, stand behind a wall, smoke a pipe and wait until the shelling stopped.

12. British trenches at Ploegsteert. This photo was taken in November 1914 and shows the village of Le Gheer in the background. Note the rum jar and tin-cans littering the area, plus barbed-wire entanglements in the left mid-ground. The 1st Battalion, East Lancashire Regiment, held this area for over six months from 21 October 1914 until the end of April 1915.

13. Lancashire soldiers in their winter dress, February 1915. The goatskin coats were not popular with the front-line troops, who christened them 'louse traps'.

14. Le Gheer, March 1915. The crucifix at the crossroads.

15. Remains of a barn at the crossroads in Le Gheer, with Ploegsteert Wood in the background.

16. La Paix Estaminet in Le Gheer, March 1915.

17. The remains of Le Gheer Convent in March 1915.

18. *(above)* In the trenches at Le Gheer, near Ploegsteert, early in 1915. The battalion had occupied these trenches for six months and were shortly to be moved to Ypres. The photo shows, left to right: Sgt Woodger, Lt W.Y. Paton, MC, and Cpl Kirk.

19. *(above right)* Second Lieutenant Frederick Thornton Knight. He was Private Roe's Platoon Commander and was killed in action on 13 May 1915 at the Second Battle of Ypres. He is mentioned in the diary.

20. *(right)* A view from the 1st East Lancashire trenches at Shell Trap Farm towards the burning town of Ypres, 11 May 1915. The soldier in the foreground is in the line of shallow trenches and breastworks which the Battalion defended between 9 and 15 May during the Second Battle of Ypres at a cost of 17 officers and 370 other ranks, including many of the surviving pre-war regulars.

21. Mudros Bay on the Greek island of Lemnos was the advanced base of the Mediterranean Force. Roe writes, 'A person unaccustomed to such sights would imagine that one half of the world's shipping was assembled in the bay and that a mighty host were encamped upon the island.'

22. The stores at Suvla Bay, Gallipoli. Roe writes of the large amount of stores that had to be burnt prior to withdrawal from Gallipoli, but not before the dumps were thrown open to the troops to fill their valises and sandbags with all manner of edibles. The APM had, however, taken the wise precaution of smashing one hundred cases of rum!

23. Paddle steamers on the Tigris in Mesopotamia. Barges were lashed on each side of the steamer and these were used for conveying troops and stores up the river.

(HMSO)

24. Shaik Saad camp. The advance base of the Tigris Army Corps in its attempt to relieve General Townshend's force besieged in Kut.

25. A unit of the Tigris flotilla. The flotilla consisted of gunboats of the 'fly' class.

26. The camp at Wadi on the banks of the Tigris in February 1916. Moored by the camp are *mahallas* used to bring supplies up the Tigris. Note the height of the river above the camp. *(HMSO)*

27. Aircraft of the Royal Flying Corps in Mesopotamia. For most of the campaign the RFC had only one squadron of obsolete aircraft used for reconnaissance and artillery observation. Roe often writes of their disadvantage against the Turks' German-built planes, which were lighter and faster. This disadvantage continued until the supply of new 'Spads' to Mesopotamia in late April 1917. *(Topical Press)*

28. British troops in captured Turkish trenches, April 1916.

29. Aerial view of Sannaiyat on 23 April 1916. The Suwaikiya Marsh (impassable) is shown on the right of the photo and the Suwada Marsh in the background, with the Tigris on the left. The darker ground in the middle of the photo is "no man's land," with the British trenches in the foreground and the Turkish positions beyond.
(HMSO)

30. A hospital barge, attached to a river steamer, arriving at Amara. This is how Roe was evacuated from Orah after being wounded at Sannaiyat.

31. Inside a hospital hut at Amara.

32. British troops marching over "Whitley's Bridge," Ashar, near Basra.

33. British soldiers bargaining for a boat on the Tigris.
(A.B.W. Holland)

34. Artillery observation ladder. In the advance to Baghdad in February 1917 Roe commented on how the Turkish rearguard artillery made a good attempt to knock down these telescopic observation ladders as soon as they were erected. *(HMSO)*

35. The Arch of Ctesiphon is the remains of the vaulted roof of the great hall that was part of the White Palace of Chosroes I. Built around AD 540, it is a fine example of Sassanian architecture. Ctesiphon was also the site of the battle on 22 November 1915, following which General Townshend retired back to Kut where he was subsequently besieged. *(HMSO)*

36. A painting of the North Lancashires fighting for a bridgehead on the Diyala, 8 March 1917. The embankment shown was captured and used as a defensive position for 36 hours against repeated counter-attacks. When finally relieved, of the 112 men who originally landed there were only 39 left alive, and most of these were wounded.

37. The pontoon bridge across the Diyala, which was built as soon as the bridgehead was established. The Indian cavalry then crossed and followed the Turks as they retired to Baghdad. *(HMSO)*

38. A photo taken in Baghdad shows Edward Roe on the far right of the front row with a puppy on his lap. The board declares that these men of the East Lancashire Regiment had served on the three different fronts of France, Dardanelles and Mesopotamia during the Great War.

39. A *gufar* crossing the Tigris at Baghdad. Several times Roe comments on these ferries, which were of a basket construction covered inside and out with bitumen to make them watertight.

13 January: Nothing doing.

14 January: Draft from Egypt joins the Battalion. My Company now boasts of seven sergeants, who no doubt will make their presence felt at the next rum issue.

15 January: Continuous and heavy rain all night last night, which turned our camp into a quagmire. Kit, blankets, etc. floating all over the island.

16 January: (Sunday) Digging operations all day in order to drain [the] camp. Rumours of a move to Egypt.

17 January: At 9.00 am orders have been issued to strike camp at 7.00 am in the morning and speculation is rife as to our probable destination. Well, Hell or Flanders is preferable to Mudros of the three plagues – flies, vermin and sandstorms.

18 January: Reveille at 5.00 am. Strike camp at 7.00 am. March out of camp at 9.00 am. We are loaded like pack-mules. The going is soft and slippery and the swearing hard.

Embarkation for Egypt

The inhabitants seem downhearted as the source of their profit slide and glide past. The Battalion boards the *Waterwitch*, which takes us out to the transport *Tuscania*.[2] We are told off to messes as we file on board and the conviction grows stronger that we are not bound for Salonika, but Egypt is our probable destination.

19 January: Set sail at 7.00 am.

20 January: Calm. Sergeant Kay, after swearing four of us to secrecy, informed us that we had been chased by a U-boat during the night, but begged us to 'keep it dark for God's sake as the boys might get panicky if they knew'. We opinioned that Charlie had consumed what was left from the last rum issue on retiring to his 'doss', hence the submarine dream or vision.

21 January: Anchored in Alexandria harbour at 9.30 am. It almost equals, if not exceeds, Mudros Bay for shipping. We are not disembarking here. We set sail at 4.30 pm today [and] for the first time I noticed that we have a French officer as passenger.

Port Said

22 January: Anchored off Port Said at 7.00 am. The Suez Canal will play an important part in the Great War, as it is rumoured that the Turks are making great preparations to attack the canal, and if only held for a week by the enemy, or long enough for them to obstruct the passage of ships by demolition, [it] could seriously inconvenience our communications with India and with forces operating in Mesopotamia.[3]

[The] Battalion disembarks at 11.00 am and pitch camp on a desert patch near the docks and close to [an] Arab town. No NCO or man was allowed to leave camp until orders were given to that effect; nevertheless thirty men succeeded in evading picquets and police and got drunk in quick time on spirits. This escapade had the useful effect of doing away with spirits, as it was poison the Port Said cafe proprietors were serving up. A few glasses of this 'stuff', drunk by men with weakened constitutions, sent them stark raving mad. Of course it is very hard to restrain men who have been cooped up in a hell like Gallipoli for months.

The Band of the 11th Battalion East Lancs played selections from 6.00 until 7.00 pm in the evening (I believe it was the 11th Battalion).[4]

23 January: (Sunday) Roman Catholic Church service held in the International Church in town. I went out for a walk in the afternoon and had a good time. This is the most cosmopolitan town in the East. Returning to camp in the evening I met a gharri or barouche being driven furiously in the direction of the French quarter by a sergeant who wore a *tarboosh* or Egyptian head-dress. Two other sergeants were reclining peacefully in the interior of the vehicle, oblivious to the dangers connected with furious driving. As the vehicle drew level with us we recognized the driver! 'Twas my Platoon Sergeant, Charlie Kay. We stared in amazement, like the heroes in Virgil when the harpies descended upon them. Cox muttered, 'Can it be he?' 'It's him sure enough,' I replied, 'for there is no mistaking that carbuncle on the right side of his nose.' In a spirit of joviality, and inspired by Port Said beer, he had evidently annexed the barouche, jettisoned the driver and *borrowed* his head-dress, He was apprehended by the GMPs later on in the evening.

24 January: Nothing doing. I can't even get a civil answer to a question from anyone, as all seem to be suffering from swelled heads and liver, owing to the attractions of Port Said, liquid and ——.

25 January: Owing to strong wind and the sandy site of [the] camp ordinary tent pegs are about as useful as darning needles. All the tents are down and keep coming down as fast as they are re-pitched. When the wind settled it commenced to rain in real monsoon style. Such weather would even make saints pray.

26 January: Surf bathing.

27 January: My Company ('D') is sent on detached duty over to some salt works[5] on the Asiatic side of the harbour. The town is *verboten* (forbidden) to all except officers, so our pleasure is at an end. The salt is extracted in the crude from pits dug in the desert and refined in the works. I never had time to study the process.

28 January: The Company stood to at dawn. The nearest enemy outpost is 40 miles away.

29 January: I form one of the Canal guard, a popular duty owing to the number and variety of shipping which pass to and fro. We are close to a camp of wretched Armenian refugees.[6]

30 January: It is with feelings of deep regret that I chronicle the downfall of my Platoon Sergeant, Charlie Kay, from the lofty and dignified position of platoon sergeant to humble private's estate. When we of his platoon tendered our sympathy, he expanded a 30 inch chest and, with a dextrous movement of the tongue, shifted an insignificant stump of a Woodbine from the port to the starboard side of his mouth, cursed women and wine as the root of all evil and wound up the debate by muttering 'Kismet'. Poor Charlie, he was an optimistic soul and always looked on the silver lining side of the cloud, particularly after rum issue.

31 January: Physical and arms drill.

1 February: On patrol duty in the desert at 4.00 am, return to camp at 9.00 am.

2 February: Swedish drill 'spasms'.

3 February: Inspected by the GOC [General Officer Commanding].

4 February: Company rejoins the Battalion at 4.00 pm. Medical inspection at 5.00 pm.

7 – 10 February: Usual camp routine.[7] Port Said has gone dry, or to be more precise, [has been] drunk dry. We have not had an issue of underclothing or socks for the last four months, so we are having pretty 'lively' times.

11 February: Four of us induced 'Horatius', who does not know much about Army regulations, to put in for a four days pass in order to see the pyramids, with the result that the Company commander threatened to incarcerate him in a mental ward. As usual I got the major portion of the blame and Irishmen in general are considerably lowered in his estimation.

12 February: Iron rations inspection. It is rumoured that the Division will move shortly towards the Persian Gulf.

The native quarter of this town is the dirtiest in existence, inhabited by the vilest types of humanity it has been my lot to gaze upon. Every other Arab one meets is blind or nearly so, one-eyed, cross-eyed and they all suffer from ophthalmic disease to a more or lesser degree owing to inter-marriage between relatives and other causes.

Like all oriental or occidental cities, it looks picturesque and beautiful from a distance (but from a distance only). When inspected at close quarters it is extremely dirty and evil smelling.

The Egyptian police are a smart body of men and turn out spick and span.

13 February: (Sunday) Divine service for the RC persuasion was held in the Regimental canteen, which is 50 yards long and roughly 20 yards wide. Mass was being celebrated at one end, whilst at the other end the 'Jippo'

(Egyptian) contractor was doing a roaring trade selling both fried and boiled eggs for other denominations' breakfast. I made six attempts to say the Lord's Prayer, but could only get as far as 'give us this day our daily bread' owing to interruptions such as, 'Give us four fried eggs, boy', 'Give us four boiled eggs, boy' and so on. I gave it my best when an inspiration hit me (Bruce and that intelligent insect the spider). So I made the seventh attempt and this time I got as far as 'and lead us not into temptation', when Peter Casey (who should be on his 'benders' [knees] like myself but 'squared' the orderly sergeant) came back with two boiled eggs which he had previously purchased for breakfast. They contained chicks, which owing to some flaw in incubation had not the necessary initiative to break their shell. Well, language???? Offensive!

I closed my prayer book and gave the rest of the service over to meditation. Bruce's spider succeeded; I failed.

Sailing for the Persian Gulf

Battalion paraded at 1.00 pm, marched to the docks, and embarked on the hired transport *Corsican*.[8]

14 February: Set sail at 3.00 am. Great military activity along the canal. Engineers are at work pumping water from the canal into the desert on the Asiatic side for a considerable area around Port Said, which is flooded. Gare-de-Kantaru is a strongpoint. The Ismalia sector of the canal is held by the 'Auzzies'. Our men don't like the Australians; professional jealousy I presume. Discipline amongst the 'Auzzies' is practically non-existent, yet initiative is not lacking. I have known instances in our own Army where, owing to excessive bullying, men lost initiative, spirit and soul (if they had got one?), and didn't care whether they lived or died. I'm not exceeding the limit when I state that they prayed for death as the only means by which their miseries could be ended. I consider the Australians a magnificent body of men who landed on and evacuated Gallipoli in a halo of glory.

15 February: Anchor off Suez town at 2.00 pm. Set sail at 4.00 pm.

16 February: Calm; alarm practice daily but we do not expect to encounter U-boats in the Red Sea, as they cannot possibly get through the Suez Canal. The only alternative is by circumnavigating the Cape of Good Hope, if they have fuel bases, or else sent in sections to be assembled on some uncharted cove on the Aribistan coast.

17 February: Heat excessive; the messing on this transport, as on all hired transports, is only fit for Kaffirs or Basutoes. A Napoleonic maxim seems to be ignored here that 'an army fights on its stomach'. When and where we land, I'm afraid we'll have to crawl on ours.

18 February: Steam past the 'Twelve Apostles' at 8.00 pm.

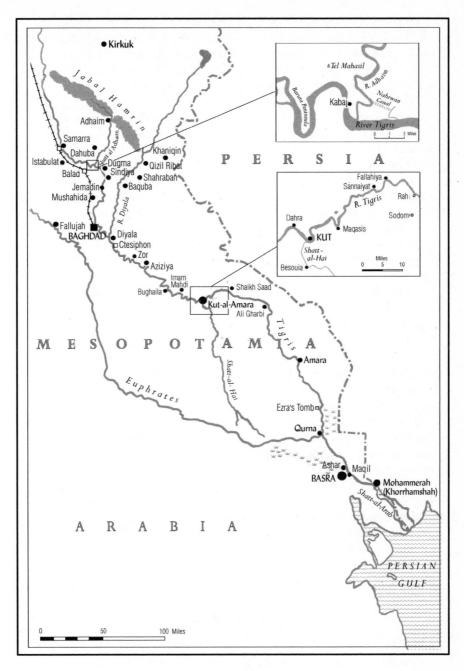

6. Mesopotamia

143

19 February: Steamed through Hell's gates at 2.00 am. The mountainous and desolate coastline of Arabia is visible from the deck of the troopship. We could just discern the grim and forbidden fortress of Aden at 6.00 pm. (as Kipling aptly quoted, " 'Twas like an old coal-box that had not seen black-lead for many and many's the year"). Boxing competition at 7.00 pm until 9.30 pm.

20 February: (Sunday) Divine service parade at 9.00 am. Carsonites and Redmondites on the port side, fancy denominations on the starboard side of the ship.

21 February: The finals of the boxing tournament were from 2.00 pm until 5.00 pm under protective awning erected by naval experts in order to protect competitors and spectators from the excessive rays of the sun. The finals produced a couple of Charlie Chaplins, but no white hopes.

22 February: The old skipper is hugging the coastline all day.

23 February: Sports are held on the aft well deck, a bit cooler for a change.

24 and 25 February: Nearing the end of our voyage. Anchor at 9.00 pm off a large native town.

26 February: The large Arab town of Koweit [Kuwait] (another town of mud hovels) is on our port bow and is about two miles from our Transport. The harbour swarms with Arab dhows or sailing vessels of shallow draught, which are sometimes engaged in the profitable occupation of gun running. Cargoes that escape the vigilant eyes of our Naval patrols find their way into the hands of the frontier tribes via Aribistan, Baluchistan and Muscat.

27 February: Voluntary Church service. Padre Lenehan told the parade off over gambling and using ungrammatical adjectives.

28 February: Still aboard.

29 February: Stormy wet and cold. My friend 'Horatius' is suffering from a bad attack of inertia and has played the role of Kipling's 'absent minded beggar' for the past week.

On the night of the 28th a raid was made on the beer store by a few daring spirits who got away with 400 pints of beer. Last night the raid was repeated, with cigarettes and tobacco being the objective. It ended in complete failure and three of the looters are under lock and key awaiting trial by FGCM [Field General Court Martial].

Wonderful lightning display after dark, such sights are common in those regions.

The Shatt al-Arab

1 March: The shallow draught steamer *Thongwa* draws alongside at 4.20 pm, trans-shipping stores and regimental impedimenta from 7.00 until 11.00 pm.

2 March: Trans-shipping continued.

3 March: All troops are aboard the *Thongwa* by 11.00 am. We were not sorry to see the last of the *Corsican* as the Allan Line upheld their reputation for 'generous' messing. Owing to the 'spacious accommodation' on the *Thongwa*, we have re-christened her 'The Black Hole of Calcutta'.

4 March: Entered the 'Shat-el-Arab' [Shatt al-Arab] at 1.00 pm.[9] The river banks are clothed with a growth of scraggy date palms, the water is yellowish in colour and sand banks are numerous.

5 March: Anchored off 'Mahomerah' [Mohammerah] a large Arab town on the left bank of the 'Shat-el-Arab'. It is the headquarters of the Persian oil company. I believe a pipeline runs from the 'Schuster oil fields'[10] to 'Mahomerah', a distance of some 60 miles. The fortifications consist of two mud forts.

Steam up at 4.00 pm; the river wends its way through a forest of evergreen date palms. Mud and reed villages inhabited by Arabs, who to judge by their attire had been in the retinue of Moses, Ezra and other Biblical Saints, adorn the river's banks.

The Turks made an ineffectual attempt to bar the passage of large steamers by sinking three small steamers in the navigable passage of the river. Wildfowl is abundant. Anchor at 4.00 am on March 6.

6 March: Steam off at 8.00 am, anchored off Busrah [Basra] at 11.00 am. The river was crowded with Transport and supply ships. Busrah is reputed to be the birthplace of the mythical 'Sinbad the sailor'. If the length of the war depends on the preparations they are making here – well – the old age pensioners will take part in the final push; Cigarette and tobacco famine at an end.

7 March: Unloading stores.[11]

By Steamer up the Tigris

8 March: My Company ['D'] embarked at 2.00 pm on lighters, or to be correct barges. Small river steamers with a barge lashed to port and starboard is the method for conveying troops, stores and transport up river.[12] [We] anchor at midnight [and] sentries are posted on barges in case of Arab attack.

9 March: Steam up at 6.00 am. [The] country [is] flat and under cultivation [with] numerous Arab villages on the right bank of the river. [We] anchor at 9.00 pm.

10 March: Warm; flies are numerous; good pasture land on each bank of the river. Anchored off Amara at 10.30 pm.

11 March: Plenty of wounded are coming into Amara. Twenty different races uphold the muddy dignity of Amara. Persian *Lurs* are most conspicuous. From what I can gather from the wounded we are not making much headway on this front.

12 March: (Sunday) Showery; steam up at 6.00 am. Numerous Arab villages with dilapidated mud forts adorn both banks of the river. Anchor at 10.00 pm.

13 March: Steam up at 6.00 am. The country is low lying and swampy. Indian troops are encamped on the right bank of the river. In the northeast a lofty range of mountains stands out in bold relief against a clear sky. Anchor at 9.00 pm.

Shaikh Saad

14 March: Our Company disembarks at Shaikh Saad[13] and joined the Battalion, which arrived on the 13th. The Corps Commander rushes troops to the advance base, but nobody seems to see to the commissariat or hospital arrangements of such. The Turks in the last Balkan war were about in the same state of chaos.

15 March: Battalion engaged in digging a model of the Um-el-Hannah [Hanna] position, which was photographed by aeroplane. We are going to attack this position.

Last night the Arabs stole nine rifles from the Gurkhas and Indian hospital orderlies.

16 March: Brigade field day; my Company were destined to skirmish over a sector of the battlefield of Shaikh Saad, which battle was fought last January.[14] Exigencies of the service did not permit of the burial of the fallen, therefore hundreds of skeletons, picked to the bone by vultures and jackals, grace the battlefield, gruesome relics of man's inhumanity to man. The stench was unbearable and owing to the heat the younger 'crowd' soon emptied their water bottles. Ignoring the advice given to them by their elders, they drank water from waterlogged trenches, in which trenches the defunct attackers' and defenders' bodies floated in a shadowy condition. Cholera and enteric of course could come afterwards – so long as they satisfied the wants of the moment.

17 March: St Patrick's Day, but no opportunity of drowning the shamrock on Mesopotamia's arid plains.

18 March: Brigade rendezvous at 2.00 am and march on markers at 2.30 am. Men are warned that they must not fall out under any circumstances during the 'stunt' as the country swarms with hostile Arabs. The column marched about 8 miles in the direction of the firing line. On our right, on the Tigris, four of our river monitors are sending some Turks to the 'Garden of Allah'. Maher, who had some naval experience, but evidently found discipline extremely disagreeable, 'skidaddled' and blossomed forth as one of

'Tho'wd sixth', informed me that our monitors were using 6 inch guns. Brigade dismissed in camp at 9.00 am.

Hostile Arabs fire on camp after dark which forces the garrison to man the perimeter, or defence works, until dawn.

19 March: Showery, the troops are compelled to patronize Gopal Singh of the Sikhs, a commercialized sepoy who makes chapattis, or pancakes, nightly. It is humiliating to see British soldiers crowding around an Indian, fighting for chapattis. I was often told that hunger breaks pride – it looks like it here – thanks to commissariat leakages.

20 March: Rumours of a move to Orah tomorrow, which is an advanced base.

Forward to Orah

21 March: It rained from 8.00 pm last night until 1.00 am this morning. The camp is knee deep in mud and all tents are down owing to the soft nature of the ground. Tent pegs 3 feet in length would be needed in this country during torrential floods.[15]

Brigade marches out of camp at 11.00 am and arrived in Orah at 2.00 pm.[16] Our new 'paradise' [Wadi Camp] is alongside the aviation ground, no doubt we will receive some attention from Turkish aeroplanes.

22 March: Guns active during the early hours of the morning. Our river monitors[17] and land armament shelled Turkish positions all day.

23 March: Usual camp routine.

24 March: Bayonet fighting. Coming events cast their shadows before [they happen]. This country is very flat indeed and affords no cover for advancing infantry. Marshes, nullahs and irrigation canals form serious obstacles to advancing infantry and particularly cavalry.

[There are] swarms of flies whose feelers and other aids to locomotion, when not in flight, are coated with adhesive layers of 'Tom Tickler's Plum and Apple Jam'. They give us no peace during the day, and night is hell without a mosquito net as millions of mosquitoes and sand flies (both armour piercing) give us their undivided attention.

Captain '28' and our Gallipoli MO [Dr Akerman] rejoined today. It is needless to say that our spirits sank to zero.

Considerable artillery activity all day.[18]

25 and 26 March: Attack practices.[19]

27 March: A German machine of the Fokker type flew over our camp today. I reckoned 'twas about 7.00 am when he paid us a visit (less visiting card) at a mighty altitude. Machine guns loosed forth belts of wasted ammunition on him and our anti-aircraft battery needs a hell of a lot more judging

147

distance at aerial objects. He dropped a couple of 'eggs' [bombs], but the altitude was so great that, from our point of view, his expectations did not come up to the parson's [curate's] proverbial egg – good in places – as he only succeeded in wounding a mule.

It is rumoured that we are going to attack very soon. The Divisional Commander [General Maude[20]] gave the Battalion a lecture at 2.00 pm on the forthcoming attack. He explained to us that all that was necessary was a bayonet rush, a mighty British cheer, and we were through to starving Townshend in Kut.

We discussed the General after dismissal and came to the conclusion he was a born optimist. We sincerely hope, although we do not believe, that the Turkish defences and defenders will collapse like the walls of Jericho. Anyhow, we'll have to adopt the 'wait and see' policy.

28 March: Attack practice. The 'Suicide Club' (bombers) were busy detonating bombs all day.[21]

Notes

1 Portianos Camp at West Mudros.
2 Regimental history (p.326) states that the 6/East Lancs embarked on HMT *Tunisian*.
3 The rumours were true and in late January, with German encouragement, the Ottoman Fourth Army under General Ahmed Cemal were crossing the sands of the Sinai desert to attack the Suez Canal. On 3 February aircraft detected the Turkish forces and the British were well prepared. The fighting lasted a week but British resistance and the failure of the Arabs to rise to Turkey's support caused the Ottoman army to retreat back across the Sinai. The outcome of the campaign was to keep a large British garrison in Egypt for the defence of the canal.
4 It was indeed the 11th Battalion, the 'Accrington Pals', who were in the next camp at that time. Their band was virtually wiped out on 1 July 1916 when all but one of the bandsmen were killed or wounded acting as stretcher-bearers on the first day of the Battle of the Somme.
5 Part of the Suez Canal Defences.
6 The Ottoman government had an undeclared campaign of genocide against their Christian Armenian subjects which, between June 1915 and late 1917, led to the deaths of nearly 700,000 men, women and children.
7 'From 1 – 12 February the Battalion was involved with training and re-equipping.' (6th Bn War Diary, February 1916)
8 In 1914 the Anglo-Persian Oil Company supplied seventy-five per cent of oil used by the British Navy. Though the wells and pipelines were in Persia, they were so near the border that they seemed likely to fall an easy prey to the Turks unless defended by the British Army. Thus, in November 1914, an expeditionary force, with a mission to protect British oil interests, landed on the mouth of the Shatt al-Arab and captured Basra. Both the Turks and the British sent reinforcements to the area. General Townshend with the 6th Indian Division marched steadily up the River Tigris but the tide turned at the Battle of Ctesiphon and Townshend became besieged at Kut-al-Amara. There were still great

hopes, despite previous failures, of relieving General Townshend's force besieged in Kut, and the 13th Division was to take part in a new attempt.

9   The Shatt al-Arab is a fine river – one and a half miles wide at the mouth and narrowing at Basra, 62 miles upstream, to about six hundred yards.

10 The Anglo-Persian oilfield was at Maidan-i-Naftun, about 26 mile south-east of Shushtar in Bakhtiari territory.

11 'At the Maqil wharf , Basra – Basra was the base of the Mesopotamian Expeditionary Force.' (Regt.Hist., p.327)

12 The river Tigris was the indispensable line of communication for the army.

13 Shaikh Saad was barely 26 miles, as the crow flies, from the besieged General Townshend at Kut-al-Amara but the only line of advance was up the river and twice the distance.

14 Shaikh Saad was a successful, but exhausting action, occurring from 6 – 9 January 1916 against entrenched Turkish positions by 7th Division under Major-General Younghusband.

15 In mid-March the River Tigris had a heavy flood produced by a thaw and rainfall in the country south-west of Lake Urmia. This flood caused difficulties to both the British and Turkish armies. One consequence was the problem of supplies reaching the British army as some roads became impassable and there was a shortage of river transport. Floodwater also inundated trenches of both sides.

16 'The East Lancashire marched in Brigade to Wadi Camp, some 9 miles up-stream.' (Regt.Hist, p.328)

17 The naval flotilla present consisted of four gunboats (*Mantis, Mayfly, Sandfly and Waterfly*) and the armed despatch boat *Flycatcher*.

18 'On 24th the River Tigris rose again to what was generally believed to be its maximum level. An air reconnaissance reported that the flood was causing considerable trouble to the Turks, especially at Hanna and on the 24th General Gorringe's artillery partially destroyed dams constructed there to keep the floods out of the trenches.' (*History of the War: Mesopotamia*, Vol 2, p.367)

19 From 22 – 31 March the Battalion was engaged in Brigade training for the impending attack on the Hanna position.

20 Major-General F.S. Maude, Commander of the 13th Division, which was composed of 38, 39 and 40 Brigades. 38 Brigade, commanded by Brigadier-General J.W. O'Dowda, had the 6th East Lancashire (with Private Roe), 6th King's Own Royal Regiment, 6th South Lancashire and 6th Loyal North Lancashire Regiment.

21 'There was much bombing practice, on which the Brigadier [O'Dowda] was very keen.' (Regt.Hist., p.327)

XII

The Attacks on Hanna and Sannaiyat

(5 – 9 April 1916)

Army Orders of the Day – Advance to the Firing Line – Hanna – Walking
into the Barrage – Death of 'Horatius' – Digging in – A Mirage – Night
Attack on the Fallahiya Redoubts – Attack at Sannaiyat – 'Stand to' –
The Advance – Mown Down – Wounded Again –
Turkish Counter-Attack – Two Brave Men

Army Orders of the Day

A copy of the Tigris Army Corps' Orders of the Day:
   'General Townshend, and the gallant troops under his command, who
won the Battle of Ctesiphon against heavy odds, have now been besieged in
Kut by greatly superior numbers for over three months. They have witnessed
the failure of two determined attacks to break through to their assistance but
they still implicitly rely on their comrades of the Mesopotamia Expeditionary
Force to do all that is humanely possible for their relief. In appealing to the
officers and men of the Tigris Column to continue their devoted and self-
sacrificing efforts, the Army Commander would remind them that the whole
Empire, while realizing the difficulties which they have to face, relies with
the greatest of confidence upon the courage and endurance of all ranks to
successfully carry out the task entrusted to them.'
   29 March: Great aerial activity all day.[1] Also rumours of a beer issue.
   30 March: A big fun day – the beer issue materialized.
   31 March: The bombers are having a rather busy time of late. Mail up.
   1 April: Raining all day; move postponed.[2]

Advance to the Firing Line

2 April: Camp is chin deep in mud. 'C' and 'D' Companies parade at 5.00
pm for the firing line. We arrive in the fire trenches at 10.00 pm.[3]

3 April: Our artillery heavily bombarded the enemies advanced lines from 2.00 until 4.00 pm this afternoon. The Battalion was hard at work all day carrying bombs (Mills) and ammunition up a two miles communication trench from the advanced dump.

It looks like more rain; we are praying for it to keep off, as to attack knee deep in mud will add to our losses by at least twenty per cent.

4 April: Our artillery shelled the Turkish position all day. The Turks replied with a couple of field guns, they must have shifted their heavy guns well to the rear.

At 2.00 pm a white flag was hoisted over the Turkish first line trench and our artillery ceased fire. A Turkish officer and two NCOs were blindfolded in no man's land and led to our headquarters. It was rumoured that they requested a four hours truce in order to bury their dead. Of course this was only a ruse, as their objective was to find out if possible our intentions. Although blindfolded, the trained ear can detect a lot and, as we were still carrying on with preparations for an attack at dawn, we could not let those gentlemen go back with the required information. So now they are on the road to safety for the remainder of the war. They did not seem very much upset over it. They chatted, laughed and smoked cigarettes energetically.

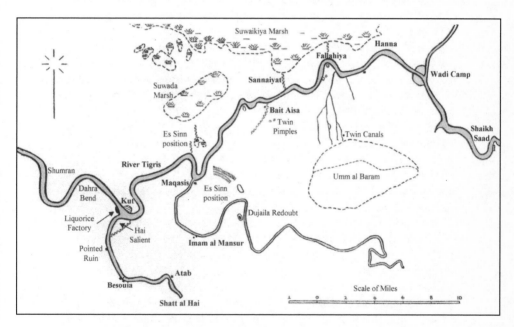

7.   Illustration of Operations between 18 March and end of
April 1916 and 7 December 1916 and 16 February 1917

151

This may be my last entry, but I have great faith in God and still less in the Corps Commander.

Hanna

5 April: At 1.00 am the Battalion assembled in the second line trenches ready for attack.[4] The King's Own[5] are in the first line, their objective being the enemy's first line. We (East Lancs) have got to rush through them and secure the second line. The 39 and 40 Brigades are on our left and are also assembled for attack, or to be correct [they are] in battle position.[6]

When the first two lines are taken, the Division must remain for twenty minutes in the captured position in order to give our artillery time to give the Turks a shaking in their second position, which is roughly 700 yards from the first and well connected by deep communications trenches. The bombers are to barricade the communication trenches, which connect the enemies' already captured first and his second line in order to prevent a bombing attack whilst we consolidate.

At 4.00 am we consume our rum issue. Each man draws a tin of 'bully' and four biscuits. Water bottles are filled from pannikins. In addition to our 150 rounds of pouch ammunition we were strangled with an extra 150 rounds in bandoliers and two Mills bombs carried in the trouser pockets of our shorts.

At 4.20 am belts are tightened, bayonets fixed and some silent prayers go aloft. Everyone wears an air of cheerfulness (assumed). We might as well. Bad as this world is, and particularly 'Messpot', yet not one of us would like to 'kick the bucket'. In a bayonet charge, under a hail of bullets and your comrades falling thickly on either side, you've got no time to think of heaven, home or hell. Get there as quick as you can, the quicker the better. In the last few minutes of suspense before you go 'over the top' you can recall a lifetime.

Our artillery are not going to bombard the enemy's first line as roughly speaking 50 yards separate Briton from Turk, which is much too close for an artillery barrage. The Turks seem to have 'smelt a rat' as they have kept up a well-sustained rifle fire until 4.20 am.

At 4.30 am the whistles sounded and over we go. Only a few stray and ill-aimed shots greet us instead of the hail of lead, which we expected, and the first two lines are taken with trifling loss. We are deafened by the detonations of hundreds of shells of all calibres, which are bursting on and over the second Turkish position. The air seems to be full of express trains.[7] The Turks retired through their excellent communications trenches to and through their third position, just in time to dodge our attack and barrage,[8] but left a few Turks behind that had already qualified for old age pensions to make a show; also a machine gun, which had already passed the stage of usefulness, manned by a very ancient machine gunner. Both gun and gunner were captured by the Warwicks.

Walking into the Barrage

On meeting with no opposition our officers lost their heads and, instead of obeying orders by remaining for the stipulated twenty minutes in the captured Turkish trenches, flourished their revolvers and yelled, 'Come on boys, we've got them on the run. We won't stop until we get to Kut.'[9]

The Division advanced in what we call in army slang 'columns of lumps', the grandest target an artillery or machine gun commander could wish for. As we advanced we came across Sergeant Major Ferguson who was in a horrible mess through shell wounds, yet he had the sense to exhort us to 'open out for God's sake'. We made a dive for the first line in the enemy's second position and of course came under the fire of our own artillery. Men were sent to Kingdom Come in bundles of eight by our howitzers and river monitors. Our artillery or monitors could not be held responsible as they were under the impression they were sending Turks by the dozen to share the glories of Allah.

A private of the King's Own mounted a trench parapet and, amidst the whine of shrapnel, the dull detonations of HE [high explosive] and the clouds of battle smoke, kept on waving a large red flag in hopes that our artillery observers might notice it and cease fire, until he was badly wounded by a Lyddite shell, an heroic figure amidst an upheaval of iron foundries. Dawn broke, the smoke clouds drifted away, and better still our artillery came to the conclusion that we'd had enough and ceased fire. Out of the confusion entailed by disobedience to orders some kind of order was restored. The Division reformed on a front roughly 900 yards in width by 600 in depth and the advance was resumed.

The Turks had just recalled a light 4-gun battery, as the opportunity was too good to miss, and persecuted the advance with shrapnel.

Death of 'Horatius'

I made up one of a party of six men who were detailed under Lieutenant Bailey to bring up ammunition from our original line of attack. We got hold of a box of SAA [small arms ammunition] each from the dump and proceeded in the direction of our advance. When we passed the Turkish second position I observed a mutilated 'lump' of humanity lying in the open 20 yards on my left. I digressed in order to ascertain who it was. It turned out to be my friend 'Horatius', who had got a whole shell to himself, both legs almost blown away, an arm badly shattered and abdominal wounds. I

153

dropped the box of SAA and asked, 'Can I do anything for you?' although I knew it was only a matter of minutes. He recognized my voice and, as I leaned over him, replied, 'You can do nothing for me, Ned. I'm past human aid. Get up with the ammo – the lads may be running short in the firing line.' I pressed his hand, shouldered my box and staggered forward. The exigencies of the moment would not allow of sentimentality. Well at any rate my friend 'Horatius' crossed the great divide and did not 'whinge' over it. If I survive, the passing of 'Horatius', gentleman that he was, will be ever prominent in my memory, a landmark of heroism and self-sacrifice to look back upon.[10]

Digging in

The Brigade have 'gone to ground' (to use a fox hunting term), as I cannot see a soul in front,[11] yet an intermittent chatter of musketry continues and the gentlemen behind the Turkish guns give us six overloaded mortals their undivided attention. Salvoes of shells are directed against us with amazing accuracy for Turkish gunners. One salvo forces us to down ammunition boxes and nose-dive into a providential Turkish trench at the expense of a crushed helmet[12] on my part. When the whizzing and buzzing ceased we climbed out of our temporary haven of refuge and resumed our trek, with the Turkish gunners still in attendance.

I felt a supreme lack of mobility, as, apart from the box of SAA, I carried 150 rounds of SAA in my pouches, was garlanded with three bandoliers, two Mills bombs (one in each pocket of my shorts), and a shovel GS for consolidating purposes; therefore I could not 'duck'. By 'ducking' I mean that when advancing under enemy shellfire you can hear the shell forcing a passage through the air (a not very pleasant sensation). Everyone imagines that that particular shell was solely moulded for his benefit, therefore you incline your head, hump your shoulders and do an oblique (or corkscrew rugby) sprint; in fact some men even resemble Praying Mantas [Mantis]. The shell may expend its energy 600 yards in the rear, yet you are consoled by the idea that you have dodged it. The same is applicable when advancing under badly directed machine gun or rifle fire. If the fire of either is well directed – well!

We reached Battalion headquarters and I handed my box of SAA (.303) over to the Regimental Sergeant Major, whom I found in a very deep and cosy irrigation canal. He was inspiring the Battalion, who were 'digging in' some 300 yards away in the open, and about 800 yards from the Turks who were holding the Falahiyah [Fallahiya] Redoubts. They [the Battalion] were under heavy rifle and machine gun fire. The ammunition party doubled forward and took up the spaces evacuated by the casualties. All were on their bellies throwing up head cover with their engineering tools. The bullet is the finest incentive in the world for making men dig. I noticed ten of the 'Wilts'[13] lying in the open about 150 yards in front (every Regiment wore a distinctive flash, also their regimental flash below the epaulettes on each arm); at first I thought they were a covering party.

When I got knee deep and pretty secure I had a 'blow'. The majority of the men by this time were suffering from thirst and, in spite of all warnings, were dashing in one's and two's to a salt marsh [Suwaikiya] 200 yards on our right rear. Some were shot down. The 'unlucky' ones who returned safe were thirstier than before, and 'twas a 100 to 1 chance that they did not contract cholera, as the marsh was decorated with the bloated bodies of mules and Turks who had passed the putrefaction stage. Yet Turkish bullets or visions of a cholera epidemic did not act as a deterrent; they still kept on 'chancing their arm'.

At 2.00 pm a solitary shell came sailing slowly for our left rear. We could tell by the rasping noise it made that it was due to expire on, or just to the rear, of our line. All got well down. It came to earth 20 yards in front of our hastily constructed line. 'Twas a high explosive lyddite shell. Dead silence until the yellow fumes cleared away – 'Anyone hurt?' – 'No, well carry on with the digging'. After five minutes suspense, three more HEs came from the same direction [from British guns] and eased the agony by going aground some 500 yards in front. This form of salutation did not seem to be appreciated by the Turks, who slated our line with more energetic machine gun and rifle fire. They were even so unmannerly as to send a brace of shells across, which harmed nobody.

A Mirage

Our casualties were just what one might expect and would undoubtedly have been heavier had not a merciful haze or mirage obscured both positions from noon onwards.[14] As it was, we were secure from rifle fire at noon. The people who 'stopped' one afterwards may thank themselves for aping about.

At 4.00 pm word is passed along the line to prepare to advance, ten minutes later the order is cancelled.[15]

Well, I thought, it was about time to look out for another helmet as my own was useless owing to taking a 'header' into a Turkish trench in the morning. So I doubled out to the right where there were three men who would need helmets no more. My luck was out as they were a size too small. I regained my position in safety and was contemplating exploring the left flank with a similar object in view, but by doing so I would be executing a flank march, so to speak, across an enemies' front and therefore offering a better target (if I may use the word) to the heavy and random small arms fire of the Turks. Our line was not continuous. Every man dug his own hole (I'm not ambiguous), a kind of every man for himself and God for us all 'stunt'.

155

The ten 'Wilts' had not moved a muscle all day. Rather strange, I thought, and two of the ten were without helmets, so I did a 150 yards sprint straight to my front. The second man from the left, a lance corporal, took a size 7½, my fit. Poor fellows they were all dead, caught about the stomach by a lucky traversing burst of machine gun fire. I did the return journey in record time, consoled with the idea I would not pass out by the agonizing process of heat stroke.

Dillon, the man in the hole on my right, was offering up various and heart-felt prayers to Guardian Angels and Patron Saints for the safety of his 'sowl'. Does religion make us cowards, I wonder?

Night Attack on the Fallahiya Redoubts

At 7.00 pm our artillery put up the semblance of a bombardment on the Turkish redoubts.[16] Under cover of this bombardment the Battalion emerge from their 'funk holes' and form up in line and in advance of them.[17]

Our Colonel (Lieutenant Colonel H. B. McCormick DSO) takes advantage of the temporary distraction caused to the enemy by the detonations of our HE to address the Battalion. I cannot write it down word for word owing to the noise made by the guns in our rear when they loosed off salutes and the bursting of projectiles in front, but the trend of this peroration ran something like this: 'Lancashire Lads, you have driven the enemy out of almost 5 miles of entrenched positions since dawn with the bayonet. You are going to attack again with the bayonet – no man will charge magazines.' He dilated on some episodes in the Peninsular Campaign. I had a faint recollection of Sir John Moore's retreat to Corunna, Waterloo and other notable achievements in which our gallant forbears of the East Lancs won renown.

Our gallant Colonel's address was rather inaudible in its latter stages owing to the attentions of the Turks, who, as soon as they got over the first demoralizing shock of the bombardment, worked their three machine guns, if not with disastrous yet with demoralizing effect upon the 38th Brigade, who were formed up in four lines of battalions with 50 yards interval between the lines. Anyone who has had the bad luck to come under well directed machine gun fire will inform the ignorant that one machine gun with a good field of fire equals a battalion of infantry. The Irishmen and Cockneys who formed forty per cent and Scottish and Welsh ten per cent of our Colonel's battalion thought it rather a lapse of memory on his part (reference some encouragement) – but still we'll carry on. His final admonition was – 'at them lads and drive it (the bayonet) well home!'

Our aeroplanes and spiritual leaders were conspicuous by their absence all day.

The Brigade advanced in four lines. My Regiment formed the last line.[18]

The Turks kept up a heavy machine gun and rifle fire on the advancing Infantry and men were falling fast. The tendency to close up (only natural I suppose) could not be controlled when under such a heavy fire and we found ourselves on the heels of the Regiment in front and got intermixed. A crescent moon did not give us much assistance in the matter of light. 'Twas the longest 1000 yards I ever 'goose-stepped'. When the leading battalion (the North Lancs I believe) got to within charging distance they 'let themselves go'. The Turks fought their machine guns to the last and conveniently retired along well-constructed communication trenches under cover of darkness. Our bombers[19] occupied the vacant trenches and in the confusion mistook each other for Turks and commenced to lob bombs at each other. A Regiment on our right front lost their direction, and heads as well, mistook their rear line for Turks and opened fire on us. Lieutenant Hopwood, a veteran of the South African War, fortunately was in command of my Company ('D') and used his brains, as he ordered his company to man a Turkish advance trench, charge magazines and prepare to repel a counterattack. We were all in a 'blue funk', bombs continually detonating in front, burst of rifle fire, stray shots and shouts of command that were drowned in the din and confusion of a night attack. No matter how well planned night attacks may be, yet a certain amount of confusion prevails.

This attack was not rehearsed; we simply walked into the void so to speak. I don't believe that one of the many officers, senior and junior, who led the attack had the faintest idea of the plan or construction of the Turkish defences, as no aerial photographs were available. We simple walked 'into it' (risking our reputation on the empty Um-el-Hannah victory of the morning.)

After 'doing ourselves in' for nearly an hour, Sergeant Sarzan of the King's Own (an Armenian) with courage (rare in his race, and he understood Turkish) went right through the entrenched position using his linguistic qualifications by shouting out commands and entreaties in Turkish, but got no response. So he returned and reported that the Turks must be miles away as the position was completely evacuated. His report led to a concentrated whistle blowing contest and firing ceased as if by magic. Of course everyone stood up (except those who could not) and congratulated each other on another empty victory – no prisoners, no machine guns captured. The Turks inflicted heavy losses on the attacking force, owing to us not knowing the ground and inadequate artillery support. Their casualties were unknown to us.

Another dearly bought lesson on the futility of night attacks unless everything is worked out in the minutest detail before embarking on such hazardous enterprises. 200 well-led and determined Turks, who were well acquainted with the lie of the ground, by a well-timed and determined

157

counter-attack would have thrown the whole Brigade back to their original line of formation for attack.

We collected as many of our wounded as time would permit, and at midnight retired through the 7th [Indian] Division, who were going forward to resume the advance.

[The] Brigade halted for a few hours and bivouacked about three miles in rear of our point of attack.[20]

In the 6/East Lancs we had 2 officers killed and 10 wounded. Captain Bartlett was shot and Lieutenant P. [Phillips], the Bombing officer, was blown to fragments by one of his own bombers by mistake in the confusion that prevailed. 120 other ranks were killed and wounded.[21]

6 – 7 April: Burying dead and collecting rifles, bombs and equipment, which were scattered all over the scene of attack. Our stretcher bearers told us of a Turkish machine gun which caught a whole platoon of North Lancs in line twenty yards from their redoubt and laid them all out for good including the officer.[22]

Attack at Sannaiyat

8 April: Division is to attack at dawn in the morning. Move up about four miles at 7.00 am after a rather light breakfast, which consisted of two biscuits and a half pint of rather washy tea. We lay alongside the river all day. The *mahallas* (country river boats) which convey our packs and blankets are in close attendance and anchored or secured by stakes driven into the ground on the right bank of the river.

At 10.00 am the Turkish FOO [Forward Observation Officer] observes masts of *mahallas*. Result – a Turkish battery opens fire on the *mahallas*. Consternation amongst the Arab navigators who slip their cables and beat it like hell downstream, leaving their mooring stakes malleted down hard and fast on the right bank of the river. We endured a generous spraying of nose caps, pieces of shell casing and shrapnel bullets but no one was hit.

At 2.00 pm my section's attention was drawn to four *drabbi wallahs* who were deeply interested in some souvenir one of them had picked up. They were standing in a circle and seemed to be listening when suddenly there was an explosion and the Tigris column was less four 'other ranks'. One of them picked up a Mills bomb and he, or one of the other three, spotted the pin and removed it, and then – – – – .

It is rumoured that the 7th Division got a rough handling at Sannaiyat and were heavily repulsed.[23] This is the second big attack [there] that failed.

At 4.30 pm all officers assemble at the Commanding Officer's 80lb tent.

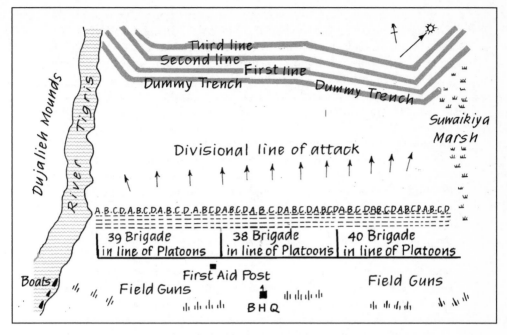

**8.   A sketch map and comments of the Turkish position at
Sannaiyat, 8 April 1916**
From the diary of Edward Roe

The nature of the ground was a flat as a billiard table. The Machine-Gun Corps
was across the river in emplacements on the Dujalieh Mounds. Their task was to
aid the attack with overhead fire. The Brigades were drawn up in line with the
men at two pace intervals and twenty yards between the lines of platoons. The
average strength of the platoons were under twenty-five men owing to previous
casualties and the withdrawal of stretcher bearers and bombers. Roe particularly
points out that the guns were silent, part of the plan of the surprise attack.

After a 'conflab' lasting fifteen minutes the Battalion are ordered to fall in.
The Company Commander calls for Platoon Commanders. As there are not
enough officers to go around, senior NCOs act as Platoon Commanders.
After explaining the plan of attack OC Company dismisses Platoon
Commanders to their Platoons. The devoted Platoon Commanders gather
the twenty-five or thirty of their lousy, unshaven commands around them in
a circle and explain the plan of attack (in no instance was a platoon over thirty
strong, including bombers).

'We are going to make a surprise attack on the key to Kut (the Sannaiyat position) at dawn in the morning. We are going to attack en masse on a frontage estimated at 3500 yards. The Turkish position is flanked on the right by the Tigris and on the left by the Suwaikiya Marsh; therefore a flank attack is out of question. It must be a frontal attack. There will be no artillery preparation as an artillery bombardment preceding the infantry attack would put the Turks on their guard and the element of surprise would be nullified or lost. The Machine Gun Corps have all their guns in emplacements on the Dujalieh [Dujaila] Mounds, which are on the right bank of the Tigris, and are going to support the attack with overhead fire.'

When this overhead or covering fire is going to start or finish, we are not informed. If they start too soon the Turks will be on the alert and if we take the Turks by surprise and get through their position we are going to come under it. We are half beaten before we move off to battle position. Fifty per cent of us have been under machine gun fire and know what it means. One machine gun well handled and directed has a more demoralizing effect on any attack than the fire of a whole battalion of infantry, and why no artillery bombardment to distract and demoralize the defenders? If we get within 50 yards of the Turkish position without being observed then we don't stand an earthly as we will be shot down like grouse on the twelfth of August before we cross bayonets with the enemy, and he is bound to have patrols and listening posts out. A light hearted venture indeed, undertaken without the slightest consideration for the defensive power of machine guns, backed up by a well entrenched and stubborn enemy who well knows that Townshend cannot hold out much longer. They hold the key to Kut, and by holding that key the reward is the capitulation of Kut, the capture of General Townshend and the gallant defenders, and a severe blow to British prestige in the Middle East.

Move off at 7.00 pm [to be] in position for attack, 1000 yards from enemy, at 11.00 pm. It took the Division two hours to get settled down as there was such an infernal amount of dressing on Brigade markers, shuffling and re-shuffling – 'Dress up' here and 'Get back' there, 'Ease off to your left', 'Get back in the centre,' 'Fall in to your right'. The Suicide Club (bombers) got lost for half an hour, then picks and shovels had to be unearthed for consolidating purposes. At last we are properly dressed, lie down in line of platoons and await the dawn or zero hour.[24]

The night was bitterly cold as we get both extremes in 'Messpot' at this time of the year, extreme heat by day and cold by night. We shivered and shook in our KD shorts and tunics. The mosquitoes were with us of course. The Turks, as far as the ear could detect, were abnormally sound sleepers.

Stand to

9 April: At 4.00 am a shivering Division stood to. Every man shivered as if he had a dose of ague. We were wet to the skin with the heavy dew.[25] No three tablespoonfuls of rum to warm us up. Being Senior Soldier, I had the honour forced upon me of performing the duties of Section Commander or leader (pro tem). God knows, I was never born to lead as I lacked both moral courage and initiative; therefore I was always quite content to plod along and leave the leading and responsibility to someone else. Whether they were better suited or not was a matter of indifference to me. I'm not ambitious.

I had occasion to check four of my maiden command whom I discovered 'wolfing' their day's rations (which consisted of four biscuits and a tin of 'bully' between two). I reprimanded them thus: 'What do you men mean by eating your day's ration before we kick off? It's only 4.10 am now and we may have to fight all day and may not get either rations or water tonight. Hunger you can endure in 'Messpot', but thirst you cannot'. One man replied and expressed the other culprits' minds as well as his own: 'Well tha' knows, Paddy, we're eating whilst we may as we mean't need any more biscuits or water!' 'Oh, cheerful indeed!' I replied. 'Carry on, there may be something in your logic or pessimism, but just remember that the Turks can't see us all off at the short trail.'

I deserted my new command for a few minutes in order to wish Corporals Smith of '15' Platoon and Cunningham of '16' Platoon the best of luck, as we had some rare old times in Poona, Mhow, Karachi and Cape Town together, and also to ask them what they thought about it. Corporal Smith replied, 'Well Ned, between you, Mick and I, whoever is not killed or wounded will be on the road to Ankara tonight – not as victors but prisoners.' Of course he only voiced our own opinion. All the old hands who had seen any fighting knew in their heart and soul that we were walking to our doom. Sannaiyat had a sinister reputation and before it famous divisions had tried and failed. We kept our opinions to ourselves, as it would not be playing the game to dishearten the youngsters who formed seventy per cent of the Battalion.

I rejoin my pessimistic section and presumed that by now there was not a biscuit amongst them. 'Twas apparent that impending fate interfered in no way with their appetites.

About 4.20 am I 'nipped' up to the leading platoon to see Sergeant Heald and old Jacques. The stillness of a graveyard prevailed all over Sannaiyat. The Turks never fired a round or betrayed their presence in any way since 11.00 pm last night. This gave some the impression that they had retired. Heald asked me, 'Do you think they have retired?' I said, 'Probably they have', and whispered in his ear, 'LIKE HELL' (meaning that they had not).

The listening posts have been withdrawn and there is another five minutes to go. I reviewed my past life. To be candid, it was nothing to be proud of. I remembered in past attacks and bombardments all the good resolutions I made (re) living a better life if I pulled through. Did I ever make an attempt to carry out those good resolutions, which I made when death stared me in the face? No, I did not! When opportunity offered I reverted to the same old mode of living. Companions and drink, combined with that old song 'Landlord fill the flowing bowl until it does run over,' made me forget all hardships and dangers, and with them of course the good resolutions vanished. Well, I'll have to woo providence once more.

The Advance

4.30 am [and] the word 'Advance' is whispered from '13' to '16' Platoon. The Company Commander is in front, and signaling with a white handkerchief (the only one amongst us, I believe), and the suspense is over. It's surprising the amount of noise that is made, although the day before we lashed our entrenching tool helves to our bayonet scabbards so as they could not come into contact with each other and rattle. Mess tins are carried in the haversack and not on the haversack straps. All are at the high port.[26]

The Divisional line at 200 yards lost all semblance of alignment, shoulder to shoulder in some places and 6 yards between files in other places (the loops or bends in the Tigris were to a certain extent responsible for this). It was a hopeless task trying to keep the 20 yards distance between lines. Roughly 80 yards should separate '13' Platoon from '16' Platoon; at 50 yards it had dwindled down to 30 yards. The front line bulged in the centre, receded and bulged again; the flanks in turn and simultaneously lost ground, causing the centre to halt until they came into alignment. I attributed all this to lack of ceremonial drill.

At frequent intervals I heard bolts pulled back and the familiar sound made by the magazine platform and spring. Of course they were loading up with five rounds, one in the 'tunnel' and four in the magazine – it simplifies long and short points and parries. If some idiot, when he forces the bolt home, forgets to pull back the safety catch and accidentally presses the trigger, good morning surprise attack.

We advanced about 700 yards and still the Turks give no signs, when suddenly on the Brigade left centre and on the Brigade's right, two officers commenced to roar at the top of their voices, 'Steady in the centre', 'Close in to your right' and so on. Everyone remarked 'Who the hell is making that row', 'Shoot them', 'Put them out of "mess"; they're blind drunk and are giving the whole show away.' Whoever they were, they were certainly blind drunk and deserved to be shot out of hand, or 'brained'.

Old 'Hoppy' [Lieutenant E.J. Hopwood] came back to the leading platoon and passed the word down: 'Get ready, we're almost on them now.' I heard whispered comments such as, 'Those two officers must think we are attacking a position held by deaf mutes', and. 'It's not much use trying to be silent now', as they could be heard at least half a mile away easily. Dawn had not yet broken, so I slipped a 'charger' [a clip of bullets] in.

Mown Down

At 800 yards, or it might be a little more, a solitary shot was fired on our left. I reckoned it was very close to the Tigris. The double report of the Mauser had no sooner died away than the whole Turkish line from the Tigris to the Suwaikiya Marsh sent up Very lights; 'twas like one man pressing a switch.[27] By their ghastly flares their position was revealed to us and we to them. The Turks were shoulder to shoulder in the trench. Machine guns were embedded on the parados, as also were Turks in the kneeling and standing positions. Before the flares expired their shrapnel was on us good and hard. A cyclone of bullets from machine guns and rifles battered and tore great gaps in the closely packed lines. Men fell by the dozen. You could hear the continual thud of the bullets as they came into contact with human bodies. Men bayoneted each other when falling dead or wounded.

I remember poor old Hopwood shouting 'Charge' – and away he went, never to be seen again.[28] A few of the leading platoon followed him[29]. Dawn was breaking. All was confusion. We were trying to make up a second line from what was left of the third and fourth, with the enemy still pumping lead and shrapnel into us. Some had already charged 'the other way'.

Wounded again

I got a bullet through the left arm – stars! – and I dropped. I distinctly heard a cultivated and authoritative command given in front and thrice repeated: 'Retire, retire, you damned fools, retire'. That finished the charge. The survivors did not need telling, in fact. I lay where I fell as I might as well get shot by the Turks as get bayoneted by some of our own men, as they were running about like men demented with bayonets at the charge. 'For Christ's sake keep those bayonets up' – No use imploring them to do so.

Bombs are detonating in front. I know they are not ours, they are fused 'golf ball' bombs used by the Turks.[30] A machine gun right on my front opened fire. I dug my head well into the ground as I could have sworn that the stream of bullets were going through my hair. It sounded to me like an immense wing of snipe flying over my head – I mean it was something similar to the noise their wings would make. The gentleman behind the gun must have had a stoppage; so I take the opportunity afforded by reconnoitering my front.

Turkish Counter-Attack

By God! The Turks have left their trenches and are advancing. Our Division wore helmets; those men have a sort of glengarry on for headdress. Some are throwing bombs as they advance, and incidentally searching our dead and wounded. On those who resist they use the butts of their rifles. Their machine guns and artillery are following up the groups of retiring infantry.

I consider it's about time I made a move. I arose and doubled about 50 yards, stumbled and fell, [and] repeated the process again. This time I can hear bullets whizzing around me. Our guns have spotted the Turks and opened fire for the first time. I make for the left, that is the Suwaikiya Marsh flank, as if I carry straight on I'll get shot by our own men, who no doubt by now have formed some sort of a line. Can't double any more, so I have to walk. Dead and dying all over the line of attack. On my left there are over 50, or maybe 80, men who have run into the Suwaikiya Marsh. They are almost up to their middles in it, some over, and the Turks are picking them off. I hear a cackling on my right – the Machine Gun Corps on the Dujalieh Mounds are giving us overhead fire; Well, you may save your powder, machine guns; it's all over.

I spot a hastily constructed kind of trench on my left and make for it at the double. I run over the parapet and fall on top of four badly scared and juvenile Warwicks.[31]

I asked, 'Wounded?'

'No'.

'Well what are you doing here?'

'We had orders to retire.'

'Oh, so you've been had also.'

I told one of them to keep a look out as the Turks were advancing. I told them straight, had I been a Turk I could have blown the lot to blazes as no one was keeping a look out. I got one of the others to cut my sleeve off at the elbow, break the ampoule of iodine, spill it over the entrance and exit wounds and 'clap' the field dressing on anyhow.

I had a squint over the top and discovered to my relief that the Turks had fallen back to their lines. Our guns are using Lyddite [and] as the enemies' first line is wreathed in yellow vapour, roughly 200 yards on my left rear, what is left of the Division are digging themselves in. Stretcher bearing parties have gone out to collect wounded but the Turks open fire on them and they are forced to retire, carrying their own wounded with them.

One of the Warwicks drew my attention to the Turkish position. He said

164

the Turks are coming out of their trenches again. I had a look. They were not Turks, but their Arab allies who came out to loot the dead and wounded.[32] They are collecting rifles, taking our men's equipment off them, and it appears to us that they are also taking the puttees, boots and clothes off them. We can see some of our men struggling with them and the Arabs dancing around them in a frenzy and clubbing our fellows with the butts of their rifles. I ordered the four Warwicks to put their sights to 800 yards, take a steady aim and fire. Of course we were risking shooting our own wounded; if we did, it would be a more merciful death than having their brains dashed out by the butts of those infernal savages' rifles. They fired, and the volley did not seem to make any impression upon them. I could get no observation. We were going to try another volley at 750 yards, [but] in the meantime two Turkish officers dashed out of the trenches and drove the Arabs from their traditional pastime of murder and loot into the trenches.

A lively half hour's counter battery duel now ensued between our gunners and the Turks.

About 11.00 am another attempt was made by a large party of stretcher-bearers (Indians included), under the Red Cross flag, to bring in the wounded but the Turks would have 'none of it' as they opened fire on them. I'm not quite sure whether the Turks were justified in opening fire or not, but the fact remains that the Division carried on digging a defensive line under cover of the Red Cross flag.

Two Brave Men

About noon the Turks opened fire on our trench with shrapnel and rifles. We kept well down and no one was hit. I noticed quite a number of wounded crawling painfully back by inches towards our line. I saw two officers out amongst the dead and wounded. They brought several wounded in and appeared to be dressing others. They bore a charmed life, whoever they were.

Firing had practically ceased, so I made for the advanced dressing station after advising the four Warwicks to make for the line the Division were digging, one at a time, and report to the first officer they came across, providing there were any left. Failing to find an officer, report to a sergeant major or sergeant and obtain a chit from whoever they reported to, as otherwise they might stand a good chance of getting shot. In any case some of their unit should be on the right flank as they advanced from that flank.

I reached the dressing station OK and had my arm properly dressed. It was there I learned who the two officers were who were out in no man's land on their own: Father Lanehan, the RC Padre, and the C of E Padre.[33] 'Two of the bravest men in Messpot,' remarked a wounded Sergeant of the North Lancs whom they brought in.

There are quite a number of Indian stretcher-bearers wounded and the Turks commenced shelling the battery in position on the left rear of the advanced dressing station. Their gunnery is of a haphazard character. The bell tents are perforated with shrapnel; stretcher-bearers going for, and coming down with, wounded are killed and wounded [themselves]. The low bursting shrapnel fails to find the objective (the battery) but gives everybody above ground a rather anxious time.

About 3.00 pm half a dozen AT carts (a divine form of transport over rough ground) arrive for the wounded and we move off for the clearing station, roughly 2½ miles away and close to the Tigris.

Notes

1   These will be reconnaissance aircraft. As more aircraft would be ready for action on 4 April 1916, General Gorringe postponed the assault on Hanna until that date so that his combined Air Force (Royal Flying Corps and Royal Naval Air Service) would be eight aeroplanes and three seaplanes.

2   'Instructions received to march up to take over Hanna trenches at 5.40 pm but storm on night 31 March – 1 April and throughout 1 April rendered going so bad . . . move post-poned 24 hours.' (6th Bn War diary, 1 April 1916) 'Flood water swept away the pontoon bridges over the Tigris by Wadi Camp' (Regt.Hist., p.328)

3   'Crossed river [Tigris] over pontoon bridge and took over portion of the line held by 125th Napier Rifles, 19 Brigade' (6th Bn War diary, 2 April 1916)

4   'General Gorringe's [Commander of the Tigris Corps] projected programme of operations was outlined as follows: On the first day [5 April] the 13th Division, supported by the 7th Division and with the 3rd Division and Corps artillery co-operating on the right bank, would seize the Hanna position [consisting of five entrenched lines one behind the other covering a depth of about one and a half miles with a number of guns positions behind the third line]. He would then establish his pontoon bridge over the Tigris just below Thorny Nala and move up his boat bridge alongside it. He calculated that by the fourth or fifth days he could first capture the Abu Rumman position on the right bank with the 3rd Division, supported by the 7th, and then take the Sannaiyat with the 13th Division supported by the 7th on the sixth or seventh day.' (*History of the War: Mesopotamia*, Vol 2, p.365)

5   6th Battalion, King's Own Royal Regiment.

6   'About 150 yards from the Turkish front line at Hanna were the 13th Division infantry. 38 Brigade were on the right, 39 in the centre, and 40 on the left, each brigade having one battalion in the front line . . . Forty-six guns were in position in rear of the 13th Division' (*History of the War: Mesopotamia*, Vol 2, p.372)

7   'At 5.00 am a large artillery bombardment opened up together with massed machine guns on the flanks and beyond the Turks third line.' (6th Bn War Diary, 5 April 1916)

8   'Evacuating the Hanna lines the Turks retreated to Fallahiya, about four miles distant, leaving only rearguards to delay the British advance. It was said that flood water had obliged them to take this course.' (Regt. Hist., p.328)

9   'So quickly were the first two lines of trenches taken that casualties were suffered from the

British barrage, which had not yet lifted from the third line and the zone beyond.' (Ibid, p.328)

10 Private Harold Eustace Bundy died of wounds on 6 April 1916.

11 [Having taken the Hanna lines] '40 Brigade was sent on to secure a position in front of the Fallahiya line, and at 8.40 am, 38 Brigade having reorganized, followed on. The East Lancashires used a wide communication trench for the first part of their advance, which eventually brought them forward on the right with their flank on the Suwaikiya Marsh. In the rear 39 Brigade extended the line of 38 Brigade to the river.' (Regt. Hist., p.329)

12 This was a tropical helmet, not the steel variety which had yet to be issued at this point in the war.

13 5/Wiltshire of 40 Brigade, 13th Division.

14 'Lancs dug in . . . the position being only 600 yards from the enemy and under heavy shrapnel and machine gun fire . . . . The casualties were only slight owing to a mirage, which prevented enemy seeing our troops unless they were standing up.' (6th Bn War Diary, Appendix, 1–5 April 1916)

15 'Orders came for an immediate attack upon the Fallahiya position but these were cancelled.' (Regt Hist., p.329) 'At 11.00 am General Gorringe went forward to the 13th Division Headquarters to ascertain the situation and found that General Maude had issued orders for an attack on Fallahiya to be made at 12.30 pm. The day had grown very hot, the mirage had become strong, and as the attack would, owing to marsh and river, have to be a frontal one over ground devoid of cover, orders were issued under instruction of General Gorringe at 12.15 pm that the attack was to be postponed till nightfall, the infantry in the meantime maintaining their positions.' (*History of the War: Mesopotamia*, Vol 2, p.377)

16 'At 7.00 pm the bombardment began and lasted for 45 minutes, the last 10 minutes being intense fire.' (Regt. Hist., p.329)

17 'At 6.00 pm orders received for attack on Fallahiya – which was successfully carried out, the position being taken and cleared of enemy by 9.30 pm.' (6th Bn War Diary, 5 April 1916)

18 'The 39 and 38 Brigades moved at 7.30 pm in lines of battalions, the East Lancashire being in the third line. It was soon found that the enemy was present in considerable force, 39 Brigade being hotly engaged. Thanks to a previous reconnaissance by Captain R.N.O. Bartlett of the 6/East Lancashire, it was discovered that the Turkish left, near the marsh, was but lightly held, so 38 Brigade . . . were able to break in and turn the enemy flank. Before 9.30 pm the whole position was captured.' (Regt. Hist., p.329)

19 The Regimental bombers were grouped and designated as Brigade bombers.

20 The Battalion, now reduced to 19 officers and 691 other ranks, withdrew to bivouac near Sandy Ridge on the river bank.

21 'The casualties of the battalion on 5 April amounted to 10 officers and 180 other ranks, the great majority being wounded.' (Regt Hist., p.329). 'Captain R.N.O. Bartlett was mortally wounded (died of wounds 6 April 1916). Second Lieutenant A. Phillips [the bombing officer] was killed 30 yards ahead of his men in the Turkish trenches.' (6th Bn War Diary, Appendix 1, April 5 1916)

22 This is an exaggeration; total casualties of 6/Loyals in the action were 97, including 2 officers and 10 other ranks who died of wounds.

23 The 7th [Indian] Division assaulted Sannaiyat, without success, on 6 April.

24 'On the left was 40 Brigade, the East Lancashire being next on the inner flank of 38 Brigade. Each company in the two brigades was on a frontage of one platoon, the whole force in four lines at 50 yards distance with bombers behind the second and fourth lines and machine-guns in rear. Every man carried 200 rounds of ammunition; magazines were charged but rifles were not loaded.' (Regt. Hist., p.331)

25 'It was a cold night and when all were in position the troops – lying motionless in the open, for all movement and noise were sternly prohibited – soon grew benumbed.' (Ibid, p.331)

26 'The distance to traverse was 650 yards [for the front platoons]; the brigades were to advance in quick time, breaking into double time when within charging distance of the hostile line.' (*History of the War: Mesopotamia*, Vol 2, p.390)

27 'The advance began but collision with a Turkish patrol had already given warning to the enemy; when the leading line was still 250 yards from the hostile trenches a red flare went up from a spot near the marsh. Almost at once the whole scene was lit by flares and a devastating fire from artillery, and from machine guns and rifles, opened on the British.' (Regt. Hist., p.331)

28 Lieutenant E.J. Hopwood was one of the four Battalion officers killed, with total casualties of 9 officers and 137 other ranks. Aged 47, he was a South African War veteran and is buried in Amara CWGC.

29 'Some groups of men were able to reach and enter the first Turkish trench where for a time they maintained an unequal struggle.' (Regt. Hist., p.331)

30 'Turkish officers rallied their men and started a bombing attack on the British invaders' [in their first trench line]. (*History of the War: Mesopotamia*, Vol 2, p.391)

31 9th Royal Warwickshire Regiment, part of 39 Brigade of the 13th Division.

32 'Turks and Arabs were seen to leave the hostile trenches and club the British wounded until driven in by fire.' (Regt. Hist., p.331)

33 The second padre was in fact the Reverend W. R. F. Addison, Chaplain of 6/Loyals, who was awarded the Victoria Cross for his gallantry on this occasion.

XIII

Down the Line to Basra

(10 April 1916 – 25 June 1916)

Casualty Evacuation – Orah – Cholera and Isolation Camp – The Fall of Kut – No Passage to India – 'Fly-Swatter' – 'Shellitis' – Light Duties in Basra – Death of Kitchener – Reinforcements and Heatstroke – Jacques and the 'egg diet'

Casualty Evacuation

10 April: It had rained during the night and the ground is in a very 'sticky' condition. There are twelve casualties in my tent, representing eights units of the Division. Apart from wounds, four are in a bad way with dysentery.

A General paid us a visit today. Some say it was Maude;[1] others swear it is Gorringe.[2] We know that there are generals of such names in 'Mess-pot', but we never 'clap' our eyes on Divisional 'Brass hats'. Brigadier-General O'Dowda[3] is ever with us and is affectionately dubbed 'thow'd "Brig",' although he is a comparatively young man as generals go. We did not know who was GOC in Chief; in fact we were not acquainted with our Divisional Commander, as we never saw them. O'Dowda we all knew.

General 'whoever-he-was' exhorted us to get well quick, come back and get our own back on the Turks, and told us that yesterday's 'scrap' was similar to a game of hockey or football in as much as one side had to lose. He also asked us did we hear the order given to retire? We told him we all heard the order given. He commented, 'Well it's damned mysterious'.

When he took his departure, his suggestion to get well quick was put to a vote and his 'get your own back' motion was unanimously voted down. We all assumed that he was the man that was responsible for the SURPRISE attack, unique in its audacity and silly in its conception.

It is rumoured that Townshend was one of the relieving force that rescued the Chitral garrison, of which Maude was a member.[4] Maude is reported to have used the expression 'I will take Kut if I have to make orderly men officers.' If it was sentiment that prompted him to send a division against a

169

strongly held and defensive position without artillery support, all we can say is that it was a damn foolish and costly sentiment indeed.

Orah

I left for Orah with a batch of wounded by river steamer at 6.00 pm.

14 – 16 April: Still in Orah. The wounded are starved and neglected, and the blankets are alive with black lice, a species quite new to me. The slightly wounded remove the dressings of the more seriously wounded, pick the lice off the edges of the bandages, and re-dress them. There are seriously wounded cases here who, unfortunately, are also suffering from dysentery. All are lying on the ground. Millions of flies persecute them by day and we have the mosquitoes and sand flies by night. The Major i/c [in charge] clearing came around today and told us that he quite understood the conditions, but he could get no medical supplies or comforts and all that he could do for us was to get us down river as soon as possible to Amara or Basrah, where we could obtain a bed at least and proper medical treatment. Bad as our conditions were, we had to sympathize with him, as he seemed a thorough gentleman and had more than his share of worry.

17 April: I can hear the big guns pounding away all morning.[5] 'Scrounged' a quarter tin of biscuits from a young SSgt [Staff Sergeant] of the S & T [Supply and Transport] and gave my tent a 'burst up'.

18 April: Large numbers of wounded coming in; also some bundles of rags which, on closer inspection, turned out to be Turkish prisoners.[6] The patient on my left is a young lad of the Wilts, just turned eighteen, who had his heel blown away by a piece of shell casing at Sannaiyat on April 9th. The wound has begun to fester and stink, and the flesh around the wound is turning blue. It means that he is going to lose his life if his foot is not amputated within forty-eight hours. Quite a number of wounds are turning septic owing to men scratching around their wounds. This is unavoidable as the edges of the dressings are strongly held by vermin.

19 April: Heavy gunfire all morning. More wounded arrive. Our advance is held up and the general belief is that the Kut garrison cannot hold out much longer.[7]

20 April: I embark with a party of wounded on River Steamer *P3* at 6.00 pm. Steam up and away at 10.00 pm.

21 April: Anchored at Sheikh Saad at 1.00 am, resumed voyage at 2.00 am and arrived at Amara at 4.00 pm. A road and a light railway are in course of construction on the right bank of the river. Forty slightly wounded cases are taken ashore. I was confidently informed by a much be-badged and bearded Indian hospital orderly, who had eaten *maunds*[8] of government salt, that Amara was a 'both crab' hospital as nine out of every ten men died who were operated upon. I immediately took cover behind some grain sacks on the under deck of the barge until we steamed off for Basrah. I also stood a better chance of a trip to India from Basrah.

Owing to being on 'short commons' up the line a couple of wounded men 'wolfed' two loaves of white bread each with disastrous results to their digestive organs.

22 April: Steam up at 7.00 am. Appalling conditions prevailed on the steamer and barges. Men who are badly wounded are in some cases suffering from dysentery. Sanitary arrangements are non-existent. There are a couple of artillerymen doing their best to perform the duties of hospital orderlies, and one harassed and overworked doctor on board. The wants of nature are relieved by the simple process of two men holding a sick or badly wounded man over the sides of the barges or steamer, the sides of which are encrusted with excreta. Keen senses of smell are stowed away pro tem. In some cases wounds have not been properly dressed since we came aboard with the result that they are turning putrid.

Cholera and Isolation Camp

Cholera has broken out on board the convoy. [We] arrive in Basrah at 9.00 pm and anchor alongside a jetty. All walking cases are ordered to disembark. We file down the left bank of the Shat-el-Arab for about 400 yards and proceed to embark on a hospital ship bound for Bombay. All were in 'high jinks', when a medical officer suddenly appeared and gave us all the impression that he had just finished a marathon. He shouted an order in a very agitated voice to the assistant surgeon and medical orderly on the gangway: 'For God's sake, don't let any of those men aboard!' Our visions of India and good cheer vanished utterly. At least my visions of salubrious Bangalore, and 'Meekins' or 'Steel and Coulson's' ale, both light and dark did! We are shepherded back to our barges, which, as soon as we get aboard, were towed out to mid-stream where the quarantine flag was hoisted both fore and aft on the steamer. All wounded are assembled on the port barge. Red Cross motor launches, flying the quarantine flag, steam alongside and remove some stretcher cases from the steamer, dead included.

23 April: Those of us who are not dead were inoculated and moved to an isolation camp on the right bank of the river.

24 April: This camp is entirely surrounded by water, the Shat-el-Arab on our front, an irrigation canal on our right rear, whilst a marsh which boasts of millions of toads, the majority of whom are approaching the accouchement stage, complete the quadrangle. These frogs maintain an uninterrupted chorus of 'croaking' the whole night long, and the mosquitoes are legion.

25 April: No news from the front.[9] Our cooks are about as well versed in

171

the culinary art as our sweeper is in algebra. I have not had a smoke for the past ten days.

26 – 27 April: No news from the front. Arab traders in *balams* draw up alongside our camp and offer the contents of their medieval *balams* for sale. I gaze with longing eyes on sticks of 'Belle of Virginia' tobacco, but have no money to purchase same. Neither have I any article of kit to barter in exchange. Therefore I continue smokeless. Without a doubt the same mode of progression by inland water was in vogue in the days of the mythical Sinbad the Sailor, and later when Alexander the Great of Macedonia returned to die in Babylon after his victorious march and conquest of a portion of India and Egypt.

28 April: No news. This is a very difficult country in which to conduct a campaign as flanking movements, even on a small scale, are out of question owing to no raised roads capable of carrying vehicular transport and lack of water. An AT cart drawn by a couple of good mules and a driver (of course) will find their way to hell, but not through 'Mess-pot' in wet weather. Therefore we have to rely almost entirely on pack transport.

Both sides to a great extent have got to rely on the two main lines of communication – the Tigris and Euphrates – and all actions of any importance are fought in contiguousness to the rivers above mentioned. The use of cavalry on a large scale is out of question owing to scarcity of water and ancient irrigation canals, which intersect the country. When the Turks are driven from their position by a frontal attack they break down the banks [river and canal], with the result that the trenches we wrested from them are flooded and the country in the rear also. Parties have to set to work and close the breaches under shell and small arms fire. It is not unusual to bivouac in mud and attack at dawn through an artificial swamp.

The shellfire might be described as mild. The Turkish shrapnel bursts too high but the climatic conditions are infinitely worse than in France.

29 – 30 April: No news from the Tigris column. Fishing and 'lousing' are our chief occupations.

The Fall of Kut

1 May: Bad news today. Townshend was forced to capitulate.[10] It is all the more disheartening when one dwells on the futile and bloody sacrifices made by the relief force who fought their way to within almost a stone's throw of Kut.

Tonight the river steamer *Julnar* made a valiant attempt to run the gauntlet of the Turkish defences to the beleaguered garrison with supplies and ammunition. She was sandbagged and defended by machine guns [but] she got disabled by Turkish gunfire off Maqasis fort.[11]

172

Lack of reinforcements and guns for the relieving force, with the forces of nature, sealed the fate of Kut and its gallant famine-stricken defenders. In fact, from our position at Sannaiyat we could see our aeroplanes from a great altitude dropping food to the beleaguered defenders.[12]

2 May: No tobacco or cigarettes to be had. The pipe smokers dry-brewed tea-leaves as a substitute for tobacco. Thank God tea-leaves are plentiful.

3 May: Heat increasing. Our cook made dumplings today by way of a treat, as he informed us. God help the consumers; no doctor could!

No Passage to India

4 May: A party of wounded were selected for India this morning. As usual, my luck was out as I was away fishing at the time of the selection. I asked in a very dispirited tone, 'Is it all over?' I was told that I was 'pushed' by an hour, so I picked up three muddy be-whiskered fish and cast them into their natural element, the Shat-el-Arab. The rod followed suit. I swore there and then that I would never indulge in Isaac Walton's favourite pastime again. The men who were on Gallipoli were selected first. My God! and to think that I missed India for the sake of three mudfish, the combined weight of which did not exceed ¼lb. I skillfully dodged Amara, risked cholera, and all my scheming came to naught – enough to make a man do something desperate!

5 – 6 May: Our period of quarantine expires. I, in company with twenty others, am removed to No3 British Field General Hospital on the left bank of the Shat-el-Arab. The hospital was formerly a palace and belonged to the Sheikh of Mahomerah who kindly placed it at the disposal of the British authorities, who converted it into a hospital. The Sheikh is an independent ruler, although he should owe allegiance to the Shah of Persia. He has a gathering of about 4,000 Arabs, dignified by the name of the 'Sheikh's army'.

7 May: What a pleasure to get on a spring bed again and have eggs and bacon for breakfast but I'm afraid my sojourn here will be of the briefest as my wound has healed up all too soon. The Matron is Scotch and a 'stickler' for discipline and fads. A twenty minutes lecture for having a crease in your blanket is considered a mild form of verbal castigation. I've got the impression that I am in her bad books already.

'Fly-Swatter'

8 May: Matron gives me an employed job – fly catching, or fly destructor. I am issued out with a swish, such as you would see ladies and gentlemen use when riding on the Maidan Mall in Calcutta during the dry season. The

Matron is very broad Scotch (which I can hardly understand) and gives me my instructions (re) my duty as fly 'swatter', and emphasized with the index finger of her right hand the consequences that would attach to me if she ever saw a live fly in the ward whilst I was so employed.

A truce has been arranged between the Turks and ourselves. Sick and wounded from Kut are to be exchanged for an equal number of Turkish prisoners.[13]

9 May: Will the public ever realize how the campaign is conducted here, or the appalling losses those little sideshows, as they are termed, cost us?

Matron comes around at 10.00 am. The flies conspired against me. No sooner had she entered the ward than two buzzed around her. As it so happened, at the time I was at the other end of the ward trying to put a very elusive customer out of action, when I heard about ten voices in unison shouting 'Fly-swatter!' I looked in the direction of the voices and saw the Matron who seemed to be in a towering rage. She gave the signal to advance with an imperious gesture of her right hand. Old Jaques remarked in a sotto voice as I passed his bed, 'You're in for it now Roe.' In fear and trembling, I approached the Matron who upbraided me thus:

'You lazy good for nothing, you're not doing your duty. You were chasing an imaginary fly at the other end of the ward because you saw me coming. The patients at this end are eaten alive with them. You're not worth the porridge you eat in the morning,' and so on.

I got exasperated before she finished her tirade and respectfully told matron that I had killed about one hundred yesterday, [and] that the element of surprise was lost, the flies were getting wise. 'In any case, Matron, I'm not the Angel Gabriel, as when they had flown out of reach I was minus wings and could not continue the pursuit.'

I lost my employment, and with it the spring bed and also the eggs and bacon for breakfast. At 4.00 pm I am transferred to the stationary hospital ship *Karadenig*, which is anchored in midstream. This vessel formerly belonged to the Austrian Government. I hope there are no sisters abroad, at least no Scottish sisters.

'Shellitis'

10 May: Medical inspection at 10.00 am. A queer-looking medico, adorned with a wig, false teeth and wearing glasses, barely glances at me and marks one 'X' against my name. I am informed by those who are (in the know) that a single 'X' denotes a speedy exit to a convalescent camp ashore, two 'XX' a trip to India, three 'XXX' 'Blighty'.

The messing on this old tub is extraordinarily good. It is incredible the number of 'lead swingers' that are wallowing in Basrah. They complain of

174

heart disease today, gastritis the following day, rheumatism the day after, and so on; in fact they can invent a disease for every day in the year. If they get 'well in' with the matron or sisters in hospital or in other words 'dug in' behind a petticoat, the College of Surgeons could not shift them.

Eventually a new and fearless MO takes over, makes a tour of the hospital and asks Brown, 'How long have you been here?'

'Seven months, Sir',

'What did you come come down the line with?'

'Fever, Sir',

Doctor: 'Why, your medical chart shows that your temperature has been normal for the past month. What are you complaining of now?'

Brown: 'Pains in the head, Sir and pains in the chest, Sir.' (Doctors cannot see pains.)

MO: 'Well Brown, I consider that you have been long enough in here. You had better "pack your traps". I will give you a week's light duty. In fact, Brown, some work might do wonders with those pains.'

The new MO interviews several of Brown's caste ('Pillow Flatteners') with the result that there are quite a number of vacant beds next day.

Brown has not played all his cards yet by any means. When those two nerve wracking letters 'M & D' [Medicine and Duty] is entered on his sick report, this means that Brown may be warned at a moments notice to proceed with a draft to the firing line.

Next day Brown reports sick and produces his master card, TEETH. Before Brown was passed fit in England he was fitted up with a set of false teeth to enable him to masticate army biscuits of concrete firmness and at the public expense. Brown states to the MO that on the night he got 'M & D' he removed his false teeth before retiring [and] placed them in a cup of water beside his head on the floor. He was awakened about 2.00 am by a noise in proximity to his head. He struck a match and by its dim light saw a jackal scampering through the door. On lifting up his cup he found, to his dismay, that it was minus water and – teeth. Apparently this particular 'Jack' was very thirsty, drunk the water contained in the cup and wound up the operation by annexing the teeth.

MO sarcastically: 'You don't fight Turks with your teeth. Neither do you eat Turks. In any case, take this card across to the dentist.' Brown laughs [to himself], another six months at least at the base. In the meantime, if he can get a billet such as Colonel's groom or QM store-man, he can, with influence, be made permanently unfit for all eternity.

Jackals are audacious animals when hungry. Who trained this particular 'Jack' I wonder? In any case, Brown gets another set free. The set the marauding 'Jack' is credited with annexing is peacefully reposing in cotton wool in a tin box in the bottom of his kitbag.

175

I have known men who were 'fixed' up at home with dentures and on arrival at Basrah stated to the MO on medical inspection, when asked where were their false teeth, 'Sir, I was suffering from *mal-de-mer* (seasickness) in the Bay of Biscay I was hurriedly forced to vomit over the side of the trooper. With the force of vomiting the clasps of the dentures became loose and over the false teeth went – to the bottom of the Bay'. Of course it means another set of dentures and six months at the base. The dentures that are supposed to lie on the bottom of the Bay are in his kit bag.

Anything [will be said or done] before getting within range of those beastly shells and naughty little Mauser bullets. About 45 in every 100 [in Basrah] are afflicted with 'Mauseritis and shellitis'.

A rush through medical inspection at 5.00 pm. I am marked fit for light duty.

Light Duties in Basra

11 May: Sixteen light duty men are transferred to Makina convalescent camp. This camp contains thirty huts, built of bamboo, and boasting of mud roofs. Each hut can contain sixty men. Quite a number of Japanese and Chinese carpenters are employed here erecting temporary huts, offices etc.

12 – 13 May: Basrah produces a ferocious type of flea that attacks with the élan of the French and never admits defeat. The nights might be un-officially described as lively on all fronts – and backs.

14 – 15 May: Having an easy time. We get six issues of tea per diem. Two issues of good tea would be more appreciated than six issues of shaving water. The tea planters should have long purses by the time the war ends.

16 May: [The] temperature [is] 115? in the shade. All drinking water is boiled and chlorinated before consumption.

17 May: Medical inspection at 9.00 am and marked fit.

18 May: Twenty per cent of the men in this camp are in hospital with heat stroke.

19 – 20 May: Today the *Basrah Times* (an official organ newspaper) reports that five Turkish Divisions are cut off between Baghdad and Mosul by the Russians (Cossacks).[14] At this rate the *Basrah Times* will not take long to dispose of the Turkish army.

21 – 26 May: I am employed on Camp Police. Hell, we are told, is some-where about the centre of the earth. Well, the scientist that invented that joke never visited Basrah during the hot weather season.

27 May: A small Russian cavalry force from General Baratoff's left wing find contact with British forces at Ali Gharbi.[15]

A fatigue party of thirty men was kept out all afternoon in the terrific heat, pitching tents; ten were wheeled to hospital suffering from heatstroke.

176

28 May: Had a walk into the village of Ashar this morning. The old Turkish barracks are in fairly good condition. The bazaar boasts of a profound and unforgettable stench.

29 – 31 May: Heat unbearable, millions of flies and billions of mosquitoes make life a living hell both day and night.

1 – 2 June: Everyone is talking about Verdun and the wonderful stand that the French are making.[16]

3 June: The Basrah Valiet [Vilayet][17] has improved out of all belief since it has come under British military and political sway. Money is plentifully lavished. Roads are being made and swamps drained. The light railway, in course of construction on the right bank of the river, will be a Godsend when completed. What we want in 'Messpot' are good lines of communication, and they must be very good and reliable lines. Without a doubt twice the number of men could be employed in this country, but the problem is could they be maintained as the line of communication exists at present? Supposing we crumpled up the Turkish defence, could the advancing force be supplied with rations, a good supply of ammunition, fodder for the animals, ordnance stores and a host of other items? An abundant supply of these is absolutely necessary to ensure success.

I remember, when at Sheikh Saad, having a controversy with a Conductor on the Supply and Transport whom I was acquainted with in India in the balmy days of peace. In a spirit of banter, I asked him how much he was making out of this deal? 'Why, you're starving us Mr F . . s. Do you call four biscuits per man per day, a 1lb tin of 'Bully' between three men, a 12oz tin of jam between thirteen men, 4ozs of cheese between six men and a ½ounce of bacon per man [sufficient]? Two soldier ants could see our sugar ration off at the short trail, the tea ration will never effect our nervous system or digestive organs, when we get bread it's four to a loaf, and no biscuits to help the bread out. We should get at least three biscuits along with the ¼lb of bread per man. Do you call that feeding us, Mr F . . s? Have your 'tribe' not made enough in the last two campaigns on the frontier?'

Mr F . . s replied, 'Admitted you're on "short commons", but it should not be as bad as all that. We've got to fight damned hard to get anything up via the river. The artillery want shells and fodder, the Royal Engineers want barbed wire, mauls, picks, shovels and so forth, the Ordnance want everything from horse shoe nails to five ton anvils. The Director of Medical Services, No.9s, castor oil, iodine, calamine, stethoscopes, lint, field and shell dressings and a host of odds and ends necessary for even a field hospital. Then your reinforcements, both British and Indian, use the same line of communication (the river). All those vast piles of firewood you see around here came up by the river, as have all the ration dumps you may have noticed on your way up. So don't be too hard on the Supply and Transport. If we give you plenty of rations you will go short of ammo and vice versa, so you cannot have it both ways.'

'I agree with you to a certain extent,' I replied, 'but full stomachs and ammunition should be twin brothers, so said Napoleon.'

To assist in preserving law and order a force of Arab police are being formed. Personally I have not much faith in the Arab policeman. If there was any looting going on he would be the first man I would expect to be on the scene, not to prevent others from looting but to help himself. [They are] a notorious-looking lot of scallywags and cut-throats. Well, all Arabs are alike and somebody has got to be a policeman. Under the un-progressive Turk there was very little law and order. The Arab could do as he liked with the result that now they resent law and order in its mildest form. Life was cheap and justice easily bought when the Turkish Governors ruled the Valizet [Vilayet] of Basra.

4 – 5 June: The rate at which U-boats are sinking our mercantile marine is causing us some alarm for if the U-boat campaign succeeds we will lose the war.[18]

6 – 7 June: Rumours of a naval action in the North Sea.[19] No official report so far.

8 – 9 June: The official version of the action is very vague and gives us the impression we got the worst of it. The general impression amongst us 'land lubbers' is that the German Fleet sallied forth from their bases, inflicted heavy losses on the Cruiser and Battle-cruiser squadron and scuttled back to their bases before the main Battle fleet arrived on the scene without sustaining anything like an equivalent loss.[20] Nibbling tactics, and von Scheer[21] must not be allowed to repeat the dose, or our two power standard will revert to a one power standard,[22] and then – - – - ?

Death of Kitchener

10 June: A shadow of gloom has been cast over the camp by the untimely end of one of England's greatest soldiers and organizers, Lord Kitchener, a soldier the Nation can ill afford to lose in the present critical crisis in her history.[23] He might have pulled the disorganized Russians together. If it could possibly be done, he was the man to do it.

I remember when he was C-in-C in India. He drove into our barracks in Karachi (in 1907) in a four-anna gharrie. No one knew he was coming. He had the 'assembly' sounded. I never remember such a scare.

'Hi! The C-in-C is in barracks!'

'Oh, go to hell, whose leg are you pulling?'

'Hurry up and get dressed and get on parade. He is not knocking back "burra pegs" back at Simla; No, he's here!' And there he was, sure enough.

As a general rule, when the 'brass hats' intend to inspect a unit's institutes or barrack rooms we get ample warning, a plentiful supply of lime and brushes are issued, all rocks and stones within the barrack area get a liberal coating, and everything is spick and span. 'K of K' was an exception; he revelled in paying surprise visits just to see for himself how things stood.

He brought out the 'Kitchener Test', when every man had to carry ten lead weights, the equivalent of 100 rounds ball ammunition, march 15 miles in a given time and attack a position afterwards. If a man fell out he lost his 'tanner' a day service pay. His heart and soul was in fieldwork; he was not a barrack room soldier or a drawing room strategist.

11 – 13 June: Great Russian victory in the Bukovina.[24] The Russians saved Paris in 1914 by invading East Prussia at the request of the British and French General staffs, although they were unprepared for such an invasion at the time. They paid dearly for their venture at the Battle of Tannenburg on the Masurian Lakes when von Hindenburg, 'the old man of the lakes', cut the Russian army to pieces.

Reinforcements and Heatstroke

14 June: Thousands of reinforcements are arriving weekly from England. It is midsummer now and these youngsters and old men are dying like flies from heatstroke. For every hundred rifles that leave England thirty reach the firing line on this front. This may be attributed to:

Sending out old crocks.

Sending out men who have not had a proper medical examination at home and when they arrive at the base their physical disabilities are brought to light on getting proper medical examination.

Not acclimatizing those drafts, say, for three months in India before sending them to 'Mess-pot'.

The 'lead swinging' element has got to be taken into consideration. A certain percentage of every draft, when they arrive at the base, manufacture imaginary diseases and convince the MO that they are suffering from such, unless he is a wary 'old bird'. Then there are the men whose dentures found a resting place on the bottom of the Bay of Biscay, or in a Jackal's den.

15 – 17 June: The death rate has been very high for the past three days, the latest arrivals from home being the victims, and no wonder, as they disregard all instructions laid down for them for the benefit of their health. I have had to chase 100 men who were bathing in a creek at 12 noon (the temperature was only 125? in the shade) back to their tents. I had barely turned my back when there were another twenty men in. This is a daily occurrence. They walk about at mid-day minus helmets and with only a Port

179

Said singlet on. Results: twenty or thirty in the heat stoke station by 6.00 pm in the evening and five or six are dead by morning. The survivors, if they had a bad 'tap', have to be sent out of the country. They will 'gorge' themselves with any kind of fruit, whether it has been washed in chlorinated water or not and drink any damned kind of water. It does not matter so long as it is 'wet'. Chlorinated water they will not drink because they do not like the taste of the chlorine. Criminal disregard of the rules laid down and lectures given for the health and welfare of the soldier are responsible for thirty per cent of the deaths here.

18 June: Quite a number of Indian shopkeepers have arrived in the country and have opened up shops and supper bars. They are a blessing in a sense, although their prices are thirty per cent dearer than in India and we know they are profiteering. The Provost Marshal is supposed to make out a price list of every article in shops in this area in order to stop profiteering, but it seems it is not in his or anyone else's interest to do so. The old system that was in vogue in the days of Warren Hastings and Clive still carries.

19 – 21 June: It is as much as we can do to keep alive owing to the terrific heat.

22 June: Fifty per cent of the camp are casualties owing to heatstroke. The majority have only got slight 'taps'.

Jacques and the 'egg diet'

23 June: Old Jacques of ours, who is rather eccentric, sleeps on my right on the floor. Beds are a luxury unless you were one of the heaven's blest and wangled a job in quartermaster branch. In the afternoons, when I am off duty and feel inclined to doze, I'm regaled by the said Jacques with adventures of his courting days that should read well in 'Peg's Paper' or the 'Flappers' Journal'. Space will not allow me to relate all his adventures. He finished his reminiscences this afternoon (the third) by ousting a formidable rival in a fistic combat that might be called Homeric and married the Lady of his affections – thank God that's over. Dear Madam Jacques, you have my sincerest sympathy. Jacques might be described as a 'supreme bore' – and what in the name of the Creator induces a man of over forty years of age to relate the love affairs and indiscretions of youth in a damned country like 'Mess-pot' I cannot imagine. His first date season, and the sun, have got a lot to do with his mental condition.

In some respects he is as cunning as an old dog fox and 'pulled my leg' for a week. I will relate the circumstances. When he came out of hospital, in which he had a good 'spell' with a mere scratch, he 'planked his body' along-side of me (he put his ground sheet down between another man and I as we were sleeping on the floor of the hut). On the following day he suggested a diet of eggs. These could be obtained on the outskirts of an Arab village roughly half a mile from camp. The village and vicinity were out of bounds. In a lengthy peroration he extolled the miraculous qualities of half-boiled hen eggs as body building material. They contained an overwhelming amount of vitamin B, very essential to men in our run-down condition. He wound up by suggesting – in fact it was between an order and a suggestion – that I should purchase one dozen hen eggs each day for a week. They only cost 8 annas per dozen and he would buy the eggs the following week. I readily fell in with his suggestion, although I ran the risk of being 'nabbed' by the GMPs.

I started mess caterer on Monday. I skilfully evaded the attentions of the GMPs and we consumed three eggs each for breakfast and ditto for tea, half-boiled of course as per professor Jacques's instructions. Duds were rare and an old helmet (Wolseley pattern) performed the duties of egg basket.

Half an hour after breakfast on Sunday morning [six days later] friend Jacques commenced to writhe and groan on his bed. I gazed upon him in consternation and was under the impression that he had a touch of colic, or worse still, cholera. I asked, 'What on earth is the matter with you?' After making a few awful grimaces he faintly gasped 'Eggs!' Hello I thought – what's the little game? After a few minutes he seemed to get his breath (but not until he had consumed 8 annas worth of hot tea, which I obtained from the coffee shop). He then commenced a damning indictment against all kinds of eggs, and hens eggs in particular. His oratory was profound and almost convincing, as he brought the four parts of grammar to bear on the subject: Orthography, Emtology [sic], Syntax and Prosody. He even quoted eminent medical authorities' opinions from a medical journal named the *Lancet*. Eggs caused indigestion, dyspepsia, headaches, boils and carbuncles, I almost expected him to state that they were responsible for in-growing toenails. I have never heard such a torrent of abusive invective hurled against the in-offensive egg that could not speak up for itself (although we came across one or two that almost could).

I spotted the ruse. It was Jacques' turn to buy the eggs the following week. Jacques, being a much older soldier than I, I did not indulge in recrimina-tions. I meekly told him that he might have exposed the poor nutritious value of the egg at least six days earlier, that he had not perused the *Lancet* since he came out of hospital; therefore he must have been aware of the ills people who eat eggs were heir to. I rounded off by telling him that he should not have waited until it was his turn to purchase the eggs before bringing medical journals to his aid in condemnation of the egg. 'As messing is concerned, you diet yourself to suit your taste and constitution, and I will do likewise.'

24 – 25 June: Two hundred men of my unit were paraded for medical inspection this morning. One hundred men are required to proceed to my unit as reinforcements. Ninety-six were passed as fit. The remaining one hundred and four made all sorts of petty excuses and complaints to the MO. The majority played on lack of dentures – yes – dentures, which were in their kit bags. Shell shock is prevalent amongst men who have never heard a shot fired and who don't intend to if they can possibly avoid it.

Notes

1   Major-General F.S. Maude CB, CMG, DSO, Commander of the 13th Division.
2   Lieutenant-General Sir G.F. Gorringe KCB, CMG, DSO, Commander of the Tigris Corps. He took over command of the Corps on 11 March 1915 from General Aylmer following the latter's failed attempt to relieve Kut-al-Amara and suffering heavy losses at Hanna in January 1916 and at Dujaila two months later.
3   Brigadier-General J.W. O'Dowda, Commander of 38 Brigade of the 13th Division.
4   This rumour had some historical truth but got totally twisted and confused, as it was Charles Townshend, then a Captain of the Central India Horse, who was besieged in Chitral Fort, 3 March – 20 April 1895. The siege of Chitral was one of the great epics of the later Victorian period. The relief-force was under the command of Major-General Sir Robert Low and included a certain Major Fenton Aylmer who, as Lieutenant-General Sir Fenton Aylmer VC, was given command of the Tigris Corps in Mesopotamia on 8 December 1915 and was ordered to the relief of General Townshend (again) at Kut-al-Amara. The rumour must have confused General Aylmer for General Maude as well as having twisted who was besieged and who relieved.
5   [6/East Lancs were detached temporarily from 13th Division in support of 3rd Division] 'Under cover of a heavy artillery bombardment 3rd Division pushed forward and captured three successive lines of Bait Aisa and Nalas.' (6th Bn War Diary, 17 April 1916) 'In the evening . . . the Turks counter-attacked and drove the Indian [3rd] Division back.' (Regt. Hist., p.332)
6   They were most likely prisoners from the action at Bait Aisa on the previous day.
7   'At 7.10 am on the 19th April, after a twenty-five minutes artillery bombardment, 39 Brigade moved forward to attack the Turkish line, which ran along a canal some 600 yards away. But the Turks by flooding had converted much of the intervening ground into a boggy marsh, and this, with the heavy enemy fire, effectually stopped the advance and forced 39 Brigade to withdraw to their trenches.' (*History of the War: Mesopotamia*, Vol 2, p.422)
8   A *maund* was an Indian weight, usually reckoned as equal to 80 pounds.
9   'On April 23, following another unsuccessful attempt to carry the Sannaiyat position, General Lake [Lieutenant-General Sir Percy Lake, KCB, KCMG] Commander-in-Chief in Mesopotamia, reported that his forces were worn out and incapable of further effort to relive Kut.' (Regt. Hist., p.334)
10 'After withstanding a siege from 2 December 1915, at 11.40 am on 29 April 1916, General Townshend telegraphed to General Lake [General Officer Commanding in Mesopotamia] that he had destroyed his guns and most of his munitions and that he was ready to surrender. The strength of the Kut garrison amounted to 13,309, of whom 3,248 were Indian non-combatant followers. (Combatants: British officers 277, Indian officers

204, British rank and file 2,592 Indian rank and file 6,988)' (*History of the War: Mesopotamia*, Vol 2, pp.457–459)

11 [Roe has most likely entered the story the *Julnar* on the date it was told to him although it actually occurred a few days earlier.] 'The attempt to revictual Kut by the *Julnar* was regarded by the navy as a forlorn hope. The *Julnar* was secretly prepared at Amara, although many, it appears, knew her destination, including the enemy. She was covered with protective plating, cleared of all possible woodwork, and filled with stores. At 7.00 pm on 24 April, carrying 270 tons of supplies, she started upstream from Fallahiya, her departure being covered by all possible artillery and machine gun fire in the hope of hiding the noise of her engines and of distracting the enemy's attention. The sky was slightly overcast and there was no moon, but in spite of the darkness she was soon discovered by the enemy and against the strong current she could not attain a speed of more than six knots … Maintaining her progress the *Julnar* kept on under heavy fire until, opposite Maqasis, she struck a cable and swung round with the current towards the right bank, grounding immediately opposite Maqasis fort. Here all attempts to get her off failed and she was forced to surrender.' (Ibid, pp.435–436)

12 'British aeroplanes had been dropping supplies into Kut since 15 April.' (Ibid, p.437)

13 [In Kut-al-Amara] 'on 29 April [day of surrender] there were 1,450 sick and wounded in hospital. Of these the worst cases, numbering 1,136 were exchanged and sent down the river from Kut.' (Ibid, p.459)

14 'General Baratoff's force [Russian] occupied Qasr-i-Shirin on its advance to Khaniqin [between Baghdad and Mosul] on 7 May 1916.' (*History of the War: Mesopotamia*, Vol 3, pp.8–9)

15 'On 20 May, a Russian Cossack patrol of 113 officers and men had arrived unexpectedly at Ali Gharbi from General Baratoff's force.' (Ibid, p.13)

16 Verdun was in the centre of the French defensive line and had been an exceptionally quiet sector since the counter-attacks in Champagne in the late Autumn of 1915. The Germans employed 35 divisions, or 700,000 men, against Verdun. The attack began on 21 February 1916 but failed to advance beyond Fort Douaumont. They then attempted to turn the French flanks, failing on the east, through Vaux, but meeting with some success on the west of the Meuse. On 21 May 1916, after months of terrible fighting and heroic French resistance, General Nivelle led a successful French counter-attack that regained Douaumont and undid two months of German gains. It must be the reports of this successful attack that Roe and his comrades were discussing.

17 Under Turkish rule the country was divided into administrative areas called Vilayets. There were three, Mosul, Baghdad and Basrah, each under a Vali or Governor.

18 The U-boat threat was a very great and real threat to Britain for much of the war. Maritime Law required commerce raiders, whether surface or submarine, to stop merchant ships, allow the crew to take to the boats, provide them with food and water and assist their passage to the nearest landfall before destroying their vessel. The German naval staff [under Admiral von Holtzendorff] had statistically calculated that a rate of sinking of 600,00 tons of Allied, but largely British, shipping a month would, within five months, bring Britain to the brink of starvation. Germany therefore adopted an 'unrestricted attack' policy that allowed U-boat captains to sink by gunfire or torpedo at will. During 1915 German U-boats sank 227 British ships (855,721 gross tons). In the first half of 1916 they

sank 610,000 tons of shipping of all flags, but the sinkings declined sharply when, after May 1916, the German Admiralty reverted to stricter observance of maritime law. This was produced by the threat from President Woodrow Wilson of America to use American naval power following the sinking of the *Lusitania* and loss of 1,201 passengers of whom 128 where American. Unrestricted sinkings began again in February 1917 and the total losses rose month by month, soon exceeding Holtzendorff's target of 600,000 tons per month. The British Admiralty's major successful solution to the problem was the development of convoys, the first of which sailed in April 1917. The German decision to recommence unrestricted attacks also produced an American reaction that far exceeded the German expectations. Following several direct attacks on American shipping Congress resolved that war should be officially declared against Germany (6 April 1917).

19 Battle of Jutland, 31 May 1916.

20 This was the largest naval battle of the war between the British Grand Fleet and Battle Cruiser Fleet against the German High Sea Fleet. After the action both sides initially claimed a victory, but now, after much analysis, it cannot be denied to have been a British victory of some sort. Though the German High Sea Fleet had lost fewer ships than the Grand Fleet it had suffered more damage to those that survived and the British remained in command of the North Sea. The battle was summarized by a German journalist as an assault on the gaoler followed by a return to gaol. Roe and his friends' impression was about right.

21 Admiral Reinhard von Scheer, Commander of the German High Sea Fleet.

22 This 'two power standard' refers, I believe, to the policy that the Royal Navy should be capable of defeating the next two largest naval powers.

23 On 5 June 1916, Field Marshal Horatio Herbert Kitchener, Secretary of State for War, en route to Russia on an official visit, was drowned when the cruiser *Hampshire* struck a mine north of Scotland. He had been invited by the Tsar to meet some of the Russian Generals and to inspect work on the reorganization of the Russian army.

24 On 4 June 1916 the Russians took up the offensive on the whole of their southern front, from the River Pripet to the Bukovina on the Rumanian border – a distance of 250 miles. On the whole front the Russians took over 40,000 prisoners and nearly 80 guns in the first three days, together with enormous stocks of materials of all kinds. With the German campaign against Verdun and the Austrian invasion of Italy this was the first move of a concerted plan of campaign between England, France, Russia and Italy. The Germans finally counter-attacked but only after Austrian troops returned from the Italian front and German divisions were withdrawn from France.

XIV

Life Behind the Line

(26 June – 29 November 1916)

Turkish Prisoners – Return to Shaikh Saad and the Battalion – March to
Amara – Rifles Stolen – Amara – Gifts from Bengal – Beer Issue – Porridge
– A Race Meeting – A Case of Beer – Quinn and the 'Jiniral'

Turkish Prisoners

26 June: One hundred NCOs and men including one officer, Mr
Thompson,[1] embark on a river steamer a 7.00 pm. One hundred Turkish
prisoners, for exchange, are proceeding with us.[2] Those prisoners came
from India and do not relish the idea of becoming active members of the army
of resistance. They were captured when Townshend made his spectacular
attack on Amara and have been having a good time in India since.

27 June: Steam up at 5.00 am [and] anchor at Kurna [Qurna] at 4.00 pm.
The confluence of the Tigris and Euphrates below this village forms the
Shat-el-Arab, which flows into the Persian Gulf. [The Tigris and Euphrates
meet at Kurmat Ali and not at Qurna]. The Garden of Eden was reputed to
be in Kurna. If the same climatic conditions prevailed in Adam's days as now
– well – he should be exonerated for partaking of the forbidden fruit.

The Turkish prisoners we are convoying for exchange are a sturdy lot of
men. They have a profound faith in Germany and state that if Germany is
beaten the cause of Islam is lost. Sixty per cent hail from Constantinople or
Istanbul, the remainder are a wiry tribe from Angora. The Istanbul Turks
can speak French and there are one or two disciples of Karl Marx amongst
them.

Ten men of my draft have been evacuated to hospital here – a good start.

28 June: Steam up at 5.00 am terrific heat accompanied by a Sirocco like
wind makes us feel as if we were on a floating furnace.

Steam past Ezra's tomb at noon. Ezra was an old biblical saint of some
kind and his ancient and decayed mausoleum, a relic of ages now long past,
stands on guard over the turgid and muddy Tigris. Anchor at 8.00 pm.

The Turks have given us no trouble so far.

185

29 June: Steam up at 5.00 am. The Arab population has increased since I came down river. They are a treacherous race and are always on the winning side.

During my stay at Basra I noticed that missionaries were trickling in. I attended one lecture given by a missionary on customs and religions in the coastal area of the Persian Gulf. I asked this foolish old gentleman what was his objective in coming to Mess-pot. 'Oh!' he replied with great confidence, 'now that the British are here we intend to preach the word to the Arabs and bring them into the fold.' I asked him had he indented for any machine guns, light armoured cars or trench mortars, as without the aid of such implements of warfare he and his bible would come to an untimely end. He seemed offended when I told him that there was only one method of preaching Christianity to those sheep and camel stealers, and that method was through the muzzle of machine guns.

30 June: Steam up at 5.00 am. It is getting slightly cooler as we proceed up river. Anchor at 8.00 pm.

1 July: Steam up at 5.00 am. Furnace-like winds blowing all day. One of the Turks has just died from the effects of heat stroke.

Enver Bey[3] is a second Napoleon in the eyes of the Turks but they do not like the idea of rejoining his standard. I sincerely hope that if it is ever the lot of any of my comrades or I to fall into the hands of the Turks, wounded or unwounded, that we will be treated with the same respect, consideration and chivalry as the British Tommies treated them.

Ismay Noureddin decorated my notebook with what he tells me is his signature. He is an out and out socialist and hates war and states that capitalists make wars to enrich themselves. He made a solemn agreement that if we ever met in an attack we would not fire on each other. Well, I would not like to trust you just the same, Mr Noureddin. I think I would try and get the first one in.

Anchored at 6.00 pm at Shaikh Saad.

During the trip up river the Turks and ourselves were accommodated on the upper deck of the steamer, with the exception of a few men who got 'well in' with the sergeants and were supposed to be acting in the capacity of batmen (in the field). [They] were quartered on the lower deck. The Turks could have escaped any night had they so desired. Two sentries were posted at each end of the deck with fixed bayonets between 12.00 to 2.00 am and 2.00 to 4.00 am. They usually left their arms lying against the deck rail and dozed. I have seen the Turks on three occasions, when Mr Thompson was coming up the ladder to visit the sentries, get hold of the sentry's leg and shake him into the position of alertness. If they did escape they knew that their freedom would be short-lived, as the Arabs would detain them and hand them over for the monetary reward.

Steam up at 11.00 pm and all the Turkish prisoners are blindfolded before we reach the firing line. The steamer flies a white flag and the prisoners are handed over to an escort of ours, who are also carrying white flags. Not a shot from any army disturbs the stillness of the night; the blood-curling howl of the jackal is all that one hears. The Turks 'tipped' us handsomely when we guided them across the gangway; 5 rupees was the lowest tip. They left several bundles behind in the form of souvenirs. When these bundles were examined they were found to consist of complete new sets of the mounted arm of the Service's saddlery (ours). How the devil did they manage to bring the saddlery from India to Sannaiyat without being detected? They must have had plenty of sympathizers in India as every Turk had rolls of notes. They swore that Colonel Subbi Bey surrendered Basra and Amara for a *maund* of rupees. I'm thinking it's a good job for Subbi he died in Burma.

Return to Shaikh Saad and the Battalion

2 July: Reached Shaikh Saad at 6.00 am [and started] unloading stores from the steamer.[4]

3 July: Draft joined the Battalion at 7.00 am. Brigadier General O'Dowda inspects the draft at 6.00 pm.[5]

4 July: Lecture by RSM Carrington on 'How to keep fit'.

5 – 9 July: Battalion finds escort for convoys from Shaikh Saad to Sodom and Orah once in every three days as mounted Arabs attack convoys that are unguarded.[6]

No one is allowed out of their tents from 10.00 am until 5.00 pm on account of the heat. If a man leaves his tent and does not return at a reasonable time, two men have got to turn out and look for him. He is usually found 'flattened' out in the sand from heatstroke.

10 – 13 July: Temperature 118 degrees in the shade.[7] On an average, within the Brigade, five funerals take place every evening. The corpses are sewn up in blankets, dumped on an army transport cart and taken to the burial ground.

14 – 15 July: One man committed suicide this morning by putting the muzzle of a loaded rifle in his mouth and pressing the trigger. He made quite a decent job of it.

16 July: Divine service at 6.00 am.

17 July: Everybody seems dull and low-spirited. The slightest exertion causes a man to sweat until what clothes he has on are saturated. The bread ration (when we get it) has got to be wrapped up in a wet towel to keep it moist; otherwise you might as well try to eat a lump of granite when teatime arrives.

18 July: The reinforcements we are receiving of late are badly trained.

Some men cannot even load a rifle or perform the elementary movements of squad drill, with the result that we've got to do a parade every evening, punishing a whole Battalion for the sake of some sixty odd men.

19 – 22 July: A blinding sandstorm has been raging for the past four days[8] and those everlasting Bully and D F Mutton stews for dinner do get on the nerves. Mutton is passable by way of a change, but when it comes to boiled goat!

23 July: Divine service at 7.00 am. All are sorry to hear that our chaplain has been sent down the line with fever. (Father Lanehan was a Gallipoli hero.)

24 July: Sandstorm again.

25 July: The Brigade ammunition dump caught, or went on fire, owing to the awful heat. Jacques attributes it to spontaneous combustion. The irregular explosions of .303 and the dull crash of exploding grenades caused panic in the tents. We were all in a state of deshabille. The sergeant majors and sergeants were all shouting, 'Turn out at once!' whilst we were trying to drag on shorts and wind putties around pipe-stem calves amidst remarks such as, 'The Arabs have attacked the camp', 'They've taken us by surprise', and so forth. On looking through the door I noticed a dozen or more running like hell towards our outpost line in the rear of the camp. They were without equipment or rifles and were running away from the direction of the exploding ammunition dump. Eventually the Battalion fell in on the parade ground and the cause of the panic is explained to us. The fire fizzles out in half an hour and we are dismissed. Luckily no one was injured.[9]

26 – 28 July: Nothing doing for the past three days owing to sandstorms.

29 July: Beer issue.

30 July: On escort duty with a convoy to Sodom camp.

31 July: Rations of very poor quality. The usual daily sandstorm is raging.

1 August: A draft from England joins the Battalion at 9.00 am.[10] It is astonishing the number of men who are over age that are passed fit for active service. They fill the base hospitals in the various theatres of war, cost the state enormous amounts of money and in the end are invalided as medically unfit. The same wastage applies to food. In Basrah I have seen scores of loaves of bread burned in incinerations whilst the men in the firing line were living on half and sometimes quarter biscuit rations.

2 August: A very disturbed night last night. It seemed as if all the ghosts in ancient Mess-pot took it into their ghostly noddles [heads] to visit the vicinity of our camp. The Company on piquet on the breastworks commenced firing at midnight and kept it up at intervals until two in the morning. When dawn broke there was nothing to show for the expenditure of ammo save a decrepit grey Arab pony, lame, and peacefully browsing on camel thorn 200 yards from the perimeter.

3 – 4 August: Our Colonel has gone down the river sick. His successor Colonel D[av]y of the Gloucesters,[11] imagines that we should be as proficient in drill, musketry and fieldwork as a peacetime regular battalion. Under existing conditions this is impossible as fifty per cent of the Battalion are raw Derbyites and every reinforcement is alike. Those men are not to blame as they are called up, rushed through a couple of months training, lack discipline, can't load their rifles properly or hit a target at 100 yards. Their knowledge of Company, Platoon, Section drill and extended order drill is very remote. In the piping days of peace it took six months hard 'graft', three months at the depot and three months at the Battalion under veteran instructors before you got dismissed drills and was classified as a trained soldier. Bear in mind it took six months under perfect conditions to turn out a trained soldier. Can it be done now in six weeks or two months when everything is in a state of chaos? Admitted they are dressed up in khaki, have rifle and equipment, small books, emergency rations and first aid dressings, but they are not trained. It takes time to turn out the finished article.

5 – 6 August: Sandstorms. The Arabs have a rather provoking habit of galloping to within rifle range of the camp and loosing off about thirty rounds nightly and clear away again, to the detriment of the tentage. Apart from making us 'stand to', it is not a very nice sensation to be lying in a tent when a couple of Arab bullets 'plop' through the tent and about 6 feet from the ground.

7 – 13 August: Regiment on mobile column [duty] for the past week – That is 'standing to' ready to turn out at a moment's notice.

14 – 16 August: No parades for the past three days owing to sandstorms.

17 August: Night operations [training] from 7.00 until 10.00 pm.

18 – 20 August: A small mounted force of hostile Arabs is threatening the camp from the West. The camp is 15 miles from the firing line. Turkish airmen have not troubled us up to the present.

21 August: Our airmen are improving of late as I saw one looping the loop this morning.[12] Quite an unusual occurrence on this front.

22 – 26 August: Usual routine[13] and daily sandstorms.

27 August: The Division has begun a gradual move to Amara. Some units have already left. It will be a welcome change.

My Company ('D') relieve 'B' Company at 'New Fort' a strong point on the right bank of the river and a veritable Mecca for mosquitoes.[14] The Persian hills 60 miles away break the monotony of the rolling plain. The Russians are 'somewhere' in the North East.[15]

28 August: The wise Hakims of the medical profession have discovered a new kind of fever (Sand Fly).

29 August: It is rumoured that Rumania [Romania] has declared war on the Central Powers.[16]

189

30 – 31 August: Nothing doing. Sleep is out of the question by day owing to heat and flies and by night owing to sand flies and mosquitoes. We are not in possession of slacks (long khaki drill trousers) and have to wear shorts and putties all night and have no mosquito nets. We are eaten alive, so to speak.

1 September: 'New Fort' abandoned. The Company rejoins the Battalion.

2 September: Rumania's declaration of war has cheered everybody up considerably.

3 September: Sunday. No divine service.

4 – 6 September: For the past three days we have been exercised in carrying out sham attacks on entrenched positions.[17]

7 – 9 September: During the past three days we have been engaged on moving our camp closer to the river[18]. Our airmen are doing a lot of night flying.

10 – 15 September: Usual camp routine.

16 – 20 September: The Battalion is under orders preparing to move down to Amara.

Quite a lot of firing by sentries takes place every night. Bullets are flying in all directions and no one feels safe. You might fall asleep in your tent in the pink of condition and, to use an Irishism, 'wake up dead'. All this firing is without results as there are no dead or wounded Arabs in front of the barbed wire or piquet lines next morning. So the firing may be attributed to extreme nervousness and imagination.

March to Amara

21 September: Battalion parades at 3.00 pm [and] marches out of camp at 3.30 pm. The camp [is] left standing. [We] cross a pontoon bridge to the left bank of the river. March continued until 8.00 pm when the Regiment bivouacs for the night.

22 September: Move off at 2.30 am [and] pitch camp at 8.00 am as too hot to march between the hours of 9.00 am and 4.00 pm.[19]

23 September: Move off at 3.15 am. Our left is flanked by a mirage, a most extraordinary phenomena in the form of a placid lake dotted with small tree-studded islands. The Persian hills, some 60 miles away, seemed only as many yards.

24 September: Move off at 3.30 am. Pitch camp at 7.00 am.

25 September: Move off at 3.00 am. Pitch camp at 8.00 am. An RAMC [Royal Army Medical Corps] orderly got drowned whilst bathing in the Tigris this morning.

26 September: Move off at 3.00 am. Pitch camp at 8.00 am. A stiff march.

190

Road very bad. Arabs hovering around camp all night. Sentries have orders not to fire.

27 September: Move off at 3.15 am. Pitch camp at 7.30 am. Arabs again seen prowling around camp at 8.00 pm. The sentries still have orders not to fire.

Rifles Stolen

28 September: Move off at 3.00 am. Pitch camp at 7.00 am. The Arabs broke into camp during the early hours of the morning and stole seven rifles from my Company ['D'] and two from 'C' Company.[20] Wonderful thieves those Arabs, in fact they could give the Pathans of the North West Frontier points when it comes to lifting rifles or blankets.

The camp might be described as a laager as three sides of the camp were protected by army transport carts [placed] wheel to wheel. The Tigris protected the rear. 'A', 'B', 'C' and 'D' Companies slept at night in the open and in lines of platoons. The rifles were secured around the right leg of the owners by the web rifle sling. Sentries were posted outside the laager only 3 yards apart. They heard and saw the Arabs several times during the night but could not fire as orders were to the contrary; neither could a sentry leave or quit his post to charge them with the bayonet as he would most probably get knifed and his rifle and ammunition taken from him. To cut the long story short, they got inside the laager and helped themselves to the first seven men's rifles of the front rank (they did not touch the rear rank) and got clean away. They cut the web slings and secured the rifles without awaking the owners. Sentries stated that they heard the metallic sounds made as if two or three men were running and carrying two or three rifles in their arms but what could they do? They had orders not to fire.

The following morning the victims thought someone had played a joke on them and kept on shouting, 'Come on, play the game, "low" those rifles up, who's been larking around here?' My friend of Basrah and 'Lancet' fame (Jacques) was one of the victims. When no rifles were forthcoming the bivouac was thoroughly searched without result and the seven victims were put under close arrest.

Amara

29 September: Move off at 4.40 am. and arrive at Amara at 7.30 am. The Divisional camp[21] is three miles up river, or above the town to be more precise.

The men who lost their rifles by neglect are to be tried by General Court Martial. Had the sentries been allowed to fire on the Arabs no rifles would have been lost and no casualties could possibly be inflicted on the Brigade personnel either, British or Indian, as everyone was inside the laager. The sentries would naturally fire outwards into a vast expanse of rolling plain without any habitation whatsoever. The wily Arabs, who were hovering around the bivouac for two nights and were not fired on, naturally became more audacious and, aided by the absence of the moon, 'chanced their arm' and won.

30 September: Battalion drill and kit inspection. As a punishment for losing seven rifles the Battalion have to sleep on the square in front of the Officer's Mess (tent). It means that every NCO and man has to carry his bed, kit bag and rifle on to the square at 9.00 pm and 'bed down' in the open in lines of platoons. In this country we get two extremes, heat and cold, and it is bitterly cold between the hours of 1.00 and 3.00 am. As I have previously written down, we have no KD [Khaki Drill] trousers or 'mozzy' nets so we get down to it in full marching order (i.e. boots, putties and shorts). Our rifles are secured to our legs by the web sling and four sentries are posted on the outer edges of the square. About 11.30 pm or 12 midnight the officers emerge from the mess tent in a jocular mood (to draw it mild) and try to enact the role of Arab 'loose wallahs' by stumbling through the sleeping lines endeavouring to abstract the men's rifles from underneath their blankets. The 'Old Man' indulges in this annoying pastime also. We arise at 4.00 am already dressed, take our beds, rifles and kitbags back to our company lines and make the beds up in line outside our tents. This form of punishment is known in the Army as 'finding Scapegoats'.

Had the Brigadier, or Colonel, issued the necessary orders that were essential when marching through, I may say, a hostile country, no rifles would have been lost and this unnecessary punishment averted. It has been assumed by the NCOs and men of the Battalion that the reason why the sentries were not allowed to fire was that the Brigadier and the Colonels would be awoken by the firing. Apparently the protection of life and property was only a secondary consideration.

1 October: Divine service parade at 7.00 am.

I had a walk into Amara this afternoon. The appearance of the streets is improving owing to enforced sanitation. One third of the Army Corps effectives are employed on the lines of communications. All men so employed are strangers to the firing line [and] don't know what it is like to go short of water or rations. [They] sport white shirts and shoes, can make sixty breaks on steeple-chasing billiard tables and send home glowing accounts of the fighting to their respective local papers. I came across a few professional 'scroungers' who seemed to be brought into this world to fight for their country's causes at Mudros, Basrah and Amara.

I met Dick S[pence]r in the main street. He was never in the line in France.

192

He remained behind in Mudros, the base for operations in Gallipoli. He remained behind at Basrah and now he is a full-blown GMP at Amara. I greeted him cheerfully – in fact I fussed over him as if he were a long lost brother. It was only diplomacy, as I was well aware that GMPs could always 'wangle' a drink and Mess-pot fosters an almost unquenchable thirst. I enquired about his health and was informed that the 'ticker' (heart) was giving him a lot of trouble. He seemed rather depressed and I asked the reason why. He informed me that he was for medical inspection on Tuesday and if marked fit would be sent up the line.

'Oh!' I said 'that is bad news indeed. I suppose you have a "cushy" time here.'

He replied, 'Very'.

'I don't suppose you want to go near the firing line?' I queried.

He answered in the negative.

I put him wise to a stratagem that often worked, although I never had recourse to it:

'Get a round of ammunition, Dick, extract the bullet then abstract the strands of cordite and chew them for fifteen minutes before you appear before the MO, taking care of course to expectorate before going in, in case he might examine your teeth as he is almost sure to do. You cannot play on teeth, Dick, as you already have had two sets up to date. Cordite lessens the heart's action and gives you a temperature.'

He invited me into a shop and we proceeded upstairs to a room. He said something in Arabic to the shopkeeper (My God, I thought, he's even had time to learn Arabic and a World War on). Before you could say Jack Robinson, there was a dozen bottles of *Ashi* beer (Japanese) on the table and two glasses.

I took my departure for camp at 5.00 pm in a jovial and generous mood. I meet the brother W's on my way to the river front [and] ignored those two out and out 'scroungers'. In a spirit of generosity I gave the *balimshi* (boatman) one rupee instead of 8 annas, his legal fare.

2 October: Last night one of our sentries was fatally stabbed in the back by an Arab. His rifle and ammunition were stolen.[22]

3 – 6 October: Platoon drills and skirmishing.

7 October: Brigade dig a model of the Turkish entrenched position at Sannaiyat.[23]

All were inoculated against enteric at 4.00 pm.[24]

8 – 10 October: The Regiment is struck off duty on account of inoculation.

11 October: Rumours of a beer issue. The Battalion is still 'wobbly'.

12 October: A large reinforcement from home join the Battalion today.[25]

13 – 14 October: Brigade operations [training].

15 – 16 October: Musketry practice. The atmospheric conditions that obtain in this country make long range shooting anything but accurate.

17 – 18 October: Usual camp routine.

Gifts from Bengal

19 October: Another consignment of gifts arrived from the ladies of Bengal today (Lady Carmichael's organization). Those gifts are not issued out free to the men as those generous-minded ladies intended. On washing days on the banks of the Tigris shirts and socks are liable to get lost, particularly when they are nice and dry. Some other person thinks he is more entitled to them than what you are and away they go. You report the loss and get issued with a gift shirt and a pair of socks on payment. They are not army pattern and already have been paid for twice. On the next kit inspection the Company Commander asks you:

'Where did you get your shirt from?'

'I got it issued on payment sir'

'Well more damn fool you for taking it. It is not an army pattern shirt. Put him down for a new shirt, Quarter.'

When the gifts arrive from India they are sent to Division. They have first choice. Then they are sent to Brigade, and Brigade helps itself. From Brigade they are forwarded to Battalion Headquarters where they undergo another ransacking. Company Quartermaster Sergeants [CQMS] are then sounded and what is left are taken to Company Headquarters. The CQMS, sergeant major and storeman select what they require and stow the articles out of sight. Then the CQMS bellows out at the head of the lines, 'Platoon Sergeants, come and draw your gifts!' Enter the Platoon Sergeants. 'Sergeant Clarke, you're 13 Platoon Commander – that's your little lot there.' Sergeant Clarke surveys his Platoon's gifts with an experienced eye and remarks, 'I could do with this', and 'I could do with that'; 'Here, storeman, put those to one side for me.' 14, 15 and 16 Platoon commanders follow the example set by Sergeant 'Paddy' Clarke from Accrington.

The gifts are then taken to the platoons. When the platoons fall in they are from twenty to thirty strong and there are two shirts, three pairs of socks and two handkerchiefs to be distributed. If Sergeant Smith of 16 were a Solomon he could not work the oracle without leaving about twenty men dissatisfied. Say he gave a shirt each to Roe and Robinson and a pair of socks each to Deardin, Turner and Jones, the remainder would 'crib' like hell. The Sergeant is a man of the world and evades the responsibility of issuing out the two shirts and three pairs of socks by asking who has got a pack of cards. He is offered about ten simultaneously. The cards are cut and the five highest cards take the gifts. It is the only way in which the problem could be solved and it obviates grousing.

20 October: Compass march from 8.00 until 11.00 pm.

21 October: The Middlesex concert party gave a performance at Battalion Headquarters from 7.00 until 10.00 pm – a good show.

22 October: The Commanding officer considers that we have atoned for the loss of the seven rifles which the Arabs 'pinched' on the line of march and graciously allows the Battalion to sleep in their tents tonight.[26]

23 October: Regimental Boxing Tournament from 7.00 to 11.00 pm – a good night's sport.

24 – 25 October: Battalion Sports.[27]

Beer Issue

26 October: Battalion cross country run.

Beer issues commenced today. Every man is allowed one bottle and pays one rupee for same. The issue takes place at 5.00 pm each evening. Major Bull of the Nagpur Rifles, our second in command and PRI [President of Regimental Institutes],[328] initiated the beer scheme. Without a doubt he wined and dined with some PRIs of the old Regular Army at some point in his past career, as every case contains forty-eight bottles and only cost 36 rupees. When this was brought to his notice he informed us that the extra 4 annas which were charged on every bottle was intended to form a sports fund and that we would have two days sports before we went up the line 'to be killed', and all the money would be distributed in cash prizes. We considered it a rather pessimistic explanation. What use is Rothschilds millions to a man if he is going to be killed?

I enquired in my tent who did 'not' drink beer. Four 'youngsters' informed me they were 'stonewall' teetotallers. I gave them one rupee each with instructions to parade at beer issue, draw their bottles of beer and bring them to the tent. The Company paraded at 5.00 pm. They got their bottles all right and were moving in the required direction with them when RSM Carrington shouted an order:

'No bottles to be taken away, every man must drink his beer here.'

I had the satisfaction of seeing the four bottles of beer, for which I paid, disappear down the throats of the four men who 'never drank' beer in their lives. They were very prompt in obeying that order and see the contents of the bottle off in what I considered excellent time for 'novices'. The remarks I made about [the] RSM I will omit from this chronicle of events. In any case, I had the satisfaction of knowing that I was not the only victim.

27 October: Divisional training, attacking flagged enemies, is a most provoking and exasperating method of training. Artillery formation (diamond), forming line, sectional rushes, covering fire, etc., etc., and when you are about to get the order to fix bayonets someone rides up with a band or armlet on his left arm and tells you that you have been wiped off the face of the earth and orders the Battalion to retire and do it all over again whilst the defenders are sitting on their backsides lazily waving their flags to and fro. This time we are not wiped out, so the flagged enemy slide away and take up positions about one mile on (in some cases two), and we repeat the performance.

28 – 31 October: [We hold training] attacks on the model San-i-Yat position before breakfast daily. Rifle and emergency ration inspections after breakfast, swimming or bathing parade at 5.00 pm every evening, followed by night attack [training].

The weather has gone cooler.

1 November: The Amara 'Perriot [Pierrot] Company' gave a splendid show at Brigade Headquarters from 7.00 pm until 10.00 pm.

2 November: Brigade attack [training] at dawn. Divisional sports in the afternoon.[29]

Porridge

3 November: I had occasion to report sick this morning, the second sick report since 1905. All through the night I suffered from intense pains in the stomach combined with vomiting. Our MO is a gentleman from beyond Hadrian's Wall and pins his faith in 'Porridge' (commonly known in the army as 'Scotchman's broth') to bring the war to a successful conclusion. By the way, I am a Regimental stretcher-bearer and on his staff.

When I told him what I was suffering from he asked me, 'Did I have any porridge for breakfast this morning?'

I truthfully stated that I had no breakfast.

'Well,' he queried, 'did you have any yesterday morning?'

I confessed that I had.

He remarked, 'Well a man that eats porridge cannot feel unwell. Orderly, give him a good dose of castor oil and see he drinks it. He has not got a temperature.'

I had to go on parade at 8.30 am [for] another attack on the Sannaiyat model position. During the course of the attack he made the weightiest men he came across be stretcher case casualties. I had to assist in carrying six such cases for over 1000 yards to the 1st aid post. I did not consider Captain McClelland played 'cricket' that day.

4 November: Usual routine. Still feeling bad.

5 November: Division parade at 7.30 pm General Maude pinned the VC [Victoria Cross] ribbon on the breasts of four recipients of that

196

honour in the Division. A few slight showers of rain fell today, the first since April.

6 – 8 November: Usual routine and attack practices.

9 November: Division parades at 6.00 pm, march out 6 miles, bivouac and attack the model entrenched Sannaiyat position at dawn. We all hope that our efforts will be made on some other part of the line that is new to us, as everyone shudders at the mention of Sannaiyat of awful and bloody memories.

10 November: Divisional Boxing commences at 7.00 pm and finishes by 11.30 pm.[30] General Keary (or du-Carey)[31] – I'm not quite sure about his name as there are quite a number of Generals seated at the ringside (we see them so often that we don't know their names) – made a speech in which he congratulated the competitors for their sportsmanlike display. He informed us that we were shortly to partake in sterner battles than we witnessed tonight, that we had withstood the hardest test soldiers can endure – heavy losses. In fact, he 'bummed' the Division up all round. He may be a sound strategist and a gallant soldier without a doubt, but he would make a damn poor politician. If he had to address his constituency without notes I'm afraid he would not gain many votes; he has not the oratorical gift.

If the gallant general was referring to the debacle at Sannaiyat on April 9 when the Divisional lines of attack were decimated by Turkish machine gun fire, and he is under the impression that the survivors would have confidence in the repetition of an attack over the same ghastly ground, he has misjudged human nature. The very mention of the name Sannaiyat freezes the blood in our veins. I hope the reader won't infer that I am a coward. Neither am I a brave man, but memories linger. General-du-Carey was perhaps an Oxford Blue and is probably a damn bad shot with a rifle, an indifferent bayonet fighter, and yet may be a good general.

In conclusion, if it is going to be Sannaiyat again, we're beaten before we deploy into line of attack.

A Race Meeting

11 November: A race meeting confined to military from 4.00 until 7.00 pm. I backed the Colonel's horse for a 'pauncher' (5 rupee note) and won 10 'rats' (rupees). Any person acquainted with eastern diplomacy should be aware of the fact that in Regimental gymkhanas east of Suez the Colonel is always allowed to win one race, even at the expense of noted jockeys 'pulling' their mounts. The Colonel's horse was nothing to boast about, a leggy, long-necked, short-headed brute. Well, he won, that's all that matters. Brigadier General O'Dowda also won a race. I'm not quite certain whether it was Lieutenant Douglas-Withers or Captain Peters that steered his mount to victory. I was too late to get a bet on as I was drinking the Colonel's health in the refreshment tent.

12 November: Gymkhana on the Polo ground from 4.00 until 6.30 pm.

13 November: Battalion concert at 8.00 pm. Box respirator drill during the morning.

14 – 19 November: Gas helmet or box respirator drill.[32]

20 November: Some of the Battalion are under the impression that the Turks are going to use gas against us. From my experience of the Turk he is a clean fighter and had he used gas on Gallipoli – well the survivors of that rash adventure would not be here to tell the tale He probably took pity upon us as he thought the poor devils are bad enough as they are, they're hanging on by their eyelashes.

21 – 23 November: Battalion training.

24 November: After a fatiguing morning loading and unloading refractory pack mules,[33] all of whom made desperate efforts to touch the sky with the hooves of their hind legs, 'Sig' Morton and I proceeded on Pass to Amara for the purpose of shopping. I encountered my old friend and comrade in arms Dick Spencer. Thirst is always prevalent, more or less, in the salubrious land of 'Sinbad the Sailor' and the 'Arabian Nights'. He failed to pass fit on medical inspection and was not going up the line after all; therefore, I suggested a drink to celebrate the occasion. I touchingly reminded him that it might be the last time we should meet on mother earth. He studied awhile before he sanctioned my suggestion and eventually led us to the GMPs quarters. They were under canvas in the compound of the old Turkish prison (very snug quarters indeed). An Arab coolie was requisitioned and in due course a case of beer made its appearance. After the fourth bottle and when indulging in that delightful topic, reminiscences of bygone and happier days, who should make his appearance but the Provost Corporal. He did not seem very pleased and I did not like his looks, and whispered my opinion to Dick, who seemed to concur, as he remarked – 'He is a bit of a . . . Ask him to have a drink'. Dick and I entreated. To this invitation the Corporal of Provosts dourly replied, 'I will have a mouthful'. Well, between mouthfuls he sang 'Annie Laurie,' followed by 'My Comrade of Many's a Hard-fought Field'. Dick regaled us with the 'Lassie frae Lancashire', and Morton followed up with a humorous song. I remember there was a Mr Ouster in it. To the best of my memory I think it was entitled 'Down on the Farm'. To cut a long story short, between elbow raising and singing, the shades of night fell and we were miles from camp with a hostile country to traverse. We made our adieus to our now jovial and lucky comrades, as they were at home.

Dick escorted us to the riverfront. We embarked on a *balaam* and were rowed to the home shore, a voice from the opposite bank shouted, 'God speed and safe home!' I presume it was our late comrade.

198

I remarked to Morton, 'We'll be lucky if we reach camp without being hamstrung by Arabs, and moreover, our line of direction is infested with strong points and lunettes which are occupied by Indian troops before dusk every evening. As a general rule they shoot first and challenge afterwards so let us keep on talking at the top of our voices so as they will recognize we are British'.

We proceeded about 1000 yards, when there was a sharp command. 'Halt! Who goes there?' followed instantly by the whiz of a bullet and the report of a rifle. The sentry was taking no risks; he challenged and fired simultaneously. We lay on the ground, shouting 'Friend!' at the top of our voices. 'Twas of no avail as the remainder of the post joined in the fusillade. When they had expended enough ammunition to wipe out a platoon, they ceased fire. Morton and I held a whispered confab, lying in the prone position, which resulted in a decision to retreat on Amara. We retired for about 30 yards at the crawl, then 'chanced our arm' in the erect position and eventually reached the river's bank without further sniping, crossed to the Amara shore and 'bedded down' for the night with a battery of artillery, who were billeted in a courtyard.

It is needless to add that our slumber was not reposeful under the conditions, as we had visions of a charge worded such as, 'WOAS, being absent from the Company lines from 'Retreat' until reporting to the company orderly sergeant at 6.30 am.'

25 November: With the first streak of dawn we shook ourselves and made for camp, after first each regaling ourselves with the juice contained in a tin of pineapple (a contrast to the previous evening). We arrived in camp at 6.20 am and learned with satisfaction that the previous night was a 'wet one' and no roll had been called by Sergeant C[larke]. The Sergeants had a 'do' in the mess. We were, however, reported absent from Reveille. We reported to the Company Sergeant Major's tent; he was hors-de-combat. The Company Quartermaster Sergeant demanded an explanation, which we truthfully gave. After giving us a 'severe telling' off, he let us 'away with it'.

Divisional night attack [training].[34]

26 – 29 November: Attack practices on entrenched positions.

A Case of Beer

The Officers and Sergeants are having a farewell 'bust-up' tonight. Morton, Paddy Maher (the CO's tailor), Brown (the Adjutant's servant) and I considered the ways and means of having a farewell 'bust up' as well (but in camp this time), as the Adjutant is going out sand grouse shooting at 3.00 pm and would not return until about 6.00 pm. 'Twas arranged that Brown would borrow the Adjutant's uniform and Sam Browne and act as an officer from 4.00 until 5.00 pm.

Brown had classical features, but there was a flaw in the scheme – Brown was a Cockney and dropped his 'haitches' lamentably and used such expressions as 'Gor blime' and 'Gor love a duck'. We coached him into repeating 'Top hole' and 'Jolly fine' for half an hour, and enjoined on him that he would only have to behave like an officer for the five minutes we would be in the Field Force Canteen at Amara, and to speak as little as possible to the canteen staff in case he made a 'bloomer'.

At 4.00 pm we set out from camp, Brown carrying a bundle. On the river's bank we hired a *balaam*. En voyage down river, Brown donned the Adjutant's uniform and became a full-blown Lieutenant in three minutes (rapid promotion!).

We arrived at Amara in due course and entered the FF [Field Force] Canteen. Brown ordered a case of beer and paid for same. The Canteen Sergeant asked no questions; in fact he was very respectful to Mr Brown, who in an authoritative tone of voice, ordered us to 'Come along, you men, and get a move on with this case of beer'. We transferred the case from the canteen to the *balaam* in record time, and embarked. We were thoroughly alarmed in case some officer of ours might come along and recognize Brown.

Brown once more became a private as we paddled up-stream. 400 yards before reaching the landing place used by the Brigade, we secured the case by log line, lowered it into the water on the riverbank and secured the log line to a tent peg. We drove the tent peg into the river's bank 18 inches under water. The site of the cache was marked by a solitary date palm, which grew on the bund or raised embankment. We viewed our handiwork and were satisfied no clues were left for the most critical eye to detect. We were to retrieve the case under cover of darkness and take it to an old dugout in the vicinity of our camp.

At 7.00 pm we rendezvoused underneath the solitary date palm and proceeded to retrieve the case of beer. Great was our dismay on discovering that case, log line and tent peg had disappeared. We suspected Maher for 'double-crossing' us, as there were no whales in the Tigris to gobble up cases of beer. Our suspicions did not prove correct, as later that night we were compelled to admit that we all suffered from a disastrous lack of knowledge re tidal rivers. The Tigris was a tidal river with a depth of from 6 to 8 feet between the ebb and flow. The tide went out in the evening about 5.30 pm and left our precious case high and dry to be annexed by the first eagle-eyed Arab boatman that poled or paddled by in his *balaam*. Well, we live and learn! The Officers and Sergeants had a very 'wet' night, and so would we, had it not been for 'Kismet'.

The majority of us have a rooted objection against going into action with

200

belts containing rupees, as the contents of the belts do not in all cases find their way to the deceased's next of kin. Accidents will occur. For instance, you take a trench and are counter-attacked and forced to retire, leaving your dead and wounded behind. John Turk and his Arab allies excel in the art of 'going through' the dead and wounded in record time. You cannot fight actions without casualties and yet all are optimists and expect to pull through, although 'Blighty ones' are very acceptable.

Quinn and the 'Jiniral'

It does not do in all cases to tell the truth and shame the Devil, or to all be George Washington. Here is an instance.

Whilst in Amara every man in the Division, no matter how employed, had to throw one hand grenade. Deadly instruments in defence and attack are those 'Mills' bombs, providing nervy persons are not allowed to handle them or if they are not used on each other in the confusion of a night attack.

Our Company cook, Michael Quinn by name, was exempt. In fact he was not allowed to look at a grenade. He was that intelligent that he was certain to blow himself up, which did not matter a great deal; it was the people who would go up with him that mattered.

He paid a visit to Amara one day and was pulled up by the Brigadier (O'Dowda). The Brigadier was a very inquisitive man [who] would pull any man up and ask him all kinds of unexpected questions. As a rule his victim was a person who knew damn all about semaphore (very few did anyway in those days). He pulled 'Ginger' Wilson, the cook, up one day and asked him 'how many teeth he had got?' Ginger made a guess and told the General that he had thirty-three. The General told him to report sick and get one extracted.

Everyone avoided the Brigadier whenever possible on account of his thirst for information, and only for 'Mick' was a 'bloomin' fool and was not gifted with powers of observation he would not have 'bumped' into him. When Mr Quinn came back from Amara he was boasting to everybody about the 'grate' talk he had with the 'Jiniral'. He was asked what sort of a 'Jiniral' was he? He replied that he was a tall thin raw-boned fellow and was 'ridin' a horse with a white stocking on his near fore. He was told it was O'Dowda he was 'yarnin' with.

'What was he talking to you about anyway, Mick?' Mick told us that he met the 'Jiniral' just outside the bridge before you go into Amara. He gave him a good 'chuck up' [salute] because he knew by all the red on his collar that he was a 'Big Bug'. The 'Jiniral' asked him, after he had pulled up his horse,

'Where are ye goin to my man?'

201

Quinn: 'Into Amara, Sorr.'

General: 'There is not much to see in Amara my man.'

Quinn: 'I am not going into see anything, Sorr, I'm only goin into the Post Office to send some money home to my mother, Sorr' (which was a damn lie, he went to Amara to buy drink if he could get it).

The 'Jiniral,' 'towl him he was a grate man and never to forget his parents.' The General asked, 'What engagement are ye on?'

Quinn: 'I joined up till it's all over, Sorr.'

The General: 'How long have you been in the country?'

Quinn: 'It's just 6 months yesterday since I put my foot in it.'

The General: 'Did you ever throw a grenade?'

Quinn 'You mane a bomb, Sorr?'

The General: 'Yes.'

Quinn: 'The devil a bomb ever I threw in my life, Sorr, an I would not know how to fire one, indeed, Sorr. I never feel safe when I'm within 50 mile w'them.'

The 'Jiniral' then bid him good day an' made for camp as if the Devil himself was after him.

Next day the parade was as strong as possible. The Colonel (Old Mac) wanted to know who was the man that told the General yesterday that he had never thrown a grenade and would run 50 miles from one? A certificate had been rendered to Brigade to the effect that every man in the Battalion had thrown a grenade. He could not believe that any man in his Regiment would run away from a grenade. He wound up by stating that he honestly believed that the General had mistaken the flash (the East Lancs wore a Red Diamond on each shoulder and on each side of the helmet; so there could be no mistaking that). He gave us the impression that the General was 'tight', although he did not say as much.

When we got dismissed we all gave Mr Quinn a dressing down for telling the 'Jiniral' that he never 'fired' a bomb and that it was a good job that Old Mac did not know it was him who told the 'Jiniral', for if he did he would make a mop of Mr Quinn and wipe Amara with him. Mick Quinn replied with, 'an what would I tell a lie to the Jiniral for? Wasn't I always towl to tell the truth an shame the Devil?'

So we all had to 'fire' another bomb through Mick Quinn telling the truth an' shaming the Devil.

Notes

1 Second-Lieutenant C.V. Thompson.

2 They were being exchanged for the captured British and Indian wounded of General Townshend's forces at Kut.

3 Turkish Minister for War.

4 'Shaikh Saad was now the advanced base of the Mesopotamian Expeditionary Force. Ammunition and stores of all kinds were accumulating there.' (Regt.Hist., p.335)

5 'Fresh draft . . . one officer (Second-Lieutenant C.V. Thompson) and nintey-four other ranks. These men are very much affected by climate and soon went sick in large numbers.' (6th Bn War Diary, 4 July 1916)

6 'Arab marauders were continuously active in the vicinity of our camps at night, as well as looting and attacking small or isolated parties whenever opportunity offered; . . . the greater part of the Cavalry Brigade had to be deployed in protective measures against them. But their depredations continued, causing us a good many casualties and losses and infinite trouble. The 17 mile line of communication from Shaikh Saad to Sinn was the area most affected; and it was not till September 1916, when the whole of this line was protected by wire entanglements and small posts, that the Arab depredations were really suppressed.' (*History of the War: Mesopotamia*, Vol 3, p.15)

7 'Average temperature 125 degrees Fahrenheit – Heat told very much on troops.' (6th Bn War Diary, 10–13 July 1916)

8 'A heavy dust storm, which started on the 19th and lasted forty-eight hours, stopped all training.' (Regt.Hist., p.336)

9 'Fire at the Brigade ammunition dump mentioned as being an incident in July.' (Ibid, p.336)

10 'New draft, Two officers from India, Second-Lieutenant O.W. Parkinson [would became E. Roe's platoon commander and an officer much respected by his men. With two others, Roe dedicated his diary to the memory of this officer] and H. Kelly with forty-eight other ranks join the battalion.' (6th Bn War Diary, 1 August 1916)

11 'Colonel McCormack had to go to hospital on 3 July. Three days later [6 July] Major R.M.M. Davy, from the 7th Battalion Gloucestershire Regiment, took over command.' (Regt. Hist., p.336)

12 'There was only one squadron at this time in Mesopotamia – No. 30 Squadron Royal Flying Corps. By the end of July 1916 the efficiency of the squadron had been much increased by the arrival of a number of additional and experienced pilots and of up-to-date aeroplanes. The efforts of the rehabilitated squadron were first directed to lowering the morale of the enemy's air service by air combats and bombing raids against aerodromes . . . it was not long before British supremacy in the air became thoroughly established.' (*History of the War: Mesopotamia*, Vol 3, p.23)

13 'During the month supplies of clothing and necessaries appreciably increased . . . Marked improvement in the health of the battalion . . . Special attention devoted throughout the month to the training of specialists. Every man practised throwing a grenade, which some 200 did satisfactorily before the end of the month. Lewis gun teams of one NCO and five men were trained . . . and made good progress.' (6th Bn War Diary, August 1916)

14 [The Battalion] 'took over garrison duties of 'New Fort post' from 6/King's Own Royal Regiment and kept same till end of month.' (Ibid, 13 August 1916)

15 'General Baratoff had recently been defeated and was withdrawing in north-west Persia.' (*History of the War: Mesopotamia*, Vol 3, p.27)

16 Romania went to war on 27 August 1916 following the Allied offering of an enlargement of Romania's territory at Austria's expense, particularly Transylvania where 3 million ethnic Romanians lived under Austro-Hungarian rule.

17 'Training continued and remainder of the battalion practised in bomb throwing and threw live bombs.' (6th Bn War Diary, 1 – 8 September 1916)

18 'Camp moved inside new perimeter with wire fences.' (Ibid, 9 September 1916)

19 'The march was done in short stages (10 – 11 miles) before the heat of the day.' (Regt. Hist., p.336)

20 'Seven rifles stolen – all in same night from camp.' (6th Bn War Diary, 28 September 1916)

21 'Abu Shitaib camp was a comfortable tented camp and two blankets per man were issued . . . . The whole 13th Division was to concentrate for intensive training.' (Regt. Hist., p.336)

22 'Private Fowler stabbed to death – presumably by Arab marauder – while on sentry duty at camp of Divisional train. Buried in Amara with military honours.' (6th Bn War Diary, 1 – 2 October 1916, 2.00 –3.00 am)

23 'Training began on 2 October, exercises in open warfare by day and night being carried out; and, a model of the ill-famed Sannaiyat position having been constructed, there was practice in trench-to-trench attacks.' (Regt. Hist., p.336)

24 'Inoculated with TAB at 40th Field Ambulance.' (6th Bn War Diary, 7 October 1916)

25 'Draft of three officers from 10th Battalion and seventy other ranks from 3rd Battalion joined.' (Ibid, 12 October 1916)

26 'Battalion started sleeping in tents instead of in the open. Rifles secured by means of pits in each tent.' (Ibid, 21 October 1916)

27 'On the evening of 25 October the battalion sports were held.' (Regt. Hist., p.336)

28 He is President of a welfare fund for the soldiers.

29 'In the Divisional sports the Battalion was fairly successful – winning the Obstacle Race, and gaining second place in Diving and third in Relay Swimming' (6th Bn War Diary, General – November 1916)

30 'An East Lancashire lad was the runner-up in the light weight boxing competition.' (Regt. Hist., p.336)

31 Major-General H. d'U. Keary of the 3rd (Lahore) Division

32 'All officers and NCOs in battalion attend lectures on protection against gas attacks and subsequently instruction given to the battalion in the care and use of gas helmets and goggles' (6th Bn War Diary, 14 – 16 November 1916). The box respirator was introduced in late 1916. It was a rubberized mask with a long tube attached to a filtration unit carried in a haversack.

33 'These were exercises of first line transport on the move.' (6th Bn War Diary, General – November 1916)

34 'Training regularly carried out especially as regards night operations.' (Ibid, General – November 1916)

XV

The Offensive Resumes

(30 November 1916 – 17 February 1917)

Stand to – The Lewis Gun – Move up River – Kut Sighted – The Astrologer's Star – 1917 – Made Lance Corporal – Stretcher-Bearers – Vigilance – Turkish Snipers – Aerial Combat – Attack on the Hai – An Officer and a Gentleman – Burial of a Bomber– Towards the Dahra Bend

Stand to

30 November: The 39 and 40 Brigades struck camp and marched upriver at 5.00 pm. The 6/South Lancashires of my Brigade [38] embark on a river steamer and proceed upstream.[1]

1 – 2 December: Battalion carried out field firing practices during the past two days.

3 December: King's Own of my Brigade strike camp and embark at 5.00 pm this evening. A river steamer, with one large barge lashed to port and one to starboard, is allotted to each unit.[2]

4 December: Life has been a mild form of torture in this camp. Rest is rare and I have heard men remark, 'I envy the inmates of Dartmoor and Princetown'. Sloping and presenting arms are necessary for ceremonial purposes in peacetime but are out of place in the field. All are anxious to get in action again, as this incessant drill and bullying breaks the men's spirit and tends to quench what sparks of enthusiasm that remains.

Nobody worries about our rations or how they are cooked, or has a look around at breakfast and dinner. One does get fed up with those incessant 'bully' and watery mutton stews that taste and smell like well boiled Billy-goat. Tom Tickler's Plum and Apple Jam is forever on the menu. We are almost convinced the raspberries, strawberries, gooseberries and black currants have gone on strike since the war started.

5 December: The Regiment is 'standing to', awaiting orders. Our well beloved 'Mutty' has not made an appearance this morning. We anxiously enquired as to his whereabouts and learned with dismay that he had folded

205

his tent and stole away in the night. In other words, he went down the line sick. We expected great things of him when he led us into action.

'Long' Wilson, who is employed in the Battalion Orderly Room (a pretty safe billet), reported sick this morning, evidently with a view to a trip to Basrah or India. As he did not eat porridge, 'Jock' gave him a still dose of castor oil. He seemed deeply offended and informed us that the medical services of the Army in 'Mess-pot', as at present provided for, are an absurdity. Quite a few believed, including himself, that doctors are a danger to the Army and that illness delivers a man, bound hand and foot, into the hands of a profession that is deeply to be distrusted. He wound up by stating that doctors were simply the descendants of the tribal medical man.

The Lewis Gun

6 December: Still 'standing to'. During our stay in Amara we were armed with a new weapon called the Lewis gun, or automatic rifle.[3] It is something in the nature of a toy for young officers to play about with. We have no faith in it.[4] It takes about six men, to the best of my knowledge, to each gun.[5] I think there are eight guns to each battalion.[6] Its traversing powers are practically nil and stoppages in the desert-like country are legion. Why not arm us with two machine guns per battalion and dump these toys.[7] Well we will soon see their utility, or otherwise, in the next push.

Move up River

7 December: Strike camp at 6.00 am and embark on the river steamer *P50* at 11.00 am;[8] steam off at 2.00 pm and anchor for the night at 9.00 pm. A guard is mounted on the riverbank and the steamer and barges are strongly guarded. This precaution is necessary as the Arabs are very daring and have been known to raid convoys in the past in the hopes of securing arms or any other kind of loot.

8 December: Steam up at 4.00 am. Steam past Ali Gharbi at 9.00 am; it is pretty cold and has been raining all day. Anchor at Shaikh Saad at 3.00 pm, [with the] steamer unloaded and camp pitched by 5.00 pm. Still raining with camp knee deep in mud.

9 December: Battalion shifting firewood from one dump to another until 12 noon and on ordnance fatigue in the afternoon. Everyone 'grousing' like . . .

10 December: Strike camp at 6.00 am, move off at 7.00 am, and arrive at Twin Canals camp at noon.[9] Why name the camp Twin Canals? He must be a humourist, whoever he was that gave it a name, as all the water observable is contained in one tiny stream – Well, you could just about wet your tooth-brush in it.

Troops in this neighbourhood are regularly strafed by a bomb-dropping Taube aeroplane.

11 December: General inspection at 9.30 am. We are informed that Prime Minister Asquith has resigned and that the opportunist Lloyd George has accepted office.[10] Will it mean a change from the 'wait and see' policy?

12 December: Battalion paraded at 6.30 pm. Move off at 7.00 pm and arrive at Es-Sin ridge [Es Sinn] by midnight and bivouac.[11]

13 December: Our artillery and river armament are heavily bombarding the Turkish position at Sannaiyat, which is roughly 4 miles in our rear and on the opposite bank of the river (the left). The 13th Division are going to operate on the right bank.

Outposts, piquets and an aeroplane guard have been posted or mounted.

The RC padre paid us a visit this evening and gave all the RCs general absolution. He had not time to hear confessions, for which I was extremely thankful. I made another *maund* of good resolutions, which, if I pull through, I don't suppose I will ever fulfil.

The Battalion moves out of bivouac at 6.30 pm and arrive at rendezvous at 9.20pm.[12] Rum issue at 11.00 pm. Owing to darkness and a certain amount of confusion, a good many issues went astray! We are going to attack at dawn.

14 December: Rouse at 2.00 am. Dump packs by Companies. Move off at 3.00 am and Brigade opens out for attack at 5.30 am. Objective captured without opposition. Division digs in roughly south east of Kut-al-Amara.[13]

Kut Sighted

15 December: Stand to arms at 5.00 am. Move off in artillery formation at 9.00 am. My regiment are in reserves.

We gaze upon Kut for the first time. It is about 4 miles away on our right front. It is a dilapidated looking village. The northeastern end of the village is partially hedged in by a grove of date palms. The mosque with minaret seems to be the only structure not damaged.

Fighting has commenced on our front and right flank. The Turkish artillery is throwing heavy and light 'stuff' at our advancing lines. The Regiment halts and lies down in artillery formation at 10.00 am and watch the attack. Heavy rifle and machine gun fire is going on along our front. Quite a number of Turkish prisoners are coming down, and also some wounded of ours. The Turkish gunners sent us over a salvo – just to show we were not forgotten. No one was injured.

At 7.00 pm we advance and dig in with the firing line.[14]

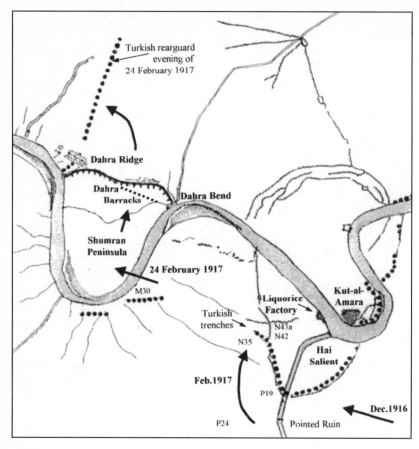

9. Operations on the Tigris from December 1916 to 25 February 1917

16 December: Under orders to move at any moment. The artillery of both sides pretty active this morning. It would seem that our flank attack took the Turks completely by surprise as we have obtained a firm footing in the Muhammad Abdul Hasan loop.

At 5.00 pm we move down to our left and take over the position held by the Worcesters,[15] who had suffered considerably from enemies' shellfire yesterday.

17 December: Digging day and night to improve our position.[16]

18 December: Battalion moved to a new position on our right. Consolidating all day, water very scarce; one pint has to last a man twenty-four hours. Our salty 'Bully' beef ration, in most cases, is thrown away owing to the thirst it fosters.

208

19 December: The enemy's trenches 1000 yards away heavily shelled by our artillery.

The Astrologer's Star

20 December: Three stretcher-bearers and I were as near shot or captured last night as damn it. We were returning from the Clearing Station after handing over a casualty. The Clearing Station, or Field Ambulance, is just over a mile from the firing line and is easily distinguished owing to a red light suspended from a pole. The difficulty lies in returning from the Clearing Station on a dark night, as the country is as flat as a billiard table and there are no prominent objects or lights to guide a person or party.

We knew by the distance we traversed that we should have reached our trench line. We halted. I wanted to go one way, LCpl. Forbes another, whilst 'Buster' Brown suggested going back to the Field Ambulance and waiting whilst dawn broke, a sensible idea but it was not carried. Friend Jacques, who by the way is a stretcher-bearer, had not said a word so far. He now declared that we were all wrong and that we were going in the right direction as he had taken his bearings before leaving the first aid post and that he was marching on the same star. He exhorted us to carry on. He being the oldest soldier, we followed, he leading the band. We kept on and on. Well, I thought, we should be half way to Baghdad by now.

Suddenly there was a hubbub in front; voices in a strange language and a burst of rifle fire. We 'flopped' on our bellies. The handles of the stretcher were shattered by a lucky bullet. We turned about on our bellies and crawled for about 50 yards. The Turks were still blazing away. Well, one cannot crawl forever, so we 'chanced it' in Indian file towards our own lines. The position was just as bad as ever as our own patrols and sentries would open fire on us under the impression we were Turks. Fortunately we got through the gap in the line, reached the Field Ambulance, where we were regaled with hot tea, and lay down until dawn when we rejoined in safety. Our blundering into the Turkish line was due to our own trench line not being continuous. There were gaps between units, we explained to the MO about Jacques' star. He laughed, and ever afterwards addressed Jacques as 'My dear Astrologer'.

21 December: A squadron of nine of our planes flew over the Turkish lines this morning. They were heavily fired upon, but succeeded in destroying the Turkish bridge of boats at Bagdalia [Bughaila].[17]

We have not had a shave for the past ten days and all are sporting beards, some in a greater, and others in a lesser degree.

The Turks are acting like gentlemen, as up to the present they have not shelled us. They content themselves by searching for our batteries.

22 December: Spasmodic bombardments by our artillery all day.

24 December: My Company ['D'] retires to the transport lines before dawn for the purpose of having a bath and general clean up. Return to trenches under cover of darkness.

25 December: Christmas day, with a rum issue. Brigadier General O'Dowda visits the firing line at 10.00 am and wishes us all sorts of joy, etc., etc. If we had a sufficiency of drinking water we would not mind.[18]

26 December: Raining all day. General 'Mud' has taken command of all operations.

27 – 28 December: Wallowing in mud and living on air.

29 – 31 December: The Brigade is entrenched on the site of a marsh. It has been raining continuously since the 26th and our position has been turned into a lake. Another two days rain and we will be cut off from our rear. Every night, from dusk until dawn, every man is working like a Trojan throwing up a bund or embankment in rear of our trench line so as we will not be flooded out.[19] I'm glad I learned to swim.

On the 30th the Turks noticed the new earth line in our rear, and now they keep up a continuous rifle and artillery fire from dusk until dawn on the working parties. The fire cannot be called accurate; nevertheless it causes quite a number of casualties.

They can only get up half rations – so they tell us – but the deficiencies are never made good.[20] We are well aware that the government allowance is ample, we are also aware that a certain amount of pilfering goes on by men in positions of trust. I truthfully state that we are half starved and over-worked. We dare not smoke owing to hunger and weakness and we know the results of making complaints . . .

1917

1 January 1917: Happy New Year to all. Rumours of a peace conference.[21]

2 – 3 January: Still more rain and cold winds.

4 January: My Company ['D'] relieved for twelve hours; out at dawn and back at dusk.

5 – 6 January: Usual routine with iron rations and rifle inspection.

7 January: Turkish lines on our right heavily bombarded.

8 January: Lively artillery actions all day. Stage an attack in the evening. It was a sham attack. We marched from left to right with rifles at the high port so as the Turks can see our bayonets and think we are going over. The ruse is to draw their fire.[22]

At midnight the trenches are fully manned and every NCO and man, stretcher-bearers included, fire 120 rounds in the direction of the Turkish trenches. We seem to have more ammunition than sense.

9 January: At 6.00 am the Brigade opens rapid fire on the Turkish trenches. On our right the 3rd Division have been attacking since dawn.[23] We cannot see anything of the fighting due to a blanket of fog. I hear that the attack has been successful, but we are told that the Manchesters lost heavily.

10 January: Our artillery shelled the Turks heavily all day. The Turks did not retaliate.

11 January: Company out for a day's rest. Those so called rests are amusing affairs, as a rest means nothing less than a series of inspections which last from the time you reach the transport lines until you fall in to march back to the trenches. We are digging a new firing line 400 yards in front of our present line, by night of course. This business is called sapping forward, and a costly affair it is proving.[24]

12 January: 'J' Battery moves to a new position on our right. We are close to the Tigris and opposite the village of Kut. I hope it will prove as quiet a position as the one we vacated.

13 January: Our new position is not as quiet as our old one. The Turks shelled us all day with light field guns, which fire a high velocity shell dubbed by the troops, or nicknamed, 'whiz bangs'. We had a few casualties.

14 January: The Battalion lost heavily in digging a forward line last night. Major Bull killed.[25] We were only 400 yards from the Turkish front line and the moon was at its full. The stretcher-bearers, of whom I am in charge, had a strenuous time. Why await a full moon before digging approach or forward lines? The Turkish river monitors gave us a hot hour this evening with their heavy calibre guns. Their ranging [shots] would make our navy men weep tears of blood.

Made Lance Corporal

15 January: I got the lance stripe, or 'dogs leg', this morning. I was 'sent for' to Mr Varvil's[26] dugout at 8.00 am. He said, 'Roe I am going to recommend you for the Lance stripe'.

I replied, 'Sir, I don't want a stripe, I have carried on for twelve years without the aid of tapes and I'm sure I can carry on for the remainder without them, and besides, I'm not ambitious.'

He replied, 'Oh! Damn it, it's not what you want or don't want, and don't talk to me about ambitions. The London Rifle Brigade in 1914 died as privates when they could have rendered better service to their country as officers.'

'Very true, Sir,' I replied, 'I was in the trenches with the Queen's Westminsters, but officers were not as scarce then as now, Sir, and I cannot speak three languages or do algebra and graphs like the Queen's.'

He replied, 'That's neither here nor there.' He then quoted Napoleon as having said that a Field Marshal's baton reposed in every private's haversack.

211

'Well, Sir,' I replied, 'I am quite convinced that the proverbial Field Marshal's baton will never repose for the infinitesimal fraction of a second in mine.'

'Perhaps you're frightened to take responsibility or lead a section?' he remarked.

'Well, if you put it in that light sir,' I replied, 'you can "lob" me in for it right away.'

He told me to fall out, and if I could not find a tape to 'shove' one on with a blue or black tape.

On returning to the stretcher-bearer's lair I found three men cleaning their rifles, as rifle inspection was on in ten minutes time. Friend Jacques was wrapped up in peaceful slumber. I shook him up and told him to 'get a wriggle on' and get his rifle cleaned. I heard him remark to a very young soldier, 'Well, Jim those new made Lance Jacks haven't half got some edge on'. I sternly rebuked him and reminded him that if I ever heard him ridiculing his superior officer again I would place him before the Company Commander. Dear reader, I hope that you will not assume that I bore malice or hiatus, in other words that I was trying to 'get my own back' on Jacques over the egg 'stunt' at Basrah. Nothing of the kind; I was simply enforcing discipline.

16 January: A Turkish or German airman (I suppose he was German) bombed our trenches at 3.00 pm. I have had no sleep for the past four days and nights as stretcher-bearers were up to their necks in it.

Stretcher-Bearers

The laws of the Hague Convention (re) stretcher-bearers are a complete farce as they are grossly ignored. My stretcher-bearers and I wear the brassard of mercy and aid to wounded, friend and foe alike. We are not supposed to be armed; yet we are fully equipped. An extra two bandoliers of ammo is worn around the neck as an extra adornment. We also carry two bombs. If the Turks attacked and carried our first line I would expect to get shot out of hand, as I would be expected to pump lead into the Turks whilst defending the trench. Tomorrow or next day I might have to go out into no-man's-land (had we attacked and were repulsed) to collect our wounded and expect the Turks not to fire on my stretcher-bearers owing to the brassards we wear. Were I not a stretcher-bearer and we attacked the Turks, and I saw one of their stretcher-bearers with a rifle in his hand, I would shoot or bayonet him, as it is a flagrant abuse of the laws laid down by the Hague Convention for RAMC or stretcher-bearers to be in possession of arms. I brought this point before the Medical Officer and he simply replied, 'You're in a hostile country and it's an order'.

212

Another point is when any casualties occur in a digging party or recon- noitring patrol, or patrols at night in no-man's-land, the stretcher-bearers have got to go out and find him, even in the Stygian darkness. The stretcher- bearers file out through a gap in the wire. I pass the word down right and left to the sentries, 'Stretcher-bearers going out; pass the word along the line from right to left or from left to right'. Of course, one would naturally expect not to be fired on coming in. You have always got to take your chance from enemies' bullets. You find your man, search for his rifle and equipment (if he has discarded both), put them on the stretcher and make for your own lines. When you get to within 30 yards of your own barbed wire a fusillade is opened on the unfortunate stretcher-bearers. You lie down and shout, 'For Christ's sake, stop firing, it is a stretcher party,' and it is not safe to arise until you get an assurance from the gentlemen behind the parapet. When you arrive at the dugout, or first aid post, the first question you are asked is, 'Have you got his rifle and equipment?' It does not matter about the man so much.

When under fire from our own lines, I often remarked, 'What damn bad shooting, I'm not surprised at the war lasting over two years.' What happens is that you order the sentries on your right and left to pass the word along. It may be passed along two or three bays and then dies a natural death, or if reaches the end of the line, it is in this mutilated condition: 'Pass the word along, get ready to move out'.

At Amara we were accustomed to one parade per week. Communication or passing of messages: You get thirty men in line at 3 paces interval. You give a message to the right hand man such as, 'Dirty and torn greybacks will not be worn on parade'. Ask the left hand man what message he received, 'Dirty and torn greybacks will be worn on all parades' As at Amara, so [it is] in the firing line.

17 January: Turkish monitor delivers the mail. No casualties.

Vigilance

A vigilance 'stunt' has come into operation, which if annoying is also amusing. From dusk until dawn all persons walking down communication trenches or main trench lines have got to be 'tackled' and interrogated. At 7.00 pm I am going down to the dressing station. Someone is coming in the opposite direction. A pair of hands grips me by the throat, almost stran- gling me.

'Who are you?'

'Lance Corporal so and so, and who are you?'

'Captain so and so'.

I thought, 'Right, I'll make sure and tackle first next time.'

Coming back from the first aid post I met a shadowy form and grabbed first: 'Who are you?'

'And who the devil are you?'

I knew I'd captured an officer so I replied, 'Lance Corporal so and so, 'D' Company, and who are you?'

'I'm your Company Commander, damn you.'

'Oh sorry, Sir, but you know the orders.'

This form of amusement, or rather annoyance, goes on all night long. It is not very nice if you're in a bad temper and wet through to be pounced upon and almost strangled by an unseen antagonist. We are told that this form of rugby tackle (although rather high) is absolutely essential as the 'Brass hats' have reason to believe that English-speaking Germans or Turks, dressed up in our uniform, get through on dark nights and stroll about the trenches, no notice being taken of them so long as they are in our uniform, and get away with a lot of vital information.

We are also requested, when out in front at night, if we trip over any ground wires to follow them to our trench line, report same and hang on to the wire until an Engineer officer arrives, as the Turks are supposed to be tapping in or using an instrument called a Dictaphone (I think that is the correct name).

Turkish Snipers

18 January: A fairly quiet day, we have been incessantly worried since December 17 by those infernal Turkish snipers, who keep pegging away all day long. Their modus operandi is: crawl out at night and dig a hole that they can just stand up in, taking care to scatter the fresh earth over a considerable area around the pit to ensure that no-man's-land appears just as usual next morning. He transplants a few bits of brushwood in front of his lair to give a natural appearance, [then] comes out the following morning before dawn and enjoys both a safe and enjoyable day.

19 - 21 January: Artilleries of both sides active during the past three days. I have seen some awful wounds inflicted by Arab bullets. The bullet weighs about 3 ounces and is not nickelled, and most probably criss-crossed in the nose by a knife. When it finds contact it spreads. If you get one in the legs or arms it means amputation, that is if you live long enough. One in the body implies that you fade away quickly; you wont bother or have time to send a billet-doux to your best girl. To gaze on a wound caused by one of these bullets, you would gain the impression that the enemy had run out of ammunition and were using up old and battered 'bully beef' and jam tins.

22 January: My Companies' day out of the trenches for a rest – as you were – I mean for inspections.

23 January: Turkish positions heavily bombarded by our artillery during the day.

Aerial Combat

During the morning we witnessed a thrilling aerial combat. Three of our aeroplanes were returning from a reconnaissance of the Turkish lines when they encountered a single Turkish plane returning from performing a similar duty over ours. They joined in combat; we can plainly hear the cackle of machine guns. Mr Turk or German was always on top of our planes. First one of ours limped for home with a smoking fuselage. The other two stuck to their guns but it was useless as the Taube could climb ten feet to our one and almost vertical at that. The second victim limped away, very wobbly, whilst the third abandoned the combat. The audacious Turk chased him right over our lines both flying very low. The throbbing of their engines almost deafened us. We could not open fire as the Turk's nose was almost on our fellow's tail and his exhaust was leaving a trail. Our man must have crashed or made a forced landing. The Taube returned and performed a series of daring evolutions over our lines for our edification and by way of celebrating his victory for fifteen minutes, despite the hail of shrapnel from field and anti-aircraft guns, which hail he seemed to ignore. When quite satisfied with his exhibition, he wound up by banking, and side-slipping, turning his plane's nose for home. A humiliating exhibition in so far as we were concerned. Our men are superior to the Turk, but for Christ's sake give them planes, not box kites.[27]

24 January: Quiet.

Attack on the Hai

25 January: The 39 Brigade are going to attack at 10.30 am this morning. Our artillery commenced the bombardment at 9.30 am. This attack took place on our left flank. At 10.30 am we watched the first line go over and disappear in the smoke clouds caused by our shells. I saw over twenty men fall from Turkish rifle and machine gun fire. They took the first and second lines, but before they had time to consolidate the Turks counter-attacked with great determination through the heavy barrage put down by our artillery and recovered the two lines of trenches, when the Warwicks advanced and drove the Turks out of the position.[28] At 5.00 pm our gunners opened up again on the Turks who were concentrating for another counter-attack, which however did not materialize.

The Turkish trenches are narrow and deep; Life Guards could stand up in them comfortably and not be exposed. The object I suppose is to lessen the effect of shellfire, particularly high explosive. I have never seen many casualties inflicted by shrapnel if one is under any kind of cover. The Turks cut footholds in the face of the trench to suit their own height.

26 January: The 14th Division attacked on the left bank of the Shatt-al-Hai and gained their objective.

27 January: Enemies' positions heavily shelled all day by our artillery. More shells have been expended since 15 December 1916, than rounds of .303 inch ball. A lot of ground has been gained and many lives saved thanks to plenty of artillery support.

28 January: At 1.00 am this morning the North Lancs and King's Own of my Brigade[29] walked over and took two lines of trenches without opposition, the enemy having retired to his main position on the left bank of the river (Shatt-al-Hai).[30]

29 January: Turkish one gun battery in action today. A large calibre gun that fires a shell, which is not quite so big as the German 'Jack Johnson'. Fortunately, accuracy is not in its gunners' dictionary.

30 January: Enemies' guns gave us a severe 'strafing' this morning. Quiet for the remainder of the day.

31 January: Enemies' works shelled at intervals during the day.

1 February: The 14th Division attacked at noon after a hurricane bombardment by our guns. The object of this attack was to drive the Turks who were still holding out across the Shatt-al-Hai. The Turks were driven into the river and fought up to their waists in water. The Istanbul Guards counter-attacked, recovered some of the lost ground and claim to have captured two automatic rifles (i.e. Lewis Guns).[31]

The 14th are a mixed Division, as British and Indian units are brigaded together[32]. It is a common belief amongst us that the Mohammedan soldiers do not like to fight against their co-religionists, the Turks.

An Officer and a Gentleman

My platoon officer, Mr Parkinson,[33] got hit in the stomach by a stray bullet as we were watching the attack. He expired almost immediately. We, of his platoon, were very sorry to lose him, as he was an officer and a gentleman. Before he would sit down in his dugout to eat his own miserable breakfast he would ensure that every man in his platoon had drawn his rations and was satisfied with them – such as they were. He was strict but just and reminded me of the old type of Regimental officer. As a rule the good are snatched away and the bad left with us. Had he been an unpopular officer (instead of having passed through Sandhurst one would imagine that certain young officers had passed through hell or bedlam, which is 7 miles below hell, before being posted to our Battalion), he could have walked through belts and belts of machine gun bullets and yet come back unscathed to worry us to death. Well, such is fate.

Burial of a Bomber

On the afternoon of 31 January two of our bombers were detonating bombs[34] in a dugout when a bomb went off. On a couple of men rushing into the dugout to ascertain the cause of the explosion they found one man in bits and the other slightly wounded.

As NCO in charge of stretcher-bearers, I had to dig the grave of the deceased some distance in rear of our trench line and await the arrival of the Padre (Church of England) to conduct the burial service. The Padre lost his direction and did not turn up. My stretcher-bearer and I had to take cover about five times during the night in the grave we had already dug owing to repeated bursts of long range Turkish machine gun fire. We buried him before dawn and I stuck a wooden cross, made from a bit of biscuit box, at the head of his grave. On the night of 1 February the Padre arrived after dusk to conduct the burial service. On proceeding to what I thought was the exact spot where I buried the man imagine my dismay when I found that someone had 'pinched' the wooden cross with a view to boiling a mess-tin of tea (wood was worth its weight in gold). We dare not use an electric torch, so I groped around on my hands and knees. I found contact with several mounds, which marked the sight of 'bully beef' and jam tins, which had lost their utility. I knew I was close to the site of the grave and yet could not find it. The Padre was getting impatient and we could not remain out all night, so I said, 'Here it is, Sir'. As I mentally argued, the prayers are intended for him whether we are at his graveside or not. The Padre donned his cassock and recited the Church of England burial service from memory. I, being a Roman Catholic and not acquainted with the service, did not know when to respond with Amen. Well to make sure, every time the clergyman paused I said 'Amen'. The service closed just as the Turkish machine gunners got 'rattled'.

We have had our Company cooks in the trenches for the past month. They cook in a dugout in rear of the lunette or strongpoint. Porridge is the main item on the menu for breakfast, a camp kettle full between twenty men. It runs a mess tin lid full for each NCO and man. There is a regular 'scrum down' for porridge. I observed four men in my platoon that in the piping days of peace turned their noses up at porridge. When seated at the breakfast table in Cape Town I would ask the orderly man to pass down a plate of porridge and the said men would sneeringly remark, 'Oh "Jock" Roe wants his "Scotchman's broth",' and in a spirit of sarcasm the full ration tin would be placed on the table before me. I gently reminded them of their hatred of

217

'Scotchman's broth' in pre-war days and that the war must have killed their prejudices and changed their palates.

At 8.00 pm my Brigade is relieved by Indian troops. [We] march back 5 miles and bivouac for the night.[35]

2 February: Weather getting warmer.

Towards the Dahra Bend

3 February: Brigade moves off at 2.00 am, cross the river Hai, march eight miles and take up position on the left rear of the 14th Division who are attacking again today.[36] We are here in case the Turkish Commander attempts to outflank the 14th Division.[37] At 5.00 pm we move two miles to our right and bivouac for the night.

4 February: Rouse at 5.00 am, move off at 6.00 am [and] bivouac at 7.00 am. The Battalion parades at 5.00 pm, marches to the firing line and relieves the Buffs.[38] My Brigade is relieving a Brigade of the 14th Division.

5 February: Daylight reveals every shell crater and disused trench filled with Turkish dead. The stench is unbearable. Even as one walks along the trench, legs and arms protrude from the sides and a springy feeling underneath reveals the fact that we are walking on corpses which are unexposed to the gaze, but not to the nostrils, owing to a thin covering veil of mother earth.

The effect of our trench mortars is in deadly evidence here and a carrion-like smell prevails all over our new position. We have twenty guns to the enemies' one and are full of confidence.

At 8.00 pm a digging party composed of Welsh pioneers and some of my unit went out into no-man's-land to dig a bombing sap. A digging party is always protected by a covering party. Both jobs are dangerous, the covering party even more so than the working party, and the Turks were infernally waspish.

Some of the digging party lost their heads, their own lives and their comrades' lives as well, by imagining they saw the Turks advancing and shouted out, 'The Turks are coming!' This caused a panic amongst the digging and covering parties and men of both parties abruptly retired on their forward line.

The Turks heard the row and imagined that we were making an attack upon them, with the result that they opened fire with rifles and machine guns and lobbed their cricket ball bombs over. We on our part thought the Turks were coming over and replied in a similar manner. Thus the remains, or what remained of the working and covering parties who stuck to their guns in no-man's-land, were decimated between two fires. The situation was critical.

Our commanding officer, Captain Townend [G.R. Treadwell], went out into no-man's-land to see for himself what was happening, and got killed (so I have been told). In twenty minutes order was restored from absolute panic. We suffered heavily, losing forty men killed and wounded, thanks to some idiot or idiots who imagined that they saw Turks walking through our armed covering party. A couple of nervous or cowardly men can stampede a whole company on a delicate night operation of such a nature.

My stretcher-bearers and I had an awful four hours work getting the wounded in to the dressing station. When they received first aid we had to carry them over a mile to the Field Ambulance over ground seared by trenches and pock-marked by shell craters. The dead we left as they fell or lay. We had no time for the dead; it took us all our time to save the living.

6 February: Artilleries of both sides active. A bombing 'stunt' on a small scale took place at 10.00 am this morning.

Our medical officer, Captain Maclellan [Macallan], would insist on assuming the role of spectator. Both Sergeant Hayes and I repeatedly implored him to absent himself from such operations, as MOs are pretty hard to come by. He was obstinate and got one through the head. 'Smudger' and I had to carry him to the Field Ambulance over open ground. The Turks potted at us delightfully. We had to run about 20 yards and when the fire became too hot throw ourselves on the ground, arise, double another 20 yards and so on until we got out of range. It would have been more merciful to let him die in peace in the MO's dugout. He expired one hour after reaching the Field Ambulance. His case was hopeless.

Two Lieutenants met their fate in a similar manner by snipers.[39]

We are steadily bombing the Turks out of their strong points; bloody work, and the ill-clad, bootless, emaciated Turks are putting up a desperate resistance. The 'suicide club' (bombers) are fairly 'going through it'.[40] Mr Thompson, the Bombing Officer, got 'seen off' today.

7 February: Fairly quiet with few casualties.

8 February: Enemies' artillery 'strafed' us for an hour with high explosive this morning. This is the bitterest close quarter fighting I've yet seen. Every inch of ground is disputed by bomb and bayonet.

Two weak willed men who were unable to stand the strain shot themselves through the hearts of their left hands this morning. They were lacking in foresight, as they did not use a folded sandbag or a first aid dressing over the muzzles of the rifles, with the result that all around their wounds the flesh was badly scorched with cordite. This gave the 'show away'. The empty cases were also found in the chambers of their rifles. Owing to shock they failed to unload.

Blowing trigger fingers and big toes off is getting 'played out'. Those wounds were inflicted with a view to getting away from the firing line. Well and good if one has the nerve and the oracle works. If found out – well!

9 February: Regiment withdrawn to reserve position at 9.00 am.[41] The King's Own and South Lancashires relieve us and are going to attack at 10.30 am. The attack is all over by 11.00 am and all objectives gained.[42]

10 February: Early this morning the Liquorice factory, or what was left of it, fell to our troops.[43] It played a prominent part in the defence of Kut.[44]

11 February: Regiment move up to position N35.[45] Heavy rain all night.

12 February: 14th Division attack on our front at 4.00 pm. The Dogras were almost wiped out by enemy's machine gun and rifle fire.[46] When the European officers of this battalion got shot down in the open, the Dogras had not the initiative to press home the attack. Instead they 'bunched' in the open and the Turks shot them down at leisure. They eventually succeeded, thanks to a platoon of the North Lancs. I will not comment any further on this attack. I can just picture what a native unit would be like without white officers to lead them.

13 February: Slow continuous fire kept up by our artillery all day. Turkish reply from left bank of Tigris [was] feeble.

14 February: Great artillery action all day.

The CO's batman and cook are eagerly sought after by certain blind strategists in order to find out, what's the next move? Well – one would not need to be a profound student of military strategy, nor yet a Hilaire Belloc, a Colonel Repington or Maurice to know what the next move is.

We have attacked the Turkish right flank and have almost succeeded in driving him across the Tigris. When he is cleared off the right bank of the river the next operation should be the forcing of the passage of the Tigris which, if successful, places two Divisions in his rear and his lines of communications are cut. Therefore Kut must fall automatically. Mr Turk must get out and be very quick about it or he will share Townshend's fate.

Therefore there is not the slightest occasion to pamper the CO's batman or the Adjutant's servant with cigarettes in order to glean a little forward information, use common sense. Both the above-mentioned gentlemen imagine they are very important personages and have at times been known to evolve a strategy of their own for their mutual benefit in the 'cigarette' line.

'Long' Wilson, the orderly room clerk, grows more important and stuck up every day and when asked, 'What's the next move?' by at one time bosom pals, haughtily replies, 'Oh you just wait and see, old chappie'. Well, he was telling them nothing new, as Premier Asquith told us that three years ago. We are still waiting – and seeing!

15 February: A very successful day. The 14th Division and 40 Brigade of my Division attacked the remaining Turkish positions on the right bank at 9.00 am under a devilish artillery bombardment. They took three lines of Turkish trenches and 1000 prisoners.[47] The Turks fired on their own men as they rushed towards our lines waving bits of dirty white rags in token of surrender. I noticed a few haughty looking 'Jerry' officers amongst the prisoners. Turkish dead and wounded are lying all over the field. The wounded are calling upon Allah and his amorous prophet Mahomet to allay their sufferings.

In an order of the previous day, which was captured, the Turkish commander kisses the eyes of all his brave troops etc., etc., for the gallant stand they made in the Shuman and Dahra bends, against unprecedented artillery bombardments and overwhelming odds. The poor ragged devils deserved all the praise that could be showered upon them. Although they are our enemies we cannot but admire them for the magnificent show they put up. Our artillery opened appalling fire upon their positions at all unexpected hours by day and ditto by night and sometimes all night. Their only means of communication with the left bank was by boats (a very precarious line).

Brigade was withdrawn to reserve position No.19 on the Shatt-al-Hai at midnight. It is raining heavens hard.

16 February: Reserve position No.19 would give a faint impression of what the world must have been like when Noah's Ark went aground on the top of Mount Ararat in Armenia. Camp kettles floating about, blankets sodden wet and tramped in the mud. Everyone wet, cold and shivering; we are mud up to our eyebrows. A rum issue, combined with the appearance of the sun at 8 a.m., tended to liven up our gloomy spirits somewhat. We have cursed the sun almost daily but 'Mc.Ormack' is welcomed by all today. In my Battalion the sun has been re-christened 'Mc.Ormack' in deference to our commanding officer, I presume. I can assign no other reason.

At 10.10 am, crash, bang! 'What the hell is that?' A bomb yes, and a Mills, to judge by the detonation. An Irishman named D[avey] was employed as Company cook. It appears he looked after the Platoon Sergeants pretty well in the line of 'Sergeant Majors' tea and in consequence got more than a liberal rum issue. About twenty boxes of detonated bombs were about 20 yards from the cookhouse. He opened a box, extracted a bomb, closed the lid, pulled out the pin and laid the bomb on the box lid. The bomb in the course of 5 seconds naturally exploded, killing an officer's groom and wounding eleven men badly including himself. Four officers' chargers shared portions of the serrated casing and seven camp kettles completed the casualty roll.[48]

I had to turn the stretcher-bearers out and make three journeys through the mud to the Field Ambulance half a mile away. We did not pray for D[avey]'s speedy recovery. If every man received the regulation scale of rum no one could get drunk, you might feel a thrill or be temporarily elated for half an hour or so. Its effect on every man is not similar. Neither is beer for that matter. I have known men to sing and tell us all about their Pa and Ma when they had consumed three pints of beer. Again I have sat with men who, after consuming 10 pints, could discuss Ancient Rome, the decline and fall of the Roman Empire, the campaigns of Alexander the Great, the Conquest of Mexico and Peru, quote verses from the Rubbaiyat of Omar Kyyaam, etc., etc., give points on Theology to a Doctor of Divinity and, when leaving the wet canteen, give the Provost Sergeant the impression that they drank nothing stronger than a dose of health salts. It's the limit when a man pulls the pin out of a detonated Mills bomb and then stands watching it – to see how it goes off.

I noticed a pontoon train camouflaged with brushwood on the north side of our bivouac. Coming events cast their shadows before.

At 5.00 pm this evening we endured one of the worst hailstorms I have ever experienced. The hails were as big as pigeon eggs. It ceased at 6.00 pm. Words fail me to describe the condition of our bivouac. No artist could do the scene justice. Napoleon's retreat from Moscow 'was not in it'. The shades of night fell on a Battalion standing above their ankles in water, their ground sheets and blankets thrown around them to prevent them being carried away by the flood.[49]

17 February: Camp bombed at 8.00 am by an enemies' plane.

Notes

1 'It was now time for active operations to be resumed, the first task of the Mesopotamian Expeditionary Force being to clear the Turks from their well-entrenched position round Kut.' (Regt. Hist., p.337)

2 'The training camp was dismantled and then, all vehicles and horses having been sent forward by road, the battalions of the brigade began to move upstream by boat, the only troops of the 13th Division to do so.' (Ibid, p.337)

3 The Lewis was the first effective 'light' machine gun issued. Loaded it still weighed an impressive 29lb (13.1kg). With its 550rpm cyclic rate it gave the equivalent firepower of a section of infantry although prone to a bewildering number of stoppages. One manual listed thirty-three possible causes of stoppage.

4 'The Lewis gun appears to have received a disappointingly suspicious welcome from the front-line soldiers, since it was seen as displacing the greatly appreciated Vickers medium machine-gun, yet failing to offer sufficient compensating advantages in weight, simplicity or reliability.' (*Battle Tactics of the Western Front*, p.130)

5 This is correct; from the War Diary of the 6/East Lancs (4 August 1916) the battalion was training teams of one NCO and five men per Lewis gun. The gun crew was two men and the remaining riflemen of the section carried extra ammunition.

6 The infantry assault manual of 1917, SS143, assumed one gun per thirty-six man platoon, serviced by a whole section of nine men carrying thirty drums of ammunition.

7 There is plenty of evidence that when the British Army got the Lewis gun it felt it was not so much 'gaining an automatic rifle' as 'losing a superlative belt-fed medium machine-gun' . . . [unfortunately] the Lewis gun started to appear in large numbers at just the same time as . . . the four Vickers guns per battalion [were] removed to a specialist company under brigade control. (*Battle Tactics of the Western Front*, pp.130–131)

8 'East Lancs is the last regiment to move, embarking on *P50* with bakery and supply section in the morning.' (6th Bn War Diary, 7 December 1916)

9 'The battalion arrived on 10 December at Twin Canals, completing the concentration of the Brigade there.' (Regt. Hist., p.337). 'Moved with ninety army transport carts.' (6th Bn War Diary, 10 December 1916)

10 David Lloyd George replaced Asquith as Prime Minister on 7 December 1916 amid mounting criticism of Britain's conduct of the war. He pushed for a more vigorous and organized pursuit of the war.

11 A regimental 'dump' was formed at Twin Canals leaving all tents and heavy baggage. Two blankets a man were carried on reduced scale (twenty-five army transport carts, sixty-four pack mules and five Lewis gun carts). (6th Bn War Diary)

12 'The 38 Brigade, with sappers and field artillery attached, marched to Imam al Mansur, 5 miles distant. This was the point of assembly for a movement towards the enemy positions on the Hai below Kut.' (Regt. Hist., p.337)

13 A start was made at 1.00 am on 14 December, the Brigade being in mass on a frontage of two battalions, the East Lancashire leading on the left. No enemy was encountered and by 7.00 am the prescribed line was reached. Here the East Lancashire had its left on the Shatt al Hai River about 2 miles east of Besouia, the Brigade facing almost due east. The position was entrenched [with three lunettes and wired defences – War Diary] without interference from the Turks.

14 'Next morning [15 December] the rear units took up the advance, the Battalion moving in the second line in artillery formation. Fire was opened by the enemy about 11.00 am, causing the leading troops to deploy, but by the afternoon a line was occupied only about a thousand yards from the Turks holding the loop of the Hai just south of the Tigris. Consolidation began at once under brisk rifle-fire, which increased after darkness fell.' (Regt. Hist., p.337)

15 '9th Worcestershire Regiment, part of 39 Brigade. At dusk 39 Brigade . . . was relieved . . . [6/East Lancs] taking 800 yards of front. The 6/South Lancashire were now nearest the Hai, their left on Pointed Ruin with 6/East Lancashire next.' (Ibid, p.337)

16 '38 Brigade extended its right so that each battalion had to occupy 1,250 yards of front.' (Ibid, p.337)

17 'During 21 December . . . ten of our aeroplanes dropped nearly a ton of bombs on the enemy shipping and stores at Bughaila. [It is not clear if these aeroplanes did damage to the bridge of boats at Bughaila but it is likely that it was wrongly attributed, as] the British artillery bombardment during 20 December broke the enemy bridge.' (*History of the War*: *Mesopotamia*, Vol 3, p.86)

18 '[Drinking] water was a problem until it could be obtained direct from the Hai, the loan of a pump from the South Lancashire saving the situation.' (Regt. Hist., pp.337–338)

19 'A new trench was made with a bund 10 feet thick and this did keep the water at bay.' (Ibid, p.337)

20 [The probable cause of them being on half rations was that] 'Iron rations were changed at the end of the month and the new grocery tins proved most unsatisfactory, in majority of cases being by no means air tight, with result that the contents were partially spoiled.' (6th Bn War Diary, 28 December 1916)

21 In early December 1916 Germany made overtures for peace, accompanied by assertions

of the invincibility of German arms. President Wilson of the United States, still a neutral state, on 8 December delivered a note to the belligerent powers asking that concrete terms should be put forward by both sides and that all generalities in discussion should be abandoned. The allied reply had three conditions for peace; these were complete restitution (of conquered land), full reparation and guarantees against repetition – the three political "R's". The German government was unable to accept these conditions and merely restated proposals for a conference with no indication of what the programme should be. This reply cut away the ground from beneath the feet of those in England and America who had hoped for peace.

22 'Demonstration made to imitate reinforcement of line with view of drawing fire from Abdul Hassan area.' (6th Bn War Diary, 8 January 1917)

23 '3rd Division assault and capture first line of Abdul Hassan.' (Ibid, 9 January 1917)

24 '38 Brigade was now closing in upon the Turkish position in the Hai salient. This operation . . . involved continuous spadework under fire . . . every night the digging parties pushed the forward entrenchments closer to the Turk.' (Regt. Hist., p.338)

25 Major H.S. Bull was in fact wounded.

26 Lieutenant J.K. Varvill.

27 'The obsolete BE, Martinsyde and Bristol Scouts were not really fit to compete on equal terms . . . . Our authorities in Mesopotamia . . . had been representing to the Air Board in London that a newer type of machine was urgently required. But it was not until April [1917] that the Air Board found it possible to despatch some new 'Spads' to Basra.' (*History of the War: Mesopotamia*, Vol 3, p.322)

28 'On 25 January 39 and 40 Brigades attacked astride the Hai and obtained a footing in the Turkish trenches, 38 Brigade assisting with its fire.' (Regt. Hist., p.338)

29 6/Loyal Regiment (North Lancashire) and 6/King's Own Royal Regiment

30 'There now appeared to be few Turks east of the Hai, and in an advance on the night of 28 January, when 38 Brigade moved in reserve, no opposition was encountered. The 6/East Lancashire was given a portion of the captured position to consolidate.' (Regt. Hist., p.338)

31 'After ten minutes intense artillery bombardment, the 45th and 36th Sikhs of 37 Brigade [14th Division] advanced to the assault at 12.10 pm. The 45th managed without great loss to capture the both the first and second Turkish lines of trenches, but the 36th . . . suffered such heavy losses . . . they could get no further than the enemy's first line. The Turks then launched a heavy counter-attack . . . and over-weighted by numbers the remnants of both Sikh battalions were driven back.' (*History of the War: Mesopotamia*, Vol 3, p.119)

32 'On 12 May 1916 a new division, the 14th, was formed of 35, 36 and 37 Infantry Brigades and of other units from the Tigris Corps.' (Ibid, p.7)

33 Second-Lieutenant Oswald Wright Parkinson was one of two officers from India who joined the battalion with a new draft on 1 August 1916 at Sheik Saad. Killed in action 1 February 1917. Commemorated on the Basra Memorial.

34 The No 5 mills grenade had a base plug that unscrewed and the igniter set was inserted only when the bomb reached the troops. So when Roe writes in his diary that they were 'detonating bombs' he means they were inserting the igniter sets (detonators). Especially in the first half of the war, before the safety features of the time-fused bomb had been finally

224

perfected, all bombs had a fearsome reputation of unreliability. (*Battle Tactics of the Western Front*, p.113)

35 'Relieved by 3rd (Indian) Division and concentrate at R12, first line camp.' (6th Bn War Diary, 1 February 1917)

36 'The enemy's line of defence across the Dahra bend ran westward from the Liquorice factory . . . for about one and three quarter miles westward the trenches were held in strength from thence towards the Shumran bend the line was not continuous, being occupied by a series of detachments and outlying posts. To minimise losses General Maude . . . proceeded cautiously . . . [from 5 – 8 February] suitable positions of assembly had to be occupied and entrenched, communication trenches had to be dug . . . and continuous pressure maintained on the enemy, day and night, by vigorous patrolling and intermittent bombardment.' (*History of the War: Mesopotamia*, Vol 3, p.129)

37 'The whole brigade was relieved in the Hai salient on 3 February and crossed the river to the western bank where the East Lancashire was in the piquet line. The task was now to drive the Turks north-westwards towards the Dahra bend.' (Regt.Hist. p.338)

38 1/5th Buffs (East Kent Regiment) of 35 Brigade.

39 Second-Lieutenant Thompson and Second-Lieutenant O'Meara.

40 "B' Company under Captain Travis, preceded by grenadiers with North Lancs grenadiers in reserve, renewed attack on N42 and gained objective with few casualties . . . two other ranks killed, both Lewis gunners. Lewis guns especially useful during this action as affording covering fire . . . protecting flank of bombing party.' (6th Bn War Diary, 6 February 1917)

41 'The battalion is withdrawn to P24 where it remains until 10 February.' (Ibid, February 1917) [The East Lancs pioneers having completed a new front line 450 yards from the Turks.]

42 'The decisive operation to clear the Dahra bend commenced on 9 February. Preceded by an intense artillery bombardment at 10.00 am the 6/King's Own . . . traversed the 450 yards which separated them from the Turkish position and captured the Turkish line at N42 and N43a.' (*History of the War: Mesopotamia*, Vol 3, pp.130–131)

43 Captured by the 2/4th Gurkhas and 1/5th Buffs of 35 Brigade.

44 Roe is writing here of General Townshend's defence of Kut-al-Amara in 1916.

45 N35 is a reference point on a geographical position within the trench networks that covered the Hai salient. In this chapter of the diary you will read of more numbered reference points for the front-line or bivouac areas. 'The following days were spent in the ever-recurring work of consolidation and extension of trenches in preparation for a further advance.' (Regt. Hist. p.338)

46 'On 12 February, after ten minutes bombardment . . . a company of 102nd Grenadiers (35 Brigade), with another company in reserve, advanced to assault an enemy's advanced post in a strong point . . . no sooner did they start the assault than they came under very heavy machine gun and rifle fire directed from both flanks of the strongpoint . . . almost the whole company was shot down . . . The company in reserve . . . also suffered very heavy casualties . . . . A company of 37th Dogras was sent forward to reinforce the 102nd Grenadiers (whose total casualties were 297) and it succeeded in doing in face of a very hostile fire . . . After dark a second Dogra company was able to reinforce the position . . . thus depriving the enemy of an important tactical point from which he could cover most of the rest of his

line with enfilade fire.' There is no mention of the North Lancs. (*History of the War: Mesopotamia*, Vol 3, pp.138–139)

47 'The North Lancs [6/Loyal Regiment] assault and take the ruins on the river to their left front and after a dummy bombardment in front of 14th Division on the right, 40 Brigade assaulted the enemy's right centre with complete success. The East Lancs was in first reserve to 40 Brigade and move up by half battalion . . . 14th Division renewed the assault in the early afternoon and by dusk the Dahra bend was cleared up to 300 yards distance from the river.' (6th Bn War Diary, 15 February 1917)

48 'Grenade accident, by which, one other rank killed and nine wounded. Private Davey detained . . . awaiting trial.' (Ibid, 16 February 1917)

49 'Cloud burst and hail storm floods camp out and renders roads almost impossible for transport.' (Ibid, 16 February 1917)

Edmund Candler in *The Long Road to Baghdad* says: "A captive officer gave us the Turks point of view: 'We have been praying for this rain,' he said, 'for two months to hinder your advance; now it has come too late.' "

XVI

Advance to Baghdad

(18 February – 10 March 1917)

Preparation for Advance – Shumran Bend – The River Monitors – Turkish
Rearguard – Reluctant 'Heroes' – Evacuation of the Wounded – The
Colonel is Wounded – The Advance Continues – Ctesiphon Arch –
Passage of the Diyala – The Loyals Attempt the Crossing – Reserve
Bomber Gaffney –
Desperate Fighting – A Successful Crossing

Preparation for Advance

18 February: Battalion moves back and takes over some lunettes and redoubts from a Battalion of Gurkhas.[1] In character with their high standard of efficiency and discipline, the Gurkas handed over their positions as clean as the proverbial 'new pin'.

19 February: A general clean up and inspection.[2]

The Orderly Sergeant comes around for names of men who can row a boat. People who do not know what an oar is give in their names, under the impression that they are going to get a soft job. If they knew that they are to row armed parties across the Tigris so as to form a bridgehead whilst the Royal Engineers swing the pontoon bridge over, the Orderly Sergeant would get fewer names.

20 February: Battalion, relieved by Indian troops.[3] Move out a couple of miles and bivouac.[4]

Two men of the South Lancashires were shot at dawn this morning. 'WOAS [Whilst on Active Service] sleeping on their posts in face of the enemy'.[5] In this campaign men are worked until they drop from sheer exhaustion and sometimes short rations. When in the trenches it's work day and night, not one day or night but every day and every night. The arduous duties of sentry have got to be performed in addition to fatigue; time for sleep there is none. One might doze for ten minutes on the fire-step after coming off two hours listening post when some CO comes along and claims you for a digging party, or filling sand bags, or putting up barbed wire maybe. There

227

is no such thing as two [hours] on and four off, or regular system of reliefs, and in consequence men find it a physical impossibility when on sentry to keep thoroughly alert; yet there are no extenuating circumstances.

I remember in 1914, when in the trenches for twenty-one days at Ploegsteert, when I was posted as sentry I used to get hold of a spare bayonet, rest my elbows on the trench parapet, with the point of the spare bayonet under my chin. If I nodded of I got pricked by the point of the bayonet on the chin and was prevented from dozing. I was not the only one that adopted that method. I am not criticizing the findings of the Court, nor yet defending the victims of regulations that were compiled by German officers in the service of George the Fourth.

21 February: Ceremonial drill at 9.00 am.

22 February: Ceremonial drill at 9.00 am. At 10.20 am we fall in for a lecture on 'Kindness to the Arabs.' We are told that the country through which we will be operating in future is largely populated by Arab tribes, on whom we will have to depend more or less for supplies. Therefore we've got to make love to those treacherous dogs and treat them as brothers. Yes! We all love the Arabs and trust them – to a certain extent.

Shumran Bend

23 February: Brigade moves towards the Tigris at 9.00 pm and bivouac.[6] We can hear a faint cackle of rifle fire and the detonation of shells.[7]

Micky Quinn from St Helens, who joined up for the duration of the war or 'longer if it lasts', informed me today that in a letter, per last mail, it stated that all soldiers killed in battle went straight to heaven. I told him frankly that it was our only chance, as we would never reach the golden gates by any other means. The means to attain the end is rather drastic. For my part, I'd rather linger on a few more years, even with a certain hell 'tagged' on at the end. What hopes have a miserable sinner like I got of ever laying my optics on St Peter, when clergymen declare from the pulpit that it is as hard for a just man to get to Heaven as it is for a camel to get through the eye of a cambric needle. There are two species of camel; the dromedary camel with one hump and the bactrian with two. If it is the latter camel our spiritual healers mean, well I give it best now.

24 February: Brigade cross over the Tigris at dawn to left bank under enemy's shellfire. The pontoon bridge rocks and sways. One lucky shell and all who are on the bridge are in heaven, whether they like it or not.

We are in the rear of the Turkish force at Kut and threatening his line of retreat. We lie in the open all day under shellfire.[8] We are close to the pontoon bridge and as the Turkish gunners are doing their damndest to demolish the bridge, we get all the shell that fall short. The Tigris is full of dead fish floating belly upwards. They have been killed by the shock of the shells, which exploded in the river.

There is a hell of a row going on down Kut way, explosions and what not.[9] Four Turks, very ragged and minus arms (rifles), approach the Battalion from Kut direction shouting out 'Bully beef!' Our day's rations include a tin of 'Bully' between three; however, we give them a tin and some biscuits. Their only equipment consists of valises (ours) slung over their shoulders by supporting straps (ours). We noticed one Turk had something in his valise, so we made him tip his valise out. Imagine our surprise when the contents revealed six Princess Mary's 1914 gift boxes. We soundly kicked his . . ? as he yelled out 'Souvenir!' He parted with his souvenirs, also three safety razors.

A party of Turks have taken up a defensive position on our left front, with a view to holding us up whilst their rearguard slips by in the rear.[10] The Battalion forms up at 5.00 pm and advance, in two lines, on the Turkish position. The Turks fire a few shots and 'mizzle'. Battalion stand fast for the night.

We are under the impression that we have let the Turks slip through our fingers and that had affairs been forced when we forced the passage of the river on the 23rd the Kut garrison would have been captured and our advance to Baghdad unopposed. The sky is illuminated by the glow of fires in and around Kut.

The River Monitors

25 February: Our river monitors steam past and we give them a cheer. We are told that the Turks are in full retreat.[11] The Brigade falls in at 6.00 am and move off in column of route,[12] and also in line with our monitors, or river gunboats,[13] which are slowly feeling their way upstream.

At 9.00 am we get a shock as the Turks open on our gunboats, when they reached a broad bend in the river, with heavy and light artillery. The gunboats are in line ahead with about 15 fathoms interval between. The enemy are trying to sink the rear monitor so as to block the navigable passage of the river and have the other four at his mercy. By Christ, is she gone? – No! – What a close shave. We hold our breath in suspense as another salvo of 'five nines' comes over. The shells explode in the river all around the monitors, causing fountains of water, 30 feet high, to arise. We are drenched with spray. Someone on the leading monitor is semaphoring like hell and the rear monitor retires, firing as she moves, followed by the second from the rear. All monitors are now retiring, and firing as they move.[14] The Turkish gunners are making desperate efforts to get them but up to the present a

229

couple of mounds of dead and stunned fish is their only reward. We were wondering what would have happened had four of those 'five nine' shells dropped on the Battalion. We were in column of route. Fortunately, all the spare stuff dropped on the opposite bank.

The Brigade adopts artillery formation and advanced under heavy shell-fire and not a moment too soon was artillery formation adopted, as the Turks, baulked of their prey (the monitors), turned their attentions on the Brigade.[15] When the rumpus started I caught a glimpse of mules bolting. I think our mules with the packals and yakdans[16] are somewhere in the vicinity of Kut by now.

Turkish Rearguard

We come under machine gun and rifle fire in artillery formation, form line and when deployed into line the infantry advance at the double. Men are falling fast. When 500 yards or maybe more from the Turks, whom we cannot see, our line is crossed by an old irrigation dyke. The line takes possession of this, get to work with entrenching tools, and in short time it is something like a trench.[17]

The MO formed his first aid post 600 yards from our firing line and in the open. 100 yards in the rear there was a deep and dry irrigation canal. A couple of hard-working men could have made a tolerably safe first aid post in an hour. Why he did not use it I do not know. Fed up with life, I suppose.

Our artillery have trotted into action and taken up battery positions, [and] run up their telescopic observation ladders, which the Turks were highly pleased to knock down as soon as they were erected. He silenced one of our batteries in twenty minutes and his shooting on the whole was extraordinary good.

What has gone wrong with our aerial observers? For the past two days I have not seen one of our planes. Reconnaissance and staff work is at fault somewhere. Why were we allowed to come under artillery fire in column of route and machine gun fire in artillery formation? One lucky shell this morning and our river fleet would have 'went west'. We are saying all sorts of unkind things (re) our intelligence department.

Wounded are flowing in by the score. One of the first men to be wounded this morning was Sergeant Jacobs of the 1st Battalion; he was one of a voluntary draft of ten NCOs and men who joined the 6th Battalion from Quetta in 1916.

The stretcher-bearers are run off their feet. How we have not been wiped out by now I cannot imagine. The Turks shelled the first aid post, the stretcher-bearers, the horsed ambulances and the Field Hospital. He must be close to an ammunition dump or else he is firing all his reserve ammunition in order to be more mobile in retreat.

The ammunition mules have taken up position in rear of the first aid post and alongside the irrigation canal. The Turkish Forward Observing Officer has spotted them and shells are dropping and bursting all around the first aid post. The MO chased the ammo mules to blazes out of it. Three wounded men were hit a second time by shrapnel. We stuck up a big Red Cross flag, but a fat lot of notice the Turkish gunners took of it.

Reluctant 'Heroes'

At 2.00 pm, when I was coming down from the firing line with a case, I passed close to a large and providential ant heap. I found a Lance Corporal and five men, nursing a sick Lewis gun, behind it. I enquired what they were doing there and why they were not in the firing line. The reply I got was, 'gun out of action'. No one was making any attempt to remedy the stoppage. I told them there were plenty of spare rifles in the firing line whose owners will have no more use for them. I suggested that six men would be very useful in the firing line as there were a lot of casualties and they would not be cramped for space. I was promptly told that they could not leave their gun. The same NCO was afterwards awarded the Military Medal for his good work on 25 February. The people who knew the true facts 'cut their chin straps up'. Out of six or eight Lewis guns that went into action I heard only one in action all day.

Evacuation of the Wounded

The wounded were laid out in two rows at the first aid post. The MO requested us to do our best and get as many stretcher cases away as we could before night in case there was a sudden move. Any man who could walk or crawl was only too damn glad to get away from the first aid post.

The Turks have been threatening to counter-attack for the past hour. Rhodes and I got one very bad case on a stretcher. He was shot through the head, unconscious and snoring heavily. We carried him alternately at the trail and shoulder high to save time in resting. As we were struggling along at the shoulder position we heard this shell coming and instinct told us it was meant for us. It buried itself in the ground about five yards from the stretcher; the concussion threw us clean off our feet. Of course the stretcher went as well. Luckily, the shell was a dud. We picked ourselves up. I asked Rhodes was he hit? He did not know. 'Neither do I,' I replied, 'but I'm badly shaken.' When we pulled ourselves together we examined our stretcher case, he had passed away, poor fellow.

Another of our batteries on the right flank or right rear has been silenced. Our gunboats are now shelling the Turks from long range.

At 5.00 pm the Turks opened an intense bombardment, which lasted until 6.00 pm. Preparations are being made to receive a counter-attack.

At last all stretcher cases are evacuated from the first aid post. The Turkish infantry are keeping up a heavy and continuous fire.

At 6.10 or 15pm I had to assist a man who was badly wounded in the leg but refused to be carried to the Field Ambulance. It was a slow job. Night had fallen by the time I left the ambulance and the Turkish infantry were still on the bolt drill.

I made my way to the Tigris. Once I found the Tigris I knew I could find our first aid post. I found the river, [and] the deep irrigation canal but the first aid post had vanished. I shouted 'Captain Coffyn!', 'Sergeant Hayes!' several times at the top of my voice, but got no reply, and to make matters worse the firing had died down. I found the Red Cross flag, but what I wanted to find was rifle, bayonet and equipment. I tramped around and felt in every direction but without success. I thought, 'Well I'll be "cat's meat" if a couple of prowling Arabs come along. Has the line retired or advanced during my absence?' A ragged volley from Mausers[18] soon assured me that affairs were much as they were when I left, so I went forward and found the 1st aid post established in the firing line. I also found my rifle and stretcher-bearer's haversack, which contained the shell dressings.

There is still work to do and there are quite a number of badly wounded men here who have to be got to the Field Ambulance by hook or by crook tonight, as we move forward in the morning.

The Colonel is Wounded

Our acting Colonel, Major Davey of the Gloucesters, has been wounded in the foot and is hopping about. The Medical Sergeant gave me an order to assist the Colonel to the Field Ambulance. The Colonel heard him and replied, 'Never mind me, I can manage. Get those poor fellows who are lying about badly wounded away first, then attend to me.' I soliloquised, 'You're a devil in some respects, but I will always doff my turban to you after that'.

The Turkish guns have been silent since 7.00 pm [and] their infantry fire has developed into spasmodic bursts, we gain the impression that the Turks are retiring behind their infantry screen. The last burst of firing occurred at midnight, then silence.

Captain Varvil is Commanding Officer now.

'Chota' McDonald, 1st Battalion South Lancashires, went out scouting and brought back the information that the Turks were packing up; he actually saw them.[19] That valuable information eased [our minds] as to a counter-attack. The silence seemed unnatural as one gets very suspicious and you don't know what devilment they may be up to behind the screen of silence.

My Regiment had something like 100 casualties.[20]

The Advance Continues

26 February: At 6.00 am the Brigade advances in two lines with fixed bayonets only to find that the birds had flown; not a Turk to be seen, dead or alive, in the position they held yesterday. As we advanced beyond their position we captured an old Turk, who was too old and stout to keep pace with the remainder, and two lean oxen. A little further ahead we came across their gun positions, heaps of live shells, eight disabled guns, dead gunners, two defunct 'Jerries' and a pile of medical stores, mostly bandages and dressings but nothing satiable or drinkable. So Mr Turk did not have it all his own way yesterday.

My pet stretcher-bearer, Jacques, is missing and two have been wounded. I sent the Reverend Jacques and Smith with a stretcher case to the Field Ambulance at midnight on the 25th. Smith reported to me when he returned. I enquired where friend Jacques was and was informed that he refused to budge from Field Ambulance. He took cover beneath the merciful folds of the Red Cross flag. So that means more new and inexperienced stretcher-bearers.

My Battalion are on the left flank of the Brigade and are advancing alongside the river.[21] We passed quite a number of Turkish guns dumped into the Tigris. At one bend we came across six inch guns (Krupps) stranded on the river bank. They had not time to complete the job. All guns we have captured so far are Krupps. They must be hard pressed to abandon such a number. What does the turgid and muddy Tigris hide, I wonder?

Halt at 11.30 am at Iman Mahud [Imam Mahdi].[22] A *tope* or grove of scraggy date palms, a few ruins and a dilapidated mosque adorn Iman Mahud. A disabled gun, a store of cocoa, dressings, two guns partially submerged in the Tigris, one of our horsed Red Cross vans, which was abandoned by Townshend on his retreat from Cestiphon [Ctesiphon], with a badly wounded Turkish officer inside and a jumble of transport that would defy the ingenuity of a Heath Robinson to caricature were left behind by the army. Oh! I almost omitted three 'Black and White' whisky bottles (empty) from the roll of captures.[23]

Advance resumed at 1.00 pm. Halt at Baghalia [Bughaila] at 5.30 pm and bivouac.[24] The village is crowded with Arabs who pretend to be friendly, but if we met with a reverse tomorrow would eagerly join the Turks. The Arabs

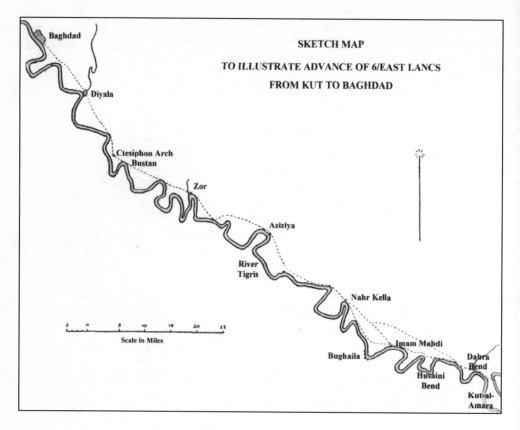

SKETCH MAP

TO ILLUSTRATE ADVANCE OF 6/EAST LANCS

FROM KUT TO BAGHDAD

Baghdad

Diyala

Ctesiphon Arch
Bustan

Zor

Aziziya

River
Tigris

Nahr Kella

Imam Mahdi

Bughaila

Dabra
Bend

Husaini
Bend

Kut-al-
Amara

Scale in Miles

10. The advance from Kut to Baghdad.

have no time for losers; they always like to be on the winning side. One of our monitors is anchored in mid-stream and has her guns trained on the village, the other four are miles ahead knocking hell out of the retiring Turks in conjunction with our well-horsed cavalry. I might as well say a word about our cavalry while I'm at it.

On the morning of the 25th on the outskirts of a ruined village I saw a Cavalry Brigade[25] formed up; squadrons of bearded Sikhs, princely Rajputs and hardy Punjabi Musselmen, splendidly mounted and appointed. The champing of bits and the stamping and impatient pawing of hooves gave one the impression that the horses knew we were winning and were eager to be after the fleeing Turk. I don't think their equal could be found in any army in the world – their superiors never. For some inexplicable reason the Regiments were mixed, that is to say, a squadron of Europeans and two of

234

Indians formed a Regiment. The Indian Cavalry Brigade formed up outside the ruined village at the Shumran bend on the morning of 25 February, 1917, will live in my memory.

The demolished Turkish boat bridge provides plenty of material for our bivouac fires. The only drawback is there is very little to cook. Our first line transport got lost in the blue, so there are neither rations nor blankets.

27 February: Resume the advance at 1.00 pm.[26] The transport was attacked by Arabs last night; the escort beat them off.

Red Cross ambulances (ours), guns, limbers, heaps of live shells and a few dead men mark the Turkish lines of retreat. Bivouac at 9.00 pm after an agonizing eight hours march through a raging sandstorm.

28 February: Brigade have out-marched supplies and cannot advance today.

1 March: One days rations arrive at 7.00 am (yesterdays). We are told to make four biscuits and a tin of 'bully' between two men last us two days, as heaven and General Maude only knows when we will get the next issue.

We are all of the opinion that General Maude could not have foreseen the extent of his victory. When he did the obvious and swung his pontoons across the river at the Shumran Bend, did he make provisions for the rapid disintegration of the Turkish forces? – or did he expect them to put up a 'show' at the Shumran Bend? Here we are, held up for want of rations whilst the Turkish army is fleeing to Baghdad as fast (or faster) than their feet can carry them, a beaten rabble pursued only by gunboats, aeroplanes and cavalry.[27] The latter are only keeping in touch with them. We are told that there is one more river to cross. If Mr Turk gets a breathing spell and digs in on the opposite bank – well – we'll have to do it all over again.

2 March: Our monitors and cavalry had a tussle with the Turks yesterday. Since 23 February we have captured 5000 prisoners, 25 field guns and nineteen machine guns. The guns and war material the River Tigris hides are not included. Still I am convinced that the Turks have a kick or two left in them yet.

Brigade resumes advance at 6.00 am. More Turkish transport and gun limbers. Bivouac at Ayzieh [Aziziya] at 4.00 pm.

3 March: No rations have arrived. Orders have been issued for the consumption of emergency rations (those that have any can eat them). [28] No advance today.

4 March: No move today as no rations have arrived. The mules are eating each other's tails off and we are faint from hunger.

5 March: Advance resumed[29] at 5.00 am. Everyone suffers extremely from thirst. The transport and pack animals are responsible for raising a thick cloud of dust, which makes it impossible for a section of fours to see the section of fours in front; the dust blinds and chokes us.

Battalion halts at 6.00 pm and bivouacs for the night.[30] Man and beast suffered on the days march. The mules make a dash for the river and the men cannot be restrained either. A couple of mules die from colic. An occasional dead Turk and mule float by, but we take no notice and carry on drinking.

Everyone's feet are in an awful condition; soles, toes and heels blood raw.

Ctesiphon Arch

6 March: Rouse at 4.00 am and move off at 5.00 am. It was given out on the line of march that the Turks had taken up a position at Cestiphon [Ctesiphon] but our cavalry routed them, capturing some prisoners and a gun.[31]

What seems to be the ruins of a high building stands out in bold relief at intervals through the mirage; it is miles and miles away. Mirages are very deceptive and it may not be a building at all.

Today has been a day of all days for me. Quite a number of men are falling out owing to bad feet and I have to remain with them and bring them along. I am carrying three rifles as well as my own [and] when the Battalion get a halt I arrive just as they are starting off again. I have not had a halt since 5.00 am this morning.

At 4.00 pm in a blinding sandstorm we arrive at Cestiphon and bivouac under the shadow of the ancient arch.[32] The arch is the only part of the palace of the Chosroes that has withstood the ravages of time and is the only monument of its kind erected to the memory of man in Mesopotamia.[33]

This is an ancient-looking and historic place. I climbed to the top of the old city walls, twenty feet high and as many feet broad. Rusty 'bully beef' and jam tins, relics of General Townshend's victory and defeat,[34] strew the ground all around the walls.

Over seventy men have reported sick with bad feet, and God knows they are bad. The MO tells them to get their feet dressed and 'stick it', as if he sent every man to hospital that should be in hospital, we would advance on Baghdad in Red Cross vans, [and] we cannot take Baghdad with Red Cross wagons.

The road or track has been fairly good for the past two marches and is carried over the deep irrigation canals by substantial brick bridges. We leave Cestiphon to its ancient glory.

Tonight, as we are dog tired and as lousy as cuckoos, we fall asleep before the first line [transport] arrives with our blankets.

Passage of the Diyala

7 March: Rouse at 5.00 am [and] move at 6.00 am [The] Regiment [is] on [the] right flank. Guard advance four miles when a halt is called. The Turks have withdrawn across the Diyalah River and it is natural to suppose he has destroyed his bridge of boats[35], so that means forcing the passage of the river. If the Turks dispute the passage, which they are bound to do, it will be a costly undertaking.

At present the Turkish Gunners are enjoying a little practice on our Cavalry Patrols in front.

We lie 'doggo' until 5.00 pm in the evening when operation orders are read out to us[36].

The Brigade is to advance in three lines at 7.00 pm on the lines of the river. Pontoons to be in the rear of the King's Own, who are to make the crossing and form a bridgehead.[37] The transport, which conveyed the pontoons, could only manage to get within 200 yards of the river. After that the pontoons had to be manhandled. If the King's Own establishes a footing on the right bank the Brigade will be across by midnight. The advance was carried out with great caution, only the pontoon train made a hell of a row.[38]

I unload the stretchers and make the bearers carry them as if anything happens and the mules take it into their heads to bolt back to Cestiphon we would be likened unto the seven foolish virgins that betook themselves to the wedding feast with no oil in their lamps. We reached the riverbank without incident or loss. The Turks never betrayed their presence even by a muffled cough. The men stood talking on the riverbank and I heard such observations as:

'Oh! he's retired.'

'He's "picked him up" again, Bill.'

'Oi Joe, isn't it a bleeding gaff!'

I observed lights pretty high up here and there some distance away. I took them to be hurricane lamps suspended on poles, which the artillery use for night firing, and at the same time I heard some good hard swearing by the King's Own as they were manhandling the pontoons towards the river. Discretion is thrown to the winds and conversation is now general. I am quite expecting someone to light a fag end; the night is fairly bright.

We were congratulating ourselves on a bloodless victory when suddenly the right bank of the river burst into flame. Hell was let loose.[37] Our Adjutant, Captain Watson[40], fell dead with the first volley, as did a dozen others. There is a general mix up and shouts of 'Lie down!' and 'Take cover!' The enemy's artillery has opened a heavy shrapnel fire on us. The machine guns and riflemen are thundering away on the opposite bank. Take cover – yes! – it's all right if you know the nature of the ground, but we don't.

The King's Own was caught in the hail of bullets and shrapnel and had numerous casualties. I can see them struggling manfully along with their pontoons through it all.

The stretcher-bearers were posted to their companies before the advance. I have been to every company looking for stretcher-bearers but cannot find any; it appears to me that nobody wants to be stretcher-bearers tonight. By the time I had got back to where I had left the MO he had gone somewhere else. I found him later on, behind a ruined mud hut, dressing casualties by the uncertain light of a half moon.

The Adjutant's body had been brought in. Our dressing station suddenly came under machine gun fire. We had to flatten out on our bellies as the mud walls tumbled about our ears. The MO decided to find a safer place. I pointed in the direction of a deep and dry irrigation canal that I fell into whilst looking for stretcher-bearers. When we got into the canal we found out we could be enfiladed; there was no other place so we had to make the best of it.

The King's Own have got the pontoons launched. We can hear an awful row going on; the bullets are beating a tattoo on the sides of the boats. Shouts, groans and curses reach our ears. What an awful experience it must be for those men in the pontoons, loaded with ammunition and bombs, reels of signalling wire, etc., and trying to cross under a converging machine gun fire. Bombs are now exploding, the machine gun and rifle increases in intensity, and the MO remarks, 'They must be landing on the opposite bank now'. The awful din was kept up for half an hour, then gradually died down to normal.[41]

Later we get the information from a wounded King's Own that some men from one of the pontoons succeeded in landing but had to return. The rowers of other pontoons were shot, the oars went overboard and the pontoons were carried away by the stream out of control. They suffered heavily as the Turks riddled the pontoons with bullets; I can just imagine it.

Our artillery gave us little support and our random covering fire from the left bank could not be of much assistance.

One to you, Mr. Turk.[42]

8 March: Later reports state that the Turks sunk four of our pontoons with rifle fire and bombs. The party that succeeded in landing had to swim back.[43] We failed and incurred heavy casualties.

The pack mules were in rear of the third line last night and when the ball opened they stampeded with the yakdans, packals and ammunition.

This morning parties of men had to go to the rear and carry picks, spades, ammunition and water to the firing line. The Turks opened fire on them and perforated a couple of packals, rendering them useless, and also inflicted casualties as the fatigue parties were in the open.

The Battalion are feverishly digging themselves in. The right bank of the river commands the left. Of course it would do, because the Turks are holding it. Our artillery made a good start this morning by dropping four howitzer high explosives amongst us.

We are using American manufactured ammunition. You can pull the bullet out of the case and tip a pinch of black powder on your hand. The amount of powder in the case would not send a bullet 200 yards.

The Regiment is not properly dug in and we are losing a lot of men from shell and rifle fire. Carelessness is responsible for fifty per cent of the casualties. The men are thirsty and risk their lives to obtain water from the river which is only two pull-through cord lengths from them; so near and yet so far.

Our artillery is shelling the Turks, as the river is roughly about 40 yards wide. The men who are holding the left bank occasionally share a premature burst amongst them.

The Loyals Attempt the Crossing

The North Lancashires are to attempt a crossing tonight at midnight, 500 yards to the right of where the attempt failed last night. My Regiment are in support.[44]

11.30 pm, first aid post pack up and make for riverbank. The Regiment are gradually easing off to the right and are lying down in rear of the point where the North Lancs are to attempt the crossing. The enemy anticipated the exact spot where the attempt is to be made and concentrates artillery, machine gun and rifle fire on it.

The first aid post takes up position in a nullah. The shrapnel fire is accurate and deadly. We no sooner got into the nullah than a shell burst over-head. I feel a thud on my back [and] my haversack is slashed with a piece of shell casing. An RAMC orderly [is] killed behind me. We are immediately engaged in cutting off coat sleeves and ripping trouser legs in order to dress up wounds.

Exactly what is going on on the river we do not know. We can hear a lot of confused shouting above the din of bursting shrapnel and rifle fire. The hollow sound of bullets beating a tattoo on wood reaches our ears.

9 March: 1.00 am, orders are issued to resume our previous positions as the attempt failed. One Company (less casualties) succeeded in gaining a footing on the right bank. The remainder were beaten back, with heavy loss and damaged pontoons.

Reserve Bomber Gaffney

The getting back business is much worse than coming forward as the Turks are distributing their fire on the frontage we hold. We move off in Indian file, the MO leading. Part of the way we are screened by a grove of date palms. I get to within 40 yards of our irrigation canal when I am compelled to nose dive into a partially dug trench owing to a sudden burst of machine gun fire. I fell on something hard. On feeling the object I found it was a sand bag half-filled with bombs and a 'God bless and save us all', (fervently), from underneath the sand bag, told me that I had flattened out on the body of Reserve Bomber Gaffney. The river embankment vibrated to the tune of Turkish high explosives. I was requested from underneath the sand bag to see 'Where that one went?' and 'Where did that one go?'

Reserve Bomber Gaffney has been prominent in my memory since December 16th. The same old Gaffney, the same old worried expression, the same old sand bag, and apparently the same old quota of bombs, the split pins of which were doubled right back over the lever. This precautionary measure was taken on his part in case a pin might work out, release the lever and send him to Kingdom come.[45] In a tight corner the bombs would be useless, as one would want a pair of pincers to straighten the pin before it could be withdrawn. If rushed by the enemy I would prefer a crateful of empty Guinness porter bottles to Gaffney's bombs. The porter bottles would make a greater impression. He always gave me the impression of a man who was carrying a time bomb on his person but did not know exactly when it was timed to go off.

Desperate Fighting

Cries in English and Turkish are borne to our ears from the right bank where the North Lancs are fighting for a foothold.[46] We can hear them shouting from across the river for more bombs. 'For Christ's sake, send us some bombs over, we've run out!' Hot work on the opposite bank [and] we can do nothing to assist them. Will there be any left by tonight, I wonder?[47]

Let those in the rear who hastily criticize the tardiness of forcing the passage of the river imagine or visualize, if they can, in an atmosphere of comparative safety and comfort, what it means. Awkward and heavy pontoons have to be carried down to the water's edge and launched under heavy fire. The landing parties have got to take their places in the pontoons under heavy and accurate fire. They are loaded with extra ammunition and bombs, reserve ammunition, bombs and signalling apparatus that has to be got on board before they shove off. Before the oars are dipped, the pontoons may be half-filled with dead and dying and waterlogged by bullet holes. When they come to within bombing distance of the river's bank they are bombed, [and] when they land, what's left have to attack the enemy with bomb and bayonet to clear them out. The position has [then] got to be consolidated in order to allow reinforcements to get across with the minimum of safety. Whilst the above is being carried out, the party engaged are being slated with good hard bullets, not snowballs. Just imagine the amount of courage and determination required to carry out such an operation. [Finally], the telephone jingles and an impatient voice, far away in the rear speaks thus, 'Not across yet! Get a move on! What the damned hell is the delay?'

All our forward positions have been heavily shelled today.

There are still quite a number of cases coming in of men suffering from bullet wounds. They must be exposing themselves in order to obtain water from the river.

Our artillery fire increased in intensity and accuracy today.

I have seen no rations for the past two days.

Artillery Forward Observing Officer wounded in our forward line this evening.

A Successful Crossing

My Regiment are under orders to cross the river at all costs tonight or in the morning. The Wilts are going to make a demonstration against the Turkish right flank. Above the confluence of the Tigris and Diyalah [there will be another demonstration], assisted by monitors.[48]

Drinking water unobtainable today.

10 March: [The] Regiment shuffles, glides and steals along to the point where we are to attempt the crossing. It is almost in the same spot as where the North Lancs made the attempt last night. Time 1.30 am. If we fail, the South Lancs are to have a try, and if they fail we all try again until we are all killed, so says General Maude. As usual the Turks were wide-awake and gave us a severe slating as we formed up.

Again the first aid post is abandoned as the MO, Medical Sergeant and I were moving up the irrigation canal in single file and heard a whiz-bang bursting just in front. Luckily we had not rounded the bend. As we rounded the bend we had to pick our steps over two wriggling headless trunks. They were caught by the shell before it exploded. They must have been sitting up against the bank. 'My God!' exclaimed the MO, 'what a ghastly start'. One was a full Corporal; I got his pay book out of his left breast pocket. It was Corporal Crookes, whom I knew very well. The other body I could not truck; it was in such a mess.

241

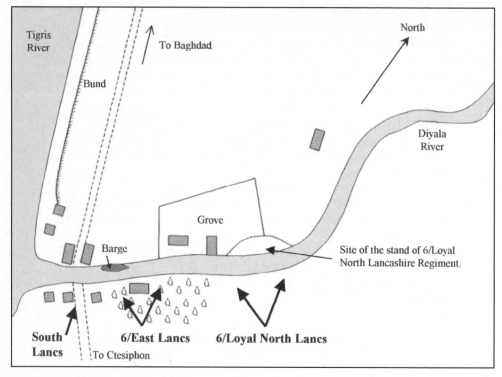

11.   Sketch Map of the Diyala Crossing, 10 March 1917
(Sketch from the letters of Buchanan-Brown)

The Turkish small arm fire is well sustained. The first pontoon is launched and crossed over, opposed by only a scattered volley.

During the preliminary preparations our artillery gave them hell.[49] As soon as the first pontoon was launched our guns 'lifted', or in other words lengthened their range.

The second pontoon followed without opposition. The Turks had surrendered as the landing party from the first platoon scrambled up the bund or embankment. Covering parties were put out and all precautions taken.

Some of the North Lancs are still alive but nearly all are wounded.[50]

A few stray shots are going off here and there. We had four or five casualties in the actual crossing.

The first pontoon crossed at 4.00 am. The medical staff crossed at 5.00 am.

One company is formed into line with fixed bayonets to charge an Arab village some 200 yards from the river in which some Turks are hiding and refuse to come out. When they see the line advancing, about one hundred Turks and two officers advance towards us with their hands up. We have taken roughly 250 prisoners, probably more; I counted six officers.[51] The Turkish dead I did not attempt to count. They were lying in heaps. I've never seen so many Turkish dead.[52]

We can see the enemy's guns galloping away in the distance.

The condition of the North Lancs dead revealed the desperate struggle that took place. Despite the incessant and desperate three days fighting, the Turks found time to strip the dead. I pointed out the condition of our dead to a Turkish officer. He replied with a wave of his hand, 'Arabs'. I told him he was a b . . liar and asked him, 'Where are your Arab dead?' 'If the Arabs were assisting you, surely out of the hundreds of dead that lie all over the position you held there would be at least one Arab. I cannot see a single dead man wearing an *Aba* (long robe worn by Arabs) or *Aqual* (a headband worn by Arabs, it consists of coils of camels hair often ornamented with gold or silver thread).' I would have given him 'one up' had not Lieutenant-Colonel Birley of the King's Own, our new commanding officer,[53] been standing on the riverbank watching us. All our dead did not die in the position and condition in which we found them. I'll say no more on the subject.

The CO gives me an order to get all stretcher-bearers together and bring in the Turkish wounded. When I assembled the stretcher-bearers I pointed out our dead and remarked, 'You see our dead and know what has happened here. Don't shed any tears over the Turkish wounded'.

The Royal Engineers swung a pontoon bridge across with incredible rapidity. In fact almost before one had time to say the Lord's Prayer, the Indian Cavalry were thundering across the bridge, formed line and were away hell for leather after the retiring Turks.

Thank God that bloody struggle is over and the road to Baghdad clear. Let us hope that is the last infernal river we will have to cross.

We brought in over fifty Turkish wounded. They were lying under shrubs, in shallow irrigation ditches and behind the mud walls of the houses in the Arab village. I came across a dead Turkish officer. I investigated his haversack and found two wheaten cakes therein, of which I made short work as I was starving. He also had a full water bottle. The fates were kind. We are dumping the Turkish wounded on the river bund. One Turkish prisoner kindly volunteered to present me with his dead officer's boots. In fact, he did not wait to see whether I would accept them or not; he began to take them off right away. I declined with thanks.

In a nullah on our right front their lies a mortally wounded Turkish officer; his guts are blown away [and] we can see his backbone. He is attended by a wounded private, his servant I presume. It is touching to watch the devotion of that wounded private to his dying officer. He will not leave him and his condition is too bad to get him on a stretcher – what a contrast.

I am told one officer and twenty men were all that were left when we came to the rescue of the North Lancs.

Battalion forms up at 9.30 am and move off (less one company who were detailed for salvage work).[54] We passed six enemy gun pits. Hundreds of shell cases are strewn around the gun positions. Our gunners must have failed to spot their positions as not a shell crater is in evidence anywhere near them.

Halt from 10.30 am until 3.00 pm when we resume the advance. At 5.00 pm the Battalion halts four miles in rear of 40 Brigade who are engaged with an enemies' rearguard who are posted on some high ground.

At 5.30 pm our Regimental Quartermaster Sergeant again came to the rescue; he rode into bivouac on a lean scraggy mount with corrugated-iron sides at the head of the ration convoy and wore the air of a man that was 'doing his bit'.

The firing on our front died away at 11.00 pm and we are soon asleep.

Notes

1. 'The 38 Brigade relieved 9 Brigade in a piquet line beyond the Hai, the East Lancashire being allotted sixteen lunettes [occupied by the 1/1 Gurkhas] with the right flank on the river in front of Besouia.' (Regt. Hist., p.339)

2. Now began fresh operations, which were to open the way to an advance upon Baghdad. The Tigris River still covered and afforded protection to the main Turkish force in its entrenched positions extending from Sannaiyat to Shumran. General Maude concluded that his best plan was to attack both enemy flanks, i.e. at Sannaiyat and Shumran simultaneously. Orders for 14th Division was to seize a bridgehead across the Tigris at Shumran bend and then construct a pontoon bridge.

3. 1/1 Gurkhas.

4. 'Camp Besouia, where training of Grenadiers and Lewis Gunners continued until 23 February.' (6th Bn War Diary, February 1917)

5. Privates Burton and Downing were the only soldiers in the whole war to be actually shot for sleeping on sentry. Instead of standing up on the fire-step they were found sitting down asleep together in the bottom of the trench. This was taken as a deliberate decision to go to sleep.

6. 'The brigade [38] moved north-westward in the wake of the 14th Division towards the Shumran Bend.' (Regt. Hist., p.339)

7. '14th Division force a crossing at Shumran Bend . . . and [construct] a bridge at M30.' (6th Bn War Diary, 23 February)

8. 'Cross the bridge [built by 14th Division on the previous day] and concentrate at a bund on the north side of the river.' (Ibid, 24 February)

9. '14th Division clear the peninsula to Dahra barracks and the [sand] ridges running west-northwest and east-southeast there from.' (Ibid, 24 February)

10. [Following the crossing of 14th Division at Shumran Bend and the successful attack by

the 7th Division on the opposite flank, at Sannaiyat, the Turkish forces were retreating to Baghdad. Roe was actually deployed against the Turkish rearguard] 'posted at the north-west corner of the Shumran peninsula and in the many canals and watercuts . . . holding on tenaciously, and making the most of its advantages of ground' . . . [and effectually allowed the main body of the Turkish XVIII Army Corps to retire.] (*History of the War: Mesopotamia*, Vol 3, p.180)

11 'On 24 February, at 7.25 pm, General Maude issued orders for pursuing operations next day. There was no doubt that the Turkish main force was in full retreat up the Tigris, though its rear guard had been able so far to check the advance of our Cavalry and 14th Divisions.' (Ibid, p.184)

12 'The advance up the left bank of the river began, 38 Brigade with artillery and engineers forming the advanced guard with the East Lancashires at the head of the column.' (Regt. Hist., p.339)

13 The naval flotilla consisted of *Tarantula, Mantis, Moth, Gadfly* and *Butterfly*.

14 'As Caesar says, "They sought safety in flight", much to the amusement of our Lancashire Brigade, who shouted to them "Back to Amara for more beer, you blighters!" and like remarks.' (Letters of Buchanan-Brown)

15 'At 11.00 am the vanguard was shelled by the Turks and the battalion was hurried forward in support.' (Regt. Hist., p.339)

16 *Packals* were water containers and a *yakdan* was a small leather box.

17 'The Turkish rear guard was holding a disused canal running to the north-western side of the Husaini Bend, and the whole Brigade deployed for the attack . . . . The Turkish shelling grew heavier and rifle and machine gun fire soon opened, the advance being checked some 500 yards from the enemy. The troops dug in as best they could with their 'grubbers', and held on while 39 Brigade came forward on the right to turn the enemy flank.' (Regt. Hist., p.339)

18 The standard issue rifle to the German Army was a Mauser rifle. The Turkish Army was supplied with these and other Mauser-action rifles. Therefore, Roe, hearing the Mausers firing, was told where the action was and that it was still occurring.

19 'Patrols were pushed out at night, but the Turks retired about 2.30 am on 26 February.' (Regt. Hist., p.339)

20 'The East Lancashire had been in the thick of the fight, advancing well ahead of the flank battalions, [apart from the commanding officer, four other officers were wounded] fourteen other ranks were killed and about a hundred wounded whilst three were missing.' (Ibid). In the close fighting that day Private John Readitt of 6/South Lancashires earned a Victoria Cross.

21 'The advance up the river was resumed next day, but made slow progress over the battle-field.' (Ibid)

22 Imam Mahdi was the Turkish advanced base.

23 '[Battalion] halted to reform. Here [at Imam Mahdi] I, and others, discovered some rather useful loot in the form of German Red Cross stores, from which I seized cocoa for my men and myself, and very good it was too, field dressings, not so good as our own variety, and a rather good acetyline lamp.' (Buchanan-Brown)

24 'Eventually the East Lancashire arrived at Bughaila where they settled down as Corps reserve.' (Regt. Hist., p.339)

25 Most likely 6 Cavalry Brigade.

26 'Proceeded to join Division at 1.00 pm and march through dust about 8 miles to point on hairpin bend about 600 yards east of Nahr Kela – where remained until the 28th.'(6th Bn War Diary, 27 February 1917

27 'General Maude had been very anxious to push on at once in pursuit of the retreating Turks, though his Chief of General Staff and his Quartermaster-General considered that the small amount of transport available was insufficient to keep the force supplied either with ammunition or food . . . . On the afternoon of 27 February . . . General MacMunn [Inspector-General of Communications] had an interview with General Maude and explained the situation fully . . . . He (General MacMunn) had had no warning that an advance towards Baghdad was imminent and he was consequently not specially prepared for it . . . he must have a few days . . . to make arrangements for a succession of temporary 'riverheads' and supply dumps. General Maude asked General MacMunn for how long he wished the halt to be made and received the answer that, if the advance was delayed till 5 March, he was prepared to give assurance by then of a sufficient and constant supply for as far as he wanted to go. To this General Made finally agreed.' (*History of the War: Mesopotamia*, Vol 3, pp.199–200)

28 'Rations very scarce' (6th Bn War Diary, 3 – 4 March 1917)

29 With the supply problem now resolved, General Maude ordered the advance to recommence.

30 'The East Lancashire arrived at Zor after a march of nearly twenty miles rendered the more trying by the fact that numerous irrigation cuts had to be negotiated.' (Regt. Hist., p.341)

31 The Turks had prepared positions at Ctesiphon but they did not occupy them. Their rearguard position was at Lajj where the 51st Turkish Division was entrenched. They were charged by the 13th Hussars, of 7 Cavalry Brigade, who swept over the first line of trenches only to come under intense rifle and machine gun fire from a second line that had been obscured. The enemy position was too strong for cavalry to capture, and after dark the cavalry division broke off the action and withdrew to bivouac on the Tigris bank. According to the Turkish account their 51st Division began its retirement at sunset, moving back to the Diyala in company with the greater part of the XVIII Corps from Ctesiphon.

32 '6 March brought the battalion to Bustan, 12 miles further on and very near the famous Ctesiphon Arch.' (Regt. Hist., p.341)

33 The Arch of Ctesiphon is the remains of the vaulted roof of the White Palace of Chosroes I.

34 [After his early successes at Basra, Qurna and Amara] 'Townshend continued his advance, and on 22 November 1915, attacked the Turkish position at Ctesiphon . . . but unbeknown to him, the enemy had been reinforced by two first-class Anatolian Divisions (the Turks previously encountered had been a poorer quality, intermixed with Arabs). In a very hard fight the Turkish first line was captured, but Townshend halted for some days, in a state of indecision. Then both sides simultaneously decided on retirement . . . . When the Turks discovered their mistake they retraced their steps and pursued the British force back to Kut.' (*Mesopotamia – The Last Phase*, p.2)

35 The Turks had two bridges across the Diyala River, both of which were removed.

36 'The Turks were reported to be holding the river line, but a reconnaissance by the

mounted troops brought little information, and at 3.00 pm the Brigade [38] was ordered to force the passage without delay. At dusk the Brigade concentrated about 3,000 yards from Diyala village, which was on the near bank at the point where the stream joined the Tigris.' (Regt. Hist., p.341)

37 '38 Brigade ordered to cross the Diyala River at night. King's Own on the left near the River Tigris and East Lancs on the right.' (6th Bn War Diary, 7 March 1917)

38 'Pontoons arrived, the carts, with their wheels creaking abominably, no doubt giving ample warning to the Turk.' (Buchanan-Brown)

39 'At 11.00 pm the King's Own seized the village, which had been evacuated by the enemy, and attempted to cross by pontoons launched at the ramp of the demolished bridge. The East Lancashire, who were to cross higher up-stream, could not get their pontoons to the bank in time as their passage was impeded by numerous ditches. The battalion therefore provided covering fire on the right for the King's Own who, however, found themselves held up by heavy Turkish fire which caused the attempt to be abandoned.' (Regt. Hist., p.341)

40 Captain T.P. Watson MC, Adjutant of the 6/East Lancashire, aged 26. 'A most gallant officer . . . he was the perfect gentle knight and beloved by all who knew him and by all ranks.' (Buchanan-Brown) He is buried at the Baghdad (North Gate) CWGC.

41 'Several boats were launched and allowed to get into midstream, there was a bright moon, and then the Turks let them have it, and all sank or had their crews put out, except one, which gained the further bank only to be bombed.' (Buchanan-Brown)

42 'Owing to the impossibility of getting boats across under heavy fire, the attempt was given up that night and the East Lancs ordered not to endeavour to cross.' (6th Bn War Diary, 7 March 1917)

43 '[One pontoon] gained the further bank, only to be bombed. All her crew were killed except one officer, wounded, and one man untouched. He, when he realized what had happened, swam back, got a tow line, returned to the pontoon, which despite galling fire was successfully towed back to our beach.' (Buchanan-Brown)

44 'During 8 March, preparations were made for a fresh attempt which was made by the Loyal North Lancashire, and at night some 120 officers and men were ferried over – the East Lancashire provided rowers – before the pontoons were all riddled with bullets and sunk.' (Regt. Hist., p.341)

45 As noted earlier, the Mills grenade had a fearsome reputation for unreliability in the first half of the war and loose safety pins could cause premature detonation. With the Mills grenade the spring-loaded striker was retained by an external lever and a safety pin. When the pin was removed the lever could be held down in the closed hand; released when the grenade was thrown, it allowed the striker to ignite a time fuse set for various delays between four and seven seconds.

46 'This time, under an artillery barrage . . . and a hot rifle and machine gun fire, some boats got across with several officers and some one hundred other ranks. Several pontoons were riddled [with bullets] and the cries of the wounded, as they drifted down to the Tigris, were heartbreaking.' (Buchanan-Brown)

47 'The hundred odd of the North Lancashire, who had crossed, occupied, with intervals . . . a length of about 300 yards of the opposite bank, encountering heavy hostile fire and then a series of counter-attacks, which caused them heavy casualties. Captain O.A.

Reid ... finding his numbers reduced from sixty to fifteen ... [combined with the other two groups of survivors] launched a bombing counter-attack [he was awarded the Victoria Cross for this action]. This cleared his front and enabled him to withdraw his men gradually downstream to a small bend in the embankment. Here with his gallant band he beat off a succession of attacks which continued till daybreak ... During 9 March, many expedients were tried ... to get ammunition and bombs across to the detachment; but they were all frustrated by the enemy's fire.' (*History of the War: Mesopotamia*, Vol 3, pp.228–230)

48 'The British 13th Division had spent 9 March in making arrangements to complete the passage of the Diyala during the night. The 38 Infantry Brigade, with 5/Wiltshire of 40 Brigade attached, was to cross the river at 4.00 am on the 10th, while the 8th Cheshire (40 Brigade) were to move up the Tigris in two motor lighters and land above the Diyala. The latter project failed. The lighters started at 11.00 p.m.; but the engine of one broke down, and the other, grounding on a sandbank, was only with difficulty hauled out of a precarious situation just before daybreak on the 10th, by the gunboats *Tarantula* and *Snakefly*. For the Diyala crossing, two columns were formed. One, composed of the 6/East Lancashire, 71st Company, R.E., one company 8th Welch Pioneers and sixty rowers from 39 Brigade with ten pontoons, was to cross over at the three places where the North Lancashire had crossed the previous night; and the other composed of the 5/Wiltshire [and attached troops] was to cross at three places about a thousand yards higher up the river.' (*History of the War: Mesopotamia*, Vol 3, p.235)

49 'After an intense eight minute bombardment, 4.40 am – 4.48 am, 6/East Lancs success-fully crossed the Diyala River with very little opposition.' (6th Bn War Diary, 10 March 1917)

50 [The North Lancs, when they were relieved] 'were very short of bombs and had an average of two cartridges a man, and were prepared to meet the next counter-attack ... at the point of the bayonet.' (Buchanan-Brown)

51 [The Battalion] 'captured 6 officers and over 180 unwounded prisoners.' (6th Bn War Diary 10 March 1917)

52 'Over 150 corpses were found close to the river.' (Ibid)

53 Lieutenant-Colonel B.L. Birley of the King's Own took over the command of the battalion on 1 March following Colonel Davey being wounded on 26 February.

54 '38 Brigade bivouacked 3 miles northwest of Diyala bridge [with] 'A' and 'C' Companies left behind to clear up the battlefield.' (6th Bn War Diary, 10 March 1917)

XVII

Operations Above Baghdad

(11 March – 1 May 1917)

Approach to Baghdad – Baghdad – To Celebrate St Patrick? – Affair at
Duqma – Operations on the Adhaim – Field Post Office – Shaving –
Crossing the Shatt-al-Adhaim – The Local Arabs – Driving the Turks from
Dahuba – Action at Adhaim – Dangers of a Stretcher-Bearer

Approach to Baghdad

11 March: Rouse at 6.00 am [and] move forward at 7.00 am. At 8.30 am we march through 40 Brigade. We are advance guard today, [with] cavalry scouting in front.

Groves of date palms and walled orchards adorn the rivers bank, whilst the domes and minarets of the mosques of the ancient and historical city of Baghdad appear at intervals over the tops of the groves of date palms, which surround the city.

At 10.00 am we could observe the smoke of several fires in the city. Otherwise all is quiet; not even the report of a Mauser disturbs the peaceful calm which surrounds this stronghold of Mohammedanism in the Middle East. I observed a noisy flock of storks that seemed to resent the change of ownership.

As the Regiment are on the right flank of the Brigade, when the order to halt is given we are about 2000 yards from the city and in line with the clock tower. We halt as the clock on the tower strikes eleven.[1] The domes of the mosques and the roofs of the buildings are covered with people. There appears to be a row going on in the city. Our troops are clearing out and rounding up the Kurds and other unruly elements that started looting as soon as the last Turkish train left at 4.00 am this morning.[2]

No sooner had we halted than we were surrounded by a crowd of Baghdadis of the poorer class who clamoured for biscuits. They seemed to be starving. We shared our meagre rations with them.

As I gaze on the city of the Caliphs that gave birth to that book of fables entitled 'The Arabian Nights Entertainments', my mind wandered back to

249

my schoolboy days when, instead of doing my home lessons such as parsing Greek and Latin roots, composition and Geography, I was reading all about Ali Baba and the forty thieves, Aladdin and his lamp and the voyage of Sinbad the Sailor. It meant a caning every morning from the old schoolmaster for incomplete and inaccurate homework. I 'stuck' the canings until I finished the book. Little did I then dream that I would be gazing on Baghdad today.

Move off at noon and bivouac 3 miles from the city.[3]

12 March: Resting,[4] only five men per Company are allowed, on pass, to the city daily. They must be fully armed, carry 150 rounds of ammunition and keep together.

13 March: Resting, we have been issued out with *Ghee* and *Chupattie* [Chapatti] meal this morning in lieu of biscuit rations. We are on short rations. By way of explanation we are informed that the left wing of General Baratoff's Russian army, which rests upon Khannikin [Khaniqin] on the Diyalah river, have got to be rationed by the British, and a fleet of Fords 'Tin Lizzies' leave Baghdad for Khannikin every other day with half our rations for the Russians.[5] So we've got to tighten up our belts and hang on for better times. The pancake making in mess tins lids was not a success.

14 – 15 March: Sandstorm raging for the past two days.

Baghdad

16 March: In company with four others I visit the historical and ancient city of Baghdad this afternoon. I entered the city by a hole in the wall dignified by the name of North Gate. Crowds of beggars assail one at every step. Thousands of dogs of the mongrel type wander at will through the streets. The city seems to be in the last stages of decay. The narrow, filthy, evil-smelling streets are blocked in places by tumble-down houses and heaps of garbage. In some streets the balconies of the houses almost meet, thus shutting out the sun.

Words fail me to describe the stench; everything solid and liquid seems to find a resting place in the streets. The Arab quarter of Port Said and the Kaffir kraals in South Africa, in so far as stench is concerned, might be described as mild in comparison to Baghdad.[6]

The mosques are marvels of ancient architecture; their mosaic domes look lovely from a distance (and so does Baghdad). We are surrounded at street corners by bevies of dark-eyed, tarnished and decidedly risky Eastern beauties, with rouged lips and darkened eyelashes that rarely solicit, although their occupation is obvious.

We visited the Maude Hotel. I suppose about a week ago it was known as the Kemal or Enver Hotel (wonderful diplomacy). We paid 4 rupees each for dinner. First course was Irish stew, backed up by one unforgettable and unbeatable pancake for second course. A large jug of pure unadulterated, unchlorinated Tigris water was flanked by an orange. I drank some of the muddy liquid from glasses embellished with the portraits of Mustapha Kemal[7] and Enver Bey Pasha[8] and paid through the nose for the privilege.

We had the headwaiter 'squared' for five bottles of beer when who should appear on the scene but Mr 'Red Tabs'.[9] The young staff officer put the 'wind up' the waiter and we had to 'pick em up' without partaking of that delectable beverage. After that dinner I felt wonderfully refreshed.

I had been commissioned by three of my comrades to purchase three bottles of whisky by hook or by crook as tomorrow was the 17th, St Patrick's Day, and we could celebrate the feast of St Patrick and the capture of Baghdad, a kind of killing two birds with one stone, if you will. We were prepared to pay 10 rupees for each bottle, or more if it came to a 'push'. I brought all my wiles and artifices to bear on various shopkeepers. 'Twas of no avail, as the APM had put his barrage down. I only wish I could get hold of that old lamp of Aladdin's!

In our wanderings after the feast at the Maude Hotel we entered one street [and] in a two-storied house with a large balcony we heard familiar tunes being played on a mandolin. At intervals a not unmusical mouth organ joined issue. We remarked 'Hello, there are some of our fellows up there.' On backing to the opposite side of the street to get a better field of view, we discovered they were 'scaly backs' (Navy men) in a very hilarious mood and dancing the Mazurka with four of Baghdad's choicest beauties. 'Lucky fellows', commented we, 'you've been drinking something stronger than muddy Tigris water from Kemal Pasha glasses.' Etiquette forbade us to intrude on the happiness, merriment and delights of the Senior Service.

We left the historic and ancient city as the muezzins were calling the faithful to prayer from the summits of tall minarets. I was profoundly disgusted and disappointed with Baghdad and the dreams and romancing of my schoolboy days I left on the heaps of garbage and filth which 'decorated' the city's streets.

Baghdad yielded booty to British arms of 650 prisoners, 4 damaged aeroplanes,[10] masses of arms and ammunition and much [railway] rolling stock.

To Celebrate St Patrick?

17 March: [It is] St Patrick's Day, a holiday.

I manoeuvred amongst the vendors of dates, oranges and what not on the outskirts of our bivouac this morning. I did not fancy dates for breakfast. The Arabs who sold eggs were bought out and had retired for reinforcements. I was on the point of returning to bivouac when I spotted a suspicious-looking hawker, dressed up in 'European language'. I approached him out of sheer curiosity and glanced into his basket. 'Oranges again', I commented.

He studied me for a few seconds, at the end of which he uttered the magic word, 'Whiskey'.

'Whiskey! What! Where?' I exclaimed.

He swept away a layer of oranges with his hand and exposed to my astonished gaze two pint bottles of 'Black and White' with the familiar silver papering covering the necks.

'Oh Heaven sent one', I murmured. If heaven did not send you, well St Patrick must have a hand in it and taken pity on one of his sons athirst in the wilderness. I whispered, 'How much?'

He replied, '8 rupees'.

I got rather sceptical as I expected the Armenian to demand 6 rupees per bottle at least. I again examined the bottles and could detect no signs of 'faking' about them. I gladly parted with 8 rupees and hid the bottles in my shirtfront. I had to execute all sorts of movements, flanking and otherwise, to get my bivouac without anyone noticing my chest development. I buried them in the sand underneath my groundsheet.

With bated breath I whispered the good news to Sergeants Tim Taylor, Clarke, Hayes and 'Boko' Murray. 'Mum's the word until 7.00 pm tonight, when we rendezvous in a nullah 200 yards north east of the bivouac.'

It has been given out that on the 14th our forces defeated the Turkish XVIII Army Corps at Mushaidie [Mushahida].[11]

At 7.00 pm I 'deliver the goods' at the place appointed. Clarke produces a cup, Tim Taylor a clasp knife, the marlinspike of which performs the duties of corkscrew. I manoeuvre into position on 'Boko's' right as the beverage is being passed around from right to left. Getting on his left means getting left with an empty mug. A cupful is poured from the bottle. Clarke tastes it and shakes his head. We all smell and taste it in turn. It is mainly composed of methylated spirits combined with mastic or arrack – No whisky, or the smell of it. The bottles are smashed and the St Patrick's night would-be-revellers disperse. I have got to bear the brunt of sarcasm and abuse. The rascally Armenian prevented us from paying full military (I mean liquid honours) to St Paddy. Let anyone come preaching to me in future about the poor downtrodden Armenians. I'll tell them in unparliamentary language what I think about them.

18 March: A day of rest.

19 March: Battalion parade for ceremonial drill from 8.00 until 9.00 am.

20 March: Inspection by Divisional Commander.

21 – 23 March: Nothing doing. Eggs very cheap.

24 March: Brigade moves to the river's bank and bivouac in a grove of date palms. Oranges and dates are plentiful and cheap.

25 March: Divine service parade. After parade the Divisional Commander[12] 'soft soaped' us by complimenting us on our great achievement and warned us not to be under the delusion that because Baghdad was captured we had finished the fighting. The latter part of his address did not go down very well.

26 March: Brigade packed up and under orders to move at a moments notice. At 4.00 pm orders are issued to move.[13] After marching 19 miles in a north-easterly direction Brigade bivouacs for the night at 11.30 pm.[14] We are told that two Turkish Divisions have crossed the Jabal Hamrin range from Persia and are advancing on Baghdad.[15]

The 39 Brigade, of our Division, is some 30 odd miles away[16] and we are going up to reinforce them.

27 March: Rouse at 7.00 am; move off at 8.00 am – very bad road.[17]

28 March: Rouse at 6.30 am; move off at 7.30 am. The heat is trying and men are falling out by the dozen. The worst offenders are the men who rejoined us at Baghdad after having a good spell in hospital. I suppose they are hankering after a nice comfortable bed, custards and rice puddings, and a nice and sympathetic sister to take their temperature thrice daily. Once men get a taste of such luxuries it is the very devil to get them to face an angry Turk. Move again at 8.00 pm; bivouac at 10.00 pm,[18] track very bad.

Affair at Duqma

29 March: The 39 and 40 Brigades are supposed to attack some time today. My Brigade moves up in the evening and dig in well in rear of 39 Brigade.[19] 'Sitting to' all night.

30 March: Turks retire under cover of darkness last night.[20] At 3.00 pm the Battalion received the order to move back to Abdul Hassan.[21] I noticed some of the 39 Brigade dead lying about. No effort had been made to bury them. They are left for the vultures and jackals.

Battalion bivouacs at 9.00 pm in a grove of palms. What are the Russians doing?[22]

31 March: A quiet day in bivouac.

1 April: No RC Church or field service.

2 April: Our Light armoured cars do patrol work by day. It is very exciting to watch them trying to creep up on the Turkish Cavalry patrols. The Turks always manage to keep out of range, when the cars advance they retire. When our cars retire; they advance, and so the game goes on.

3 – 4 April: In bivouac. Nothing doing.[23]

5 April: A party of NCOs and men have been selected to proceed to India on one months leave at a later date. We can hardly credit it, as Mess-pot is a land of lost reputations and broken promises. Only NCOs and men who have been with the Battalion since its arrival in the country are eligible. Battalion is under orders to move at 4.00 pm to Divisional rendezvous.

Our RSM has got his Commission.[24]

We are informed that the Russians have had another big victory. We are getting used to those big victories and take them with a pinch of salt.[25]

Move off at 4.00 pm and bivouac at 5.30 pm at Palm Grove, which is the rendezvous.[26]

Operation on the Adhaim

6 April: Brigade move out of bivouac at 6.00 pm. Halt at midnight.[27] We marched over some ancient ruins tonight. It seemed to me to be an ancient city, or the site of one I should say. The walls were standing to a height of over 12 feet in some places. The sky is brilliantly illuminated with stars every night.

7 April: Battalion remains in bivouac all day. Two hostile aeroplanes kept us under observation.

8 April: Sunday. Divine service parade.

We had it given out to us today that on the 18–19 March our forces occupied Ba'qubah[28] on the Diyala River, and Fallujah[29] on the Euphrates.

On 25 March our forces attacked a portion of the Turkish XIII Army Corps at Sharaban, inflicting heavy losses. On 2 April the Turks evacuate Sharaban and retreat across the Diyala River.[30]

British establish contact with the Russians at Quizil Rubat [Qizil Ribat].[31] So far so good.

At 7.00 pm we move out and take over the piquet line from the Cheshires.[32] The Turks are some 1,500 yards away on the opposite bank of the Shatt-al-Adhaim.

Our water mules, escorted by our watermen, went to the Shatt-al-Adhaim to fill the *packals*. The Cheshires had filled their *packals* there every night without interference.[33] It so happened that when the Lancs went to this quiet spot to replenish their water supply, there was a strong Turkish piquet with a machine gun posted on the opposite bank. They let a start be made and then opened fire. The mules and *packals* have not turned up, some of the *drabbi wallahs* and watermen have, and in a very scared condition. The Battalion go waterless.[34]

9 April: Parties have been sent out this morning to search for fifteen mules and thirty pannikins that got lost or strayed after last night's affair with the Turkish piquet. Some mules were found in [the] rear [area] and ten *packals* saved.

We are under orders to move after dusk. The 7th Division on the right bank have had to retire 10 miles through lack of supplies.

We are plagued for the past two days by an immense swarm of locusts. Every locust crawls in the same direction; men have to be detailed to shovel them out of the trenches by day and by night.[35]

Move cancelled at 8.00 pm.

10 April: The Turks sent over a few shells today. When the haze lifts we can see the Turkish piquets on some rising ground on the opposite bank of the river. Visibility [is] bad.

11 April: The 39 and 40 [Brigades] were in action on our right rear today. It seems as if the Turks were trying to cut our lines of communication. We do not like to hear firing in our rear.[36]

I witnessed a thrilling aerial combat this evening. Our man, by skilfully handling his plane, made a forced landing and escaped with a slightly damaged plane. When the enemy drove our man down he rose to about 4,000 feet, rolled, banked and nose dived in a spirit of elation. He heeded not the bombardment by anti-aircraft guns from our land batteries, or from our river monitor. The sailors did the better shooting. When 'fed up', he headed for home.[37] It is humiliating to relate that in all the aerial combats I have witnessed in Mesopotamia our airmen have always been driven to earth by faster and superior machines. The enemy's machines appear to possess more speed and climbing power, and their audacity knows no limit.[38] On two occasions I have seen them stick to their man until they almost landed with them.

We seem to be doing well on the right bank as the capture of Balad Railway station is reported, together with 9 Turkish officers, 200 other ranks, 3 machine guns and rolling stock.[39]

Field Post Office

Mails are very infrequent of late and I am not surprised owing to the system that prevails at the base post office, Basrah. In 1916, when discharged to convalescence camp Makina from No.3 B[ase] G[eneral] Hospital or the hospital ship *Karadenig* it was just the same. I went down to the field Post Office on the riverbank in order to see if I could find any mail belonging to me. I was directed to two EPSP tents pitched and laced together. A *Babu*[40] dozed at the doorway, I asked him, 'Can I have a look for some mail?' He waved his hand towards the interior of the tents. I went in. The floor was two foot high with parcels, papers and letters. It took me two hours to wade through the piles of letters on the floor. I found three of my own and quite a number belonging to men in my Regiment who had been killed in action. I wrote 'killed in action' on the envelopes and left them there. I suppose they remained there until they were burned. Parcels were broken open and the contents strewn all over the floor. Anyone could walk in and pick up a parcel

255

and a bundle of newspapers, tell the *Babu* they were his, the *Babu* would murmur, '*Atcha Sahib*', and you could walk away with them. It is done regularly here.

Shaving

12 April: When in the trenches one has to shave every day. The tin case, which at one time enclosed a Williams or any other brand of shaving stick, is used as a receptacle for holding our shaving water. A tobacco or cigarette tin would hold too much water. Shaving is an ordeal never to be forgotten; Quartermaster's 'Erasmic soap' and an army razor – a trying combination, and a mild form of Chinese torture. When the ordeal is completed, not without a succession of nicks and gashes, the wet shaving brush rubbed over the face has to suffice for a wash, as we cannot spare water for washing from a quart of drinking and cooking water *per diem*.

13 April: Nothing doing. We can see Turks moving about in the distance but are not within effective rifle range.

14 April: Sandstorm raging all day.[41]

15 April: Sunday. Sandstorm again. Six hungry and fed-up Turks came into our lines at dawn.

16 April: Battalion under orders to move.

Crossing the Shatt-al-Adhaim

17 April: Battalion relieved at 4.00 pm by the North Lancs who take over the piquet line. [Our] Brigade, less the North Lancs, move back to Brigade headquarters and rest for the day.[42] We are going to cross the Shatt-al-Adhaim and attack the Turkish right flank at dawn.[43]

In the morning we are issued out with two day's rations each. Think of it, two whole loaves of bread per man. Is the world coming to an end? How are we going to carry tomorrow's rations, haversack already filled to its capacity with a cardigan, socks, towel etc.? We solve the difficulty by having a real 'tuck in', the best we've had in Mess-pot. Water and brushwood was plentiful. We saved half a loaf and a tin of 'bully' between two for tomorrow, as when fighting water is all one troubles about: food is only a secondary consideration. In any case, we may all be dead tomorrow. Some of us will for a certainty.

Brigade moves off at 11.00 pm and each Regiment are allotted four pontoon boats.[44]

18 April: At 2.00 am we reach the point where the crossing is to be made.[45] Owing to the noise made by the wagons conveying the pontoons, we draw the fire of a Turkish patrol on the opposite bank of the river.[46]

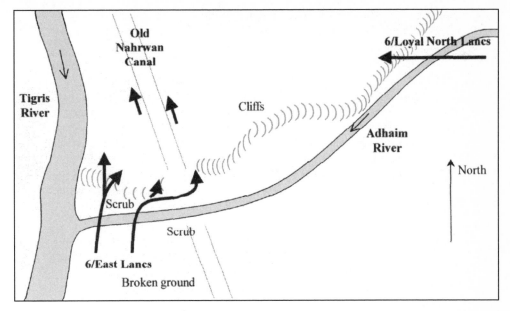

12.   Sketch map to illustrate the Adhaim crossing, 18 April 1917,
from the letters of Buchanan-Brown.

Pontoons were launched at 2.30 am and the first three Companies of each
Regiment (East Lancs, South Lancs and King's Own) get over and form line
in the brushwood on the opposite bank without a shot being fired.[47]

Some of the men soon forget the lesson taught them on the Diyalah as they
imagined they were on a boating expedition on the Thames or Ribble instead
of carrying out a difficult military operation. Although the Turks were 1,500
yards away they must have been very sound sleepers indeed or else they did
not conceive that we would cross the river and take them in the flank. The
Turkish Commander made a grave blunder when he reckoned on his flank
being secure behind the river.

The remaining companies get across without incident and the three
Regiments are formed up in two lines facing the Turkish flank, their objective being the capture of a continuation of mounds 20 feet high and roughly
1,500 yards from the river.[48]

The lines have advanced; a tall growth of brushwood conceals their
advance to within 200 yards of the mounds.

The Turks are beginning to 'smell a rat'.

The MO and staff cross last. Daylight is coming. We are fired on from the
mounds, and the bullets kick up delightful little fountains of spray around

257

the pontoon. The rowers re-double their efforts and the pontoon grounds its nose on the opposite bank. As the MO looks around for a suitable place to fix up a first aid post, scattered firing is going on in front.

We hear a cheer; the mounds are clearly visible now. Who are those men on top of the mounds? They are ours. I can tell by their helmets.[49]

[We] move forward; when we reach the base of the mounds prisoners begin to come in. The attack was a complete surprise; only a few sleepy Turks manned the flanking trenches. Turkish officers were captured in bed as they languorously sipped their early morning coffee.[50]

Parties of Turks are stubbornly holding out here and there. The fighting has developed into a series of small actions.[51] A party of Turks held out in the old river's bed until 2.00 pm when the King's Own charged them with the bayonet, taking 200 prisoners and 2 machine guns.[52]

Everyone is enduring the pangs of thirst.

Lieutenant Davey[53] killed. Our losses were slight when compared with the magnitude of the operation.[54] For once the element of surprise was not lost.

Some guns and about 300 Turks are retiring in the distance; our cavalry are across and are in pursuit.[55] I cannot estimate the number of prisoners taken.

Battalion moves off at 6.00 pm and bivouac at 7.00 pm two miles from the battlefield.[56]

A number of Arabs, who were caught on the battlefield tonight, looting the dead and collecting rifles, were shot out of hand. It is mysterious where those Arabs came from. During a battle there is not an Arab to be seen, but as soon as the shades of night fall they are prowling like ghosts all over the battlefield, looting and collecting rifles.

19 April: Brigade resting in bivouac.[57] The heat is trying from 10.00 am to 5.00 pm.

We are officially informed that the Turkish losses yesterday were: captured, 27 officers, 1,217 other ranks, one gun, 6 machine guns with ammunition and much booty. I noticed some of their gun mules yesterday had our Government brand and numbers on their hooves. Not a bad haul.

The Local Arabs

20 April: Resting in bivouac.

The country north of Baghdad is inhabited for the most part by tribes of agricultural Arabs who dwell along the rivers and canals banks. The ancient Persian waterwheel, manipulated by two bullocks, lifts water from the Tigris for irrigation purposes. The machinery consists of a bullock skin, which brings the water to the surface, and a system of ropes. It lifts about 8 gallons of water every two minutes. The water is emptied into small channels which convey it to the cultivated patches. Wheat, watermelons, tomatoes and onions are chiefly grown.

The Arabs are notorious robbers and will open up a grave and disinter a dead man for the sake of the socks he was buried with. No cross or mound marks the graves of the British dead on the battlefields, as a cross or mound would indicate to the Arabs that someone was buried there. The graveyards at Baghdad, Kut, Amara and Basrah are wired in and guarded at night by an Arab watchman.

21 April: A big battle [is] going on, on the right bank of the river in the direction of Samarra.[58]

Driving the Turks from Dahuba

22 – 23 April: Brigade under orders to move at a moments notice.[59]

24 April: Brigade moves out of bivouac at 1.30 am and marches in column of route in a northeasterly direction.[60] Halt at dawn.

We can discern groups of men on or right flank. Who are they? – Oh, they are the West Kents.[61] At the same time fire is opened on us from the front and right flank (queer West Kents, those!). Well, they must be Turks! Yet we were told the Turks are miles away. The Brigadier seems quite surprised.[62]

Our artillery comes into action under heavy machine gun fire and the Brigade opens out for the attack[63]. The North and South Lancs attack in two lines, the King's Own are in supports, the East Lancs are in reserves.

Our cavalry have galloped around our left flank, well out. The Turks are posted on a line of small mounds 2000 yards away on the right flank of the Brigade's original line of advance. The ground is as flat as a billiard table. The mules are off-loaded, [and] one solitary shell sails over and explodes in rear of the pack animals. For a wonder none of them bolts.

The fight is in full swing by now. It is an inspiring sight to see the North and South Lancs advance across the open ground by sectional rushes. The covering fire was accurate and well maintained and carried out with the coolness and precision of a field day 'stunt' for the benefit of some inspecting General. Our artillery are on the mark. The enemies' bullets are kicking up dust all around the advancing lines. At last a bayonet charge and the Turks 'leg it like Hell', except two machine gunners who fired their guns to the last, then put up their hands and asked for mercy from the King's Own – They got it.[64] Fifty prisoners taken, and the stretcher-bearers of the units that attacked seem pretty busy.

Brigade bivouacs on battlefield for the day.

This scrap was a mutual surprise to both parties as when we found contact with the Turks they had advanced some miles forward from their position as reported on the evening of the 23rd.

The Turkish XVIII Army Corps were heavily defeated at Istabulat[65] on 21–22 [April]: 20 officers, 700 other ranks, 15 guns, 2 machine guns, 540,000 rounds of small arms ammunition, 1,240 rifles, 16 railway locomotives,[66] 240 trucks and 2 barges captured.

25 April: Regiment moves at 1.00 pm. We are escorting General Marshall's second line transport.[67] Arrive in bivouac at 6.00 pm.[68]

The 7th Division on the right bank of the Tigris have captured Samara.[69] The Roman Emperor Julian is said to be buried in Samarra[70] and Alexander the Great died in Babylon. I credited both Julian and Alexander the Macedonian with more brains than to die in a country like Mess-pot. Another Greek General, Xenophon, and his forces got lost in the dim and misty past in the marshes of Mesopotamia. I expect he too died.

26 April: Brigade moves at 6.00 am. Bivouac at 10.00 am.[71] If operations last much longer we will all be in hospital with heatstroke.

27 April: In bivouac.[72]

28 April: Brigade moves at 4.30 pm advance six miles and post outposts.[73] Our mules are almost played out for want of sufficient food.

It is rumoured that the XIII Turkish Army Corps are advancing towards us.[74] We are moving up tonight to support the 35 Brigade, who are going to attack at dawn.

29 April: Brigade relieved at 6.00 pm by an Indian Brigade. The plan of operations has been altered and we are going to attack at dawn in the morning.

Thirty NCOs and men per Battalion left Brigade Headquarters tonight for a month's leave in India – 'Lucky fellows.'

Brigade moves at 7.00 pm, fords a stream and halts at midnight. We are promised '*lacs*' [lakhs] of artillery support.[75]

Action at Adhaim

30 April: Brigade in position at 3.00 am.[76] Artillery opens up at 5.00 am; we advance under cover of the bombardment.[77] Through some error the shells are dropping short on the right. Sergeant Jacobs and three men were killed and two wounded by our own shells. The line halts to allow artillery to lift.[78] The barrage lifts and we advance. Enemies' piquet line on mounds rushed with a few casualties.[79]

Further advance held up by strong rifle and machine gun fire from enemy's main position. His artillery has chimed in and things are getting hot. We are hanging on by our eyebrows to the position vacated by the enemy's piquet.[80]

At 7.00 am the 40 Brigade are fighting around an Arab village about 2000 yards away on our left flank.[81]

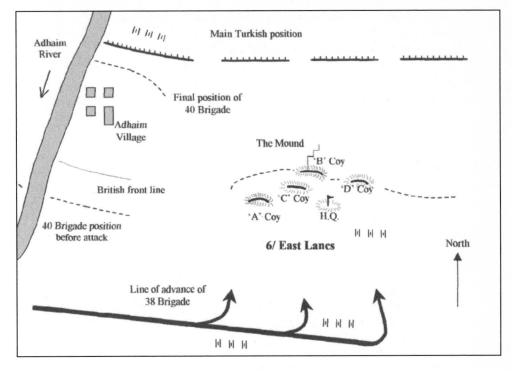

13. Sketch map of the action at Adhaim showing the Mound and the
final position of the advance, 30 April 1917,
from the letters of Buchanan-Brown

The Turkish guns are numerous, well handled and are giving us an awful time on the exposed mounds. Two batteries of ours in action on our right rear had to be abandoned as the Turks got on the mark and smothered them with high explosives at 8.00 am.

One Company of ours under Mr X, a very young Lieutenant, who was not afraid of death, doubled forward in line, the objective being a nullah or irrigation canal 120 yards in front. He or his men never got there as they were stopped by machine gun and rifle fire before they advanced 50 yards. In some parts of the line they were shoulder to shoulder, in others they were 10 yards apart. They had to lie down. They could not open fire as they were pinned to the ground by superiority of fire. Quite a number sought refuge in a shallow irrigation ditch that ran direct to the Turkish position. They were enfiladed and shot down.[82]

Our artillery is giving us very little support today.[83] From the mounds we can see the Turkish field guns and the teams in rear of the guns. His heavy guns are much further back. What a sight for a Forward Observing Officer – but there are none here.

All is quiet on our left. What has happened to 40 Brigade?[84]

At 2.00 pm the Turks form up leisurely in the open for a counter-attack. Now is the chance for the artillery but we don't seem to possess any. They advance for 200 yards at a walk then lie down. Our shooting is bad as their heavies and lights are bursting amongst our exposed men and disconcerting their aim. Thank God they are retiring. Luckily for us they have no aerial eyes.[85]

Wounded are lying by the dozen at the base of 'The Mound'. The 39th Field ambulance is two miles in rear. It takes an hour and a half to get there and back and the stretcher-bearers have more than their work cut out to get the casualties in from the firing line. The Turks are dropping shells around the Field ambulance. The Red Cross flag seems to be a rallying point for all kinds of transport, therefore under the circumstances they cannot very well be blamed.

About 3.00 pm the Brigadier, General O'Dowda came up to the firing line. With legs well apart, he pulled out his glasses and leisurely surveyed the Turkish position.[86] He showed a supreme indifference to bullets and shells. His action renewed our courage and restored our confidence. He remained with us for an hour.

At last an artillery observing officer arrives and our guns commence throwing some 'stuff' over. Firing ceased when darkness fell.

The 39th Field ambulance sent squads of stretcher-bearers to remove our wounded. During the day I noticed one brave fellow who drove a horsed ambulance all around the abandoned batteries picking up wounded. The Turks shelled him unmercifully, I expected him to 'go up' every second, but he bore a charmed life.

7.00 pm and dead silence in front. What is he doing? Is he going to attack under cover of darkness? These were the thoughts that flashed through our minds on that harrowing night.[87]

Dangers of a Stretcher-Bearer

My Regiment had one hundred casualties, including three stretcher-bearers.[88] I am determined to make an attempt to get returned off stretcher-bearing. It is no sinecure. You have got to follow up an advance and when your comrades are under cover you're out in the open, in the midst of it, dressing and carrying in wounded. If the attack is repulsed it is just the same thing. A forward digging party has a number of casualties; they are forced to retire. The stretcher-bearers have got to go out, find and bring in the wounded. A reconnoitring patrol gets to within 20 yards of the Turkish barbed wire. The Turks opened fire and wound a couple of men, you have got to go out and bring them in without fail, and so on. You have the honour to be sniped at, shot at and probably shot, yet you have not the privilege of putting a rifle to your shoulder and retaliating.

Pollard[89] got one through the head today. We soldiered together, went to France together, came out to Gallipoli together, have been through this Mess-pot 'stunt' together, and he goes and stops one at last. What bad luck, or is it fate. We were going to have a good time on our month's leave in India, but the fates decreed otherwise.

1 May: The Brigadier informed us at dawn that the Turks had retired through the passes in the Jabal Hamrin and were well 'well away' by now. Our aeroplanes and cavalry are in pursuit.

Our overconfidence, or indiscretion rather, was nearly our undoing yesterday; 2,000 infantry attacking 5,000 well-entrenched Turks with 37 guns to back them up, is beyond a joke.

I picked up one of our wounded this morning. He was lying in a shell hole since early yesterday morning with a broken thigh. He seemed quite cheerful in spite of his privation and experience. It appears that when the SWBs [South Wales Borderers] took the Arab village yesterday morning, the Turks counter-attacked up a nullah, took them by surprise, threw the whole line into confusion and took some prisoners.[90]

The Jabal Hamrin range is only seven miles away.

Notes

1 'At 9.30 am the [13th] Divisional commander received orders not to enter the city.' [The 35 Infantry Brigade was ordered to garrison Baghdad] (*History of the War: Mesopotamia*, Vol 3, p.247)

2 'The King's Own and Corps cavalry were ordered into Baghdad for police duties.' (Ibid)

3 'The East Lancashire . . . marched round east of the city and camped at Es Salek [lake], 2 miles to the north.' (Regt. Hist., p.342)

4 'The Battalion rested and efforts were made to make up for the large number of casualties in the specialists – the bombers, Lewis gunners and scouts. Training of these specialists and PT [Physical training] and squad training filled up the time.' (6th Bn War Diary, 12 – 25 March 1917)

5 Roe is partially mistaken here. He was either given the wrong information, or he has misinterpreted what he heard. 'On 13 March General Maude learnt that Baratoff's main force . . . was nearing Bisitun on 8 March . . . and might reach Khaniqin on 20 March. . . . . On the 15th the Chief of the Imperial Staff telegraphed that, although the advantages of co-operating with the Russians might be considerable, he did not wish General Maude to take undesirable risks . . . . On 16 March orders were issued for an advance towards Khaniqin of a force under the command of General Keary (3rd Division) . . . . One hundred and fifty Ford vans' [which Roe comments upon] 'carry supplies for his force [Keary's].' (*History of the War: Mesopotamia*, Vol 3, pp.272–273)

Extra confusion to the story, and for Roe, was that, 'on 4 April Colonel Rowlandson [the British liaison officer with the Russians] left Baghdad to rejoin the Russians, taking with him forty-six lorries loaded with supplies sent by General Maude for the Russians' Force [at Qizil Ribat].' (Ibid, p.298)

6   The general feeling among the troops was that Baghdad was a great disappointment. 'There were no sanitary nor scavenging arrangements, noxious smells abounded and hundreds of diseased and half-starved dogs roamed everywhere. The miserable-looking and rather dilapidated houses of mud-brown brick, and the narrow filthy streets completed the disillusion.' (Ibid, p.248)

7   Mustafa Kemal Atatürk – The most famous Turkish military commander of the First World War, making his reputation in the Gallipoli campaign. He emerged after the war as the first president of the new republic of Turkey, 1924–38.

8   Enver Pasha – Turkish minister of war in World War I.

9   Slang for a staff officer.

10 '6 Cavalry Brigade . . . occupied Kadhimain [just north of Baghdad] where they captured a hundred prisoners and four damaged aeroplanes.' (*History of the War: Mesopotamia*, Vol 3, p.247)

11 On 14 March General Cobbe's column, consisting of two squadrons of the 32nd Lancers, the 7th Division and some artillery, executed a flank attack on the Turkish XVIII Army Corps who had halted to cover the withdrawal of ammunition and stores, etc., from Mushahida railway station. The action caused the Turks to retreat abandoning ammunition and equipment.

12 'General Cayley addressed the battalion, complementing it on the work it had done.' (Regt. Hist., p.342)

13 'The Turks were now reported to be in position some 50 miles north of Baghdad in the direction of the Jabal Hamrin hills and the whole 13th Division moved out on 26 March to disperse them.' (Ibid, p.343)

14 'Bivouac at Khan Jadidah' (6th Bn War Diary, 26 March 1917)

15 The Turkish 51st and 52nd Divisions.

16 At Jadida.

17 'Reached Jemadin at 2.00 pm . . . 38 Brigade had covered a distance of 34 miles in twenty-two hours, with the usual hourly halts and one rest of eight hours at Khan Jadidah. The circumstances were trying, with blinding, choking dust . . . . Considering all things, very few men fell out.' (Buchanan-Brown)

18 'The Division closed up to the front . . . which brought the East Lancashire to Jadida and thence to bivouac at Khan Nahrwan after darkness had fallen.' (Regt. Hist., p.343)

19 'General Cayley, commanding 13th Division, arranged to combine a frontal attack [by 40 Brigade] against the enemy's left centre, east of the Nahrwan canal, with an outflanking movement [by 39 Brigade] against his extreme left at the ruins . . . .The 40 Brigade drove the enemy from a line of rifle pits . . . and dug themselves in, apparently a few hundred yards short of the enemy's main line . . . but the enemy's position could not be accurately located through the mirage . . . [it was] decided that 40 Brigade should suspend its advance until the result of the 39 Brigade advance became clear. The 39 Brigade made a general attack with all three battalions . . . carried out with great dash over an absolute bare and flat plain . . . and met with complete success.' (*History of the War: Mesopotamia*, Vol

3, p.292). 'The 38 Brigade had little part [in the attack] . . . the East Lancashire were sent to protect the [gun] batteries on the right flank where they had come into action only 1,200 yards from the Turks.' (Regt. Hist., p.343)

20 During the night the enemy, the Turkish 52nd Division, evacuated its position and retired to the line of the Adhaim River.

21 Roe has made a mistake here with the name, as the East Lancashires were ordered to retire to Abu Tamar to be in Divisional reserve. 'Owing to the transport being late, we did not start to retire till afternoon, being escorted on the flank by an armoured car, which effectively frightened away some of the Turkish mounted Arab irregulars which might have given trouble on our left flank'. (Buchanan-Brown)

22 'General Maude heard on 30 March that two of the Russian Corps . . . would undertake an offensive towards Mosul, commencing probably about the end of April.' (*History of the War: Mesopotamia*, Vol 3, p.294)

23 'Weather getting much hotter than usual . . . Drinking water and washing water very scarce. PT [physical training] parades before breakfast and a short drill parade after breakfast with a bathing parade in the evening.' (6th Bn War Diary, 1 – 4 April 1917)

24 Second-Lieutenant Herbert Carrington MC, DCM, (formerly Regimental Sergeant Major) was commissioned on 2 April 1917. Promoted to Lieutenant on 2 October 1918, he retired 18 October 1919 with the honorary rank of Captain.

25 This information given to the troops is most likely about General Baratoff's advanced troops having reached the vicinity of Qasr-i-Shirin. The British command still had high hopes of a co-ordinated campaign against the Turks once the two armies met, which were soon to be dashed by the effects of the Russian Revolution. We now know the troops were right to be sceptical about the report.

26 '38 Brigade concentrate north of Palm Grove' (6th Bn War Diary, 5 April 1917)

27 'In an effort to assist the advance of the Russians through Persia a blow was now to be struck at the Turkish concentration on the Adhaim river, and General Marshall's column, which was to operate on the left bank of the Tigris, included the 13th Division, with cavalry, artillery, engineers and aeroplanes.' (Regt. Hist., p.343) 'The battalion arrived at Kuwar Reach at 10.30 pm where the 13th Division concentrated at the spot on the left bank and the 7th Division opposite on the right bank.' (6th Bn War Diary, 6 April 1917)

28 'Troops of the 3rd Division, under the command of General Keary, occupied Baquba on 18 March' (*History of the War: Mesopotamia,* Vol 3, p.268)

29 'General Maude issued orders for the I Corps to despatch a brigade group to Falluja on 18 March' [which was successfully taken on the same day] (Ibid)

30 The dates Roe was given, or recalls, for the action at Shahraban are wrong by two days. The Turks were holding an entrenched line west of Shahraban. 'General Keary received a message from General Maude : "It looks very much as if enemy [is] slipping away . . . Utmost importance that you should pin him to his ground and, if he will not be so pinned and retreats, you should attack him vigorously . . . ". General Keary, decided to make a frontal attack next morning . . . the Turks, however, withdrew in the early hours of 23 March. The 47th Sikhs occupied Shahraban at 7.00 am; and an advanced guard of one squadron of cavalry, a field battery and two battalions of infantry engaged and followed up the Turkish rear guard till checked by artillery fire along the line of the Haruniya canal.' (*History of the War: Mesopotamia,* Vol 3, pp. 275–276)

31 'On 1 April a detachment of General Keary's column reached Qizil Ribat unopposed; and next morning a *sotnia* of Russian Cossacks [of the I Caucasus Cavalry Corps] also arrived there, accompanied by Lieutenant-Colonel Rowlandson, the British liason officer.' (Ibid, p.297)

32 '38 Brigade move to Shatt-al-Adhaim and take over outpost line from 40 Brigade. North Lancs and East Lancs [provide the] piquet line.' (6th Bn War Diary, 6.30 pm 8 April 1917) 8th Cheshire Regiment, part of 40 Brigade, was the regiment relieved by the East Lancs.

33 '40 Brigade [informed us] that a certain place in the river was perfectly safe to obtain water.' (Ibid, 9 April 1917 at 2.00 am)

34 'A battalion headquarters party, without taking due precautions, led its water *pakhal* mules down to fill up at the river and came under heavy fire which caused a stampede and the loss of sixteen mules with their thirty-two *pakhals*. These must have been gathered in by the ubiquitous Arab.' (Regt. Hist., pp.344–345)

35 'An appalling plague of locusts which literally covered the ground, and cliffs, and they were able to inflict quite a painful bite.' (Buchanan-Brown)

36 'About 5.30 am a large body of Turkish Infantry was seen by 6 Cavalry Brigade moving south-west in column along the Delli Abbas-Diltawa road . . . . The enemy, with his guns well up, came on rapidly . . . . The Cavalry Division was gradually driven back . . . . [About 8.00 am] General Cayley ordered Colonel Cassel's Cavalry Brigade to occupy a line of mounds about three and a half miles west of Chaliya and to hold this position until the arrival of 40 Infantry Brigade . . . . The 39 Infantry Brigade was following the 40 in echelon to the left with a view to attacking the enemy's right. About 10.00 am the 40 Infantry Brigade, just forestalling the Turkish infantry, occupied the line of mounds . . . The 40 Brigade stopped and drove back the enemy right . . . . The 39 Brigade continued its advance in a turning movement against the enemy's right flank. Before this movement the hostile infantry began to fall back.' (*History of the War: Mesopotamia,* Vol 3, pp.313–315)

37 'While we were on the piquet line, one of our aeroplanes was up, when along came one of the Turks most up to date and fastest machines. Our fellow gallantly decoyed the Turk over our anti-aircraft batteries although in imminent peril of being shot down. Unfortunately the Turk got away.' (Buchanan-Brown) [Two different interpretations of the same event.]

38 'Twelve new [German] aeroplanes, half of them Halberstadts, were expected to reach Mosul early in April . . . . On 3 April two of the latter were encountered [for the first time by the RFC on this front. The RFC still had only the one squadron of obsolete aircraft although some new 'Spads' were on their way to Mesopotamia]. From the single squadron, on 19 March 1917, a flight was sent to work on the Diyala front, another went up the Tigris and the third (of Martinsydes) remained at Baghdad for General Headquarters work.' (*History of the War: Mesopotamia,* Vol 3, pp.261, 289, 322)

39 'On 8 April a detachment of General Fane's column, under command of General Davies, moved forward from Sumaika to occupy Balad station . . . . We captured 3 machine guns about 200 prisoners and some 30 railway trucks.' (Ibid, pp.307–308)

40 An Indian clerk.

41 '38 Brigade ordered to cross Shatt-al-Adhaim and occupy heights above – operation postponed.' [presumably due to the sandstorm] (6th Bn War Diary, 14 April 1917)

42 'Relieved by one company of Loyal North Lancs [the Battalion] marched back to brigade headquarters with a view to crossing the Shatt-al-Adhaim, and occupy the heights above, in the early morning.' (Ibid, 17 April 1917)

43 [At 5.00 pm on 17 April] 'General Marshall issued his full and final instructions . . . the 6/East Lancashire and 6/South Lancashire, each with four pontoons and a machine gun section . . . were to start ferrying across the Adhaim, about half a mile above its mouth, at 2.20 am. On reaching the further bank they were to form up facing north with their left on the Tigris and to advance and assault at 4.30 am the cliffs across the north end of the Kabaj peninsula. The 6/Loyal North Lancashire and a machine gun section . . . south-east of 'High Point' were . . . to wade across the ford there and at 4.30 am assault the cliffs opposite.' (*History of the War: Mesopotamia*, Vol 3, p.327)

44 'At 11.00 pm [on the 17th] South Lancs leading and East Lancs, each with four pontoons on light carts, move to river for crossing. Roads very dusty and difficult to maintain touch as night was very dark. Last half mile to river was through very thick bush and direction was rather lost. This fact and the difficulty of off-loading and launching the pontoons delayed the ferrying.' (6th Bn War Diary, 17–18 April 1917)

45 'The river bottom was muddy, and although the actual stream was only 80 feet broad the riverbed was much wider: the steep cliffs, 30 to 40 feet high, on either bank were nearly a mile apart.' (Regt. Hist., p.345)

46 'Just as we neared the river bank we were surprised to hear some shots ring out to our right flank . . . however the march continued and we proceeded to off load our pontoon. Unfortunately indescribable confusion at first reigned on the bank. The same "beaches" were allocated to several companies . . . also there was a good deal of noise, and now was the time, as pontoons crashed down the steep bank into the water, for jolly Turk to open the ball with an effective machine gun fire. But not a sound came from the other shore.' (Buchanan-Brown)

47 'The height of the bank delayed the launching of the pontoons and the embarkation of the men . . . . By the time the assault was due to be delivered only two-thirds of the battalion had crossed, and the South Lancashire had done no better; but it was decided not to wait.' (Regt. Hist., p.345)

48 'It was imperative to advance from the other bank so as to arrive under the enemy's cliff position before daylight and the South Lancs and East Lancs (taking with them as many men as had landed) advanced at 4.15 am.' (Ibid, 18 April 1917)

49 'The enemy were practically surprised and though they opened fire at 150 yards the men rushed to the assault with a cheer and the cliffs were ours.' (Ibid, 18 April 1917)

50 'One or two heavy sleepers were surprised between their blankets.' (Buchanan-Brown)

51 'The Turks were obviously taken by surprise and soon fled, so the advance was able to proceed. Next to the Tigris the South Lancashire had fairly easy going; on their right the East Lancashire had to negotiate the nullahs along the old Nahrwan canal. Nevertheless the whole line made some 600 yards and were then confronted by the Turks in position on some mounds astride the canal some 400 yards away. Further up the Adhaim the Loyal North Lancashire had waded the stream, and behind the other battalions the King's Own had now been ferried over. At 12.15 pm, in the torrid heat, after an effective artillery preparation which had opened at noon, the East Lancashire, the King's Own, who had come up in the centre, and the South Lancashire, advanced to the assault and drove the

267

Turks into the waterless plain north-west of the junction of the two rivers.' (Regt. Hist., p.345)

'It was decided to drive the Turks up the old canal bed, and to drive their snipers, and small posts, in from the numerous nullahs running parallel to, and into the canal, at its west bank. We began to move and started the most exciting and sporting show I have ever taken part in, but unfortunately just about this time, Colonel Davy, our CO, was wounded in the foot and for a long time this very gallant gentleman persisted in hobbling on, after our advancing groups . . . . As a first phase of our operations 'C' Company, working back to the foot of the cliffs, managed to cross the mouth of the canal unperceived. The Turks had quite a strongpoint on an eminence on the East bank there, a few hundred yards from the cliff edge, which 'C' Company, under cover of a most effective barrage of machine gun fire, rushed and captured . . . . Then prior to the advance there was a fifteen minutes intense artillery preparation, which was a joy to watch. The eighteen pounders field artillery especially took my fancy, spraying the ridge. . . . The 'heavies' meanwhile had put up a big barrage of crumps on the edge of the west bank of the canal, under cover of which the 4th Foot [King's Own] now came up . . . preparatory to an advance.' (Buchanan-Brown)

52 'A cheer rang out and we saw the incredible sight of three officers and some twenty men, rushing and capturing some two hundred Turks. It was some of the 4th [King's Own].' (Buchanan-Brown)

53 Second-Lieutenant H. Davey – killed about the same time as Lieutenant-Colonel Davy was wounded. 'With his death we lost a real good fellow, and the battalion a most gallant officer'. (Buchanan-Brown)

54 'Casualties during the operation: killed, Second-Lieutenant H. Davey and six other ranks; wounded, Lieutenant-Colonel Davy and nineteen other ranks.' (6th Bn War Diary, 17–18 April 1917)

55 'The cavalry went through and troops of a gallant Indian Division [35 Brigade of the 14th Division] . . . were vanishing in the distance in close pursuit . . . . All the time we were at rest there was the usual stream of troops and guns . . . attending a rapid advance, for once again our RE [Royal Engineers] had not been slow in throwing a bridge' [across the river at the point where the old Nahrwan canal joined the Adhaim]. (Buchanan-Brown). 'By noon a bridge had been thrown and the 35 Brigade and Cassel's Cavalry . . . crossed by it . . . turning retreat into rout . . . .The Turkish 52nd Division was practically annihilated, 1,250 prisoners being taken.' (*Mesopotamia – The Last Phase*, p.45)

56 'Battalion concentrated and marched 1½ miles to Tel Mahasil where 38 Brigade concentrated.' (6th Bn War Diary, 18 April 1917)

57 The East Lancashire went into reserve for a few days, apart from 'A' and 'C' Companies which held part of the piquet line across the Burura Peninsula.

58 On 21 April began the first day of a two day battle for Samarra, an ancient town, at one time the capital of the country and still of some local importance though much reduced in size. 'The Turks intended to hold Istabulat as their main Tigris line of defence during the hot weather . . . stubborn defence was offered by the Turkish XVIII Corps . . . their 51st and 52nd Divisions are said to have been engaged . . . . Capture of this position by our troops involved severe fighting [by battalions of the 7th Division] during two days of

extreme heat' General Cobbe occupied Samarra on 24 April. (*History of the War: Mesopotamia*, Vol 3, pp.344–345)

59 'General Maude's intention was to deal with the Turkish XIII Corps [2nd and 14th Divisions] if it should continue its movement on Barura and to pursue the XVIII Corps [51st and 52nd Divisions] as far up the right bank of the Tigris as supply arrangements would permit.' (Ibid, p.346)

'The next operation [for the East Lancs] consisted of an advance up the Adhaim with the intention of driving the Turks from their position at Dahuba, west of the river.' (Regt. Hist., p.345)

60 'The 38 Brigade, with cavalry [1 troop] and artillery [4 field batteries] attached, moved at 2.00 am on 24 April.' (Ibid, p.345). In the order from General Maude, issued at 7.30 pm [23 April], 'the enemy's advanced troops [14th Division] ... were said to be preparing a position north-west of Dahuba .... General Marshall's main force was to attack this position early next morning and capture it before Turkish reinforcements could arrive.' (*History of the War: Mesopotamia*, Vol 3, p.349)

61 'During the night we had noticed lights on our right flank, which some had said were Turkish posts, but others had smiled and said it was only some Arab encampment. But now, as it got lighter, these mounds, some two thousand yards away, were seen to be dotted with men, which at first were taken for our flank guard, but some shots falling short soon undeceived one. There was dear old Johnny Turk, waiting for us.' (Buchanan-Brown)

62 'The position of the Turkish 14th Division had been incorrectly located.' (*Mesopotamia – The Last Phase*, p.50)

63 'All was movement again and we quickly got into battle order, the manner in which the gunners got into action, and their rapidity, were superb.' (Buchanan-Brown)

64 'At 5.15 am the column halted and the North Lancs and King's Own advanced in extended order and with artillery support drove the enemy from the mounds, when they retired to the main body [of Turkish XIII Corps] at Band-i-Adhaim. During this operation the battalion [East Lancs] were in reserve.' (6th Bn War Diary, 24 April 1917)

65 This was the battle that Roe heard on the right bank of the Tigris on 21 April.

66 'At Samarra railway station much rolling stock was captured, as this was the terminal station of the Baghdad – Samarra railway.' (*Mesopotamia – The Last Phase*, p.47)

67 'Northward march was resumed, the battalion escorting the second-line transport of General Marshall's column. The heat was trying in the extreme but the advance was made in fairly easy stages, and plenty of water was available.' (Regt. Hist., p.346)

'Second-line transport was calculated to carry one day's rations, one blanket and one waterproof sheet per man, cooking pots, officers' baggage (20lbs per man) and one day's forage for animals.' (*History of the War: Mesopotamia*, Vol 3, p.65)

68 'Bivouaced at Tulul en Nor.' (Regt. Hist., p.346)

69 Following the battle at Istabulat, General Cobbe's Column (7th Infantry Division) occupied Samarra on 24 April.

70 The Roman Emperor Julian is said to have died of his wounds there in AD 363.

71 'No great distance was covered on the 26th as there was a danger of out-running the supply train ... the next few days were occupied in making dispositions for attack.' (Regt. Hist., p.346)

72 'Battalion resting' (6th Bn War Diary, 27 April 1917)

73 'Battalion reinforce an outpost held by the 35 Brigade' (Ibid, 5.00 pm, 28 April 1917)

74 Following their defeat at Dahuba the Turkish 14th Division fell back towards Turkish 2nd Division effectively concentrating the Turkish XIII Army Corps (which had originally advanced and threatened General Marshall's column, but was now retreating).

'At 6.30 pm [24 April] General Marshall issued orders to continue operations against the Turkish XIII Corps and deal with it decisively.' (*History of the War: Mesopotamia,* Vol 3, p.353)

[On the 26th] 'the enemy was located holding a position astride the river through the village of Adhaim, and extended for about two miles on each bank, the flanks being refused.' (*Mesopotamia – The Last Phase*, p. 51)

75 'Battalion was relieved at 3.00 pm to cross the Adhaim preparatory to attack in the morning.' (6th Bn War Diary, 29 April 1917). 'As dusk fell, after a short address from our CO, we were marching off. After fording the Adhaim, we struck up over the cliffs and started to march in earnest. Throughout the night our guns, at certain set times, fired on the enemy, but one is inclined to believe that they did little more than to give him a restless night. A little after midnight we had our last halt and pow-wow, and saw that all was ready to proceed to the place of deployment and for the subsequent assault.' (Buchanan-Brown)

A lakh is an Indian measure of 100,000, usually applied to rupees.

76 'We deployed [East of the "Three Ridges"] into waves of one company, of each unit engaged, to each wave, and lay down.' (Buchanan-Brown)

'38 Brigade formed up for the attack . . . East Lancashire in the centre, King's Own on the right and South Lancashire on the left. The Loyal North Lancashire in reserve.' (6th Bn War Diary, 30 April 1917)

77 'Some moments before dawn, an intense bombardment, of all the British guns, broke out along the whole front, and we began to advance'. (Buchanan-Brown)

78 'By some unfortunate error, some battery west of the river kept dropping shrapnel over some of our men as they advanced. They soon checked their fire, but not until they had inflicted some loss'. (Ibid)

79 'The East Lancs advance was directed on a redoubt known as 'The Mound' and by 5.30 am they had captured this redoubt.' (*History of the War: Mesopotamia,* Vol 3, p.360)

'The first wave soon disposed of the Turkish piquet on the first mounds with surprisingly little loss and I remember turning to a sergeant and saying, "Why this is going to be quite a picnic!" I never made a greater mistake in my life.' (Buchanan-Brown)

80 'The Mound had been reported as the left of the enemy's main line. But it was found that the Turks were only holding it lightly as an advanced position and that they had dug another line in rear, as well as to the northward of it. On reaching 'The Mound' the 38 Brigade came under heavy fire from the north.' (*History of the War: Mesopotamia,* Vol 3, p. 360)

81 'In the 40 Brigade the Cheshires were on the left and the South Wales Borderers on the right. The Cheshires pushed straight on as far as the river bank without orders, capturing both lines and the village [Adhaim] and several hundred prisoners; they had lost their CO and his place was taken by a captain from the Machine Gun Corps . . . .The South Wales Borderers had also pushed on beyond the first line and past the village.' (*Mesopotamia – The Last Phase*, p.52)

82 Buchanan-Brown mentions the ditch in his letters. 'By an unfortunate error, an impetuous officer, who obviously thought that the trench, leading towards the Turkish lines, which was shallow and finally came to a dead end, was an ordinary deep communication trench, started a rush up it yelling, "Bomb the – – – out!" A hail of lead was directed on the trench, which soon became a veritable shambles but never the less we managed to establish a post out there in a deep zig zag.' (Buchanan-Brown)

83 'A dust storm arose [early in the assault] and lasted for over two hours, preventing artillery co-operation.' (*Mesopotamia – The Last Phase*, p.52). 'No aeroplanes were able to get up in the high wind today . . . . At 7.35 am it was reported: "dust storm is getting worse and visibility is little more than 400 yards".' (*History of the War: Mesopotamia,* Vol 3, p.362)

84 [Around 7.45 am] 'The Turks launched a counter-attack against the Cheshire and South Wales Borderers, which checked the British advance completely. This counter-attack, carried out apparently by the 1st Regiment of the Turkish 2nd Division, advanced under cover of the dust storm.' (Ibid, p.362)

85 'Taking ground to the right [of 'The Mound'] the three Lancashire battalions were just in time to stop a Turkish counter-attack.' (Ibid, p.360)

86 'General O'Dowda reported that his infantry [38 Brigade], were under enfilade machine gun fire from the westward, were engaged with the enemy in a strong position to the north-ward and that the cavalry reported enemy working around his right flank.' [This last part of the report was contradicted some time later.] 'He was told in reply for the 38 Brigade to stay were it was.' (Ibid, p.363–364)

87 'The Turks withdrew during the night and their whole force retired into the Jabal Hamrin.' (Ibid, p.364)

88 'In this action the battalion casualties were two officers and thirteen other ranks killed, five officers and sixty-eight other ranks wounded with two missing.' (Regt. Hist., p.346)

89 Private Fred Pollard (6578), born Burnley, Lancashire. Killed in action, Mesopotamia 30 April 1917.

90 See earlier footnotes about the action; the Turks took 150 Welsh prisoners from the counter-attack. (*Mesopotamia – The Last Phase*, p.53)

XVIII

Months of Rest

(2 May– 17 June 1917)

Sindiya – Sandstorms and Winds – The Countryside –
The Seasons – Medical Problems -
A 'Dear John' – Mr 'Hells Bells' – One Month's Leave –
Local River Craft – Down the Tigris

Sindiya

2 May: Resting

3 May: Brigade move back 5 miles in the evening and bivouac.[1]

4 May: Move out of bivouac at 4.00 pm, halt for the night at 7.00 pm.

5 May: No move today.

6 May: Brigade move out of bivouac at 6.00 am. Bivouac at 10.00 am. All moves since 3 May are retrograde, or backwards.

7 May: Move at 5.00 am. Bivouac at 10.00 am. 'McCormack', or rather the sun, is making it pretty uncomfortable for us.

8 May: Move off at 5.00 am and arrive at Scindia [Sindiya] at 9.30 am.

9 May: Pitching summer camp on the banks of the Tigris .[2]

10 – 12 May: Tidying up around camp. All have been inoculated against enteric.[3]

13 May: Regimental concert at 8.00 pm. I omitted to mention that Colonel Davy rejoined us just in time to get wounded again on 18 April. Major Houghton of the . . . is at present commanding the Battalion.

14 May: No parades are allowed between the hours of 9.00 am and 5.00 pm owing to the heat. Scindia might be described as an oasis in the desert. Groves of date palms meet the eye and break the monotony of the flat never-ending desert. Fruit is plentiful and cheap.

Of course, all fruit has to be dipped in chlorinated water [and] this is provided by the Medical Officer, or rather the Sanitary Sergeant, at the place set apart for the hawkers, who are an evil, filthy-looking crowd indeed.

I suppose we will have an orgy of inoculations, vaccinations, medical and dental inspections now that we are in a standing camp.

272

15 May: Brigade hard at work for eight hours tonight, establishing defensive works north of Scindia.[4] This will go on for months, we are told, as the Turks are concentrating at Mosul with a view to a dash on Baghdad at the commencement of the cold weather season. Well, it will be a change to be on the defensive and let somebody else do the attacking.

16 May: The sick paraded at 7.00 am this morning. I went out of the medical tent to collect the sick reports from the BOC [Battalion Orderly Corporal]. I glanced along the ranks of sick for new faces. I spotted my friend Mr Quinn from St. Helens; he looked in perfect health but seemed worried. He was a cook and not a bad sort of a fellow as any time I would pass the cookhouse he would give me the 'nod' to go into the cooks' tent. There he would regale me with a mug of Sergeant Major's 'tack'. One good turn deserves another, so I called him to one side and asked him what was his complaint? He told me it was 'pantomime' poisoning.

' "Pantomime" poisoning,' I gasped, 'have you been "scoffing" any tinned stuff?' I asked.

'No', he replied, 'but I ate 4 annas worth of dates last night with my tea.'

'Did you wash the dates in chlorinated water?' I queried.

'No', he did not know fruit had to be washed before consumption.

'Well', I replied, 'you deserve to be "pantomime" poisoned. Are you aware that you might have been the origin of a cholera or enteric epidemic that might ravage the whole Army Corps and cause hundreds of deaths through your carelessness in disobeying instructions laid down by the medical authorities? Don't tell the MO that you have eaten dates without first washing them. In fact, you had better not mention dates at all. Complain of pains in the stomach.'

He did! – and a stiff dose of castor oil shifted the 'pantomime' poisoning. Someone told him he had 'pantomime' poisoning for a leg-pull.

I have seen men eat dates and grapes just as the filthy Arabs handed them over the barrier to them, with the result that dozens were coming sick every morning with all sorts of abdominal troubles and a policeman had to be detached for duty on the hawkers' stall to ensure that all fruit purchases were washed in chlorinated water.

Sandstorms and Winds

17 May: At 2.00 pm the sky became darkened. On looking toward the North West we saw a dark wall advancing. At 2.30 pm the sandstorm was upon us. The sun became obscured and a blanket of darkness descended on the camp. We were engulfed in an avalanche of sand backed up by a 40 mile an hour wind. We rolled blankets around our heads to keep the sand from blinding us. Tents went down like skittles. Blankets, shirts and suits of khaki drill were

273

whirled away and never seen again. At 3.00 pm daylight reappeared, and with it plenty of work; the tent floors were inches deep in sand, sand everywhere.[5] The unit encamped a mile in our rear, and in the path of the storm, reaped a harvest in blankets, shirts, khaki drill, etc.

18 May: Draft from India arrives today. Some of them have been in beautiful Bangalore since we arrived in Basrah in 1916. Concert at 7.00 pm.

19 – 20 May: Sandstorms. The prevailing wind is from the North and North West. The East wind, or '*Sharqi*', brings a high temperature. We get the '*Shamal*' in June; it blows from the North and North West, dries the atmosphere and affords some relief from the intolerable heat. The South wind is invariably oppressive and is accompanied by dust.

All winds raise dust and increase the difficulties of observation for ground forces and airmen, and affect their engines by choking them up. Its effects are the same on mechanical transport. The pulling for artillery teams is heavy in places, even where the surface is good. At first it soon cuts up and becomes heavy if a succession of vehicles attempt to make a track. Mechanical transport of any weight, where such can be utilized, soon breaks through the desert crust and gets bogged in mud beneath. In wet weather mechanical transport is useless.

The Countryside

Lack of wood and total absence of stone present great difficulties; both have to be imported. There are no metallic roads in the country beyond those made by the Indian Expeditionary Force.

All the houses are built of sun dried brick and are no benefit to us as they are rarely where they are most wanted. They are wretched, badly ventilated hovels without cooking or sanitary arrangements of any kind. Indeed, before we came to Mesopotamia the open street was the public latrine.

No natural shade of any kind exists, for trees are scarce and date palms give poor shade. No trees means no wood for building or burning, and all wood has to be imported from India and elsewhere.

The palm belt area is always deep and damp and the humid heat takes it out of man and beast.

In the hot weather, potatoes and other vegetables rot in a short time, onions sprout, and local supplies are not sufficient. Grass for animals cannot be depended upon and rarely grows where it is most needed.

The Seasons

The 'flood season' has nothing to do with rains and is caused by the melting of the winter snows in the Caucasus and in the highlands of Asia Minor, hundreds of miles away. The rivers commence to rise in January and reach their level at the end of March. The floods occur in April and May.

March, April and May are the best months for military operations. [There is] little rain and fairly reasonable temperature, but these advantages are nullified by floods whose subsidence is followed immediately by the awful heat of June, July and August which render military operations impossible.

Medical Problems

Everyone suffers from a plague of flies; men who chuck refuse down anywhere, *saises*[6] who do not burn their horses' dung, a faulty latrine system or a dirty camp, increases the plague. You pick up some at Basrah. You are met by reinforcements when close to Amara. At successive camps you get more and more, till it culminates with a plague at the most advanced positions. The experts inform us that there is no natural production and the plague is due to faulty latrines and a faulty disposal of refuse and dirt.

Apart from the fly, there is the danger of typhus from lice; nor must we forget the sand fly.

Malaria is the principal disease in this country. It is prevalent during the floods and in the autumn.

Epidemics of cholera and plague rarely occur.

I have only outlined a few of the military and medical problems which confront an Expeditionary force in Mesopotamia.

21 May: Fruit season in full swing.

22 –24 May: Usual camp routine. Mosquitoes and sand flies are causing a lot of fever. The second furlough party left for India on the evening of the 23rd. [7]

25 – 28 May: Heat intolerable. We are just alive and gasping, and no more.[8] A Turkish airman paid us a visit this morning; he did not drop any 'visiting cards'.

A 'Dear John'

29 May: Mail up. I got a letter from Noreen. It was posted nine months ago; a rather affectionate epistle. As I read on, I came to a paragraph, which stated that Wilfred was taking her to the pictures twice weekly and did I mind? The friendship was purely platonic, and so on. I was flabbergasted. Who the devil was Wilfred, anyway, or what was he? Platonic friendship, forsooth! – there is no such thing as platonic friendships. The letter ended with a little more than the usual 'barbed wire adornments' and a trifle more affectionately.

I thought and smoked hard for an hour, I weighed the situation up from all angles. If I pulled through, got home and married Noreen (that is, if she was not already 'tied up' to 'Wilfy') 'Wilfy' might be best man. Without a doubt 'Wilfy' would be invited to tea on occasions. 'Wilfy' would claim that he poured balm on Noreen's aching heart whilst I was 'doing my bit' for King and Country in the deserts of Mesopotamia – and the eternal, or infernal, triangle would be formed.

I came to a decision and wrote Noreen a very plainspoken letter. I did not like breaking away, but under the circumstances I had no option. It took me hours to compose it. I told her it was no use hanging on for me as the war might last for years yet. I might get home with a whole skin or I might get home blinded or crippled. If not blinded or crippled, I might be minus a leg or arm, or both legs or arms. Again, there was a possible chance that Mesopotamia might claim me as a landowner until Gabriel sounded the trumpet. [She was] to think of me only as a friend, to marry 'Wilfy' if she liked him, to take a chance whilst she had one. I gave her her freedom, without prejudice and for her own good, I released her unconditionally, although I would always cherish tender memories of Belle Vue Gardens. I made one stipulation, and that was that when the war ended in years to come, and if I got home safe, I would consider it a privilege to stand as sponsor or godfather to the second or third 'Wilfy' or Noreen, whichever providence liked to send.

In any case it is cruelty encouraging her to cling to an almost forlorn hope. Of course there are other girls in Mesopotamia but none to equal Noreen. Of course that is only my opinion. In any case the decision is irrevocable as the censor, Mr 'Hells Bells' (it is his turn for censoring letters this week), will be callous enough to chuckle over my pessimism and sentimentality, I suppose, when he peruses it.

Mr 'Hells Bells'

30 – 31 May: Usual camp routine, with 5 sandstorms per day thrown in.

A young officer was posted to my unit when we got settled down at Scindia, we'll call him Mr 'X'. In him the clerical profession lost a shining star. 'Hells Bells' is his strongest and only swear word, if it can be called a swear word. Some of us believe that it is between a prayer and the mildest form of swearing. A prayer word in a sense that it brings before our memory Hell and what Hell stands for.

In our schoolboy days we all received a certain amount of religious instruction, more or less. We were taught that God made Hell and populated it with Lucifer and his platoon of fallen angels who had rebelled against him. The angels were deprived of their wings and other celestial trappings and were converted into 'stokers' or devils. All men who lead bad and unruly lives go to hell when they die, and I suppose women too. Quite a number of us in this Regiment (myself included) have almost forgotten that there is such a place as Hell, or Heaven for that matter, although we hear Hell mentioned often enough. The sights we've seen and hardships endured have made us callous. The war has not put the clock of Christianity forward; it has shoved it back.

If Mr 'X' fell into a deep irrigation trench on a compass march he would simply ejaculate 'Oh Hells Bells', nothing more. If Mr 'X' awoke in the morning and found that some poor benighted Arab, suffering from kleptomania, had annexed all his kit and left him with only his pyjamas, he would simply mutter 'Oh, Hells Bells'. Most annoying incidents have occurred in which, had St Thomas, Peter, Patrick or John been in his place, [they] would have sworn heartily, but Mr 'X' simply 'Hells Belled' it. We all admire him for his self-restraint and the grip he's got over his emotions. He is as free from temper as a frog is from feathers.

He has set a good example to the Regiment. As, for instance, I was watching Cook Brown chopping up firewood the other day [when] the axe slipped and dinted his shin badly. I expected a torrent of invective, but he simply muttered 'Hells Bells'. A camp kettle full of water is almost on the boil, it slips and puts the fire out. Cook Jones simply mutters 'Hells Bells, that's caked it'.

Patrick Maher, the Commanding Officer's breeches maker, whilst criticizing his superiors to an onlooker, sticks a needle half way through his thumb. Does he 'D and B' the needle? No, he 'Hells Bells' it.

Private Gent, the Quarter Master store-man, in a fit of aberration, issues 'A' Company out with a pair of socks too many. When he discovers his loss does he fill the EPIP tent with swear words? No, he murmurs " 'Hells Bells', they've done me for a pair of 'Almond Rocks'."

Mr 'Hells Bells' deserves the OBE (jocularly referred to by the troops as the 'Order of the Boiled Egg') for cleansing the Regiment from foul-mouthed expressions and forcible adjectives. I'm afraid he would be too modest and unassuming to accept it. All are 'Hells Belling' it now. It is more pleasing to the ear to hear that simple ejaculation uttered than a sentence containing the full quota of luminous adjectives such as D's, B's, F's and H's.

1 June: Sand fly fever and dysentery [are] prevalent in camp.

Spuds are 'loved' up in a new formation now, (i.e.) tinned, just as biscuits are, and are termed desiccated potatoes. They are sliced, brown in colour, and when boiled resemble a mess of boiled turnips and smell like an artificial manure called Guano, a product of the Pacific Islands. They are not popular and are called 'desecrated spuds' by the troops.

When the ration boats fail to navigate bars and shifting sandbanks on the Tigris, we are forced to live on the products of the country. For instance, we have apple stew for dinner today and date stew for breakfast tomorrow. Cook Sergeant Doman is a wizard. His apple and date stews they are fine, and as

277

a working medicine they beat the famous No.9 (a pill in general use in Mesopotamia for people who suffer from indigestion. Its qualities might be described as violently active, although I've known people who were supposed to be suffering from heart disease and bronchitis to be 'doped' with them).

2 – 3 June: Nothing doing. Fighting is over until September, when the cold season starts. We are expecting aerial visitors as shelter trenches have been dug and Lewis Guns mounted.

4 June: The Arabs are behaving very well; we have lost no rifles so far.

5 June: It is rumoured that Austria and Bulgaria have asked for an armistice. We live on rumours out here.[9]

6 June: This is a great poultry rearing and fruit growing district, Eggs 6d [old pence] per dozen and chickens 1 shilling each. They would give you the impression when eating one that they had escaped from Noah's Ark during the flood.

One Month's Leave

7 June: Hurrah! I form one of a party of thirty NCOs and men who are proceeding to India on one months leave under Captain Varvil.[10]

Embark at 7.00 pm on a small river steamer at Scindia, I was in charge of 'D' Company's quota. Mr Carrington[11] asked me, when we were about to march off, 'Have you got 'D' Companies rations?' 'I have sir', I replied. Well, I had not. 'Hells Bells', who is going to worry about a tin of 'Bully' and three biscuits? We are only too glad to get away from the sandstorms and sand flies of Scindia.

8 June: Steam up at 4.00 am and disembark at Shatadan Camp at 9.00 am. Embark on another steamer at 5.00 pm.

Local River Craft

9 June: Steam up at 4.00 am; arrive at Baghdad at 9.00 am. The local river craft are ancient and interesting.

The *Goofa [Gufar]* [12]: a round basketwork affair, covered inside and out with bitumen to make it watertight. When launched it spins deliriously. The trick of controlling it is by paddling first one side and then on the other to stop its revolving tendencies. They vary in size and hold from two to twenty men and are as old as the days of Assyria and Babylon.

Kellecks: goatskin rafts, they can be deflated and carried on pack animals until required.

Mahayla [Mahailas] [13]: a short broad river sailing boat with high curving bow and stern, common on the Tigris below Baghdad.

278

Mashoof: a framework of thin reeds covered with bitumen.

Bellum: a canoe-shaped affair with curving bow and stem (two to twenty men).

Disembark at 10.00 am and proceed to rest camp on the south side of the city. The Turkish bridge of boats is undergoing repair.

10 June: Awaiting orders at rest camp.

11 June: In rest camp, Captain Varvil 'sticks' [gives] the leave party a case of beer.

Down the Tigris

12 June: Embark on river steamer PS *No2* at 7.30 am; steamed past Ctesiphon at noon, anchor at 7.30 pm.

13 June: Steam up at 7.00 pm. [The] River [is] low and sandbanks [are] numerous; past Kut at 7.00 pm; what was no man's land a couple of months ago is now covered by tents.

The hundreds, in fact I might venture on a thousand or more, of our comrades who lie beneath the sod on both banks of the river are but a memory.

The famous Sannaiyat position is as still as a graveyard tonight. Last February thousands of men were dug in, scores of guns belched death and destruction. The air resounded with the deadly rattle and rat – tat – tat of machine guns by day and night as men waited for Maude to give the word – Go!

Steam past Maqasis point at 7.30 pm; somewhere near here the *Julnar* ran aground late on 16 April in a gallant but unsuccessful attempt to run the gauntlet of the Turkish defences with provisions for the starving Kut garrison.

Anchor at 8.00 pm. Somewhere on my right front lies 'Horatius', and in line with my right shoulder lies Mr. Parkinson. In eternal sleep, may they rest in peace.

14 June: Steam up at 4.00 pm. Anchor at Shiek Saad at 9.00 pm. I lost 50 rupees playing Nap today. I indulged in Crown and Anchor tonight with a view to retrieve my losses at Nap. I lost another 20 – no more.

15 June: Steam up at 4.30 am and anchor at Amara at 10.00 am. Steam off again at 2.00 pm. Anchor above the Narrows at 9.00 pm.

The river at this point is illuminated for miles by electric light. The block system is in operation and only one steamer can pass through at a time.

The light railway in course of construction from Basrah to Amara is in full working order up to this point.

Steam through the Narrows at 11.00 pm, a difficult stretch to negotiate as the river is low.

16 June: Steam up at 4.30 am. River navigable for large steamers up to Kurna. Anchor at Basrah at 1.50 pm and disembark at 2.30 pm and proceed to British base depot.

17 June: Awaiting orders at base camp. Rifles, ammunition and equipment handed in.

Came across one of the Walsh brothers today, just the place I would expect to find him.

Notes

1 'The East Lancashire marched back by easy stages to their summer quarters at Sindiya, on the Tigris about 40 miles north of Baghdad.' (Regt. Hist., p.346)

2 'Marking and pitching new camp for summer quarter. EP tents are provided with four officers or sixteen other ranks per tent.' (6th Bn War Diary, 8 – 10 May 1917)

3 Typhoid fever.

4 'Working parties were employed in the cool of the evenings on the Sindiya – Abu Tamar defence line.' (Regt. Hist., p.347)

5 'On 17 May at about 1.45 pm a very violent dust storm – almost a cyclone – smote the camp and almost wrecked it, over twenty tents being blown down. For half an hour the darkness was intense and it was impossible to remain in the open during the height of the storm.' (Ibid, p.346)

6 Indian term for a groom.

7 'Twenty-three NCOs and men proceeded to India on leave.' (6th Bn War Diary, May 1917)

8 'Average temperature during the month of May was 103° Fahrenheit.' (Ibid).

9 This was an optimistic and unfounded rumour.

10 Captain J.K. Varvil.

11 Captain H. Carrington – Battalion Adjutant (formerly RSM).

12 The Gufar is like a coracle.

13 'Mahailas were employed to supplement the steamer service [on the Tigris] but they were an uncertain means of transport; and many of them had to be employed to accumulate gradually a much required reserve of supplies at Amara.' (*History of the War: Mesopotamia*, Vol 3, p.31)

XIX

India

(18 June 1917 – March 1918)

Embarkation for India – Baghdad Re-fought – Leave Parties in Bangalore –
The Corporals' Room –
New Uniform – Madras – Dinner with the Mahratta Rifles –
No Moderation – Ladies of the Kirk –
A Tea Party – 'Leave' Life – Return to Bangalore –
Reporting Sick – Venereal Disease – Bangalore Garrison

On looking over my diary I find that I was not engaged in any further actions, although I came back to Mesopotamia. I did not keep a daily record of events, save here and there. I have generalized more or less from 17 June 1917 until 4 June 1919 when my month's demobilization leave expired.

Embarkation for India

18 June: Embark on HMS *Edavana* at 7.00 am. Steam up at 11.00 am.
Hadrahs [were] numerous on the lower reaches of the Shat-al-Arab. A *Hadrah* is a simple Arab device for trapping fish. It consists of an enclosure made of reeds, which often covers a considerable area. The fish come in with the tide, which covers the reed traps. When the tide recedes the fish are left flopping about in a foot or so of water and are picked up by the Arabs. Anchor at 5.00 pm outside the bar.
   19 June: Steam up at 10.00 am. Bombay is our next anchorage.
   20 – 21 June: Very stuffy on board, not even a breeze to cool the atmosphere.
   22 – 24 June: Heavy swell with showers. The monsoon is breaking over the Persian Gulf. Gambling in full swing.
   25 June: Anchor in Bombay harbour at 10.30 am. This is my fifth acquaintance with Bombay. At 11.00 am a tug tows the *Edavana* into Alexandria docks. Disembark at 2.00 pm. Entrain on troop train at 4.00 pm

281

for Bangalore. This is my first experience of a troop train (trains specifically constructed for the conveyance of troops), and I must admit that they are very comfortable indeed.

26 June: The country wears a refreshing appearance, thanks to the monsoon.

Baghdad Re-fought

27 June: The line ran through rugged mountainous country today; two engines have been on since 6.00 am.

Owing to the facilities afforded, at almost every station of any importance, for obtaining whiskey at 7 rupees per bottle, the Battle of Baghdad was fought o'er again today between the 'Jocks' (Black Watch) and the 'Lancs'. Both parties assumed the offensive in turn and were repulsed. Casualties were numerous, but no stretcher cases. The fight ended in a draw as the fifth station up provided a fresh supply of Johnnie Walker. Neutrals used their influence to good effect and we agreed to share Baghdad between us. Peace was signed and sealed, and 'Jocks' and 'Lancs' quaffed bottles and bottles of Mr Walker in peace and amity.

Several persons in my carriage gave 'boys' 10 rupees to fetch bottles of whisky. The boys never turned up, or the whiskey, or the 10 rupees, at least not until the train steamed out of the station.

Leave Parties in Bangalore

28 June: Arrive at City station Bangalore at 6.30 am.

We of the East Lancs were surprised and delighted to see our dear and well-beloved 'Mutty' once again. We thought he had got swallowed up in the fleshpots of Egypt. He was Conducting Officer and sported the nattiest pair of jodhpurs from the Himalayas to Cape Comorin. He left us quite unexpectedly on 5 December 1916.

The Depot band played us up to Hebbal Camp. We met some old friends in the wet canteen at 12 noon and made some new ones.

We were amazed to meet certain people who bought – well! – postcards at Port Said in 1916 and were sent to India when the Battalion reached Basrah – floating about, some with two stripes up and others with sashes on. Well, well!!!

6.00 pm: We, who had journeyed from afar, from a land called Mesopoluvia, were looked upon as moneyed men and Capitalists by they of Bangalore. We did not lack vessels from which to slake our thirst as the Bangalorites produced a formidable array of enamel pots and basins, some with handles, some without. One and all of the receptacles provided by the hospitable Bangalorites would give one the impression that they had just recently survived a severe dose of smallpox. All they needed was filling, and we of Mesopoluvia did not need asking.

7.30 pm: The Buzz of conversation is general and deafening. Trench systems are being roughly sketched on every table from the overflow of beer from the mugs and basins. The muddy Tigris, the swift flowing Diyalah and the sluggish Shat-al-Arab and Shat-al-Adhaim appeared before my vision once again in facsimile, but [in] more congenial surroundings. Basra, Kut and Baghdad sprang into existence by simply dipping the index finger of the right hand into a mug and making a blob on the table and on the required bank of the river; match-stalks dipped in beer drew thinner lines to represent trench systems.

The accuracy in detail would amaze even a Hilaire Belloc. 'We was here! and the Turks was there'. 'Yes! – there's the bombing sap you got wounded in, Tom, and Bill was killed in this trench by a sniper. There was an old dug out here where we buried Joe when he stopped that nose cap'. 'Here's the dug out that the Sergeant Major slept in'. 'Harry! – do you remember that night we 'pinched' his water bottle full of rum? Christ! – didn't he get a 'liver on' when he went for a swig and found it was gone?'

More beer, more reminiscences and less accurate trench systems.

By 8.40 pm the Tigris, Diyalah and the two Shatts have overflowed and obliterated the trench systems. The tabletop resembles a marsh. Dead and gone comrades are forgotten pro tem as singing has commenced. The talent was fairly good; the songs, 'The Lassie from Lancashire' and 'McAffery',[1] were rather stale.

9.00 pm: They're all jolly good fellows and so say all of us. Enter the Provost Sergeant and his staff – Mesopoluvianites and Bangyites, after swearing eternal friendships and numerous handshakes, slowly file out of the canteen and part with a good night.

The leave party had a line of tents all on their own, on the right flank as you face the camp. Sergeant 'Mick' Cunningham,[2] Corporal 'Jumper' Wilde and 'Crackie' White of the 2nd Battalion visited my tent at 9.20 pm. I thought they were all dead. Reminiscences again, of Preston, the Curragh, India, South Africa, France and Gallipoli. We were mutually regretting the fact that we had nothing liquid with which to celebrate the re-union when who should stagger into my tent but two of my stretcher-bearers, Peter Casey and 'Dusty' Rhodes, each carrying a camp kettle full of beer. 'Mick' Cunningham remarked, 'Well, the devil looks after his own'. We 'cheerioed', 'ching chinged' and 'tu-ra-lued', we talked about officers, quartermasters, and a certain CQMS that charged us twice for shirts we were put down for at Sheikh Saad in 1916 and who had dead men on the pay sheets. We may be still paying for those shirts for all we know.

There was a certain RQMS on the retirement from Mons. When halted in a French village for a few hours one night, we all slept around the transport. He accused us of allowing the Dublin Fusiliers to 'pinch' our bacon and rum. The next morning we knew for a fact that there was not a Dublin Fusilier within a radius of 10 miles.

We talked and drank ourselves 'squiffy'.

Colonels we had soldiered under: Johnny Nick[3] was a "soldiers' Colonel" and so was Le Marchant. W.O. G[4] was not bad, but Colonel L[awrence] did not care a damn about his men and never looked after their interests. Opinions varied.

I asked, 'What about the police?' 'Oh – don't bother about the police. They never interfere with leave parties. In fact, it is a wonder they are not in here now, having a drink,'

'Crackie' White related how he 'lifted' the Queens Westminster's rum issue in the trenches at Ploegsteert in 1914.

Corporal 'Jumper' Wilde, an amateur strategist, with the aid of the tent floor which was of sand, soon made a sand model of the land of the two rivers and illustrated to us how, had he been in General Maude's shoes, he could have captured Baghdad and the whole Turkish army with the approximate loss of a platoon, four mules and two sweepers. The brain-wave came too late.

11.30 pm: Au-revoired and retire to bed. All the tent dreamed of floods and monsoons.

29 June: Leave party wearing 'the morning after the night before' aspect.

There are quite a number of pet monkeys in camp and as soon as the time gun is fired at 12 noon they grab their owner's mug or basin of his box and lope away to the wet canteen. The Lancs have trained them well. It is also advisable not to put your change on the table [as the] monkeys have a peculiar liking for 8 and 4 anna bits, which they deposit on the owner's tables.

Irrigation[5] from 12 noon to 1.00 pm; 'camp kettling' it in the afternoon (getting beer in camp kettles from the canteen during prohibited hours). At 6.00 pm I went to the 'wet' [canteen] with the stretcher-bearers. I fell into the hands of the Philistines. I was not half an hour seated when the Provost Sergeant and Corporal appeared and called me outside.

I was asked, 'Was I an NCO?'

'Yes'

'Well get out of here and go into the Corporals' room.'

The Corporals' Room

I had to obey. In any case it was much better in the Corporals' room. One had more room, one had bearers and one got half an hour extra in which to drink up in when time was called. I suspected Corporal 'Jumper' Wilde of snitching (informing) to the Provost Sergeant. Beer flowed freely as the night progressed. 'Twas a songsters' night as everyone had to sing a song or give a recitation; failing to give either meant 'sticking' drinks around.

Corporal Patrick Maher [was] a tailor from Athlone and a corporal by virtue of his abilities with the needle. He was our Commanding Officer's unofficial breech maker and turned him out in jodhpurs beyond compare in the broad lands of Mesopotamia. They were the envy of the General Staff. In other words, noted 'lady killers' on the General Staff (although unfortunately there were very few ladies to kill in Mess-pot) viewed Colonel McCormack's jodhpurs with envy.

The chairman, Corporal 'Marrowbone' Smith in a high pitched treble, called Corporal Maher. Corporal Maher sung a song which extolled the virtues of all Irishmen who had been generals in the British Army. Each one had a verse all to himself; Kelly Kenny, Kitchener, French, dear old Roberts. Wellington came last on the roll. He made a supreme mess of the 'Iron Duke'. This is the concluding line of the song as he sang it:

'And an Irishman named Blucher won the Battle of Waterloo.'

I became rigid; my heart stopped beating. Had he gone mad? Did he ever read history? Did the Englishmen hear him? No – they could not, as they were all applauding. A couple might, but they glossed over it. I shook the finger of admonition at him across the table. I told him to go to school again. 'You have not credited a single English General with winning a battle. You have labelled Blucher, a grumpy, gouty old Prussian Marshal, an Irishman and gave him credit for winning the Battle of Waterloo, whereas he did not arrive on the field until the French were beaten. Granted he took up the pursuit – anybody can pursue a beaten and disorganized rabble. If the Iron Duke heard you tonight he would turn in his grave. Give up singing, Maher, and learn how to play a tin whistle.'

New Uniform

30 June: Leave party fitted out with new clothing so that we can go on leave respectable.

There are only a few places open for leave parties. Madras is closed, Mhow is too quiet and I have been stationed there. Calcutta is open. Well, Calcutta then – the majority are for Calcutta.

1 July: Elbow raising.

In Hebbal Camp alone there are about 2,000 men, in the prime of manhood, well drilled and disciplined. All have arrived straight from England, some have been here eighteen months, some less. How is it that they have not been sent up to relieve some of the men in Mess-pot who have been at it from March 1916? Men who have been wounded twice and three times are turned out of the hospitals in Mess-pot with wounds just healed and packed off back to the firing line and kept at it until they were invariably 'seen off'. There is old Gasgoine of ours, fifty-two years of age and has three sons fighting in France. Could not one of those young fellows replace him in the firing line? Every man should take an equal risk.

2 July: Twenty furlough men entrain for Calcutta at 8.00 pm. Sacks of beer bottles are taken on board. I 'squared' the CQMS, one of my old Battalion, for two greenbacks (100 rupee notes). Some of them won't have much left to spend when they arrive in Calcutta at the rate they are 'bottling it'.

Madras

3 July: Arrive in Madras at 6.00 am. We were received by GMPs who took us all around Madras 'doing the sights'. The train for Calcutta does not leave until 7.00 pm [and] we are not allowed to enter Fort St. George as there are some of our men there on leave and we might be inclined to remain.

At 6.00 pm I met Sergeants Clarke and Kelly in the De Angeles Hotel. They informed me that you could get no pay in Calcutta. In Madras you can always get an advance of 100 rupees. I took 'Dusty' Miller into my confidence with the result that we decided to give the leave party 'the slip' and remain in Madras if possible. Sergeant Clarke takes Millar and I to the Fort and lent us two of his tunics. When the police were looking for the two absentees from the leave party we were having a high time in the Devon's Sergeants' mess in the Fort. At midnight we reverted to a Private and a Lance Corporal again and were 'fixed up' with beds in the Fort.

4 July: [We had] a refresher in the Sergeants' mess at 6.00 am, [then a] shave and brush up and away to 'square' the Station Staff Officer. We told him we missed the train. Of course we knew what he thought, that we got drunk and went 'somewhere' or that we went 'somewhere' and got drunk. We told him our dearest pals were on leave in Madras, pals we had soldiered with in peace and fought with in war. That we would be under a life long obligation to him if he could use the long arm of influence and allow us to remain in Madras. He was a decent sort of chap, though he reminded us that disciplinary action could be taken against us. He spread his protecting mantle over us, took our numbers and names and said he would 'fix it up'. He wished us a good time and warned us against visiting certain places in Madras and what the results would be if we did. If we thought he was trying to put the 'wind up' us, all we had to do was to take a trip to the hospital and see for ourselves.

We thanked him profusely and left. The interview exceeded our expectations as we fully expected him to 'bundle' us off to Calcutta by the 7.00 pm train under police supervision. We reported to the attached section and were put in rations.

5 July: Spend the day on board a minesweeper in harbour.

Dinner with the Mahratta Rifles

6 July: All NCOs and men on leave from Mesopotamia have been invited to a dinner given by the Colonel and Officers of the Southern Mahratta Railway Rifles at 7.00 pm. Their Boxing Tournament is on tonight also. This social function takes place at Perampur, about 4 miles from the Fort.

Taxis, *gharries* and rickshaws are supplied gratis. The party detailed for rickshaws have to leave three-quarters of an hour earlier than the main body, as the rickshaw is a slow mode of conveyance. I, being a Lance-Corporal, drive in state in a *gharry*.[6] The Sergeants claimed the taxis.

At 7.00 pm we file into a long hall and take our seats. Before the first course is served the Commanding Officer enters and made us welcome in an appropriate and witty speech. The array of cutlery in front of each man was rather bewildering when one considers that knives and forks were rarely used by many of us since 1914. Mr Quinn, naturally, wanted to know what they were all for? Could not a man eat a dinner with one knife, one fork and one spoon just as well as with half a dozen of each?

The first course appeared on the scene. Out of the tail of my eye I saw Bugler Billy Begs with his plate in both hands and drinking the soup therefrom. I tapped him gently on the shin with my right boot and told him to use the big spoon in front of him.

The third course came along, Mr Quinn fancied it and, instead of taking a helping from the dish the bearer brought around, Quinn wanted to 'dump' the lot on his plate. I whispered, 'Take a little and let him pass it on'.

He asked me, 'What "tool" am I going to start on this with?'

I replied, 'Any, so long as you don't use your fingers'.

I was taking my cue from Private 'Tex' Richards who sat opposite to me. 'Tex' was a member of the Rechabites in South Africa and used to go out to bun-fights and dinners, which a fair number of the opposite sex graced by their presence, and his table manners left nothing to be desired.

Midway through the dinner Staff Sergeants made their appearance and placed a bottle of 'Johnnie Walker' between every two men.

Bearers placed tankards of Tennants beer shoulder to shoulder along the whole length of the table.

The last three courses were rarely touched by any, and declined by most, in preference for the liquid part of the dinner. Men were drinking whiskey in the same quantities as if it were beer. The stately bearers removed the debris of the feast in a twinkling of an eye, leaving only bottles, glasses and tankards. The Colonel and officers came in and we gave them three cheers and then carried on with the good work.

I would give 10 rupees to be able to hear the bearers' remarks in the compound the following morning on the table manners of the Mesopoluvians.

At 9.00 pm we filed out to the boxing and were accommodated with reserve ringside seats. We did not see much of the finer points of the game. We could see two men moving around the fistic arena. We applauded when the crowd applauded, but did not know who won or lost. By 11.30 pm, when the last fight took place, the ring was simply a blur. We were colour-blind.

All arrived in the Fort by 12.30 am [with] no casualties.

7 July: After breakfast this morning I was detailed by Sergeant Clarke to collaborate with Private 'Tex' Richards in drafting a letter of thanks to the Commanding Officer and officers of the Southern Mahratta Railway Rifles on behalf of the 6/East Lancs, on leave in Madras from Mesopotamia, for their kindness and hospitality which was greatly appreciated by all. Sergeants Clarke and Kelly duly appended their signatures to the letter when compiled.

Sweltering heat confines us to our bungalow by day.

No Moderation

8 July: Sergeants Clarke, Kelly and I are invited on board a 'Yankee' cargo boat in harbour and had a good time. That good in fact that when she cast off, we were still 'bottling it' in the saloon. We had to swarm down ropes or else go on to Calcutta.

9 July: Having a glorious time. When the native cook brings the camp kettle of gunfire[7] in the morning, someone invariably empties two bottles of whisky into it; a good day's start. It is no use protesting about easing down or we will all be dead before our furlough is up. You are told you missed your vocation, you should have been a 'sky pilot', and so on. What did we come here for? To have a good time of course, and we're going to have it. In two month's time we will be back in Mess-pot and may get 'seen off' in the first 'scrap'. What is the use of being miserable? Enjoy yourself while you're in it; you will be a long time dead!

The above is the argument brought forward every time anyone suggests moderation.

Ladies of the Kirk

10 July: The Ladies of the Scottish Kirk gave us an invitation to a bun fight this evening. We all went – to please them. The young lady who brought the invitation gave us to understand that there would be no religion attached to it, and no drink.

We had a very nice tea. I told Bugler Begs to get next to me and he could have all my buns. After tea we had a treasure hunt and a guessing competition. You were blindfolded and then led forward to a line, on which a lot of bags were hung, by a young lady (less) Scottish accent. You had to guess what each bag contained, whether it was salt, pepper, rice and so on. The correct number of guesses won a cigarette case, or I should say the man who had the most number of guesses correct won a cigarette case. 'Tex' Richards got the prize, and we were not surprised as he was a-billing and a-cooing all the evening to the young lady who acted as his guide. She lovingly whispered the contents of each paper bag into his ear. 'Tex' was always a Lady's man.

At 7.30 pm we saw a dear old lady send a boy in the direction of the Kirk. He came back with a bundle of books, which looked uncommonly like hymn books to us. Darkness was no obstacle to hymn singing as the old Presbytery lawn was illuminated by two incandescent lamps. She might request us to sing one little hymn. Well, that could lead to two, and if 'Tex' Richards got going he would not stop until midnight, and that would mean no sleeping draught. So, after a mixed game of Blind Mans Buff, Miller, Clarke, Casey, Kelly and I took leave of our charming hostesses on the plea of an urgent engagement. The urgent engagement was at the De Angeles Hotel. We only had two hours to go.

A Tea Party

11 July: Our RQMS has been on leave in Madras for the past week. He came to the Fort today and invited all East Lancs to a tea party at the bungalow in which he resides. We had a jolly good time and he spared no expense to make it a success. We had a 'sing song' after tea. He gave us his favourite ditty, 'Down on the Yei Yei-o, or Yehio'. It is a river in China, I know, in which an old fellow named McDoodle and a lot of cows, pigs and goats figure prominently. On conclusion, he was tumultuously applauded. The song was very ancient, his voice slightly cracked, but still it was policy to applaud him. Mr Patchett dismissed the parade at 7.30 pm, which gave us ample time to pay a visit to the De Angeles.

'Leave' Life

12 July: Atmosphere close and muggy. The European residents do not emerge from their bungalows until the evening. I would prefer the clear atmosphere of Mesopotamia, even though it is hotter, to the mugginess of Madras.

13 July: Got 100 rupees advance today from the officer commanding attached section. The old pay book won't stand much more.

14 July: Madras seems to be an East Lancs stronghold. There are no men from any other Mesopotamian unit here. The Jocks are in Dum Dum, just outside of Calcutta. Thank God they are not here, as it would only mean endless squabbles over Baghdad and Kut and what not.

15 July: A prominent Madrasite took us around this evening and pointed out places that the German raider *Emden* bombarded during her visit to Madras.[8] There was not a gun mounted to reply. He told us they loaded up a few old muzzle loaders and fired them to give the inhabitants confidence. Her objectives were the destruction of oil tanks and wireless. After the second shell had been fired he informed us the Madras Guards bolted for Bangalore. I have been in their canteen on several occasions for a quiet drink. They are Eurasians and sport names such as Murphy, Doolan, Donovan, Casey, O'Rafferty, Flynn, O'Shea, etc., etc., so I came to the conclusion that Madras must have been a favourite station for Irish Regiments in the past. I was profoundly disappointed, as I expected men who sported the above names to put up a bit of a stand.

Our fellows agree very well together and help each other out financially.

16 July: Bugler Begs [was] recalled by wire today. He has to proceed to Mesopotamia at once. Some wiseacre has just discovered that he was one of the men whose rifle was stolen by Arabs on the march from Sheikh Saad to Amara in 1916 and that he was not entitled to leave in India. He was not going to comply with the order. We told him not to be 'silly', as to disobey the order implied that he would go back to Mesopotamia under escort and lose all privileges. Casey and I saw him to the station to ensure that he would not change his mind.

17 July: Feeling bad. No inclination to keep a diary up. Hospital here is full of VD [Venereal Disease] patients. None of ours so far. Every opportunity is offered here for indulging and no safeguards after exposure. If there is a prophylactic room here, it has been pointed out to nobody.

28 July: I have given daily notes a miss for the past eleven days.

During our stay in Madras the civilian element did everything possible to brighten our furlough. In fact, in some cases they were too kind. We were well treated wherever we went. The military element treated us as if we were non-existent. Not a man was awarded a day's CB [Confined to Barracks].

Return to Bangalore

Entrain at Madras for Bangalore. The Calcutta mail arrives, bringing the remainder of our furlough party back from Calcutta. They were 'stony' broke and had been so for the past fortnight. They could not get any pay, so Miller and I were lucky to dodge Calcutta.

One of our civilian friends must have a big pull with the railway officials as he got a first class sleeping apartment for Clarke, Kelly and I. He gave us a basket containing three bottles of whiskey, a dozen sandwiches, a box of cigars and three tins of Gold Flake [tobacco], so we could not complain on the journey from Madras to Bangalore.

29 July: Arrive at Bangalore station at 6.30 am.

Reporting Sick

30 July: Medical Inspection at 7.00 am:

Major Kelly: 'You don't look very well'.

'I have been troubled with my stomach, Sir, for the past week'.

'Put out your tongue – Oh Good God!'

He pulled down my lower eyelids, told the orderly to give me a Calomel powder and told me to get my belongings together, make a will if I had any money to leave to anybody, and to report sick in the morning, and upbraided me thus:

'You leave men from Mesopotamia come here with pocketfuls of money. You get another pocketful to go on leave with, you indulge in all kinds of excesses, particularly drink. You have no regular meals, if you have any at all. You behave as men who had only one month to live, spend all the money you've got recklessly in gratifying your passions and come back physical wrecks. If you are not in possession of a packet of VD you've got gastritis or some other ailment brought on by your excesses, and we have got to make you whole and well again.'

I was glad to get out of that medical tent. Major Kelly only spoke the truth.

31 July: Arrived at the station hospital at 8.30 am. I was sent to Captain Brittain-Jones's ward. Another telling off, I suppose. When the MO came around he only remarked, 'Leave man from Mess-pot?' 'Yes Sir'. 'H'm.'

I candidly state and admit that it is nothing to boast about. It happened, so I must write it down. The leave men from Mess-pot crowded three years of a soldier's peacetime life into one month. 600 rupees was the least sum of money that any of my party went on leave with. If we pooled our resources it would average 800 rupees per man for the month. We shared and shared alike. Eight of my party had over 1000 rupees each in their possession. Of course they had big wins gambling. We got up when we liked, went to bed

291

when we liked, stopped out all night when we liked, got beer and whiskey from Moore market in any quantity and when we liked. The male population of Madras killed us with kindness and whiskey. We were in a grip of fatalism. The war might last another two years, and there were no signs of a speedy or victorious conclusion. We were going back to Mess-pot; there would be fighting and still more fighting; we might get killed in the first 'scrap' on returning, or we might get 'seen off' on the eve of peace. We might never get another chance of enjoying ourselves. We played up to the slogan – 'Let it rip' whilst we may, let's have a good time whilst we're here.

We would have been fitter and cleaner men had we remained in Scindia on a diet of 'Bully', rice, dates and 'desecrated' spuds.

Venereal Disease

I must mention VD, not a very palatable subject, yet I must write down what I've seen or it would not be a true reminiscence or diary.

After being cooped up on that hell (Gallipoli), they dumped us at Port Said in 1916, the ancient land of the Pharaohs, whose cities for centuries had the reputation of being the most contaminated in the world. We were unprepared for contact with a cesspool reeking with indescribable depravity and filth. Was it any wonder that young fellows released from the graveyards of Helles, Anzac and Suvla, in their hours of leave on pass and with money to spend in novel Eastern surroundings, should satisfy curiosity and fall victims to the hordes of cosmopolitan vampires infesting the city and its underworld? Compulsory prophylactic treatment did not exist and the scourge claimed its quota of victims. In a lesser degree the same is applicable to India today; no brothels under medical supervision as in the days of Kitchener. Infected prostitutes wander and solicit without let or hindrance along the highways and byways of Bangalore, Madras and Calcutta, apart from the permanent and dense population of the brothels. Is it any wonder that hospitals are filled to overflowing with VD cases? In Bangalore forty EPSP tents had to be erected in the hospital compound to accommodate the increasing number of cases. Calcutta is very bad, Madras bad and Bangalore not so bad. Ninety per cent will tell you that they 'kopped out' when they were drunk, or nearly so; twenty per cent are married men and have wives and children at home. VD embraces all ranks in its fold. Take Bangalore, for instance, as a base for statistics, I expect it is general throughout India. There must be at least seven or eight thousand men affected, including men who have been discharged from hospital and who are attending for treatment (this embraces all India).

I am not a saint, neither am I preaching morality. I was just as bad as the remainder – only I was lucky, that's all.

1 August: Sleepless night. Matron is a thorough lady. I am told there is only one thorough disciplinarian amongst the sisters and her sphere of influence is the surgical ward.

2 August: I developed a temperature [and was put on a] soda and milk diet.

The famous Sergeant 'Gipsy' Carroll of the South Lancs is two beds away on my right. Our complaints are similar. He was also on furlough in Madras. He was not in the attached section but was living in 'private quarters'.

It is not worth wasting paper on hospital routine, the same old ward boys, the same old orderlies, the same old, very old, chicken, etc.

31 August: Discharged, fit and well.

Bangalore Garrison

Bangalore is a very nice station. It might be called salubrious, [with] plenty of enjoyment and plenty of football, cricket and hockey in season. It contains a large garrison. The necessary qualifications for remaining in Bangalore for the duration of the war are:

(a)   A good footballer
(b)   A good hockey player
(c)   A good bat, wicket keeper or fielder
(d)   A super bowler, as they possess half a dozen already, two of who are county players
(e)   A fair tennis player, but you must show signs of rapid improvement
(f)   An excellent ping pong player
(g)   An excellent billiard player. To gain the distinction of being an RE fixture you've got to make not less than fifty every time you 'poke'.
(h)   A good ring or dart player
(i)   You must be able to clear 6 foot (high jump)
(j)   Run 100 yards in 10 seconds
(k)   A devoted batman to the RSM
(l)   Be very chummy with the Lance Corporal who acts as the MO's orderly and confidant. Every time there is a medical inspection he will put in a good word for you.

I have not quite exhausted all the qualifications, but the above will suffice.

Drill every day and all day, Sundays included. The Turks must be taking it pretty easy in Mess-pot, as there are no drafts leaving here. I have been marked fit long ago.

Christmas came and went and so did the New Year. You're in charge of a squad of recruits in the forenoon and in charge of [the] company in the afternoon on company drill. I was never intended for this kind of business and am fed up.

'Durban' Kelly has been here for over twelve months. He manages to dodge every draft. He is 'square feeling' a young lady of very doubtful antecedents, I think ladies of her hue are called '14 annas to the rupee', meaning, I take it, that they are not pure whites. Every time I go out for a walk in Bangalore I meet scores of these girls, '8 annas to the rupee', hanging on soldiers' arms and giggling, a truly disgusting sight. It lowers the prestige of the white race.

January 1918: Field days and trench digging. Night attacks are rather prevalent of late.

February 1918: Depot sports on or about the 20th. As there are four Regimental depots here, the North and South Lancs are in the upper camp and the King's Own and East Lancs in the lower camp. Entries were numerous and competition keen.

March 1918: I did not pay 8 rupees this year for two bottles of methylated spirits on the 17th. The Corporals and Lance Corporals of the upper camp gave a smoker on St. Patrick's night and Corporal Maloney was at his best. Smokers are a common feature of camp life here.[9]

Notes

1   Private P. McCafferay was executed in 1862 for the murder of two officers. His story was made into a poem, and later a ballad, which became popular in the East Lancs.
2   Sergeant J.H. Cunningham was wounded at Beit Aisa in April 1916, earning a Mention in Dispatches.
3   'Johnny Nick': Lieutenant-Colonel C. L. Nicholson, Commanding Officer 2/East Lancashires on the outbreak of war. He became Major-General Sir Lothian Nicholson KCB CMG, Colonel of the East Lancashire Regiment 1920–1933.
4   W.O.G. was presumably Lieutenant-Colonel Green.
5   Drinking in the 'wet' canteen.
6   A gharry is an Indian cart (Hindustani).
7   A camp kettle of 'gunfire' is a kettle of tea, or coffee, laced with rum and traditionally served at Christmas.
8   The *Emden* was a German light cruiser of 3,540 tons displacement carrying ten four-inch guns. At the outbreak of war she was on the German China station. In September 1914 she cruised the Bay of Bengal sinking several merchantmen. On 22 September she appeared off Madras and set two oil-tanks on fire by shelling from the four-inch guns. She was finally sunk on 9 November 1914 at Keeling, Cocos Islands by the Australian cruiser *Sydney*.
9   A 'smoker' is a shortened term for a 'smoking concert' when all ranks relaxed and took it in turn to sing a song or give a recitation.

XX

Return to Mesopotamia

(19 April 1918 – 6 March 1919)

A Small Draft – Basra 1918 – Influenza Epidemic –
Turkey Surrenders – A Bad Parade –
'Cooking' Oil – Germany Surrenders – The Jackal –
Remarks on Mesopotamia – Leaving Mess-pot

A Small Draft

19 April 1918: I form one of a small draft of reinforcements for Mesopotamia.

The officer in charge of the draft wired ahead to all stations not to sell beer to the troops. At noon we had an hour's halt at a large station. Sergeant 'Gypsy' Carroll asked the officer could we have a bottle of beer each. The officer said 'No!' Sergeant Carroll, with the aid of an army fork, opened the lock on the cupboard, which contained the beer in the refreshment room. The troops helped themselves. The officer came around searching for bottles [but] he did not find any.

Arrive at Bombay on 21 April and embark on the Hospital ship *Epinura*. Steam up at 10.00 pm.

Basra 1918

27 April: Anchor off Basrah after an uneventful voyage. We were posted to Basrah Base Depot, Makina, for duty. It is evident there are no operations taking place or about to take place or we would not be allowed to remain here.

YMCA's[1] and soda fountains have sprung up since I left Basrah last. These YMCA's and kindred Institutes are run by well mentally equipped and stalwart young Yanks, who instead of hymn singing and tea walloping could be better employed on the battlefields of France, helping President Wilson to make Europe safe for Democracy.

Then we've got Lady . . . who rules Basrah with an iron hand. Her 'hubby' is a 'big wig' on the political [scene]; she graces the YMCA's regularly with her presence. Shirtsleeves must be rolled down when she chooses to make a visit. If your shirtsleeves are cut at the elbows you've got to get out. Before she arrived, men who could afford and wanted a bottle of beer could obtain one bottle per diem on payment. Lady . . . stopped that. Lady . . . meets a couple of men on the road, when driving around in her barouche.[2] Lady . . . stops the barouche and tells the men: 'You men look healthy enough, why are you not up the line? How long have you been here? I'll see about this'. Lady C . . . brooks no rivals. An attractive lady in other branches of the Services is banished to Tanooma or Amara. Lady . . . wears cross batons and field boots and is <u>beloved</u> by the army of Mess-pot.

25 June: I form one of a draft, which entrains at Basrah for my unit. Entrain at 5.00 pm.

26 June: Arrive at Amara at 7.00 am. I came across two men who have been running Crown and Anchor boards in Amara since 1916. Was the war started, or Amara built, for gentlemen of this type? They have never been near the firing line and always manage to get marked unfit on medical inspections – wonderful strategy.

I made vigorous enquiries about my old friend Dick Spencer. No one appears to know about his whereabouts. I know for a certainty he has not gone in the direction I am going. He is much too clever for that.

The 'Reverend' Jacques appears to have vanished from the face of the earth. All enquiries failed to elicit any information concerning him.

Sergeant Sinnot, of my old 2nd [Battalion] company, is Sergeant Major of a Trench Mortar Battery. They are lying below Kut; I don't suppose I will get a chance to see him. Embark on P *69* at 6.00 pm.

27 June: Went aground on sandbanks five times during the trip to Kut. The light railway between Amara and Kut is not completed. As the ground is swampy the line is being laid on a causeway.

28 June: Disembark at Kut at 5.00 pm and entrain at 9.00 pm.

29 June: Arrive at Hainada Rest Camp at 7.00 am and detrain. This camp is six miles south of Baghdad. My party was detained for duties until 6 July.

6 July: Entrain at 9.00 pm for Table Mountain.

7 July: Detrain at Table Mountain at 4.00 am and proceed to rest camp for the day.

8 July: Parade again at 6.00 am and arrive at Battalion Headquarters at 9.00 am. The Regiment are encamped close to the prosperous Arab village of Deli Abbas. This is an unusually hot summer, but the conditions of the British soldier have greatly improved since 1916. We could not get enough of drinking then but now every man is issued with two bottles of soda water per diem during the summer season.

Our RQMS is a sticker for economy; you have got to be almost shirtless, shortless and jacketless before he will exchange anything for you.

Our Engineers are blasting a cutting through the Jabal Hamrin at Table Mountain in order to continue the light railway to the coalmines of Kifri. Thousands of Arabs are employed in constructing roads and irrigation canals. This should develop into a great grain growing country ten years hence if properly irrigated in some places and drained in others. The soil is alluvial. If it remains in British hands or control the British taxpayer will be well repaid.

The nomadic and warlike tribes, or say camel and sheep 'lifters', are ruled with a firm hand. They may resent it but at the present time there are no signs of unrest.

All troops are being trained in mountain warfare; evidently the Caucasus Mountains will be our next battleground.

Influenza Epidemic

September 1918: This month brought a new disease to the Land of the Two Rivers. It is called the Flu.[3] Two thirds of my Regiment are down with it; in fact all the troops in Mess-pot are suffering from it. No case in my Regiment proved fatal as the dry warm weather favoured us. I hope the Turks have got their share as well.

As a preventative the wise 'Hakims' (Doctors) invented a 'sniffing' parade, that is to say the Battalion parades as strong as possible every evening at 5.00 pm. Each man takes his mug on parade and is issued with a gill of 'Condys fluid' (Permanganate of Potash dissolved in water), which you inhale through the nostrils and spit out through the mouth. The Flu germs are supposed to be inhaled through the nostrils and the 'Condys' puts them out of action.

Had the rainy season been on our losses would have been heavy.

It is reported that the Dunsterville force,[4] of which the 39 Brigade of my Division formed a part, have had a severe set back at Baku. The cowardly Armenians and Georgians, whom we armed and fed, ran away when they sighted an angry Turk and left our fellows to fight for their freedom. What [a] waste of time and money! Raising, training, paying and feeding Armenian levies to assist us in liberating their country from Turkish oppression only to find that they run like hares when the first Turkish shell bursts 500 yards away.

Good news today. Bulgaria surrenders unconditionally.[5] One link in the chain broken. Turkey and Austria must soon follow suit.

21 September: Battalion under orders to proceed to a new camp at Abu-Saida on the Diyalah.

22 September: Laying out and pitching our new camp, we are quite close to the river and 2 miles from Rail Head, a mecca for mosquitoes.

Turkey Surrenders

31 October [1 November][6]: Drink up, lads. Hostilities ceased at 12 noon today with the Turks.[7] The event was celebrated at night by a display of fireworks (Very lights and rockets) and a beer issue.

1 November [2 November]: Commanding Officer's Parade, as strong as possible, at 7.00 am Battalion formed three sides of a square. The Colonel, who was mounted, made a brilliant speech in which he eulogized the traditional manner in which the Battalion blazed a trail of glory through the burning plains of Mess-pot and that he was proud to be our Colonel – 'Good old Mac. – Three cheers for old Mac'.

A Bad Parade

2 [3] November: Battalion drill at 7.00 am, executed a few movements then formed into line for arms drill. The Colonel was so pleased with the arms drill that he paid us the highest compliment that could be paid to a line Regiment – 'The Guards could not do it better' – and 'Lancashire Lads I'm proud of you. Dismiss the parade, Mr Carrington' (the Guards could do it better – but still!!).

Owing to the scarcity of tents for white troops in this country, we are overcrowded. At Reveille it is not an uncommon happening for one man's right leg and his neighbour's left to find their way into the same leg of a pair of shorts.

I forgot to record that I got my second tape some months ago.

3 [4] November: Commanding Officer's Parade at 7.00 am, [and] the Adjutant is not present for some reason or other. The Colonel always drilled us well when the Adjutant was on parade, as we could plainly hear the Adjutant prompting the Colonel as to what order to give for the next movement.

He got us moving [and] we knew what the next order should be, [but] the Colonel gave the wrong order. Two companies obeyed the order as given, the remaining two companies, through force of habit moved <u>as</u> the order should have been given. Confusion! – one half of the Battalion were moving towards Mosul and the other half towards Baghdad. The Colonel halted the Battalion, gave us an awful 'telling off', likened us unto old Brown's cows, told the acting Adjutant to give us an hour's stiff drill, and galloped off in disgust. We were crestfallen. Why, only yesterday the Guards could not do it better and today we're compared with old Brown's cows. What has come over the Colonel?

When the parade was dismissed the incident was the sole topic in the tents. Augustus Majorbanks, who only speaks thrice weekly, remarked that the Colonel was *Volté Facé*. He would not enlighten us as to the meaning of the words, as he appeared to be under a vow not to speak for the next three days, so we had to appeal to 'Long' Wilson of the Orderly Room staff. 'Long' Wilson told us that our parents should have paid for our education as his had to pay for his, and grudgingly informed us that *Volté Facé* meant a change of front. So the Colonel had changed his front! And by the way, whilst interviewing Wilson we noticed that he had the same piece of Pears' soap as he had when we landed at Basrah in 1916. He always takes it with him when going for a wash and then forgets its existence.

3 [4] November: 300 NCOs and men, including some officers, have left the Brigade for Salonica, evidently to form an army of occupation.[8] Parades are over at 8.00 am every morning since the Bulgars and Turks 'packed in'.

[6] November: Austria has 'packed in'.[9] When is 'Jerry' going to throw up the sponge?

'Cooking' Oil

Oil for cooking has ousted wood and is much more economical. It has one disadvantage; it is very dirty. The crude oil throws out a dirty vapour and our cooks resemble sweeps. It is a matter of speculation as to whether they will ever look clean again. Our Colonel takes a delight in waltzing Colonel Charleton [Charlton] of the South Lancs and Colonel Birley of the King's Own around our cook house and explaining to them the advantage of crude oil.

8 November: When the war ends, as it must do soon, the miners are expecting to get away first. Therefore a great many who have never seen a coal mine in their lives now profess to be miners.

At various times during the campaign, Division used to send through for men with a knowledge of engine driving. [Suddenly] market gardeners and scenic artists by the dozen knew all about engine driving. When Division sent through for men with a knowledge of boiler making, architects and draughtsmen turned boilermakers. When Division sent through for men with a knowledge of gardening, with a view to growing vegetables for the troops, painters and decorators took up the job (any job to get away from the firing line). We never saw any vegetables and I don't suppose Division did either. Steeplejacks were most unfortunate and had to resign themselves to the hardships and glories of the firing line.

Germany Surrenders

11 November: We were informed at 7.30 pm that Germany had signed the Armistice; everybody shook hands with everybody else. The sky, from

Basrah to Mosul, was illuminated by Very lights and rockets. At last the slaughter is over.[10]

8.30 pm: Mr. B came around with a jar of rum. Each tent he came to he enquired 'How many men in that tent?' – twelve or fifteen as the case might be, he gave every man a good issue. My tent got a double issue as half the men were on guard. I was not in at the time; I was in the Orderly Sergeant's tent. I had my share there.

The Jackal

I got to my tent at 9.30 pm and found the 'Don' and 'Maggie Ann' on the floor pummelling each other. It being Armistice night, I did not like to consign the pair to the 'Bird Cage', and fights were very rare indeed. I undertook the role of peacemaker and was in the act of separating them when the spluttering candle, which rested on an overturned mess-tin, gave up its ghost. Simultaneously I was made receiver general as I 'stopped' a hefty wallop in the eye under cover of darkness. Instinct told me that it was the 'Don' who took advantage of the darkness 'to get his own back' on the Corporal. I let go in the direction of where 'Don's' head should be and I found contact below his nose. At the same time I ordered someone to strike a match; a light duly appeared. I warned an escort. The 'Don' asked me for a chance. I considered for a while and then remarked – 'Well, considering it is Armistice night and everyone is rejoicing, save our late enemies, I'll overlook it this time.'

I had to put up a bit of a bluff in case they might conspire and report me for striking a private. Although no one saw me retaliate, evidence is easily manufactured.

12 November: Port optic [left eye] badly 'bunged' up and I am Orderly Sergeant. The 'Don's' lips are cut and swollen, and one of his front teeth has gone adrift. He and 'Maggie Ann' are quite chummy this morning – 'Struth!' – he never dreamt 'Maggie Ann' carried such a punch! Had the 'Don' not stated a falsehood to Mr. B last night and obtained sixteen tots of rum for eight men, he would have been a tooth to the good this morning and I could see with two eyes.

The row last night was over the nationality of Virgil. What on earth had Virgil to do with the war, or what brought him to Mess-pot on Armistice night anyway? In any case, something will have to be done. The Company Sergeant Major, the RSM, the Adjutant and the Company Commander will want to know how I came by the adornment. I can't say I fell over a tent peg. The night was too bright and I have been accustomed to tents for too long not to know the position of the pegs. In any case there have been so many injuries 'tagged on' to tent pegs that they are played out. I must invent some other story as I cannot tell the truth or I would get 'pegged' for not taking action. What about a Jackal? – the very thing. I take the tent into my confidence. Last night's incident must not be disclosed. All men in the tent must corroborate my tale. A jackal got into the tent about 2.00 am this morning, the occupants were aroused, boots were hurled at the jackal and I, sleeping next to the door, got hit in the eye by a size 10.

The Company Sergeant-Major whistled. The Regimental Sergeant-Major told me to preserve it, it was a beauty. The Adjutant wanted to know whose pet jackal it was? And the Company Commander (Captain Spense) told me to tell it to the Arab Labour Corps. Once one gets over the first day people are not so inquisitive, they get accustomed to you.

13 November: An inspiring speech by the Colonel on how we won the war. He wound up by exhorting us to kick a German up the!!!! if ever we came across one.

25 December: Xmas Day [with] Divine service parade at 8.00 am. After the parade Colonel McCormack made a speech which suited the occasion. He reminded us of the hardships of past Christmases and hoped that the next Xmas would find us all in our own homes enjoying peace and prosperity. Each NCO and man was allowed three bottles of beer with their dinner, which was all that could be desired under the circumstances.[11]

26 December: Regimental sports[12] and a beer issue of three bottles per man (beer).

27 December: Major Wynberg gave the Battalion a lecture on how Government were going to carry out demobilization. The Group system is preferred on account of the national reconstruction scheme. Farmers and miners will be the first men to get away as their work is of national importance. A hairpin bender, or a painter of dolls eyes has got to carry on for some considerable time as their trades are not essential in building up the nation's industries.

29 December: The first group of colliers entrained today for the United Kingdom.

5 February 1919: My Company ['A'] was sent down to Amara as advance party to mark out and pitch a new camp for the Battalion. Travel by rail from Abu Jisri [Abu Jisra] to Kut and from Kut to Tabar, which is 5 miles below Amara.

7 February: We arrived at the site of our new camp, a desolate looking place and swampy. Whoever chose this site must owe the Division a grudge.[13]

10 February: A heavy thunderstorm accompanied by a torrential downpour of rain turned our camp into a lake tonight. All tents are down [and] barges were torn from their moorings on the river's bank. Scores of men took refuge on the YMCA barge, which held fast.

11 February: Remainder of the Battalion arrives. The Tigris is rising with alarming rapidity. The Division is encamped on low ground [and] every man in the Division had to turn out today to throw up an embankment, or bund, 4 feet high, for a distance of 3 miles, or a length of 3 miles, in order to save the camp from being submerged.

The demobilizsation scheme is causing a lot of discontent. It is not working smoothly and again men who have done least clamour loudest to get away.

An army of occupation has to be formed. That will entail more grousing.

Remarks on Mesopotamia

The *Beni Lam* and *Al Bu Mohammed* tribes of Arabs who lie along the course of the Tigris up to Kut are about the worst tribes in Mesopotamia, with the exception of the *Shammar* who hang around Mosul and Tekrit [Tikrit].

They can give points to their brethren of the North West Frontier of India in the gentle art of lifting rifles. Our Battalion camp is roughly 120 yards square. The Battalion's rifles and Lewis guns have to be placed in the guard tent each night and withdrawn the following morning. Forty-eight men mount guard from retreat to reveille; a sentry is posted every 30 yards, and in spite of all precautions they get into camp, slit the sides of the tent with a knife and get away with kit bags, etc.

Some tribes follow the occupation of camel breeding (and all follow the occupation of camel stealing, either by force or opportunity), others buffalo and horse breeding. A certain number are agriculturists and fishermen. They are all born thieves. The Arab tribes might be described as a floating population. After the rains they migrate to the tribal grazing grounds with all their belongings – tents, cattle and their wives and dogs.

Even reed-villages are semi nomadic, shifting frequently from place to place. The puzzled mapmaker often finds his last addition to geographical knowledge removed, almost before his eyes, from the spot assigned to it in his survey and re-erected on another site.

The gold and silver smiths of Amara are very skilful. They are a Christian sect called Sabians and are mentioned in the book of Job and have some kind of a claim on John the Baptist, (surprising to find anyone in this country with any knowledge of John the Baptist). They never shave or cut their hair.

There are two sects of Mohammedans in this country. They are called Sunnis and Shias. The difference lies in a 'dust up' they had in the misty past over the succession to the Caliphate. The majority of the inhabitants of Messpot are Shias owing to early Persian influence in the country.

The Chaldeans have a colony and a church in Baghdad. Jews, of course,

302

you will always find in towns of any importance.

Basrah, Amara and Baghdad have municipalities of a kind. At least they manage to keep the streets fairly clean.

Arab police – Well, I have not much faith in them, or in any Arab for that matter.

A lot of modern agricultural implements are arriving in the country, and also missionaries. Roads are spreading all over the country; it is surprising the progress since 1916.

The Arabs don't like the railway, and for very good reasons. The advent of the railway has done away with the camel caravans that used to convey merchandise from Basrah to Mosul, Tekrit, Kirkut [Kirkuk], Baghdad and other places. It has hit a certain section financially.

The Bazaars in the towns are flooded with shoddy, cheap Japanese goods for which the Armenian shopkeepers charge the highest price. Good bargainers, those Armenians, but damn bad fighters.

At present there is a craze for Turkish watches. The characters are in Arabic on the dials. They are awkward, clumsy affairs, cost 20 rupees each, and are eagerly sought after as souvenirs of Mess-pot.

Rings, both gold and silver, with a date palm or Ezra's tomb engraved thereon, are bought by the hundred. I should imagine that a man who had spent six months in this country had seen enough date palms to last him a lifetime without carry one about with him on a ring.

Leaving Mess-pot

26 February: I have been asked by the Adjutant[14] today to extend to complete twenty-one [years] with the Colours and I would be promoted Sergeant. I refused. He told me I would regret it.

I have been acting CQMS for the past month. I hand over today as I am leaving for home tomorrow on demob. Reckoning up pay books is a devil of a job. The men have altered the figures, it is plain to be seen. A man draws 80 rupees at Baghdad, he erases the 8 and substitutes a 4. A man draws 40 at Amara, out goes the 4 and in goes a 2, and so on. The entries are made in blacklead and the trick is easily done.

27 February: I form one of a party of forty-five NCOs and men who entrain for Makina demobilization camp, Basrah.[15] The camp is overflowing with men awaiting movement orders.

4 March: Embarkation party proceed to Margill [Maqil], where all kits were fumigated and everyone had a hot bath before embarking on the *Franz Ferdinand* in the morning.

If thirty men leave a unit together for Makina it does not imply that the same party will proceed home together. There is a muster parade every morning and if your name is called out you embark on the following morning. You might be unlucky and have to remain for two months at Makina; some men have been here for over two months waiting for a boat.

Official arrangements have been made for changing your money into English currency.

6 March: Embark on *Franz Ferdinand* at 9.00 am.

Notes

1   The Young Men's Christian Association, or, as it more commonly known, the YMCA began its connection with the British army as long ago as 1901. In the summer of that year the Lancashire Fusiliers were in camp at Conway, and the YMCA erected tents there for recreation all the week and services on Sundays. Each following summer the work was carried on in Territorial camps, until in the August of 1914 the mobilization of the Territorials for active service also brought about the mobilization of the YMCA with their buns, hymn books and pianos.

2   A four-wheeled horse-drawn carriage with seats for two couples facing each other.

3   The Influenza pandemic, sometimes known as 'Spanish flu' was a worldwide disease originating in South Africa. It first appeared on the Western Front in June 1918 among the German troops and laid low nearly half a million German soldiers whose resistance, depressed by poor diet, was far lower than that of the well-fed Allied troops. It was to recur in the autumn with devastating effects and according to some estimates as many as 30 million people died between 1918 and 1920, an even heavier toll in lives than the war itself.

4   Transcaucasia might have remained a backwater in the Great War had it not contained a resource of the greatest strategic value – Caucasian oil, refined at the port of Baku on the Caspian Sea. Discovering the plan of a German-Turkish advance towards Transcaucasia in the spring of 1918, the British presence was reinforced. A column of British armoured cars under General Dunsterville ('Dunsterforce') had been started forward from Mesopotamia to the Caspian, with Baku as its objective, in January. The principal task of the force was to deny Baku's oil to the Germans and Turks. However, a Turkish advance in September 1918 drove 'Dunsterforce' from Baku and resulted in a massacre of Baku's Armenians by their Azeri enemies.

5   Bulgaria surrendered on 26 September 1918.

6   Roe has obviously been given the wrong date at some point and is a day out in his calculations for the first few days in November. The correct date is in the square bracket.

7   'At 11.15 am news came through that the Turks had signed an armistice. All further work for the day ceased; and a holiday proclaimed for tomorrow.' (6th Bn War Diary, 1 November 1918)

8   Salonika, a Greek port, was the centrepiece of the Allies' Balkans strategy during the First World War. Anglo-French forces landed there in October 1915, ostensibly to offer support to the retreating Serbian army. The Salonika Front was widely regarded as a military sideshow in both Britain and Germany and only became important in the last few weeks of the war, when Allied forces defeated the Bulgarian troops in the region, triggering the beginning of the Central Powers' collapse.

9   'During the morning we heard of the Armistice being signed with Austria-Hungary.' (6th

Bn War Diary, 4 November 1918)

10 'At about 9.00 pm (21.00 o'clock) we heard the news of the armistice being signed by Germany.' (Ibid, 11 November 1918)

11 'Xmas Day, all ranks very much appreciated the good fare, which was provided by the President Regimental Institutes in addition to gifts, which were received from India and Ceylon. Suitable replies have been sent to the Secretaries of the different Funds.' (Ibid, 25 December 1918)

12 'A Boxing Day sports fixture was very successful.' (Regt. Hist., p.356)

13 'The new camp site at Tabar Camp was a very damp one and most of the month [January] was spent in draining the camp and building bunds to prevent the river from overflowing its banks.' (6th Bn War Diary, February 1919)

14 Second-Lieutenant S.J. Widgery – acting Adjutant, as Captain H. Carrington had left the Battalion on 22 February for some leave in the U.K.

15 'Forty-five ORs [other ranks] leave for Base to be demobilized.' (6th Bn War Diary, 26–28 February 1919)

XXI

Going Home

(7 March 1919 – 7 May 1919)

Bombay – Aboard the Troopship – Suez – Mediterranean – Marseilles –
Gibraltar and into the Atlantic – Home and into Quarantine –
Demobilization – Ireland

Bombay

7 March: Steam up at 6.00 am with 1,200 troops are on board. We are all
bound for Bombay and are overcrowded, however there is no grousing for
we are going in the right direction at last.

13 March: Arrived at Victoria Docks, Bombay, after a calm voyage. All
the ships in the harbour are gaily decorated with bunting in honour of Lord
Jellicoe's visit. His flagship, the *New Zealand* is lying off the Apollo Bunder.
Bombay gave the Hero of Jutland a Civic reception.

Disembark at 10.00 am and entrain for Deolali at 2.00 pm, arriving at 8.00
pm. Thousands of troops are awaiting under canvas at Deolali for passage to
the UK for demob.

17 March: (St Patrick's day) Pretty wet. Everyone is buying brassware,
curios, silks, tablecloths and carpets here to take home as mementoes of their
visit to the East.

4 April: The authorities at Basrah gave us to understand that we would
tranship at Bombay for England. Instead, we have been here over two
weeks. Indian currency that was changed into English at Basrah has, owing
to financial stress, to be changed back again into Indian and at a loss.
People who had bought silk shawls and silks for Ethel, Mabel, Kathleen
and Mary re-sold them for a song. In the end all the men received a casual
payment.

5 April: 300 NCOs and men entrain for Bombay. Kit bags were sent on
ahead and stacked in trucks.

6 April: Arrive at Bombay at 6.00 am. Detrain at 9.00 am. A general scrum
down for kit bags. Quite a number of men did not get their kit bags as they
were claimed by people who had none and 'twas like looking for a needle in

the proverbial hay stack as trying to find them on board the *Somali*. They were never seen again.

Embark on SS *Somali* at 11.00 am, towed out of docks, and set sail at 3.00 pm. The band of a Mahratta Regiment was formed up on the quayside and we slowly glided away to the tune of 'Should Old Acquaintance be Forgot'. I felt an infinite sadness. I remained on deck until Malabar point and the last vestige of the shores of India faded from view. I had left India behind for good, India where I spent the happiest years of my soldiering. I felt lonely and depressed, I can't explain why.

We expect to make Portsmouth on the 30th, always providing we don't strike a mine.

Aboard the Troopship

7 April: The *Somali* is an old boat and a slow sailor. There are a lot of men over fifty years, going home for demob. They have been in Garrison Battalions doing duty in Burma (garrison duty). Twenty per cent of them are hobbling about and all are excused duty.

8 April: Gambling everywhere, Crown and Anchor boards everywhere one looks.

9 April: Just about getting settled down. A state of chaos existed for the first two days on board.

10 April: Very stuffy 'tween decks. There is a regular scramble to get deck space for hammocks every night, even though the 'swabbers' wash you away at 4.00 am every morning. Discipline is only a name on board. There are men from fifty different units on board. As it so happened I was lucky to get Lance Corporal of a mess composed of decent men, although one or two suggested that I should take my turn in doing mess orderly. I gave them all to understand that I was an NCO and put in charge of the mess to see that they carried out their duties.

11 April: In the Red Sea a native stoker tried to commit suicide tonight. He threw himself overboard, then changed his mind. The sea was like glass. 'Twas well for him he could swim as it took the crew an eternity to lower a boat. We were over an hour fell in at our stations before he was rescued. He might have obliged us by going over in daylight, as a little incident like that would break the monotony and we would be able to watch operations.

12 April: Arrived at Aden and anchored off Steamer Point. Mails and cargo were transferred to lighters, as there are no docks at Aden. Viewed from the deck of the trooper it does not give one a good impression. I should not like to be stationed in Aden. Anchor weighed at 2.00 pm and Aden is soon astern.

13 April: We managed to ship a cargo of flies, however, who manage to be present at all meals. Ginger W. of ours, a Woolwich man, who evidently has not changed his socks since we captured Kut, sports a ginger moustache the ends of which reach his ears, waxes it with jam as a substitute for pomade. He sleeps all day on the mess table except when meals are being issued. I am quite 'fed up' watching the flies from Aden perform acrobatic feats on the ends of his moustache. I have felt inclined on several occasions to take my scissors out of my pocket and snip the ends off.

He does not know who is in command of the British Expeditionary Force when Kut or Baghdad fell or who is in command of the forces. He is ignorant of trajectory, fields of fire and culminating points. Talk about football, he can give you a detailed history of Woolwich Arsenal FC since they were formed, what position they held in the League in 1905, the number of goals they beat 'Pompey' by in 1906, and so on. All football and no interest in his profession.

14 April: Steamed through 'Hell's Gates' on the Straits of Beb-el-Mandeb at midnight and passed the twelve Apostles at 3.00 am.

A sudden change in the weather with heavy seas and the old *Somali* shipped some. It is a welcome change from the stifling heat. Rough weather for the Red Sea in April, and quite a number are seasick.

16 April: Coastline of Somaliland in sight all day; storm abating. Three submarines pass us this morning escorted by three torpedo boat destroyers. Expect to get into Suez tomorrow.

17 April: Two more torpedo boat destroyers steam past this morning, escorting more submarines. Anchor off Suez town at 9.00 am this morning, dropped mails and cargo and take a pilot on board.

Suez

Suez town contains a few modern buildings and a grove of date palms in rear of the town gives it an oasis like appearance.

Enter the canal at 4.00 pm; the abandoned defences on the Asiatic side of the canal seem to be of great strength. The three great assets in the war, barbed wire, bully beef and sandbags grace the banks of De Lesseps' great achievement. The canal is roughly 95 miles long and takes about fifteen hours for the passage.

18 April: Anchor off Marina Palace Hotel, Port Said at 6.30 am. Harbour crowded with shipping, mostly Japanese. The Japs have done well out of this war. They have captured the markets of the East. Their mercantile marine has suffered very little, if at all and no matter into what port one sails the banner of the rising sun is most conspicuous. Steam up at 2.30 pm. Red flags on buoys indicate the position of minefields, either past or present.

308

Mediterranean

19 April: Calm, pretty cold, gambling fever dying down. Sailors go around raffling bottles of whisky. Nobody has known of anybody else to have won a bottle so far.

20 April: Easter Sunday. Curry and rice for breakfast; it was left untouched.

The mountainous island of Candia, or Crete, is plainly visible from the starboard side. The mountains appear to be about 5,000 feet high and are snow capped.

Everyone sleeps between decks now; it is bitterly cold at night.

22 April: Enter the Straits of Messina at 4.00 am. The Straits are narrow at the entrance; we could just discern the town of Messina on the Sicilian coast. Mount Etna was shrouded in mist. Reggio, on the Calabrian shore, looked splendid. We hugged the Italian coast for a matter of 10 miles. The scenery was beautiful, a panorama of white towns and villages nestling at the foot of the mountains. The mountains were well wooded.

Steamed past Stromboli, a burning mountain, at 10.00 am. She was emitting dense clouds of black smoke or vapour by way of salute. I am not surprised at the loss of life when those volcanoes are in violent eruption as towns and villages nestle at the foot of the mountains or on the slopes. The country is lovely to look at from a distance. It does not seem much of an agricultural country to me.

All on board have got 'wind up' today. All are issued out with life belts which must be worn until 8.00 pm. We are just moving, mine sweepers are about 4 miles ahead. Floating mines constitute a great danger to shipping.

Rain and heavy seas broadside on all evening and night.

23 April: Raining all morning. A large island is just discernable through the mist on our port bow. We get to Marseilles tomorrow.

In the afternoon our course took us between the islands of Corsica and Sardinia. They are separated by a strait about 7 miles wide. The islands appear to be a mass of rocks of volcanic origin. The mountains of Corsica appeared to be capped with snow. Occasional villages and patches of green swim past the orbit. Since we left Port Said we have not sighted a ship of any nationality, so this must be a very unfrequented route. Four light-houses guard the straits, which are about 12 miles in length. The villages are old fashioned and seem to be built in the Moorish style with watchtowers. The great Napoleon was born on the rocky island on the starboard bow. The island of Elba, where he was imprisoned and eventually escaped to set Europe ablaze in 1815, is somewhere in the vicinity.

The skipper has not left the bridge since 6.00 am this morning. It is bitterly cold all day with heavy showers.

Ajaccio is the chief town in Corsica. The islands seem to be sparsely inhabited.

Marseilles

24 April: The old *Somali* got a severe buffeting before entering Marseilles harbour. It reminded me of coming around the Cape of Good Hope.

Steamed past a fortified island called the Chateau d'If and anchored in the inner basin at 11.00 am. Victor Hugo was incarcerated on this island for a number of years owing to his literary works not finding favour with the political clique then in power.

The harbour has got an ancient appearance and is crowded with shipping. The Japanese are again in supremacy.

The town follows the configuration of the harbour and is about six miles in length. It is built up hill and down and is without any architectural features. The uneven nature of the ground seems to spoil the appearance of the town. Marseilles seems to be the meeting place of all nationalities, a second Port Said.

[There is a] one hour Route March in the evening for all who like to avail themselves of the opportunity of stretching their legs. I did not.

At 5.00 pm Sergeants only were allowed ashore for four hours; this almost led to a mutiny later on, [as] the men demanded to go ashore. The Officer in Charge [of troops] arrived on the scene (Colonel S) and ordered the men to their respective messes. They refused point blank to obey the order and started an argument with the Colonel. They told the Colonel that they were just as much entitled to go ashore as the Sergeants and that they helped to win the war as well as the Sergeants.

The Colonel replied it was a 'dog in the manger' attitude they were adopting. The men replied by rushing the gangway and overpowering the guard and military officer of the watch. It was then given out that we could go ashore at our own risk. Had everyone been confined to ship there would have been no trouble.

25 April: Everyone allowed ashore until 10.00 am. I took a stroll into town. The proprietors of most beer houses were serving beer behind the bar, in uniform, and everything is terribly dear.

There are a lot of German prisoners working in and around the docks; they seem to feel their position.

[There are] also a lot of Yankee soldiers who seem to give us an 'inferiority complex'. They strut about with profound swagger and a real 'We've won the war attitude'. The boulevards swarm with them.

Steam up at 12 noon. The suburbs are beautifully wooded and an

310

occasional church steeple peeps through here and there. It is blowing half a gale at present so we are expecting a rough night.

At 4.00 pm the cliffs of Southern France fade from one's vision. It is very rough and the old *Somali* is shipping seas. The storm abates at midnight, we left sixteen men behind at Marseilles. Instead of being sent to England they will join the Army of Occupation on the Rhine as a punishment, if such can be called a punishment – 'Wine and Women again'.

26 April: Calm and pretty warm. Water for toilet purposes is only turned on for three-quarters of an hour morning and evening. There is a certain type of manhood, on board, who take half an hour over their toilet, I mean washing, powdering and painting them selves up. I am quite certain Lady Willoughby-Stone Broke could get herself up in half the time it takes those male dolls to satisfy themselves that they are nice looking. Meanwhile hundreds of men are lined up two deep awaiting a chance to get a wash. The water is turned off prompt to time and hundreds remain unwashed. By way of retaliation, every time we get in the washhouse we dump their lipstick, powder and powder puffs through the porthole. The real men are disgusted with such open vanity. It's not manhood, and their place is not here.

27 April: The blue waters of the Mediterranean are like a millpond today. Mountainous coast of Spain on port side, fishing smacks numerous.

Owing to the demobilization I have been signing papers since I left Tabar Camp, below Amara. The American and French armies will be demobbed and in work before we are finished signing army forms. The accounts of the majority are in a hopeless muddle, we attribute this state of affairs to the employment of 'Flappers' in pay and record offices.

We expect to reach Gibraltar early tomorrow morning.

Gibraltar and into the Atlantic

28 April: Anchor at the Rock at 6.00 am. The coastline of northern Africa looms in the distance. There are about a score of ships in harbour, including men-o-war. Spanish rowing boats pull up alongside selling oranges, cigars and tobacco. The prices have increased fifty per cent since 1915.

Steam up at 1.00 pm. Steam past Finistere lighthouse at 4.00 pm. A dozen minesweepers are at their customary and dangerous occupation on our starboard bow. Calm so far.

29 April: Blowing a gale, heavy seas breaking over the ship. We are quite close to the coast and steaming against a strong head wind. I shudder at the thought of what would happen if we run against a mine in this sea. Few would live to tell the tale. Everyone remains below today, as it is much too cold to remain above.

Escorted by an old pattern destroyer, [there is a] large city on the starboard side. We are told it is Lisbon. We are so close to the shore we can discern houses on shore.

It has been given out that there will be a rigid customs examination when we disembark as troops smuggle cigars and tobacco. You are only allowed a certain scale. I cut up eighteen cakes of hard tobacco and fill my own and four of my comrades' water bottles with it. The custom officers are not going to get hold of it if I can help it.

30 April: Strong head wind all day. Mileage 226 miles from 12 noon yesterday until 12 noon today. 602 miles separate us from Devonport. We may get there late on Friday night or early on Saturday morning.

1 May: In the bay – [It is] pretty calm.

2 May: Rough since 8.00 pm last night. Past Eddystone at 7.00 pm with Lands End on our port bow. The low hills of Devon loom through the mist. Raining all day, poor visibility. Steam into Plymouth harbour at 8.30 pm and anchor for the night.

3 May: A cold day, at least it seems so to us. The Stars and Stripes of America fly from the masthead of several men-of-war. They have a squat appearance, nothing graceful about them. The historic Hoe is right on our front.

We have had a case of infectious disease on board, fever of some kind or a smallpox scare.

Home and into Quarantine

The *Somali* flies the quarantine flag and all on board are going to a segregation camp. The custom officials run away from us. If you approached one with an armful of cigar boxes he would run for his life.

Troops commence to disembark by lighters as the *Somali* is bound for Tilbury and is not berthed in dock. Troops entrain for St Budeaux[1] on disembarking.

Custom officers give us a wide berth. We reach our destination after a twenty minutes railway journey and are billeted in wooden huts. As we marched into our billets we met a middle-aged lady dressed in mourning. On learning that we came from Mesopotamia she burst into tears. Poor woman, I suppose a husband or son lies for good in the deserts of Mess-pot.

No arrangements have been made. No signs of a meal or a blanket. We have arrived home rather late, all the Mafeking and rejoicings are over and the war is partially forgotten.

The wet canteen opened from 12 to 1.00 pm [with] 4 pence per pint for sterilized water. I am going to be a staunch TT [teatotaller] if the quality of the beer does not improve.

312

Bread and jam at 4.00 pm and given wet blankets. We do not know how long we may be detained here.

4 May: Medical inspection at 11.00 pm all troops are allowed out until midnight. We leave for our dispersal areas tomorrow.

5 May: First party parades at 12 noon. Entrain at Budeaux for Prees Heath at 1.30 pm.

Beautiful Devonshire wears a summer aspect; it is a pleasure to see green fields again. Herds of cattle and flocks of sheep and the people are so healthy looking that it makes one doubt if they have ever been on the ration cards.

Reach Exeter at 3.00 pm, with its beautiful cathedral. Quite a number of New Zealand infantry are on the platform.

Bedminster[2] at 4.00 pm. The town gives one the impression of being rather old fashioned.

Painswick[3] at 6.00 pm, the inhabitants busy on their allotments. The cabbages don't seem very healthy.

Gloucester 7.00 pm – Australians and Canadians grace the platforms of every other station.

Prees Heath at midnight. We were kept waiting in the rain for two hours before we were detailed to our huts.

Demobilization

6 May: Parade at 4.00 am for demobilization. Form single file and give your home address at one office. File on to another where your rifles are inspected, then on to another office where your kit is inspected, with all surplus kit being taken from you. You then hand your rifles and equipment into stores, then on to another office, where you produce your duplicate dispersal certificate and are supplied with an out of work insurance policy. File on to another office, where you get a protection certificate. On to another office, where you are issued with a ration book. On to another office, where you hand your pay book in. On to another office, where you get measured for a suit of 'civvies', if you require one. On to another office where you sign a receipt for £2. On to another office, where you are grouped and told what time to parade. A padre also gives you a lecture on what to do in civilian life; you are also given a book on how to obtain employment. This bewildering parade lasts about forty-five minutes; you are on the move all the time. You have got to sit tight on your kit bag or you will be saved the trouble of taking it home with you. You are allowed to retain your tin hat as a souvenir, or in case you might forget that you took part in the Great War.

Men proceeding to Ireland parade at 9.00 pm.

Arrive in Holyhead at 1.00 am and embark on the *Slieve Gullion* at 1.30 am.

Ireland

7 May: Arrive at North Wall at 7.00 am and catch a connection at Broadstone at 9.00 am. Troops in Dublin were out in battle order and tin hats.[4] Arrived at my destination at 1.00 pm.

I felt utterly miserable during the three hours train journey. I was like a man pitch-forked into another world. I had left the world I was accustomed to for over fourteen years behind me for good. Was I wise in not taking the Adjutant's advice at Tabar Camp below Amara, or was I a fool for not taking it? I was entering a new life where they only talk hay, oats, potatoes, cows and horses. Would I ever get settled down or accustomed to the new life? I'm afraid not.

The feeling came over me when I parted with the last of my 'chums' in Dublin.

A Parish Priest got into my carriage at Kilcock and opened his Missal. He never spoke to me, only kept on reading. My dress [uniform] did not suit his eye.

At Mullingar a middle aged woman got in. She had to come to Mullingar to get a tooth extracted. She talked me to death and I was in no mood for talking – 'Where did I come from? Where was I going? What was I going to do? Was it a fact that the war was all over?' and so on. Well, I thought, it was a pity that the dentist did not make a mistake and pull your tongue out instead of the offending molar.

Arrive at my destination at 1.00 pm.

Three modes of conveyance were drawn up outside the station, awaiting me, and quite a number of my friends. I declined a seat, as to go home in Mr. F's pony and trap would give offence to the others, so I made the excuse that I wanted to stretch my legs as I had been travelling for the past month by sea and rail and wanted a walk badly.

Everyone wants to treat me. 'Come and have one with me,' 'Indeed he won't, he'll have one with me', and so on.

One and all declared that they knew I would come back safe, Mary prayed for me every night, Julia never forgot me in her prayers, Annie always said at least one our Father and ten Hail Mary's for me. If God did not hear the young women's prayers he must have heard the old one's. (I am supremely embarrassed as I owe my life to a whole parish who claim to have prayed for me, whether they did so or not.)

All who could manage to, squeeze into the public house bar. 'What was I drinking?'

'Oh – a bottle of Bass's ale'

The shop assistant, a red-haired, freckle-faced youth who was alternately selling pennyworths of snuff and half pounds of butter, stared at me when I called for the bottle of Bass and replied 'If it's Bass, porter or whiskey you want, you will have to go back to Dublin as the strongest drink I have in the house is ginger wine.'

'Hells Bells!' I ejaculated, 'so this is the land Lloyd George made fit for heroes to live in?'

Notes
1   Plymouth.
2   Bristol.
3   Gloucestershire.
4   Due to the civil unrest with 'Sinn Fein' and the demand for home rule.

Select Bibliography

Hopkinson – *Spectamur Agendo, 1st Battalion The East Lancashires Regiment, August and September 1914,* by Captain E.C. Hopkinson M.C. (Privately Published, 1926)

Regt.Hist. – *History of the East Lancashire Regiment in the Great War, 1914–1918,* Official History, Volumes 1 and 2, (D.P.& G., 2nd Edition 2002)

1st Bn. War Diary – *War Diary, 1st Battalion East Lancashire Regiment, 1914–1918,* Regimental Headquarters, Fulwood, Preston.

6th Bn. War Diary – *War Diary, 6th Battalion East Lancashire Regiment, August 1915 – October 1919,* Regimental Headquarters, Fulwood, Preston.

Lawrence – *Records of the XXXth, 1st East Lancashire Regiment, September 28th 1914 – May 21st 1915,* by Lieutenant-Colonel G.H.Lawrence (a private diary of the Commanding Officer), Regimental Headquarters, Fulwood, Preston.

Hist. of the War: Mesopotamia – *The Campaign in Mesopotamia 1914 – 1918,* Four Volumes by Brig.-Gen. F. J. Moberly, (HMSO, Official History, 1924)

Military Operations, France and Belgium, 1914, by Brigadier–General Sir James E. Edmonds (MacMillan 1922)

1914, The Days of Hope, by Lyn Macdonald (Penguin 1987)

The Retreat from Mons, by Major A. Corbett-Smith (Cassell, 1919)

Notes on the Campaign in France, 1914 by A. Kearsey (Sifton Praed)

Battle of the Aisne, 13th–15th September 1914, An official Account by order of the Army Council, (HMSO, 1935)

Battle of the Marne, 8th–10th September 1914 An official Account by order of the Army Council, (HMSO, 1937)

Ypres, An Official Account, by order of the German General Staff (Constable, 1919)

The Mons Star, B.E.F. 5th August–22nd November 1914, by David Ascoli (Harrap, 1981)

Old Soldiers Never Die by Frank Richards (Naval & Military Press)

There's a Devil in the Drum, by J.F.Lucy (Naval & Military Press, 1992)

Four Years on the Western Front, by a rifleman (Odhams, 1922)

The Royal Flying Corps in World War 1, by Ralph Barker (Robinson, 2002)

Forty Days in 1914, by Major-General Sir F.Maurice (Constable 1919)

The British Campaign in France and Flanders, 1914, by Arthur Conan Doyle (Hodder,1916)

The Western Front, Then and Now, From Mons to the Marne and back, by John Giles (After the Battle, 1992)

The Great War by Winston S. Churchill (Newnes, 1933)

World War 1 Trench Warfare, 1914 – 16, by Dr Stephen Bull (Osprey, 2002)

Battle Tactics of the Western Front, by Paddy Griffith (Yale Univ. Press, 1994)

The First World War, by John Keegan (Pimlico, 1999)

Forward into Battle, by Paddy Griffith (Crowood Press, 1990)

A Naval History of World War 1, by R. Halpern (Annapolis, 1994)

Mesopotamia – The Last Phase, by Lt-Col. A.H.Burne (Gale and Polden Ltd, 1936)

Soldiers Died in the Great War 1914-19, Part 35, The East Lancashire Regiment (Hayward & Son, 1989)

Mud, Blood and Poppycock, by Gordon Corrigan (Cassell, 2003)

Gallipoli Diary, by Sir Ian Hamilton in two volumes. (Arnold 1920)

Manuscripts:

Papers of Private Edward Roe (7041678), Army records 1905–1933

Buchanan-Brown – Private letters of 2nd-Lieutenant Buchanan-Brown, 6th East Lancs Regiment 1914 – 19

Papers of Major E.R. Collins D.S.O. 1st East Lancs Regiment

Index

320

325